NEW PERSPECTIVES ON
COMPUTER CONCEPTS

8 EDITION

by June Jamrich Parsons and Dan Oja

BRIEF

Includes access to an integrated companion Web site and an interactive BookOnCD. The companion Web site offers audio clips, labs, games, relevant links, practice tests, and more. The BookOnCD contains the entire contents of the textbook with figures that come to life as videos, software tours, and animations. See the inside back cover!

THOMSON
COURSE TECHNOLOGY

Australia · Canada · Denmark · Japan · Mexico · New Zealand · Philippines · Puerto Rico · Singapore · South Africa · Spain · United Kingdom · United States

MANAGING EDITOR
Rachel Goldberg

SENIOR PRODUCT MANAGER
Kathy Finnegan

SENIOR PRODUCT MANAGER
Amanda Young Shelton

PRODUCT MANAGER
Karen Stevens

PRODUCT MANAGER
Brianna Hawes

ASSOCIATE PRODUCT MANAGER
Emilie Perreault

EDITORIAL ASSISTANT
Shana Rosenthal

MARKETING MANAGER
Joy Stark

DEVELOPMENTAL EDITOR
Lisa M. Lord

PRODUCTION EDITOR
Jennifer Goguen

TEXT DESIGN
Steve Deschene

DTP AND COMPOSITION
Tensi Parsons

PREPRESS PRODUCTION
GEX Publishing Services

MEDIA DEVELOPERS
Donna Mulder, Fatima Lockhart,
Keefe Crowley, Tensi Parsons

PHOTO RESEARCHER
Christina Micek

PHOTOGRAPHERS
Greg Manis, Joe Bush

ILLUSTRATOR
Eric Murphy, GEX Publishing Services

NARRATORS
Chris Robbert and Michele Martinez

BOOKONCD DEVELOPMENT
MediaTechnics Corporation

New Perspectives on Computer Concepts, 8th Edition is published by Course Technology.

©2006 Course Technology, a division of Thomson Learning, Inc. Thomson Learning™ is a trademark used herein under license.

Printed in the United States of America.

2 3 4 5 6 7 8 9 10 BM 09 08 07 06 05

ALL RIGHTS RESERVED. No part of this work covered by the copyright hereon may be reproduced or used in any form or by any means—graphic, electronic, or mechanical, including photocopying, recording, taping, Web distribution, or information storage and retrieval systems—without the written permission of the publisher.

Disclaimer
Course Technology reserves the right to revise this publication and make changes from time to time in its content without notice.

ISBN: 0-619-26762-3

For more information, contact:
Course Technology,
25 Thomson Place, Boston,
Massachusetts, 02210
www.course.com

For permission to use material from this text or product, submit a request online at www.thomsonrights.com. Any additional questions about permissions can be submitted by e-mail to thomsonrights@thomson.com

Trademarks
Some of the product names and company names used in this book have been used for identification purposes only and may be trademarks or registered trademarks of their respective manufacturers and sellers.

TABLE OF CONTENTS

ORIENTATION

O-4	**Section A: Getting Started with Your Computer and BookOnCD**
O-4	Computer Equipment
O-5	How to Turn Your Computer On and Off
O-6	Windows Basics
O-7	Mouse Basics
O-9	Keyboard Basics
O-11	QuickCheck A
O-12	**Section B: Getting Started with Software**
O-12	How to Start Software
O-13	Windows Controls
O-14	Creating Documents
O-16	BookOnCD Software Features
O-17	Help
O-17	QuickCheck B
O-18	**Section C: Getting Started on the Internet and New Perspectives NP8 Web Site**
O-18	Internet and Web Basics
O-18	How to Use a Web Browser and Search Engine
O-20	Accessing the New Perspectives NP8 Web Site
O-21	QuickCheck C
O-22	**Section D: Communicating with Your Instructor**
O-22	Working with E-mail
O-23	How to Transfer Tracking Disk Data
O-25	QuickCheck D
O-26	**Section E: Security and Privacy**
O-26	Securing Your Computer and Data
O-27	Avoiding Viruses
O-28	Preventing Intrusions
O-29	Blocking Spyware and Pop-Up Ads
O-30	Protecting E-commerce Transactions
O-31	Avoiding E-mail scams
O-33	Protecting Your Privacy
O-33	QuickCheck E

CHAPTER 1
COMPUTER, INTERNET, WEB, AND E-MAIL BASICS

ON THE BookOnCD

Operating a Personal Computer Lab	14
Making a Dial-up Connection Lab	25
Browsing and Searching Lab	35
Using E-mail Lab	43
Interactive Review Activities	52-55
Interactive Figures	7, 16, 18, 31, 33

ON THE WEB

Interactive Overview, Pre-Assessment, and Learning Objectives	3
InfoWebLinks	7, 9, 13, 15, 16, 28, 32, 39, 40, 42, 47, 49, 51
TechTV Video Project	56
Projects, Study Tips, and Online Games	56
Student Edition Labs	57

4	**Section A: Computer Basics**
4	A Computer Is...
6	Computer Categories
9	Personal Computer Systems
11	Data, Information, and Files
12	Application Software and Operating System Basics
13	QuickCheck A
14	LAB: Operating a Personal Computer
15	**Section B: Internet Basics**
15	Internet Resources
18	Internet Connections
20	Internet Service Providers
22	User IDs and Passwords
24	QuickCheck B
25	LAB: Making a Dial-up Connection
26	**Section C: Web Basics**
26	The World Wide Web
28	Browsers
31	Search Engines
34	QuickCheck C
35	LAB: Browsing and Searching
36	**Section D: E-mail Basics**
36	E-mail Overview
38	Netiquette
40	E-mail Technology
42	QuickCheck D
43	LAB: Using E-mail

TABLE OF CONTENTS

44 **TechTalk: The Boot Process**
47 QuickCheck TechTalk

48 **Issue: E-mail Privacy**

50 **Computers in Context: Homeland Security**

52 **Review Activities**
52 Interactive Summary
54 Interactive Key Terms
55 Interactive Situation Questions
55 Interactive Practice Tests

56 **Review on the Web**
57 Student Edition Labs

CHAPTER 2
COMPUTER HARDWARE

ON THE BookOnCD

Working with Binary Numbers Lab	67
Benchmarking Lab	77
Interactive Review Activities	108-111
Interactive Figures	80, 83, 94, 97

ON THE WEB

Interactive Overview, Pre-Assessment, and Learning Objectives	59
InfoWebLinks	65, 71, 76, 78, 87, 92, 96, 105, 107
TechTV Video Project	112
Projects, Study Tips, and Online Games	112
Student Edition Labs	113

60 **Section A: Data Representation and Digital Electronics**
60 Data Representation
63 Quantifying Bits and Bytes
64 Digital Electronics
66 QuickCheck A
67 LAB: Working with Binary Numbers

68 **Section B: Microprocessors and Memory**
68 Microprocessor Basics
69 Microprocessor Performance Factors
71 Today's Microprocessors
72 Random Access Memory
74 Read-Only Memory
75 CMOS Memory
76 QuickCheck B
77 LAB: Benchmarking

78 **Section C: Storage Devices**
78 Storage Basics
81 Floppy Disk Technology
83 Hard Disk Technology
85 Tape Storage
86 CD and DVD Technology
88 Solid State Storage
89 QuickCheck C

90 **Section D: Input and Output Devices**
90 Basic Input Devices
92 Display Devices
94 Printers
96 Installing Peripheral Devices
99 QuickCheck D

100 **TechTalk: How a Microprocessor Executes Instructions**
103 QuickCheck TechTalk

104 **Issue: Computers and the Environment**

106 **Computers in Context: Military**

108 **Review Activities**
108 Interactive Summary
110 Interactive Key Terms
111 Interactive Situation Questions
111 Interactive Practice Tests

112 **Review on the Web**
113 Student Edition Labs

TABLE OF CONTENTS

CHAPTER 3
COMPUTER SOFTWARE

ON THE BOOKONCD

Using the Windows Interface Lab	132
Installing and Uninstalling Software Lab	160
Interactive Review Activities	168-171
Interactive Figures	120, 134, 136, 137, 139, 140, 143, 146

ON THE WEB

Interactive Overview, Pre-Assessment, and Learning Objectives	115
InfoWebLinks	127, 128, 129, 130, 133, 135, 138, 141, 142, 147, 148, 149, 150, 157, 165, 167
TechTV Video Project	172
Projects, Study Tips, and Online Games	172
Student Edition Labs	173

116 **Section A: Software Basics**
116 Software: The Inside Story
118 Programmers and Programming Languages
119 How Software Works
120 Application Software and System Software
121 QuickCheck A

122 **Section B: Computer Operating Systems**
122 Operating System Overview
126 Windows, Mac OS, UNIX, Linux, and DOS
130 Handheld and Tablet Operating Systems
131 QuickCheck B
132 LAB: Using the Windows Interface

133 **Section C: Application Software**
133 Document Production Software
138 Spreadsheet Software
141 "Number Crunching" Software
142 Database Software
145 Graphics Software
147 Music Software
148 Video Editing Software
148 Software Suites
149 Educational and Reference Software
150 Entertainment Software
151 Business Software
151 QuickCheck C

152 **Section D: Software Installation and Copyrights**
152 Installation Basics
154 Installing from Distribution Media
155 Installing Downloaded Software
156 Uninstalling Software
157 Software Copyrights
157 Software Licenses
159 QuickCheck D
160 LAB: Installing and Uninstalling Software

161 **TechTalk: The Windows Registry**
163 QuickCheck TechTalk

164 **Issue: Software Piracy**

166 **Computers in Context: Journalism**

168 **Review Activities**
168 Interactive Summary
170 Interactive Key Terms
171 Software Key Terms
171 Interactive Situation Questions
171 Interactive Practice Tests

172 **Review on the Web**
173 Student Edition Labs

CHAPTER 4

FILE MANAGEMENT, VIRUS PROTECTION, AND BACKUP

ON THE BookOnCD

Working with Windows Explorer Lab	190
Backing Up Your Computer Lab	208
Interactive Review Activities	218–221
Interactive Figures	177, 181, 184, 187, 199, 205, 213

ON THE WEB

Interactive Overview, Pre-Assessment, and Learning Objectives	175
InfoWebLinks	194, 196, 198, 201, 204, 210, 213, 215, 217
TechTV Video Project	222
Projects, Study Tips, and Online Games	222
Student Edition Labs	223

- 176 **Section A: File Basics**
- 176 Filenames, Extensions, and Formats
- 178 File Locations, Folders, and Paths
- 179 File Sizes and Dates
- 179 QuickCheck A

- 180 **Section B: File Management**
- 180 Application-Based File Management
- 182 File Management Utilities
- 183 File Management Metaphors
- 184 Windows Explorer
- 185 File Management Tips
- 186 Physical File Storage
- 189 QuickCheck B
- 190 LAB: Working with Windows Explorer

- 191 **Section C: Computer Viruses**
- 191 Viruses, Trojan Horses, and Worms
- 196 Antivirus Software
- 197 Virus Hoaxes
- 198 QuickCheck C

- 199 **Section D: Data Backup**
- 199 Backup and Restore Procedures
- 203 Disk, CD, and DVD Backup
- 204 Network and Internet Backup
- 204 Hard Disk and Tape Backup
- 206 Boot and Recovery Disks
- 207 QuickCheck D
- 208 LAB: Backing Up Your Computer

- 209 **TechTalk: File Formats**
- 213 QuickCheck TechTalk

- 214 **Issue: Computer Crime**

- 216 **Computers in Context: Law Enforcement**

- 218 **Review Activities**
- 218 Interactive Summary
- 220 Interactive Key Terms
- 221 Interactive Situation Questions
- 221 Interactive Practice Tests

- 222 **Review on the Web**
- 223 Student Edition Labs

- 224 **TECHBUZZ**

- 232 **QUICKCHECK ANSWERS**

- 234 **PHOTO CREDITS**

- 236 **GLOSSARY**

- 246 **INDEX**

PREFACE

NEW PERSPECTIVES ON COMPUTER CONCEPTS 8TH EDITION

Whether you're a complete novice or computer-savvy, *New Perspectives on Computer Concepts 8th Edition* offers an engaging hands-on approach to computers backed by innovative learning technology. The 8th Edition incorporates invaluable feedback from the New Perspectives on Computer Concepts Advisory Committee, made up of over twenty instructors, to ensure that this book contains the most current information and resources for learning about computers.

THE NP8 LEARNING SYSTEM

You have purchased more than just a book. *New Perspectives on Computer Concepts 8th Edition* includes a printed book, an integrated Web site, and an interactive BookOnCD designed to be used together to provide a cutting-edge learning experience.

Want to study smarter? The NP8 Web site offers tools to help you understand the material from all angles and to thoroughly prepare you for exams. Want to see the concepts in the book in action? The BookOnCD brings concepts to life by directly linking to videos and animations.

Throughout this book you'll see CD and Web Activities icons. These tell you that there's more to explore beyond the surface of your textbook.

NP8 BOOK FEATURES

ORIENTATION CHAPTER

If you have little or no experience with computers, this chapter will put you at ease with the essential computer concepts you need to get up and running quickly. Even if you already know how to use computers, the Orientation offers helpful tips about how to most effectively use NP8's technology-based learning tools.

viii PREFACE

CHAPTER OPENER
The Chapter Openers serve as guides to everything you'll learn and do in each chapter.

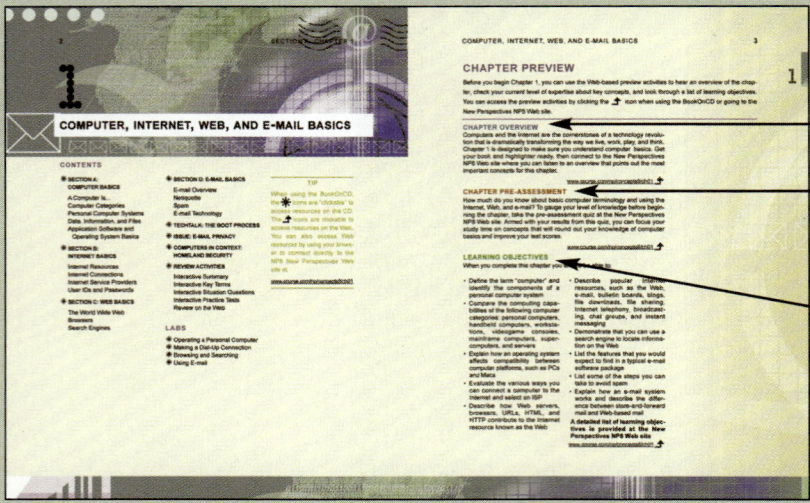

Understand key areas of focus in the chapter by listening to a 5-minute **Interactive Overview** on the NP8 Web site.

Measure your knowledge of the chapter's material by taking a short **Pre-Assessment**, accessible from the NP8 Web site.

Read the **Learning Objectives** list for an overview of the material you should understand upon completing the chapter.

CHAPTER FEATURES
Chapter features, such as **FAQs**, **InfoWebLinks**, and **QuickChecks**, help you understand concepts, put information in context, and explore topics beyond those presented in the text.

Gain a broad understanding of topics through the **FAQ** headings, which provide a relevant context for the material.

Delve deeper with structured Web research using the **InfoWebLinks**. You can use the InfoWebLinks as a starting point for research projects or simply to gather additional information about an interesting subject.

Make sure you understand each section's content with the **QuickCheck** questions. On the BookOnCD, answers to the QuickCheck questions can be saved and submitted for grading.

PREFACE

TECHTALK
Each chapter includes a **TechTalk** section that presents challenging technical information in a easy-to-understand way. TechTalk helps you delve deeper into the mechanics of how computers and computer technologies work.

ISSUE
Controversy and technology seem to go hand and hand. It's no longer enough to study what computers are, but rather how they shape our world. Each chapter explores a contemporary **Issue** and gives you the opportunity to express your opinion through What Do You Think questions.

COMPUTERS IN CONTEXT
So you're not a computer major? There are still a number of ways technology will affect you in your future career. In the **Computers in Context** section, you'll discover how technology plays a role in careers such as film-making, architecture, banking, and fashion.

REVIEW ACTIVITIES
Prove your mastery of the concepts in each chapter with the **Review Activities**, which are printed in the book and also accessible in an interactive format on the BookOnCD. The Review Activities include the Interactive Summary, Interactive Situation Questions, Interactive Key Terms, and Interactive Practice Tests. When you work on the Review Activities using the BookOnCD, you can save and submit your scores to your instructor. The Interactive Practice Tests are also available through the NP8 Web site.

REVIEW ON THE WEB
Take your knowledge of the concepts one step further with the **Review on the Web** activities available on the New Perspectives NP8 Web site. These activities, which include **Projects**, **Study Tips**, and **Online Games**, reinforce the concepts that you have learned in the chapter.

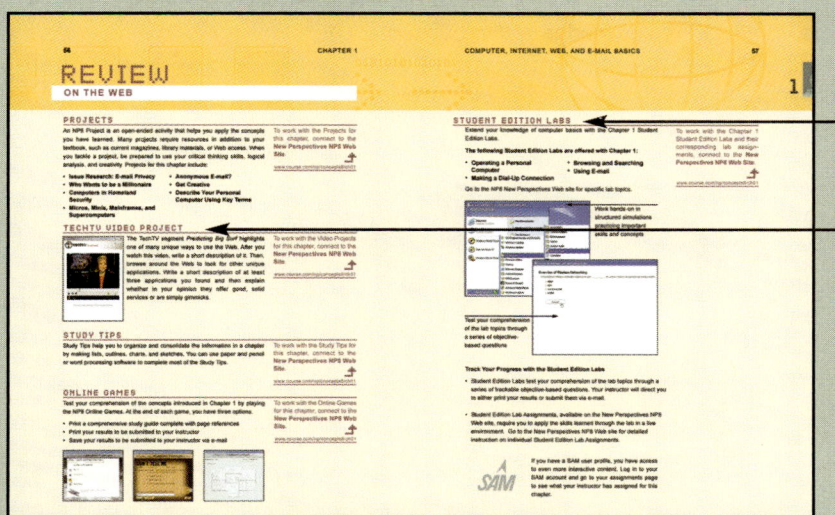

Student Edition Labs help you review and extend your knowledge through observations, hands-on simulations, and challenging objective-based questions.

TechTV Video Projects feature TechTV news clips that explore technology-related issues and trends.

TECHBUZZ
Some new technologies make a lasting impact, while others are just a flash in the pan. The new magazine-like **TechBuzz** section at the end of the book helps you follow tech trends, cutting-edge products, and emerging technologies.

PREFACE

NP8 WEB SITE

Use Course Technology's centralized login page, CoursePort, to gain access to the NP8 Web site. Web Activity icons in each chapter direct you to the NP8 Web site, which offers a wealth of online resources and study tools.

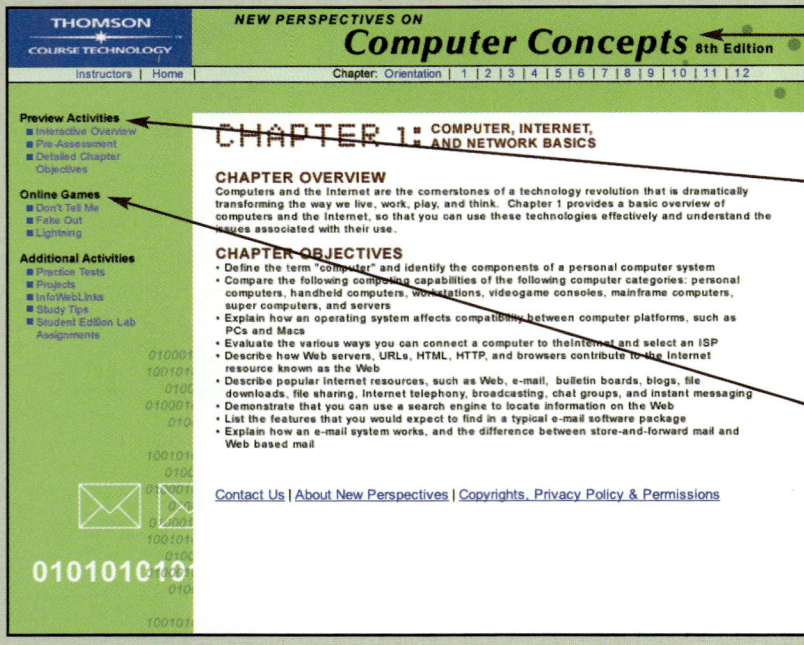

Use the NP8 Web site to access valuable resources, including the **InfoWebLinks, TechTV Library, Study Tips,** and **Student Edition Labs.**

Tailor your study plans for the chapter by using the **Chapter Preview Activities**. Listen to an interactive overview, take a pre-assessment quiz, and read through the detailed chapter objectives.

Test your comprehension with the **Online Games**, which challenge you with different interactive scenarios.

AUDIO INTERACTIVE OVERVIEW

Get your book and highlighter ready, and listen to a 5-minute **Interactive Overview**, which points out key concepts and topics in each chapter.

PRE-ASSESSMENT QUESTIONS

Use the **Pre-Assessment** to gauge your level of knowledge of the concepts in each chapter. Upon completing the Pre-Assessment, you can view and print a study guide that helps focus your study time in your weakest areas of knowledge.

ONLINE GAMES

The **Online Games** give you a rewarding interactive way to reinforce concepts taught in each chapter. Each game offers a printable study guide that points you back to specific pages in the text for review. You can also save your results from the Online Games and submit them electronically to your instructor for grading.

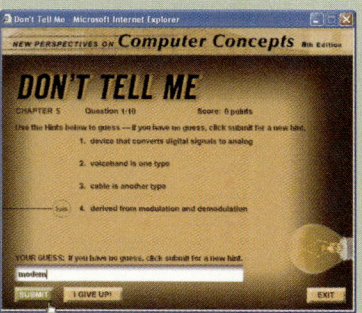

INTERACTIVE PRACTICE TESTS

Interactive Practice Tests, also available on the BookOnCD, consist of 10 multiple-choice, true/false, and fill-in-the-blank questions chosen at random from a large test bank. Each test offers a printable study guide with page references. Your test scores can be saved and submitted to your instructor electronically.

PREFACE

TECHTV VIDEO CLIPS LIBRARY

Ever wondered what it is like to program your own video game? What are the social implications of a digital system that tracks patrons at a neighborhood bar? Stay on top of emerging technologies and technology-related issues with our library of **TechTV Video Clips**. TechTV Video Projects, included in every chapter, challenge you to further investigate the issues and topics raised in the video clips.

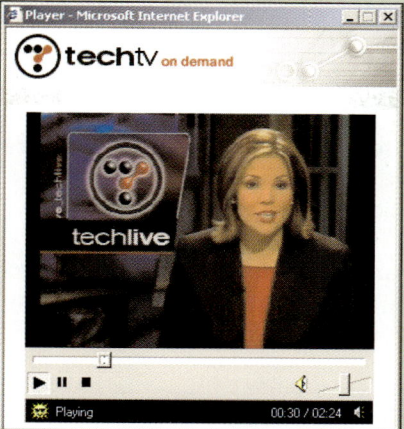

PROJECTS

Work with the NP8 **Projects** to apply the concepts you have learned from reading and lab activities. NP8 Projects are open-ended assignments that require you to research topics, apply critical-thinking skills, and produce reports, summaries, graphics, or other creative deliverables.

STUDY TIPS

Study Tips help you organize and consolidate the information in a chapter by making lists, outlines, charts, and sketches.

STUDENT EDITION LABS

You can master hundreds of computer concepts including input and output devices, file management and desktop applications, computer privacy, virus protection, and much more using the **Student Edition Labs**. The interactive Student Edition Labs help you learn through dynamic observation, step-by-step practice, and challenging review questions. Student Edition Lab Assignments challenge you to apply the skills learned in the labs to realistic case problems.

Hands-on practice reinforces important topics.

Feedback on each step guides you through the simulations.

Prepare, Observe, Practice, and Apply learning modes engage all types of learners through readings, simulations, hands-on practice and review questions.

xii PREFACE

NP8 BOOKONCD

The interactive BookOnCD includes the entire contents of the printed book and brings the concepts to life with the following interactive features:

- **Interactive Review Activities** test your understanding of the concepts presented in each chapter.
- **Interactive QuickCheck** questions check your comprehension of each section.
- **Videos**, **animations** and **screentours** throughout each chapter bring the figures to life.
- **New Perspectives Labs** give you hands-on experience applying concepts and using software.

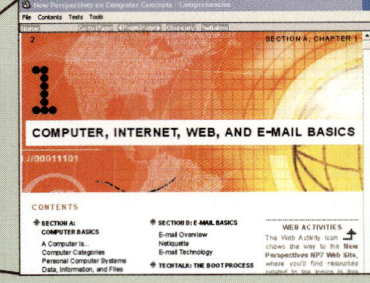

You can save or print your results from the BookOnCD Interactive Review Activities, QuickCheck questions, and New Perspectives Labs to submit to your instructor.

SAM COMPUTER CONCEPTS

If your instructor has chosen to use SAM Training and Assessment Software in your course, you will have access to interactive training simulations that reinforce the lessons presented in this text, as well as realistic hands-on exams.

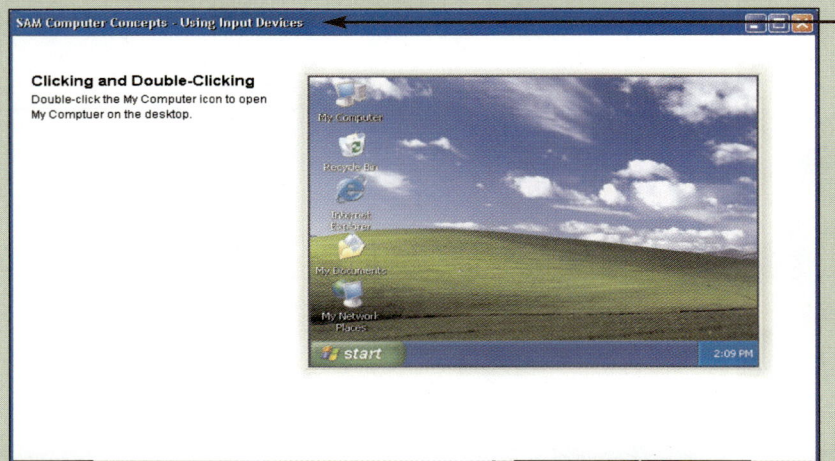

Hands-on tasks allow you to demonstrate your understanding of important computer concepts and applications.

PREFACE   xiii

NP8 INSTRUCTOR RESOURCES

New Perspectives instructional resources and technology provide instructors with a wide range of tools that enhance teaching and learning. These tools can be accessed from the Instructor Resources CD or at *www.course.com*.

INSTRUCTOR'S MANUAL: HELP IS ONLY A FEW KEYSTROKES AWAY

An enhanced Instructor's Manual offers an outline for each chapter, plus instructional suggestions and teaching tips, including how to effectively use and integrate the Web site content, CD content, and labs.

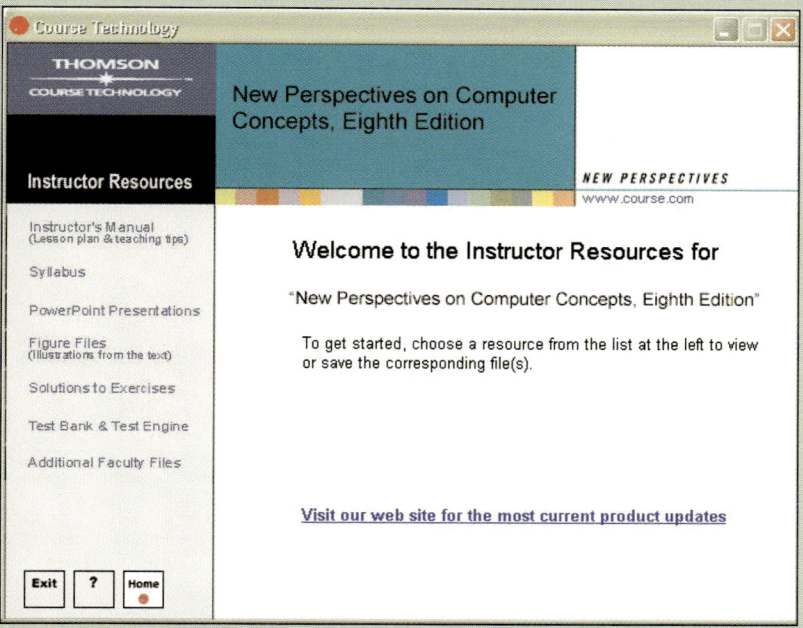

EXAMVIEW: OUR POWERFUL TESTING SOFTWARE PACKAGE

With ExamView, instructors can generate printed tests, create LAN-based tests, or test over the Internet.

COURSE PRESENTER

Instructors can deliver engaging and visually impressive lectures for each chapter with the professionally-designed Course Presenter. The Course Presenter is a PowerPoint presentation that is multimedia-enhanced with screentours, animations, and videos.

INSTRUCTOR'S EDITION

The Instructor's Edition content explains in depth the New Perspectives Computer Concepts pedagogy and technology resources. It also provides suggestions on how to use New Perspectives on Computer Concepts technology in the classroom.

BLACKBOARD AND WEBCT CONTENT

Course Technology offers a full range of content for use with BlackBoard and WebCT to simplify the use of New Perspectives in distance education settings.

FROM THE AUTHORS

Technology continues to move forward at a rapid pace. To help instructors and students stay in step with the march of technology, we produced this media-rich and Web-enhanced 8th Edition of New Perspectives on Computer Concepts. An expanded Orientation section at the beginning of the book now includes a hands-on introduction to computer security and privacy—essential information for both beginning students and those who are computer savvy. A new TechBuzz section at the end of the book gets students thinking about technology trends and the potential of new products to become the next "killer apps" or "tech turkeys."

We retained the same basic organization for Chapters 1 through 4 and updated their content to reflect current developments. Based on feedback from students, instructors, and reviewers, we focused on making technology concepts even more understandable by streamlining explanations and honing figures for the clearest presentation possible. We logged countless hours of research to bring you the most up-to-date information about new products and trends in computers, software, and the Internet. Please make sure to check the InfoWebLinks for important updates on post-publication events.

Many of today's students have substantially more practical experience with computers than their counterparts of 10 years ago, and yet other students enter college with inadequate technology preparation. The goal of New Perspectives on Computer Concepts is to bring every student up to speed with computer basics, and then go beyond basic computer literacy to provide students with technical information that every college-educated person would be expected to know. Whether you are an instructor or a student, we hope that you enjoy the learning experience provided by our text-based and technology-based materials.

ACKNOWLEDGEMENTS

The book would not exist—and certainly wouldn't arrive on schedule—were it not for the efforts of our media, editorial, and production teams. We thank Amanda Young Shelton and Emilie Perreault for tireless work on every detail of the project; Rachel Goldberg for her leadership for the entire New Perspectives series; Jennifer Goguen for managing production; Fatima Lockhart, Donna Mulder, Tensi Parsons, Keefe Crowley, Greg Manis, Joe Bush, and Eric Murphy for creating videos, screentours, interactive tests, photos, illustrations, and animations; Rebekah Tidwell for her work on the Pre-Assessments; Dave Nuscher for his work on updating the Online Games; Chris Robbert for his clear narrations; Sue Oja, Debora Elam, Deana Martinson, Karen Kangas, Jaclyn Kangas, and Kevin Lappi for checking and double-checking the alpha and beta CDs; Lisa Lord for her insightful developmental edit; Robin K. Flynn for making sure that every comma is in the right place; Keefe Crowley for designing and maintaining our InfoWebLinks site; artist Steve Deschene for a stunning interior design; and Christina Micek for her photo research. We want to thank you all!

-June Parsons and Dan Oja

PREFACE

NEW PERSPECTIVES ON COMPUTER CONCEPTS ADVISORY COMMITTEE

Dr. Nazih Abdallah
University of Central Florida

Paula F. Bell
Lock Haven University of Pennsylvania

Wendy Chisholm
Barstow College

David Courtaway
Devry University, Pomona

Sallie B. Dodson
Radford University

Philip Funk
Southern New Hampshire University

Michael Gaffney
Century College

Ernest Gines
Tarrant County College Southeast

Ione Good
Southeastern Community College

Thomas E. Gorecki
College of Southern Maryland

Steven Gramlich
Pasco-Hernando Community College

Michael J. Hanna
Colorado State University

Stan Leja
Del Mar College

Martha Lindberg
Minnesota State University, Mankato

Teresa C. Long
Valencia Community College

Dr. W. Benjamin Martz
University of Colorado, Colorado Springs

DeAnn McMullen
West Kentucky Community and Technical College

Robert P. Moore
Laredo Community College

Dr. Rodney Pearson
Mississippi State University

Lana Shryock
Monroe County Community College

Betty Sinowitz
SUNY Rockland Community College

Martin Skolnik
Florida Atlantic University

Jerome Spencer
Rowan University

We would also like to thank the reviewers from the recent past editions who helped provide valuable feedback that is still an influence on the 8th Edition:

ACADEMIC REVIEWERS

Dr. Nazih Abdallah
University of Central Florida

Beverly Amer
Northern Arizona University

Ken Baldauf
Florida State University

Mary Caldwell
Rollins College

Chuck Calvin
Computer Learning Centers

Becky Curtin
William Rainey Harper College

Eric Daley
University of New Brunswick

Robert Erickson
University of Vermont

Mike Feiler
Merritt College

Ed Mott
Central Texas College

Catherine Perlich
MediaTechnics

David Primeaux
Virginia Commonwealth University

Gregory Stefanelli
Carroll Community College

Martha J. Tilmann
College of San Mateo

Mary Zayac
University of the Virgin Islands

STUDENT REVIEWERS

Kitty Edwards

Heather House

TECHNICAL REVIEWERS

Ramachandran Bharath

Jeff Harrow

Barbra D. Letts

John Lucas

Karl Mulder

ORIENTATION

CONTENTS

SECTION A: GETTING STARTED WITH YOUR COMPUTER

Computer Equipment
How to Turn Your Computer On and Off
⌨ Turn Your Computer On
Windows Basics
Mouse Basics
⌨ Use Your Mouse
⌨ Start the BookOnCD
⌨ Open a BookOnCD Video
Keyboard Basics
⌨ Make a Tracking Disk
⌨ Complete a QuickCheck
⌨ View the Contents of Your Tracking Disk

SECTION B: GETTING STARTED WITH SOFTWARE

How to Start Software
⌨ Start Microsoft Word
Window Controls
⌨ Use the Menu Bar
⌨ Use the Toolbar
⌨ Use the Sizing Buttons
Creating Documents
⌨ Create a Document
⌨ Save a Document
⌨ Print a Document, Close It, and Exit Word
BookOnCD Software Features
⌨ Explore BookOnCD Menus
⌨ Navigate the BookOnCD
Help

SECTION C: GETTING STARTED ON THE INTERNET

Internet and Web Basics
⌨ Start Your Browser
How to Use a Web Browser and Search Engine
⌨ Access a Search Engine
⌨ Use a Search Engine
Accessing the New Perspectives NP8 Web Site
⌨ Access the NP8 Web Site
⌨ Explore the NP8 Web Site

SECTION D: COMMUNICATING WITH YOUR INSTRUCTOR

Working with E-mail
⌨ Create and Send E-mail
How to Transfer Tracking Disk Data
⌨ Open a BookOnCD Lab
⌨ Send Your Tracking Data
⌨ Check for Annotations

SECTION E: SECURITY AND PRIVACY

Securing Your Computer and Data
⌨ Check the Accounts on Your Computer
Avoiding Viruses
⌨ Get Familiar with Your Antivirus Software
Preventing Intrusions
⌨ Check Your Computer's Firewall
Blocking Spyware and Pop-up Ads
⌨ Explore Internet Explorer Security and Privacy
Protecting E-commerce Transactions
⌨ Know How to Identify a Secure Connection
Avoiding E-mail Scams
⌨ Arm Yourself Against E-mail Scams
Protecting Your Privacy
⌨ Check Your Privacy

TIP

⌨ Keyboard icons indicate hands-on activities. When using the BookOnCD, the ✽ icons are "clickable" to access resources on the CD. The ✣ icons are clickable to access the NP8 Web site.

ORIENTATION   O-3

CHAPTER PREVIEW

Before you begin the Orientation, you can use the Web-based preview activities to hear an overview of the chapter, check your current level of expertise about key concepts, and look through a list of learning objectives. You can access the preview activities by clicking the icon when using the BookOnCD or going to the New Perspectives NP8 Web site.

CHAPTER OVERVIEW

The purpose of this Orientation is to get you up and running with your computer and all the technology tools that accompany this textbook. If you have had little or no experience with computers, you'll find the basics here. If you've worked with computers before, don't skip this section. Make sure you check out the information about the BookOnCD and Web site—there's a pretty good chance it will improve your grade! Get your book and highlighter ready, then connect to the New Perspectives NP8 Web site where you can listen to an overview that points out the most important concepts for this chapter.

www.course.com/np/concepts8/ch00

CHAPTER PRE-ASSESSMENT

How much do you know about basic computer operations, using software, communicating with your instructor via e-mail, using the CD and Web site for this textbook, and staying safe online? To gauge your level of knowledge before beginning the chapter, take the pre-assessment quiz at the New Perspectives NP8 Web site. Armed with your results from this quiz, you can focus your study time on concepts that will provide you with the background and skills for making the most of this textbook.

www.course.com/np/concepts8/ch00

LEARNING OBJECTIVES

When you complete this orientation you should be able to:

- Identify the basic components of your computer system
- Turn your computer system on and off
- Identify the major components of the Windows desktop
- Use the mouse and keyboard
- Start the BookOnCD, view a video, make a Tracking Disk, and take a QuickCheck
- Start and exit a software program
- Use the menu bar, toolbar, and sizing buttons
- Create, save, and print documents using Microsoft Word
- Describe the features offered by your BookOnCD
- Describe the difference between the Internet and the Web
- Use a browser
- Use a search engine to find specific information on the Web
- Use the Internet to connect to the New Perspectives NP8 Web site
- Create, read, and reply to e-mail messages
- Complete a BookOnCD lab
- Submit Tracking Disk data to your instructor
- Secure your computer for working online
- Take steps to protect your online privacy

A detailed list of learning objectives is provided at the New Perspectives NP8 Web site

www.course.com/np/concepts8/ch00

O-4

SECTION A

GETTING STARTED WITH YOUR COMPUTER

SECTION A

When you use the *New Perspectives on Computer Concepts* textbook, you not only learn about computers, you also use computers as learning tools. You can read your textbook on-screen where many of the photos come alive as videos, where screen shots open into guided tours of popular software, and where you can take interactive quizzes to make sure you understand chapter material before encountering it on a test. In Section A you'll learn how to turn on your computer, start the on-screen version of your textbook, use your computer's mouse, start a BookOnCD video, use a computer keyboard, and take an interactive quiz.

COMPUTER EQUIPMENT

What do I need to know about my computer? Your computer—the one you own, the one you use in a school lab, or the one provided to you at work—is technically classified as a microcomputer and sometimes referred to as a personal computer. A computer runs software (or "programs") that help you accomplish a variety of tasks. A typical computer system consists of several devices—you must be able to identify these devices to use them.

What are the important components of my computer system? The system unit contains your computer's circuitry, such as the microprocessor that is the "brain" of your computer and memory chips that temporarily store information. It also contains storage devices, such as a hard disk drive.

Your computer system also includes basic hardware devices that allow you to enter information and commands, view work, and store information for later retrieval. Devices for entering information include a keyboard and mouse. A display device, such as a TV-like monitor, allows you to view your work, a printer produces "hard copy" on paper, and speakers produce beeps and chimes that help you pay attention to what happens on the screen.

Where are the important components of a desktop computer system? A desktop computer is designed for stationary use on a desk or table. Figure 1 shows the key components of a desktop computer system.

PC or Mac?

Microcomputers can be divided into two camps: PCs and Macs. The CD that comes with this book is designed for use with PCs, and the Orientation instructions apply specifically to PCs.

You can usually determine whether you have a PC or Mac by noting your computer's brand name. PC brands include Dell, IBM, Hewlett-Packard, Compaq, Gateway, and Sony. You can use the software that accompanies your textbook with these and other PC brands.

Macintosh computers are manufactured by Apple Computers, Inc. and sport a rainbow-colored logo of an apple. If you have a Mac, check with your instructor for the location of your school's PC lab.

FIGURE 1
A desktop computer system includes several components, usually connected by cables.

ORIENTATION   O-5

Where are the important components of a notebook computer system? Notebook computers (sometimes called "laptops") are small, lightweight computers designed to be carried from place to place. The components of a notebook computer system, except the printer, are housed in a single unit, as shown in Figure 2.

FIGURE 2
A notebook computer includes a flat-panel LCD screen, keyboard, speakers, and touchpad in the same unit that contains the microprocessor, memory, and storage devices. An external mouse is sometimes used instead of the touchpad.

How do I identify my computer's storage devices? Your computer contains a hard disk, housed inside the system unit. It is also likely to have a floppy disk drive and some type of drive that works with CDs. Figure 3 can help you identify your computer's storage devices and their uses.

FIGURE 3
You should use the hard disk to store most of your data, but to transport or back up data, you can use floppy disks, CDs, DVDs, or USB flash drives.

Floppy disk drive

Capacity: 1.44 million characters

Low-capacity storage, but handy for transferring work between home and school labs.

CD drive

Capacity: 640 million characters

A CD-ROM drive reads CDs, but does not allow you to store your own data on them. CD-R or CD-RW drives allow you to store data.

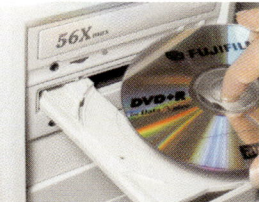

DVD drive

Capacity: 4.7 billion characters

DVD-ROM drives read CDs and DVDs, but do not let you store your own data. The R or RW versions allow you to store data.

USB flash drive

Capacity: 32 million–2 billion characters

A USB flash drive is about the size of a highlighter and plugs directly into the computer system unit.

HOW TO TURN YOUR COMPUTER ON AND OFF

How do I turn it on? A notebook computer typically has one switch that turns on the entire system. Look for the switch along the sides of the computer or on the top above the keyboard. When using a desktop computer, turn on the monitor, printer, and speakers before you flip the switch on the system unit.

Most computers take a minute or two to power up, and you might be required to log in by entering a user ID and password. Your computer is ready to use when the Windows desktop (Figure 4 on the next page) appears on the computer screen and you can move the arrow-shaped pointer with your mouse.

How do I turn it off? Your computer is designed to turn itself off after you initiate a shutdown sequence by clicking the Start button, selecting "Shut Down" or "Turn Off Computer," and following the instructions on the screen. After the computer shuts itself off, you can turn off the monitor, speakers, and printer. When using computers in a school lab, ask about the shutdown procedure. Your lab manager might ask that you log out but do not turn the computer off.

TRY IT

Turn your computer on

1. Locate the power switch for any devices connected to your computer and turn them on.

2. Locate the power switch for your computer and turn it on.

3. If a message asks for your user ID and/or password, type them in, and then press the Enter key on your computer's keyboard.

4. Wait for the Windows desktop to appear.

WINDOWS BASICS

What is Windows? Microsoft Windows is an example of a type of software called an operating system. The operating system controls all the basic tasks your computer performs, such as running application software, manipulating files on storage devices, and transferring data to and from printers, digital cameras, and other devices. The operating system also controls the user interface—the way software appears on the screen and the way you control what it does.

What is the Windows desktop? The Windows desktop is your base of operations for using your computer. It displays small pictures called "icons" that help you access software, documents, and the components of your computer system. The desktop is divided into several areas, as shown in Figure 4.

FIGURE 4
The Windows Desktop

A The main part of the desktop displays icons that represent software, files, and folders containing documents, graphics, and other data.

B The taskbar contains the Start button, Quick Start bar, and Notification area.

C The Start button is used to display the Start menu, which lists all the programs installed on your computer.

D The Quick Start bar is always visible, making it a good place for icons that represent the programs you frequently use.

E The Notification area displays the current time and the status of programs, devices, and Internet connections.

When working with your computer, you'll frequently use the Start button in the lower-left corner of the screen to display the Start menu that provides options for accessing software, finding data, configuring hardware, and finding answers to your questions about using Windows (Figure 5).

How do I manipulate icons and other Windows controls? To use the Start button and other desktop controls, you'll need to become familiar with how to use a mouse to control an on-screen pointer. The pointer is usually shaped like an arrow, but you can change to a different shape, depending on the task you're doing. For example, when the computer is busy, the arrow shape turns into an hourglass, signifying that you should wait for the computer to finish its current task before attempting to start a new task.

FIGURE 5
The Start Menu

ORIENTATION O-7

MOUSE BASICS

What is a mouse? A mouse is a device used to manipulate items on the screen, such as the controls displayed on the Windows desktop. PC compatible mice have at least two buttons, typically located on top of the mouse. Some mice also include a scroll wheel mounted between the left and right mouse buttons. Other mice include additional buttons on the top or sides (Figure 6).

FIGURE 6
For basic mousing, you need use only the left and right mouse buttons.

How do I use a mouse? Hold the mouse in your right hand as shown in Figure 7. When you drag the mouse from left to right over your mousepad or desk, the arrow-shaped pointer on the screen moves from left to right. If you run out of room to move the mouse, simply pick it up and reposition it. The pointer does not move when the mouse is not in contact with a flat surface.

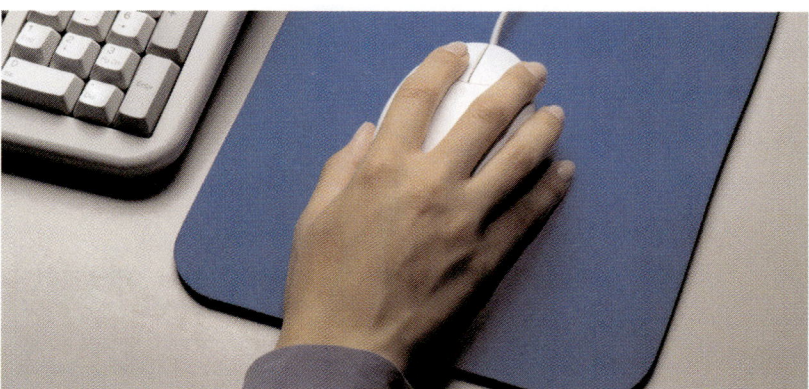

FIGURE 7
Rest the palm of your right hand on the mouse. Position your index finger over the left mouse button and your middle finger over the right mouse button.

There are several ways you can manipulate on-screen objects. Although you might not be able to manipulate every object in all possible ways, you'll soon learn which mouse actions are allowed for each type of control. The following list describes your repertoire of mouse actions.

Action	How to	Result
Click	Press the left mouse button once, and then immediately release it.	Select an object
Double-click	Press the left mouse button twice in rapid succession without moving the body of the mouse.	Activate an object
Right-click	Press the right mouse button once, and then immediately release it.	Display a shortcut menu
Drag	Hold the left mouse button down while you move the mouse.	Move an object

TRY IT

Use your mouse

1. With your computer on and the Windows desktop showing on the screen, move your mouse around on the desk and notice how the mouse movements correspond to the movement of the arrow-shaped pointer.

2. Move the mouse to position the pointer on the Start button.

3. Click the left mouse button to open the Start menu.

4. Click the **Start** button again to close the Start menu.

O-8 SECTION A

You can find out more about using a mouse by watching a video from the CD version of your textbook. The BookOnCD supplied with your textbook includes many photos like the one in Figure 8 that come to life as videos. The BookOnCD also includes diagrams that become animations and screen shots that open to guided software tours. Any figure in your textbook that displays the ✳ symbol has a corresponding video, animation, or software tour.

FIGURE 8
Use your palm to move the mouse in the direction you want the on-screen pointer to move. Use your fingers to click the mouse buttons to choose an action.

CLICK TO START ✳

How do I start the BookOnCD? Now that you know how to use a mouse, you can work with the CD supplied with your textbook. To learn how to start the BookOnCD and take advantage of its interactive features, you can follow the instructions in the box below.

EXPLORE NP8 LEARNING TOOLS

Start the BookOnCD

1. Locate the button on your computer's CD or DVD drive and push it to open the tray.

2. Insert the BookOnCD into the tray, label side up.

3. Push the button on the drive to close it.

4. Wait a few seconds until the BookOnCD main menu appears.

5. Position the arrow-shaped pointer over the option **Open the electronic textbook** and click the left mouse button one time. Click the **No** button when you see the Tracking Disk message.

Open a BookOnCD video

1. When the first page appears, click the **Go to Page** button, then type **O-8**. Hint: Use an uppercase "O," not a zero!

2. When the mouse photo appears, click ✳ to start the screen tour.

3. Watch the video to learn more about using your mouse. When the video is finished, click the **Exit** button.

4. You could leave the CD in the drive and continue to read the book on your computer screen, but for now, click the ✕ Close button in the upper-right corner of the screen to close the electronic textbook. From the main BookOnCD menu, click **Exit** before removing the CD from the drive.

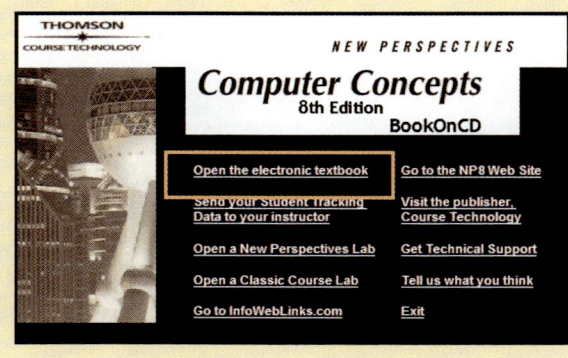

ORIENTATION

KEYBOARD BASICS

What are the important features of a computer keyboard? You use the computer keyboard to input commands, respond to prompts, and type the text of documents. An insertion point that looks like a flashing vertical bar indicates where the characters you type will appear. You can change the location of the insertion point by using the mouse or the arrow keys. Study Figure 9 for an overview of important computer keys and their functions.

FIGURE 9
Computer Keyboard

- **A** The **Esc** or "escape" key cancels an operation.
- **B** **Function keys** activate commands, such as Save, Help, and Print. The command associated with each key depends on the software you are using.
- **C** The **Print Screen** key prints the contents of the screen or stores a copy of the screen in memory that you can print or manipulate with graphics software.
- **D** The **Scroll Lock** key's function depends on the software you're using. This key is rarely used with today's software.
- **E** **Indicator Lights** show you the status of three toggle keys: Num Lock, Caps Lock, and Scroll Lock. The Power light indicates whether the computer is on or off.
- **F** The **Backspace** key deletes one character to the left of the insertion point.
- **G** The **Insert** key switches between insert mode and typeover mode.
- **H** The **Home** key takes you to the beginning of a line or the beginning of a document, depending on the software you are using.

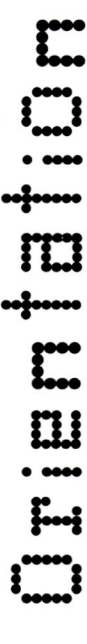

- **I** The **Tab** key can move your current typing location to the next tab stop or the next text-entry box.
- **J** The **Caps Lock** key capitalizes all the letters you type when it is engaged, but does not produce the top symbol on keys that contain two symbols. This key is a toggle key, which means that each time you press it, you switch between uppercase and lowercase modes.
- **K** The **Shift** key capitalizes letters and produces the top symbol on keys that contain two symbols.
- **L** You hold down the **Ctrl** key while pressing another key. The result of Ctrl or Alt key combinations depends on the software you are using.
- **M** You hold down the **Alt** key while you press another key.
- **N** The **Enter** key is used to indicate that you have completed a command or want to move your typing position down to the next line.
- **O** The **Delete** key deletes the character to the right of the insertion point.
- **P** The **End** key takes you to the end of a line or the end of a document, depending on the software you are using.
- **Q** The **Page Up** key displays the previous screen of information. The **Page Down** key displays the next screen of information.
- **R** The up, down, right, and left **arrow keys** move the insertion point.
- **S** The **numeric keypad** produces numbers or moves the insertion point, depending on the status of the Num Lock key shown by the status lights.

What do Alt and Ctrl mean? The Alt and Ctrl keys work with the letter keys. If you see <Ctrl X>, Ctrl+X, [Ctrl X], Ctrl-X, or Ctrl X on the screen or in an instruction manual, it means to hold down the Ctrl key while you press X. For example, Ctrl+X is a keyboard shortcut for clicking the Edit menu, and then clicking the Cut option. A keyboard shortcut allows you to use the keyboard rather than the mouse to select menu commands. For more tips on using your computer keyboard, start the video for Figure 10.

FIGURE 10
Using a computer keyboard is similar to using a typewriter. Unlike typewriters, computer keyboards include many special keys designed to simplify common tasks.

What if I make a mistake? Everyone makes mistakes. The first rule is don't panic! Most mistakes are reversible. The hints and tips in Figure 11 should help you recover from mistakes.

What Happened	What To Do
Typed the wrong thing	Use the Backspace key to delete the last characters you typed.
Selected the wrong menu	Press the Esc key to close the menu.
Opened something you didn't mean to	Click the X button in the upper-right corner of the screen.
Computer has "hung up" and no longer responds to mouse clicks or typed commands	Hold down the Ctrl, Alt, and Delete keys, and then follow instructions to close the program.
Pressed the Enter key in the middle of a sentence	Press the Backspace key to paste the sentence back together.

FIGURE 11
Most mistakes are easy to fix.

You can practice using the keyboard when you type your answers for the QuickCheck questions at the bottom of the next page.

What is a QuickCheck? Each chapter of your textbook is divided into four main sections: A, B, C, and D. Each section ends with a series of QuickCheck questions that help you assess your understanding of material you've read. You can fill in the answers on the page, and then check your answers by referring to the end of the book. If you are using the BookOnCD, you can type your answers into the boxes and your computer automatically corrects them. You can save your score on a Tracking Disk for later reference or to submit to your instructor. Follow the instructions on the next page to make a Tracking Disk, complete the QuickCheck at the end of this section, and access your Tracking Disk summary.

TIP
Whether reading from your printed textbook or working with the BookOnCD, you might get a better grasp of the material if you take a break between sections rather than attempt to complete the entire chapter in one sitting.

ORIENTATION   O-11

⌨ EXPLORE NP8 LEARNING TOOLS

Make a Tracking Disk

1. Place the BookOnCD in your computer's CD or DVD drive, and then close the tray.

2. From the main menu, click **Open the electronic textbook**.

3. When you see the message, "Do you want to check for a Tracking Disk to load Annotation and Syllabus Links?" click the **Yes** button.

4. A box titled Tracking Disk Not Found appears. Click the **Create** button.

5. Fill in the information requested (shown at right).

6. Insert a floppy disk into the drive, silver part first.

7. Click the **OK** button. Your Tracking Disk is ready when you see the first page of the textbook.

In the User ID box, enter a unique identification, such as your student ID number.

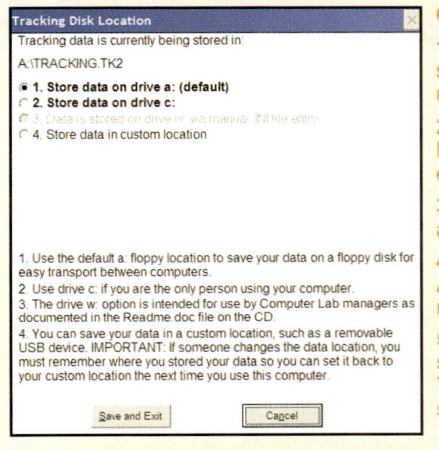

Complete a QuickCheck

1. Use the **Go To Page** button to jump to page O-11. Click the ▼ scroll button in the lower-right corner of your screen several times until you can see the entire set of QuickCheck questions.

2. Click the answer box for question 1, and then type your answer. Remember that you can use the Backspace key if you make a typing error.

3. Press the **Enter** key to jump to question 2, and then type your answer.

4. When you have answered all the questions, click the **Check Answers** icon. The computer will indicate if your first answer is correct. Click **OK** to check the rest of your answers.

5. When you've reviewed all your answers, the computer presents a summary of your score and asks if you want to save your score on a Tracking Disk. Click **OK**. When you see the Responses Saved message, click **OK** again.

View the contents of your Tracking Disk

1. Click the **Tools** menu at the top of your screen.

2. Click **Tracking Disk**. Your computer displays a summary score for the QuickCheck you completed. The list of summary scores grows as you save additional QuickChecks, end-of-chapter Interactive Summaries, Interactive Situation Questions, and Lab QuickChecks.

3. Click **Exit** to return to the electronic textbook pages. You can then exit the BookOnCD and remove the CD from the drive.

If you'd rather store tracking data on your computer's hard disk or on a flash drive that plugs into the USB port, click **Tools**, and then click **Change Tracking Location**. Select a storage location from the list shown above.

QUICKCHECK......SECTION A

1. When turning on the components of a desktop computer system, the computer's system ▭ should be switched on last.

2. Instead of using the on/off switch to turn off your computer, you should use the ▭ button to initiate a shutdown.

3. Windows icons and controls are designed to be manipulated by a device called a(n) ▭.

4. Ctrl+X means to hold down the Ctrl key, then press +, then press X. True or false? ▭

5. The ▭ key can be used to delete the last character you typed.

 CHECK ANSWERS

O-12

SECTION B

GETTING STARTED WITH SOFTWARE

Software helps you accomplish a variety of tasks, such as creating documents, generating graphs, maintaining to-do lists, and repairing old photographs. Section B begins with a quick overview of using word processing software called Microsoft Word. You might find this software handy for completing assignments and projects at the end of each chapter. This section also provides tips on using the menus and options included with your BookOnCD software.

HOW TO START SOFTWARE

How do I start a software program? You can use the Start button to launch just about any software that's installed on your computer. Clicking the Start menu displays a list of recently accessed software. Clicking the All Programs option displays a list of every software program installed on your computer. You can run a program from this list simply by clicking it. Follow the instructions in the TRY IT box to start Microsoft Word (assuming it is installed on your computer).

TRY IT

Start Microsoft Word

1. Make sure your computer is on and it is displaying the Windows desktop.

2. Click the **Start** button to display the Start menu.

3. Click **All Programs** to display a list of all software installed on your computer.

4. Click **Microsoft Word**.

5. Wait a few seconds for your computer to display the main screen for Microsoft Word, shown below. Leave Word open for use with the next TRY IT.

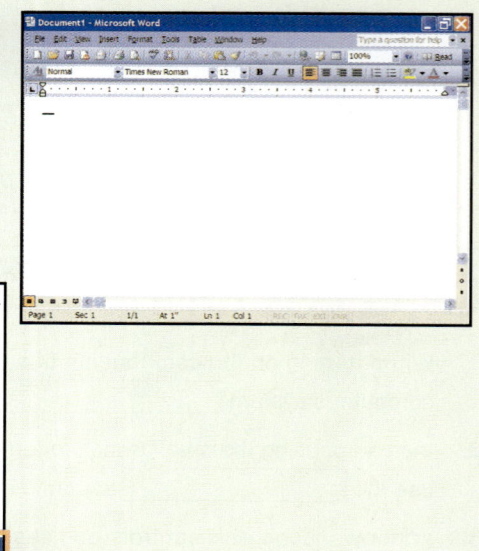

ORIENTATION   O-13

WINDOW CONTROLS

How do I tell the software what I want to do? Word processing, photo editing, and other software designed for use on computers running the Microsoft Windows operating system is referred to as "Windows software." Most Windows software works in a fairly uniform way and uses a similar set of controls.

Each software application appears in a rectangular area called a "window," which includes a title bar, a menu bar, and various controls shown in Figure 12.

FIGURE 12

The **title bar** displays the title of the software, the name of the current data file, and the window sizing buttons.

The **Minimize button** shrinks the window to a button at the bottom of the screen.

The **Maximize button** stretches the window to fill the screen.

The **Close button** closes the window and exits the program.

The **menu bar** displays the titles of menus you can click to select commands.

The **toolbar** displays a series of tools for accomplishing various tasks.

The **scroll bar** can be clicked or dragged to see any material that does not fit in the displayed window.

The **workspace** is the area in which your document is displayed.

If you're unfamiliar with Windows controls, take a few minutes to complete the steps in the TRY IT box below.

TRY IT

Use the menu bar

1. Click **Insert** on the menu bar.

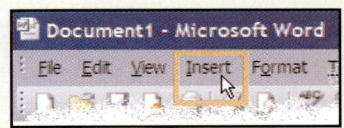

2. Click **Date and Time**.
3. Select the first option.
4. Click the **OK** button. The current date is inserted at the top of the workspace.

Use the toolbar

1. As shown below, click the **Spelling and Grammar** button on the Word toolbar.

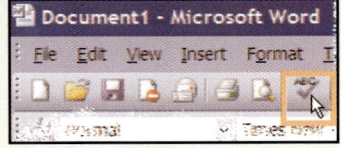

2. The computer checks the spelling in your document.
3. You didn't have any misspelled words, so click the **OK** button to end the spell check.

Use the sizing buttons

1. Click the ▬ Minimize button.
2. The Microsoft Word window shrinks down to a button on the taskbar at the bottom of the screen.

3. Click the taskbar button to make the Word window appear again. Leave Word open for the next TRY IT.

CREATING DOCUMENTS

How do I create a document? To create a document, simply type the text in the workspace provided by the Microsoft Word window. The flashing vertical insertion point indicates your place in the document (Figure 13).

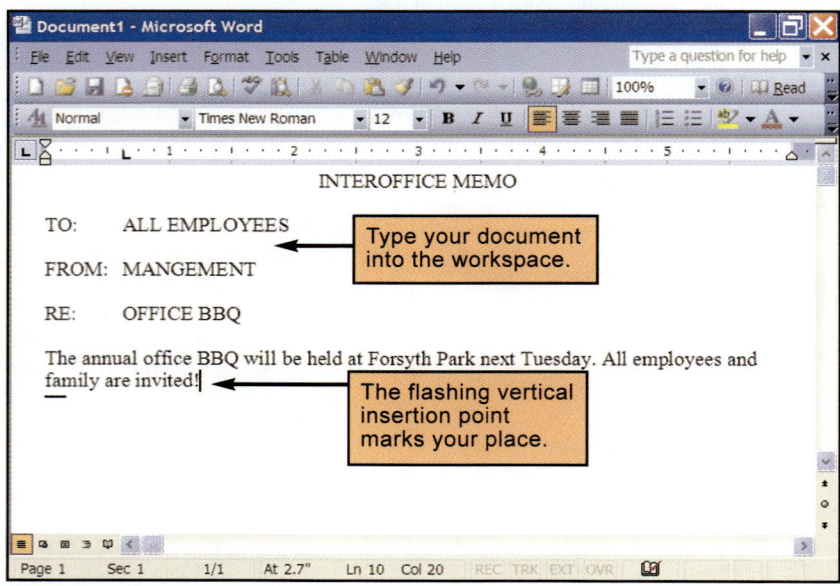

FIGURE 13

When typing text, you can use the following keys to move within the document and make revisions:

- **Backspace**: Delete the character to the left of the insertion point.

- **Delete:** Delete the character to the right of the insertion point.

- **Enter:** End a paragraph and begin a new line.

- **Arrow keys:** Move the insertion point up, down, right, or left.

How do I save a document? It is a good idea to save your work every few minutes, even if it is not finished. To save a document, use the Save option on the File menu, specify a storage location, and provide a name for the document, as shown in Figure 14.

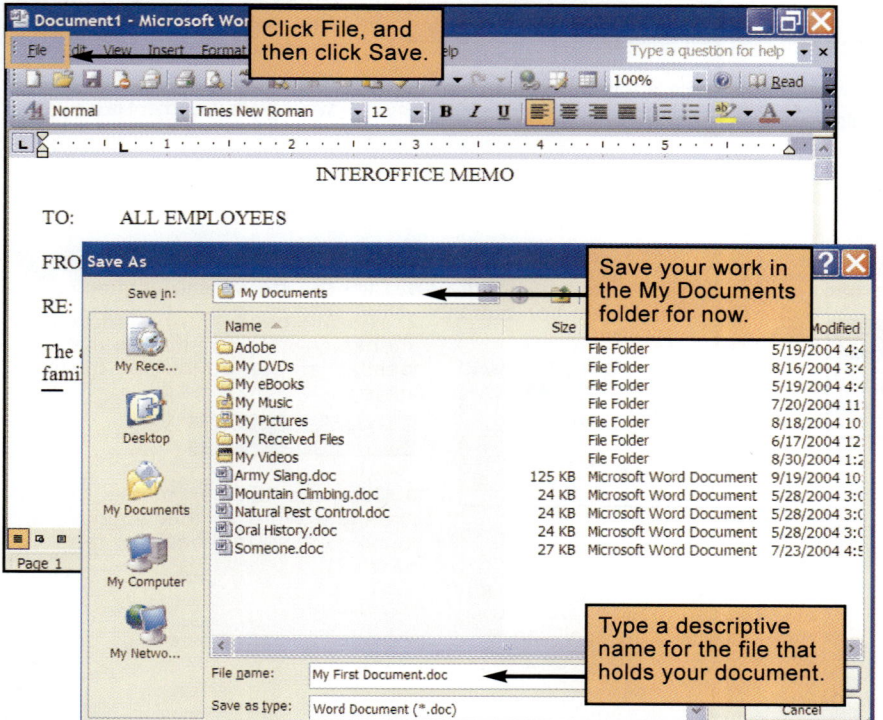

FIGURE 14

When you save a document, use the Save option on the File menu.

Your computer is probably configured to save documents in the My Documents folder on the hard disk. No need to change that until you gain more experience.

Make sure you enter a descriptive name for the document in the *File name* box. File names can be several words long; just do not use the * / \ " ' : symbols in the file name.

ORIENTATION   O-15

How do I print a document? To print a document, you simply click the File menu, and then select Print. Your computer displays a window containing a series of print options. If you want to print a single copy of your document, these settings should be correct, so you can click the OK button at the bottom of the window to send your document to the printer.

Can I send a document to my instructor? You can send a document via e-mail by using the Send To option on the File menu (Figure 15). To do so, you must know your instructor's e-mail address. You'll learn more about e-mail later in the Orientation, but keep this option in mind because it is a handy way to submit assignments, such as projects and term papers.

How do I find my documents again in the future? If you want to revise a document sometime in the future, simply start Microsoft Word, click File on the menu bar, and then click Open. Your computer should display a list of documents stored in the My Documents folder. Locate the one you want to revise and click it.

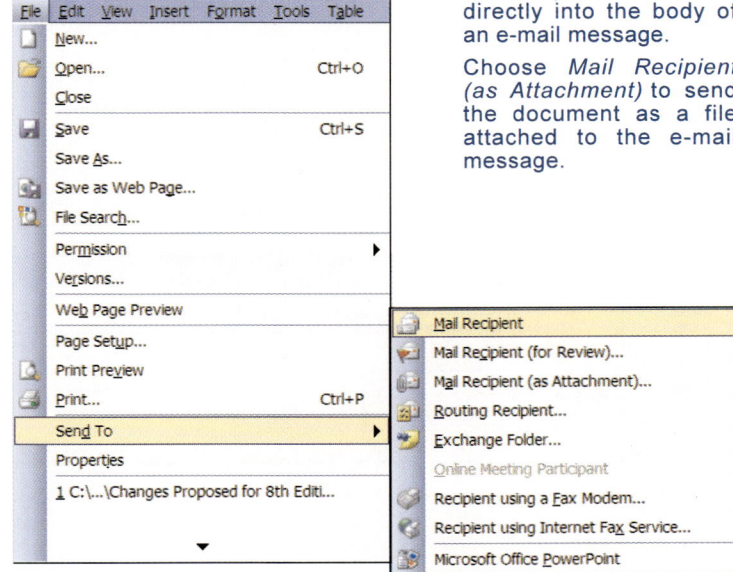

FIGURE 15

The File menu's Send To option produces a submenu of choices for sending mail.

Choose *Mail Recipient* to insert your document directly into the body of an e-mail message.

Choose *Mail Recipient (as Attachment)* to send the document as a file attached to the e-mail message.

What should I do when I'm done? When you're ready to quit, you can close the document by clicking the Close option from the File menu. When you want to close Microsoft Word, you can click the ☒ Close button in the upper-right corner of the screen.

If you have not yet had an opportunity to use Microsoft Word to create, save, and print a document, complete the steps in the TRY IT box below.

TRY IT

Create a document

1. Make sure that Microsoft Word is open.

2. Click the workspace to position the insertion point in the upper-left corner, just under the date.

3. Type a paragraph. Refer to Figure 13 for keys to use while typing and revising your work.

4. When the first paragraph is complete, press the **Enter** key to begin a new paragraph.

5. Type a second paragraph of text.

Save a document

1. Click **File** on the Word menu bar.

2. Click **Save**.

3. Make sure the *Save in* box lists My Documents. If not, click the ▼ button and then click My Documents from the list.

4. In the File name box, type a name for your document.

5. Click the **Save** button.

6. When the Save As dialog box closes, your document is saved.

Print a document, close it, and exit Word

1. Click **File** on the Word menu bar, and then click **Print**.

2. Make sure the Print Range button is set to **All**.

3. Make sure Number of Copies is set to **1**.

4. Click the **OK** button and wait a few seconds for the printer to produce your document.

5. Close the document by clicking **File**, then clicking **Close**. The workspace should become blank.

6. Exit Microsoft Word by clicking the ☒ Close button. The Word window should close and your screen should display the Windows desktop.

BOOKONCD SOFTWARE FEATURES

How do I use the features of the BookOnCD software? The BookOnCD offers you a unique learning environment full of media presentations and interactive assessment opportunities (Figure 16). To make effective use of this learning tool, you can complete the steps below to become familiar with BookOnCD menus and toolbar options.

EXPLORE NP8 LEARNING TOOLS

Explore BookOnCD menus

1. Start the BookOnCD and use the main menu to open the electronic textbook. Click **No** when asked about downloading Tracking Data.

2. Click **File** on the menu bar. The only option on this menu is Exit, which closes the electronic textbook. Do not use this option yet.

3. Click **Contents** on the menu bar. This menu lists the major sections of the textbook—preface, chapters, QuickCheck answers, Glossary, and Index. This option is most handy when you want to jump to a specific chapter.

4. Click **Tests** on the menu bar. Click **Chapter 1**. If you have a Tracking Disk, put it in; otherwise, click the **Continue** button. Your computer displays the first of 10 questions selected at random from a 150-question test bank. As you've not read Chapter 1 yet, click **Exit**.

5. Click **Tools** on the menu bar, which contains these options:

- Sound Settings: Turn off the volume when you are in a computer lab and have no earphones.
- Select Browser: Allows you to select Internet Explorer if you have multiple browsers installed on your computer.
- Tracking Disk: Displays scores stored on your Tracking Disk.
- Change Tracking Location: Stores your scores on the hard disk instead of a floppy disk.

Navigate the BookOnCD

1. Position the pointer over the scroll box on the right side of the BookOnCD page. (See diagram above.) Hold the mouse button down while dragging the mouse toward you. The BookOnCD page should scroll down. You can also click the ▼ or ▲ buttons several times to scroll the page.

2. Click the **Go to Page** button. Type **45**, and then click the **OK** button. Your computer displays page 45 of the textbook.

3. Click the **<Page** button. Your computer backs up and displays page 44.

4. Click the **Page>** button. Your computer displays page 45.

5. Click the **Glossary** button. Suppose you want to know the definition of MP3. Type **MP3** in the box and press the **Enter** key to see the definition, as shown to the right. Click the **Close** button to close the Glossary window.

6. The Syllabus and Annotation buttons appear only if your instructor has posted material for your class. You'll learn more about these features in Section D.

FIGURE 16
BookOnCD Resources

Entire Textbook
Carrying a notebook computer? Take the BookOnCD along. It's lighter than the printed book and contains every page.

Animated Figures
Specially marked figures come to life as animations, videos, and guided software tours.

Interactive Key Terms, Summaries, and Situation Questions
Help you assess your grasp of chapter material and study for tests.

Practice Tests
Take computer-graded tests with questions similar to those you'll find on in-class exams.

WebTrack
Keep a record of your scores and submit them electronically to your instructor.

New Perspectives Labs
Hands-on activities that help you explore chapter topics and apply what you've learned.

If you are unsure about the spelling of a term, click the ▼ button to see a list of terms.

ORIENTATION

O-17

HELP

How can I get help using software? If you've had problems using software, you're not alone! Everyone has questions at one time or another. Most software offers several sources of help, such as the following:

- **Message boxes.** When using software, it is important to pay attention to any message boxes displayed on the screen. Make sure you carefully read the options they present. If the box doesn't seem to apply to what you want to do, click its Cancel button to close it. Otherwise, set the options the way you want them, and then click the OK button to continue.

- **User manual.** Whether you're a beginner or a power user, the manual that comes with software can be an excellent resource. User manuals can contain quick-start guides, tutorials, detailed descriptions of menu options, and tips for using features effectively.

- **Help menu.** The Help menu provides access to on-screen documentation. Most Windows software offers a standard method for searching through its Help files. Documentation can be accessed through a table of contents, by consulting the index, or by searching for particular words or phrases (Figure 17 top).

- **Office Assistant.** Some software includes animated "assistants" that prompt you to type in simple questions (Figure 17 bottom). After you've entered a question, the assistant might ask you additional questions to refine your search, or it might display a list of documents that answer your question.

FIGURE 17
Clicking Help on the software menu bar usually produces a window, such as this one, where you can use the Contents, Index, or Find tabs to search the Help file for information.

QUICKCHECK......SECTION B

1. The ⬚ button on the Windows desktop can be used to launch just about any software installed on your computer.

2. It is a good idea to ⬚ your work every few minutes, even if you are not finished with it.

3. When you have completed work on a document, you can close it by using an option on the ⬚ menu.

4. If you've forgotten the definition of a key term in your textbook, you can use the ⬚ button on the BookOnCD.

5. The ⬚ menu provides access to on-screen documentation detailing the software's features and functions.

 CHECK ANSWERS

SECTION C

GETTING STARTED ON THE INTERNET

The Internet provides access to a vast collection of resources and information. As a student, you'll find it handy for research pertaining to many of your classes. You can also access information and activities designed to enhance the introductory computer material in this textbook. Section C shows you how to access these useful resources.

INTERNET AND WEB BASICS

What is the Internet? The Internet is the largest computer network in the world (Figure 18), carrying information from one continent to another in the blink of an eye. The computers connected to this network offer many types of resources, such as e-mail, instant messaging, popular music downloads, and online shopping.

What is the Web? Although some people use the terms "Internet" and "Web" interchangeably, the two are not the same. The Internet refers to a communications network that connects computers in every country in the world. The Web—short for World Wide Web—is just one of the many resources available over this communications network.

The World Wide Web is a collection of linked and cross-referenced information available for public access. This information is accessible from Web sites located on various computers. The information is displayed as a series of screens called Web pages. You'll use the Web for general research and for specific activities designed to accompany this textbook. To use the Web, your computer must have access to the Internet.

How do I access the Internet? Most computers can be configured to connect to the Internet by using telephone or cable television systems. Internet access can be obtained from school computer labs, local service providers, such as your cable television company, and national Internet service providers, such as AOL (America Online), AT&T, and MSN (Microsoft Network).

To expedite your orientation, it is assumed that your computer has Internet access. If it does not, refer to Chapters 5 and 6, consult your instructor, or ask an experienced computer user to help you get set up.

How do I know if my computer has Internet access? The easiest way to find out if your computer can access the Internet is to try it. You can quickly find out if you have Internet access by starting software called a browser that's designed to display Web pages.

Browser software called Internet Explorer is supplied with Microsoft Windows. Other browsers, such as Netscape, Mozilla, FireFox, and Opera, are also available. The NP8 Web site is optimized for Internet Explorer, so you should use it, if possible. Follow the steps in the TRY IT box to start Internet Explorer.

HOW TO USE A WEB BROWSER AND SEARCH ENGINE

How do I use a browser? A browser lets you type in a unique Web page address called a URL and jump from that page to other Web pages by

FIGURE 18
The Internet communications network stretches around the globe.

📠 TRY IT

Start your browser

1. Click the [icon] icon located near the Start button.

2. Your computer should soon display a window containing "Microsoft Internet Explorer" in the title bar. (Refer to the next page.)

If your computer displays a *Connect to* box, click the **Dial** button to establish a dial-up connection via your telephone.

You'll need to cancel the browser command and consult an experienced computer user if:

- Your computer displays a "working off line" message.
- Your computer displays an Internet Connection Wizard box.

ORIENTATION

O-19

using links. Links are usually underlined, and when you position the arrow-shaped mouse pointer over a link, it changes to a hand shape.

You'll learn much more about browsers in Chapter 1. Until you read that material, you can get along quite well using the basic controls shown in Figure 19.

FIGURE 19
Using a Browser

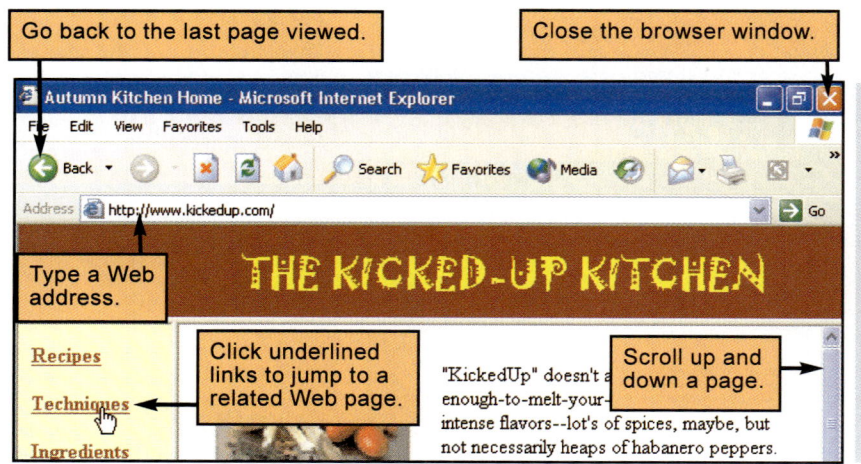

A full Web address might look like this:

http://www.kickedup.com

It is not necessary to type the http://, so to access the Kicked-Up Kitchen page shown here, you would type:

www.kickedup.com

When typing a Web address, do not use any spaces and copy upper- and lowercase letters exactly.

How do I find specific information on the Web? If you're looking for information and don't know the Web site where it might be located, you can use a search engine to find it. Follow the steps in the TRY IT box to "go "Googling" by using the Google search engine.

TRY IT

Access a search engine

1. Make sure the Internet Explorer browser window is open.
2. Click the Address box and type:

   Address: www.google.com

3. Press the **Enter** key. Your browser displays the Web page for the Google search engine.

Use a search engine

1. Click the blank search box and then type **national parks**.

2. Press the **Enter** key. Google displays a list of Web pages that relate to national parks.

3. Click the underlined **National Park Service** link. Your browser displays the ParkNet home page.

ACCESSING THE NEW PERSPECTIVES NP8 WEB SITE

What kinds of Web resources accompany my textbook? The New Perspectives NP8 Web site—NP8 Web site, for short—includes all sorts of activities and information to help you learn about computers. Figure 20 lists the resources you'll find at the site.

FIGURE 20
NP8 Web Site Resources

Interactive Overview (audio)
Listen to a 5-minute audio presentation of chapter highlights.

Pre-assessment
Take a short quiz to assess your background in the chapter material.

InfoWebLinks
Follow Web links to find the most current information on equipment and software you read about in a chapter.

Study Tips
When test time rolls around, try these tips for a complete review of chapter material.

Online Games
Have some fun while refreshing your memory about key concepts that might appear on the next exam.

Student Edition Labs
Get hands-on practice with some of the concepts presented in a chapter.

Projects
Find lots of topics for term papers and extra-credit projects here.

TechTV Video Project
Watch a video clip from a recent TechTV show and explore new tech trends.

How do I access the NP8 Web site? You can get to the Web site in several ways:

- Open your browser and type *www.course.com/np/concepts8*. Your browser will display the main page of the NP8 Web site. From there, you can click links to various activities and information.
- Open your BookOnCD and click any link. These links take you directly to the information or activity specified along with the link.

Follow the steps in the box below to access the NP8 Web site.

EXPLORE NP8 LEARNING TOOLS

Access the NP8 Web Site

1. Make sure the Internet Explorer browser window is open.
2. Click the address box and type:

   Address: www.course.com/np/concepts8

   Make sure to use all lowercase letters, insert no spaces, and use the / slash, not the \ slash.
3. Press the **Enter** key. Your browser displays the Computer Concepts main page.
4. Read the Welcome message and scroll, if necessary, to get a look at the entire page.
5. Click **Chapter 1** at the top of the screen. Your browser displays links to activities for the first chapter in your textbook.

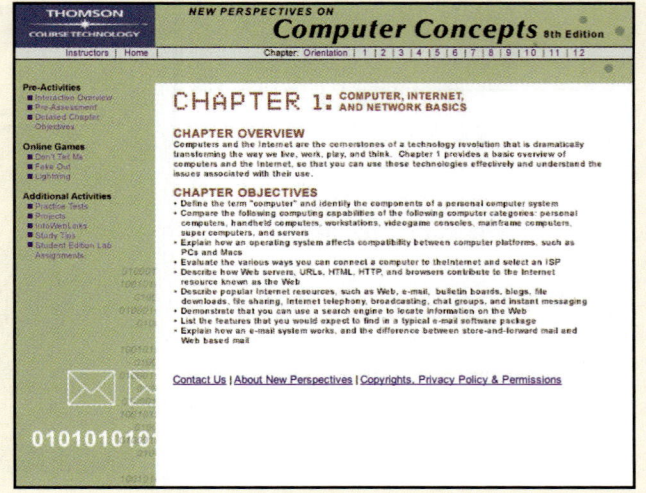

ORIENTATION

O-21

How do I use the Interactive Overview and other resources? Follow the steps in the box below to explore the NP8 Web site.

EXPLORE NP8 LEARNING TOOLS

Explore the NP8 Web site

1. Make sure your browser is displaying the activities page for Chapter 1 (*www.course.com/np/concepts8/ch01.htm*).

2. Click the **Interactive Overview** link. Listen to the chapter overview for a few seconds, and then use the on-screen buttons to return to the Chapter 1 page.

3. Click the **Pre-assessment** link. You might want to complete the quiz to see how much of the material in Chapter 1 you already know. Use the on-screen buttons when you are ready to return to the Chapter 1 page and continue your exploration.

4. Click the **InfoWeb** link. When you see a list of InfoWebLinks for Chapter 1, click the **Netiquette** link. Read the short overview, and then click the first blue underlined link. Use the **Back** button to get back to the Chapter 1 main page.

5. Click the **Study Tips** link and read through a few to get an idea of the activities recommended to help you study for a test on the material in Chapter 1. When you are ready, return to the main Chapter 1 Web page.

6. Click the link to the **Lightning** game. Try your hand at a few questions, and then go back to the main Chapter 1 Web page.

7. Click the **Student Edition Lab** link. Try this interactive lab to get an idea of how it works. After exploring this activity, return to the main Chapter 1 Web page.

8. Click the **TechTV Video Project** link. Take a few minutes to watch the video, then return to the main page for Chapter 1.

9. Use your browser's ❎ Close button to exit the NP8 Web site when your exploration is complete. If you are using a dial-up connection, you might have to manually disconnect from the Internet by double-clicking the 🖳 icon in the lower-right corner of your screen, and then clicking **Disconnect**.

InfoWebLinks provide lots of information to supplement what you've read in the textbook.

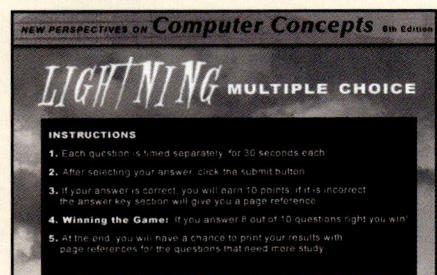

Online games, such as LIghtning, Don't Tell Me, and Fake Out provide a fun way to review chapter material.

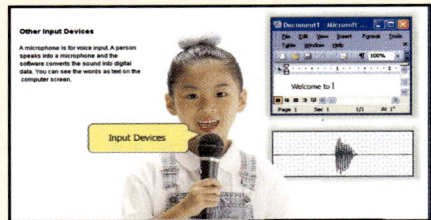

Student Edition labs give you an in-depth, hands-on look into one or more chapter topics.

QUICKCHECK......SECTION C

1. The _____ is a communications network that connects computers all over the world.

2. The World Wide _____ is one of the many resources available on the Internet communications network.

3. Software called a(n) _____ helps you access Web pages.

4. If you don't know where to find information, you can use a(n) _____ engine to produce a list of links to Web pages that might contain the information you seek.

 CHECK ANSWERS

SECTION D

COMMUNICATING WITH YOUR INSTRUCTOR

Staying in contact with your instructor is important whether you attend classes on campus or online. Section D provides a quick overview of e-mail. It introduces you to your textbook's lab, annotation, WebTrack, and syllabus features. Plus, it shows you how to send your Tracking Disk scores to your instructor.

WORKING WITH E-MAIL

What is e-mail? E-mail is a form of communication that relies on computer networks, such as the Internet, to transmit messages from one computer to another. Like regular mail, e-mail messages are sent to a mailbox where they are kept until the recipient retrieves the message. Messages might arrive at their destination within minutes, or might not arrive for a few hours. Once sent, e-mail messages cannot be retrieved.

What do I need to use e-mail? To send and receive e-mail, you need an Internet connection, an e-mail account, and software that enables you to compose, read, and delete e-mail messages. An e-mail account consists of an e-mail address (Figure 21), a password, and a mailbox. You can usually obtain an e-mail account from your Internet service provider, your school, or a Web-based e-mail provider, such as Hotmail, Yahoo! Mail, or GMail.

How do I create and send an e-mail message? Many e-mail systems are available, and each uses slightly different software, making it impossible to cover all options in this short orientation. You might want to enlist the aid of an experienced computer user to help you get started. Chapter 1 provides more detail about e-mail, too. The steps in the TRY IT box are designed for students who use e-mail software called Outlook Express, which is supplied with Microsoft Windows.

FIGURE 21
E-mail Addresses

An e-mail address consists of a user ID followed by an @ symbol and the name of a computer that handles e-mail accounts. Ask your instructor for his or her e-mail address. It is likely similar to the following:

instructor@school.edu

When typing an e-mail address, use all lowercase letters and do not use any spaces.

TRY IT

Create and send e-mail

1. Click the icon located at the bottom of your screen. The Outlook Express window opens.

2. Click the **Create** button to display a form like the one at right.

3. Follow steps 4-6 as shown at right.

4. When your message is complete, click the **Send** button. With most computers, this button places the e-mail in your Outbox.

5. Click the **Send/Recv** button on the toolbar to ship the message from your Outbox over the network to your instructor.

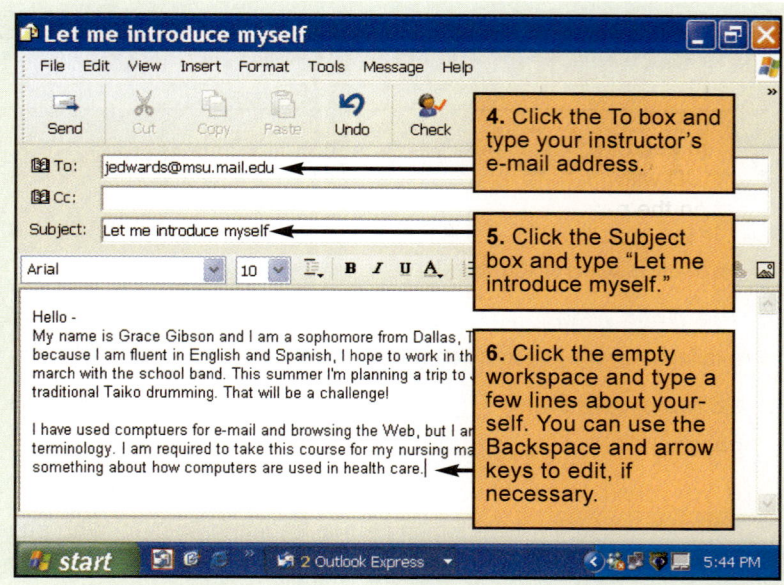

ORIENTATION O-23

How do I get my mail? As with sending mail, the way you get mail depends on your mail system. In general, clicking the Send/Recv button collects your mail from the network and stores it in your Inbox. Your mail software displays a list of your messages. The new ones are usually shown in bold type. You can click any message to open it, read it, and reply to it, as shown in Figure 22.

FIGURE 22

Most e-mail software displays a list of your messages. You can:

- Open a message and read it.
- Reply to a message.
- Delete unwanted messages (a good idea to minimize the size of your mailbox).
- Forward a message to someone else.

HOW TO TRANSFER TRACKING DISK DATA

What has my Tracking Disk got to do with communication? A feature of your textbook's technology called WebTrack allows your instructor to send you an updated syllabus and notes, called annotations, that supplement the pages in your textbook. It also enables you to transfer scores to your instructor. You can transfer QuickCheck, Practice Tests, Interactive Summary, Interactive Situation Questions, and Lab scores, as well as your opinions on the Issue questions.

Whenever you submit scores, your Tracking Disk collects any material posted for you by your instructor. For example, if your instructor has posted some annotations for Chapter 1, you'll automatically receive links to them when you send in your first QuickCheck score. The next time you use the BookOnCD with your Tracking Disk in the drive, the Annotation button will appear on the pages specified by your instructor, as shown in Figure 23. When you click the Annotation button, your computer accesses your instructor's annotation Web pages.

FIGURE 23

If your instructor has created annotations, the Annotation button will appear on your BookOnCD pages.

How do I submit Tracking Disk scores? Suppose you want to work on a BookOnCD lab, take the lab QuickChecks, and submit your score to your instructor. Follow the instructions below to find out how. Before you begin, make sure your instructor has posted some annotations for Chapter 1 and you have the following:

- An Internet connection
- Your instructor's e-mail address
- Tracking data stored on a Tracking Disk or drive C (you made a Tracking Disk or specified drive C as your tracking location in Section A)

EXPLORE NP8 LEARNING TOOLS

Open a BookOnCD lab

1. Make sure your Tracking Disk is in the drive (or you specified drive C for your tracking location) and start the BookOnCD.

2. When you see the main menu, click **Open a New Perspectives Lab** (shown at right).

3. Click the lab title **Operating a Personal Computer**.

4. Click the ➡ Continue button to view the objectives for Topic 1.

5. Click the ➡ button again to view page 1 of the lab. Read the information on the page, and then continue through the lab, making sure to follow any numbered instructions such as those shown at right.

6. After page 8, you will encounter the first QuickCheck question. Click the correct answer, and then click the Continue button. Complete all the QuickCheck Questions for Topic 1.

7. Complete the entire lab and answer all the QuickCheck questions.

8. When you complete the lab, follow the instructions to exit. Your QuickCheck Tracking Report is displayed and saved. For future reference, notice that you can print the report by using the Print button. After reviewing the report, click **Exit**.

9. From the NP Labs screen, click **Exit** to return to the main BookOnCD menu. Leave the main menu open in preparation for the next TRY IT.

In addition to Lab QuickChecks, each BookOnCD lab also includes a set of assignments located at the end of corresponding sections of your textbook. Your instructor might require you to complete these written online assignments. You can submit them on paper, on disk, or as an e-mail message, according to your instructor's directions.

Now you've completed a lab and your score has been automatically saved on your Tracking Disk. The steps on the next page guide you through the process of sending your tracking data to your instructor.

ORIENTATION   O-25

⌨ EXPLORE NP8 LEARNING TOOLS

Send your tracking data

1. Make sure your Tracking Disk is in the drive (or you specified drive C for your tracking location) and the BookOnCD main menu is displayed on your computer's screen.

2. Click the option **Send your Student Tracking Data to your instructor** (shown at right). Your computer makes an Internet connection, opens your browser, and displays the WebTrack site.

3. Click the underlined link **Click here to send your Tracking files to your instructor now**.

4. If this is the first time you have sent data, you might see a Security Warning window. Click **Yes** to download the MediaTechnics component that sends your tracking data. This operation takes a few seconds.

5. When you see the WebTrack Student Module window (shown at right), enter your instructor's e-mail address, and then click the **Submit TK2 Data** button.

6. On the next screen, confirm that your student ID is correct and then click the **Send Data** button.

7. Follow the instructions displayed on the screen to return to the main BookOnCD menu.

Check for annotations

1. If your instructor has posted annotations for Chapter 1, the Annotation button should now appear when you read the BookOnCD. Click to open the electronic textbook, and page through Chapter 1 to find your instructor's annotations.

QUICKCHECK......SECTION D

1. The special symbol used in e-mail addresses is _____.

2. An e-mail account consists of an e-mail address, a password, and a(n) _____.

3. In general, clicking the Send/Receive button collects your mail from the network and stores it in your _____.

4. It is a good idea to _____ unwanted mail to minimize the size of your mailbox.

❖ CHECK ANSWERS

SECTION E

SECURITY AND PRIVACY

Today's digital landscape is dotted with a few obstacles that can trip up unwary computer users. As with most other facets of modern life, computing has its share of troublemakers, scam artists, and identity thieves. Section E offers some tips on navigating through the sometimes rough neighborhoods of cyberspace, while keeping your data safe and your identity private.

SECURING YOUR COMPUTER AND DATA

What's at risk if my computer is stolen? A computer can be an attractive target for thieves, but the value of a stolen computer is not so much in the hardware as in the data it contains. With stolen data such as your bank account numbers and PINs, a thief can wipe out your checking and savings accounts. With your credit card numbers, a thief can go on a spending spree. Even worse, a criminal can use stolen data to assume your identity, run up debts, get into legal trouble, ruin your credit rating, and cause you no end of trouble.

How can I protect my computer data from theft? When you carry a notebook computer, never leave it unattended. To thwart a thief who breaks into your home or dorm room, anchor your computer to your desk with a specially designed lock you can buy at most electronics stores.

If a thief steals your computer, you can make it difficult to access your data by setting up a password. Until the password is entered, your data is off limits. A thief might be able to boot up the Windows desktop, but should not be able to easily look at the data in your folders.

Many new computers are shipped with a standard administrator password that everyone knows. Create a secure password (Figure 24) for this account as soon as you can. If you are the only person using your computer, you can use the administrator account for your day-to-day computing.

Your computer might also include a preset guest account with an unsecure password such as "guest." You should disable this guest account or assign it a secure password.

FIGURE 24
To create a secure password:

- Use at least five characters, mixing numbers with letters, as in 2by4s.
- Do not use your name, the name of a family member, or pet's name.
- Do not use a word that can be found in the dictionary.
- Do not forget your password!

TRY IT

Check the accounts on your computer

1. Click the **Start** button, then select **Control Panel**.

2. Select **User Accounts**. The User Accounts window shown at right displays a list of accounts.

3. If you are working on a school lab computer, close the User Accounts window without making any changes. If you are using your own computer, click the Administrator account and make sure it has a secure password.

User accounts are displayed at the bottom of the window.

ORIENTATION

AVOIDING VIRUSES

What's so bad about computer viruses? The term "virus" has a technical meaning that you'll learn in Chapter 4, but many people use the term loosely when referring to malicious programs that circulate on disks, in e-mail attachments, and on the Internet. This malware, as it is sometimes called, can steal your data, destroy files, or create network traffic jams. It might display an irritating message to announce its presence, or it might work quietly behind the scenes to spread itself to various files on your computer or mail itself out to everyone in your e-mail address book.

After a virus takes up residence in your computer, it is often difficult to disinfect all your files and make sure it is eliminated. Rather than wait for a virus attack, you should take steps to keep your computer virus free.

How can I keep viruses out of my computer? Back when viruses were less sophisticated, computer users were commonly warned not to download pirated software or open e-mail attachments from unknown senders. These two common sources of viruses still exist, but virus creators have found ways to make pirated software look legitimate and to affix your friends' names to e-mails that carry infected attachments.

Although it is a good idea to avoid pirated software and stay alert when opening e-mail attachments, the best defense against viruses is to install antivirus software and configure it to run continuously whenever your computer is on. At least once a week your antivirus software should also run a full system check to make sure every file on your computer is virus free.

You should make sure your antivirus software is set up to scan for viruses in incoming files and e-mail messages. As new viruses emerge, your antivirus software needs to update its virus definition file. It gets this update as a Web download. If you've selected the auto update option, your computer should automatically receive updates as they become available.

FIGURE 25
Popular Antivirus Software

Norton AntiVirus
McAfee VirusScan
Kaspersky Anti-Virus
F-Prot
Softwin BitDefender
Panda Antivirus
Trend Micro PC-cillin

TRY IT

Get familiar with your antivirus software

1. Click the **Start** button, and then select **All Programs**. Look for antivirus software (refer to Figure 25 for a list). Open your antivirus software by clicking it.

Can't find any? If you are using your own computer and it doesn't seem to have antivirus software, you can connect to an antivirus Web site and download it.

2. Each antivirus program has unique features. The figure on the right shows the main screen for Norton AntiVirus software. Explore your antivirus software to make sure it is configured to do the following:

- Scan incoming e-mail
- Run continuously in the background—a feature sometimes called Auto Protect
- Block malicious scripts

3. Check the date of your last full system scan. If it was more than one week ago, you should check the settings that schedule antivirus scans.

4. Check the date when your computer last received virus definitions. If it was more than two weeks ago, you should make sure your antivirus software is configured to receive automatic live updates.

PREVENTING INTRUSIONS

Is it risky to go online? The Internet offers lots of cool stuff—music downloads, movie reviews and trailers, online shopping and banking, consumer information, chat groups, news, sports, weather, and much more. Most Internet offerings are legitimate, but some downloads contain viruses, and shady characters called "hackers" control programs that lurk about waiting to snatch your personal data or infiltrate your computer. The longer your computer remains connected to the Internet, the more vulnerable it is to a hacker's infiltration attempts.

If a hacker gains access to your computer, he or she can look through your files, use your computer as a launching platform for viruses and network-jamming attacks, or turn your computer into a server for pornography and other unsavory material. Hackers have even found ways to turn thousands of infiltrated computers into "zombies," link them together, and carry out coordinated attacks to disrupt online access to Microsoft, Bank of America, and other Internet businesses.

How do hackers gain access to my computer? Intruders gain access by exploiting security flaws in your computer's operating system, browser, and e-mail software. Software publishers are constantly creating patches to fix these flaws. As part of your overall security plan, you should download and install security patches as they become available.

How can I block hackers from infiltrating my computer? Firewall software (Figure 26) provides a protective barrier between a computer and the Internet. If your computer is directly connected to the Internet, it should have active firewall software. If your computer connects to a local area network for Internet access, the network should have a device called a router to block infiltration attempts.

When a firewall is active, it watches for potentially disruptive incoming data called "probes." When a probe is discovered, your firewall displays a warning and asks what to do. If the source looks legitimate, you can let it through; if not, you should block it (Figure 27).

Where do I get a firewall? Windows XP includes a built-in firewall called Windows Internet Connection Firewall (ICF) or Windows Firewall. If your computer uses an earlier version of Windows, you can download a third-party firewall.

FIGURE 26
Popular Firewall Software

Tiny Personal Firewall
McAfee Firewall Plus
Zone Alarm Pro
Sygate Firewall Pro
Norton Firewall
Black Ice Defender
Mac OS Firewall
Outpost Firewall

FIGURE 27
When your firewall software encounters new or unusual activity, it asks you what to do.

TRY IT

Check your computer's firewall

Finding out if your computer has an active firewall requires a little detective work. Try one or more of these three methods. If your computer doesn't seem to have a firewall, you might want to download one and install it.

For non-XP users:

Click the **Start** button, click **All Programs**, and then look through the program list for firewalls such as those in Figure 26. If you find a firewall listed, start it and explore to see if it has been activated.

For Windows XP Service Pack 2 users:

Click the **Start** button, then click **Control Panel**. Double-click the **Security Center** icon and then make sure the Firewall is on.

For Windows XP users:

Click the **Start** button, then click **Control Panel**. Click **Network Connections**. Click the connection you use for Internet access. Under Network Tasks, click **Change Settings for this connection**. Click the **Advanced** tab and look for a check mark in front of *Protect my computer and network by limiting or preventing access to this computer from the Internet*.

ORIENTATION

BLOCKING SPYWARE AND POP-UP ADS

Are some Web sites dangerous? When you access Web sites, data is transferred to your computer and displayed by your browser. Most of this data is harmless, but malicious HTML scripts, rogue ActiveX components, and spyware have the potential to search your computer for passwords and credit card numbers, install viruses, block your access to legitimate Web sites, or surreptitiously use your computer as a staging area for illicit activities.

Spyware is the most insidious threat. It often piggybacks on pop-up ads and activates if you click the ad window. Some spyware can begin its dirty work when you try to click the Close button to get rid of an ad.

FIGURE 28
Some pop-up ads contain fake warnings about viruses, spyware, and intrusion attempts.

How can I block spyware? The first line of defense is to never click pop-up ads—especially those that carry dire warnings about your computer being infected by a virus or spyware! (See Figure 28.) To close an ad, right-click its button on the taskbar at the bottom of your screen, and then select the Close option from the menu that appears. Some browsers can be configured to block spyware and pop-up ads. Your antivirus software might offer similar options. You can also install software specially designed to block spyware and pop-up ads. Figure 29 lists some popular titles.

What other steps can I take to browse the Web safely? Most browsers include security features. You should take some time to become familiar with them. For example, Internet Explorer allows you to specify how you want it to deal with ActiveX components. You can also specify how to deal with HTML scripts, cookies, security certificates, and other Web-based data. If you don't want to be bothered by these details, however, Internet Explorer offers several predefined configurations for Low, Medium, and High security. Most Internet Explorer users set security and privacy options to Medium.

FIGURE 29
Popular Antispyware and Ad-Blocking Software

Webroot SpySweeper
Ad-Aware
Spybot S&D
SpyHunter
SpyRemover
Pest Patrol
Spykiller
Pop-up Defender

TRY IT

Explore Internet Explorer security and privacy options

1. Start Internet Explorer. Click **Tools** on the menu bar, then select **Internet Options**.

2. Click the **Security** tab. Typically, your security setting should be Medium.

3. Click the **Privacy** tab. Typically, your privacy setting should be Medium.

4. Check the bottom of the window for a Pop-up Blocker option. If your version of Internet Explorer offers this feature, make sure its box contains a check mark so that it is activated.

5. If your version of Internet Explorer does not offer a pop-up blocker, check your antivirus software to see if it can provide protection. Otherwise, you can use the Start button to see if the software listed in Figure 29 has been installed. If your computer seems to have no antispyware or ad-blocking software, you might want to download some and install it.

PROTECTING E-COMMERCE TRANSACTIONS

Is online shopping safe? Online shopping is generally safe. From time to time, shoppers encounter fake storefronts designed to look like legitimate merchants, but that are actually set up to steal credit card information. You can avoid these fakes by making sure you enter correctly spelled URLs when connecting to your favorite shopping sites.

How safe is my credit card information when I shop online? Online shopping is no more dangerous than using your credit card for a telephone order or giving it to a server when you've finished eating in a restaurant. Anyone who handles your card can copy the card number, jot down the expiration date, and try to make unauthorized charges.

That's not to say that credit cards are risk free. Credit cards are surprisingly vulnerable both online and off. Thieves can break into merchant computers that store order information. Thieves might even pick up your credit card information from discarded order forms. Despite these risks, we continue to use credit cards.

Many people are concerned about their credit card data getting intercepted as it travels over the Internet. When you wrap up an online purchase and submit your credit card information, it is transmitted from your computer to the merchant's computer. Software called a packet sniffer, designed for legitimately monitoring network traffic, is occasionally used by unscrupulous hackers to intercept credit card numbers and other data traveling over the Internet.

How can I keep my credit card number confidential? When you submit credit card information, make sure the merchant provides a secure connection for transporting data. Typically, a secure connection is activated when you're in the final phases of checking out—as you enter your shipping and credit card information into a form and click a Submit button to send it. A secure connection encrypts your data. Even if your credit card number is intercepted, it cannot be deciphered and used. To make sure you have a secure connection, look for the lock icon in the lower-right corner of your screen. The Address box should also display a URL that begins with shttp:// or https:// (Secure HTTP), or contains ssl (Secure Sockets Layer).

TRY IT

Know how to identify a secure connection

1. Start your browser and connect to the site: **www.walmart.com**.

2. Select any item and use the **Add to Cart** option to place it in your online shopping cart.

3. Click the **Proceed to Checkout** button.

4. At the checkout screen, do you see any evidence that you're using a secure connection?

5. Close your browser so that you don't complete the transaction.

ORIENTATION

AVOIDING E-MAIL SCAMS

What are e-mail scams? From time to time, you hear about con artists who have bilked innocent consumers out of their life savings. The Internet has its share of con artists, too, who run e-mail scams designed to collect money and confidential information from unsuspecting "marks." E-mail scams are usually distributed in mass mailings called spam.

What do I need to know about spam? The Internet makes it easy and cheap to send out millions of e-mail solicitations. In the United States, the CAN-Spam law requires mass-mail messages to be labeled [SPAM] in the subject line. Recipients are supposed to be provided with a way to opt out of receiving future messages. Legitimate merchants and organizations comply with the law when sending product announcements, newsletters, and other messages. Unscrupulous spammers ignore the law and try to disguise their solicitations as messages from your friends, chat room participants, or co-workers (Figure 30).

FIGURE 30
Some spam is clearly labeled, whereas others are not.

Is spam dangerous? Many spam messages contain legitimate information, including daily or weekly newsletters to which you've subscribed. Some spam messages, however, advertise illegal products. Others are outright scams to get you to download a virus, divulge your bank account numbers, or send in money for products you'll never receive.

Beware of spam containing offers that seem just too good to be true. For example, you might receive a message from an African businessman who is seeking your help to transfer a large sum of money from his country to yours (Figure 31). These messages are frauds.

FIGURE 31
Many variations of this African money-transfer fraud—complete with deliberate grammatical errors—have circulated on the Internet for years. Victims who responded to these preposterous e-mails have found their bank accounts raided, their credit ratings destroyed, and their reputations ruined. According to the FBI, some victims have even been kidnapped!

What's phishing? Phishing (pronounced "fishing") is a scam that arrives in your e-mailbox looking like official correspondence from a major company, such as Microsoft, PayPal, eBay, MSN, Yahoo!, or America Online. The e-mail message is actually from an illegitimate source and is designed to trick you into divulging confidential information or downloading a virus. Links in the e-mail message often lead to a Web site that looks official, where you are asked to enter confidential information such as your credit card number, social security number, or bank account number.

The following are examples of phishing scams you should be aware of:

- A message from Microsoft with an attachment that supposedly contains a security update for Microsoft Windows. Downloading the attachment infects your computer with a virus.

- A message from America Online, complete with official-looking logos, that alerts you to a problem with your account. When you click the AOL Billing Center link and enter your account information, it is transmitted to a hacker's computer.

- A message that's obviously spam, but contains a convenient opt-out link. If you click the link believing that it will prevent future spam from this source, you'll actually be downloading a program that hackers can use to remotely control your computer for illegal activities.

How do I avoid e-mail scams? If your e-mail software provides spam filters, you can use them to block some unsolicited mail from your e-mailbox. Spam filters are far from perfect, however, so don't assume everything that gets through is legitimate. Use your judgment before opening any e-mail message or attachment.

Never reply to a message that you suspect to be fraudulent. If you have a question about its legitimacy, check whether it's on a list of known scams. Never click a link provided in an e-mail message to manage your account information. Instead, go directly to the Web site and access your account as usual. Microsoft never sends updates as attachments. To obtain Microsoft updates, go to *www.microsoft.com* and click Windows Update or Office Update.

TRY IT

Arm yourself against e-mail scams

1. Start your browser and connect to the site **www.antiphishing.org**. Scroll down the page and become familiar with the list of recent phishing attacks.

2. Open your e-mail software and find out if it incudes spam filters. You can usually find this information by clicking Help on the menu bar and then typing "spam filter" in the search box.

3. Explore your options for configuring spam filters. If you use Microsoft Outlook for e-mail (shown at right), you can find these settings by clicking **Actions** on the menu bar, pointing to **Junk E-Mail**, then clicking **Junk E-mail Options**.

Spam filters sometimes catch legitimate mail and group it with junk mail. You might want to keep tabs on your spam filters when they are first activated to make sure they are set to a level that eliminates most unwanted spam without catching too much legitimate mail.

ORIENTATION

O-33

PROTECTING YOUR PRIVACY

How much information has been collected about me? No matter what steps you take to protect your privacy, information about you is stored in many places and has the potential to be consolidated by government agencies, private businesses, and criminals.

Some databases are legitimate—those maintained by credit bureaus and medical insurance companies, for example. By law, you have the right to ask for a copy of these records and correct any errors you find. Many other databases, such as those maintained at e-commerce sites and those illegally acquired by hackers, are not accessible, and you have no way of checking the data they contain.

Can I control who collects information about me? To some extent, you can limit your exposure to future data collection by supplying personal data only when absolutely necessary. When filling out online forms, consider whether you want to or need to provide your real name and address.

You should also be careful about revealing personal information in chat rooms and other online forums. Many chat room participants are not who they appear to be. Some people are just having fun with fantasy identities, but others are trying to con people by telling hard luck stories and faking illnesses. Never reveal personal information, such as your full name, address, or phone number. Resist the temptation to meet face to face with chat room participants. Taking these simple steps to protect your privacy is an important part of your overall security plan.

FIGURE 32
Security Checklist

- Use a password to protect your data in case your computer is stolen.
- Don't leave your computer unattended in public places.
- Run antivirus software and keep it updated.
- Install software service packs and security patches as they become available, but make sure they are legitimate.
- Install and activate firewall software, especially if your computer is directly connected to the Internet by an ISDN, DSL, satellite, or cable connection.
- Do not publish or post personal information, such as your physical address, passwords, social security number, and account numbers, on your Web site, your online resume, or other online documents.
- Be wary of contacts you make in public chat rooms.
- Don't click pop-up ads.
- Install and activate anti-spyware and ad-blocking software.
- Do not reply to spam.
- Ignore e-mail offers that seem too good to be true.

⌨ **TRY IT**

Check your privacy

1. Start your browser and go Googling by connecting to www.google.com. Enter your name in the Search box. What turns up?

2. Connect to www.peopledata.com and click the **People Search** option. Enter your name and state of residence. Click the **Search** button. Notice all the information that's offered.

3. Connect to www.ciadata.com and scroll down the page to view the kind of information anyone can obtain about you for less than $100.

4. Connect to the Federal Trade Commission site:

http://www.ftc.gov/bcp/conline/pubs/credit/crdright.htm

At this site, you can read about your rights to view credit reports.

QUICKCHECK......SECTION E

1. The best defense against viruses is to use a phishing filter before opening e-mail attachments. True or false? [   ].

2. Intruders can access your computer by exploiting [   ] flaws in a computer's operating system, browser, or e-mail software.

3. [   ] is an online threat that compromises your privacy by piggybacking on pop-up ads and collecting personal information.

4. E-mail scams are usually distributed in mass mailings called [   ].

✦ CHECK ANSWERS

NEW PERSPECTIVES

Computer Concepts
8th Edition

COMPUTER, INTERNET, WEB, AND E-MAIL BASICS

CONTENTS

SECTION A: COMPUTER BASICS
- A Computer Is...
- Computer Categories
- Personal Computer Systems
- Data, Information, and Files
- Application Software and Operating System Basics

SECTION B: INTERNET BASICS
- Internet Resources
- Internet Connections
- Internet Service Providers
- User IDs and Passwords

SECTION C: WEB BASICS
- The World Wide Web
- Browsers
- Search Engines

SECTION D: E-MAIL BASICS
- E-mail Overview
- Netiquette
- Spam
- E-mail Technology

TECHTALK: THE BOOT PROCESS

ISSUE: E-MAIL PRIVACY

COMPUTERS IN CONTEXT: HOMELAND SECURITY

REVIEW ACTIVITIES
- Interactive Summary
- Interactive Key Terms
- Interactive Situation Questions
- Interactive Practice Tests
- Review on the Web

LABS
- Operating a Personal Computer
- Making a Dial-Up Connection
- Browsing and Searching
- Using E-mail

TIP
When using the BookOnCD, the ✻ icons are "clickable" to access resources on the CD. The ✝ icons are clickable to access resources on the Web. You can also access Web resources by using your browser to connect directly to the NP8 New Perspectives Web site at:

www.course.com/np/concepts8/ch01

COMPUTER, INTERNET, WEB, AND E-MAIL BASICS

CHAPTER PREVIEW

Before you begin Chapter 1, you can use the Web-based preview activities to hear an overview of the chapter, check your current level of expertise about key concepts, and look through a list of learning objectives. You can access the preview activities by clicking the ✣ icon when using the BookOnCD or going to the New Perspectives NP8 Web site.

CHAPTER OVERVIEW

Computers and the Internet are the cornerstones of a technology revolution that is dramatically transforming the way we live, work, play, and think. Chapter 1 is designed to make sure you understand computer basics. Get your book and highlighter ready, then connect to the New Perspectives NP8 Web site where you can listen to an overview that points out the most important concepts for this chapter.

www.course.com/np/concepts8/ch01 ✣

CHAPTER PRE-ASSESSMENT

How much do you know about basic computer terminology and using the Internet, Web, and e-mail? To gauge your level of knowledge before beginning the chapter, take the pre-assessment quiz at the New Perspectives NP8 Web site. Armed with your results from this quiz, you can focus your study time on concepts that will round out your knowledge of computer basics and improve your test scores.

www.course.com/np/concepts8/ch01 ✣

LEARNING OBJECTIVES

When you complete this chapter you should be able to:

- Define the term "computer" and identify the components of a personal computer system
- Compare the computing capabilities of the following computer categories: personal computers, handheld computers, workstations, videogame consoles, mainframe computers, supercomputers, and servers
- Explain how an operating system affects compatibility between computer platforms, such as PCs and Macs
- Evaluate the various ways you can connect a computer to the Internet and select an ISP
- Describe how Web servers, browsers, URLs, HTML, and HTTP contribute to the Internet resource known as the Web
- Describe popular Internet resources, such as the Web, e-mail, bulletin boards, blogs, file downloads, file sharing, Internet telephony, broadcasting, chat groups, and instant messaging
- Demonstrate that you can use a search engine to locate information on the Web
- List the features that you would expect to find in a typical e-mail software package
- List some of the steps you can take to avoid spam
- Explain how an e-mail system works and describe the difference between store-and-forward mail and Web-based mail

A detailed list of learning objectives is provided at the New Perspectives NP8 Web site

www.course.com/np/concepts8/ch01 ✣

SECTION A
COMPUTER BASICS

Whether you realize it or not, you already know a lot about computers. You've picked up information from commercials and magazine articles, from books and movies, from conversations and correspondence—perhaps even from using your own computer and trying to figure out why it doesn't always work!

Section A provides an overview that's designed to help you start organizing what you know about computers, give you a basic understanding of how computers work, and get you up to speed with a basic computer vocabulary.

A COMPUTER IS...

How old is the word "computer"? The word "computer" has been part of the English language since 1646, but if you look in a dictionary printed before 1940, you might be surprised to find a computer defined as a person who performs calculations! Prior to 1940, machines designed to perform calculations were referred to as calculators and tabulators, not computers. The modern definition and use of the term "computer" emerged in the 1940s, when the first electronic computing devices were developed.

What is a computer? Most people can formulate a mental picture of a computer, but computers do so many things and come in such a variety of shapes and sizes that it might seem difficult to distill their common characteristics into an all-purpose definition. At its core, a **computer** is a device that accepts input, processes data, stores data, and produces output, all according to a series of stored instructions.

Computer **input** is whatever is typed, submitted, or transmitted to a computer system. Input can be supplied by a person, by the environment, or by another computer. Examples of the kinds of input that a computer can accept include words and symbols in a document, numbers for a calculation, pictures, temperatures from a thermostat, audio signals from a microphone, and instructions from a computer program. An input device, such as a keyboard or mouse, gathers input and transforms it into a series of electronic signals for the computer to store and manipulate.

In the context of computing, **data** refers to the symbols that represent facts, objects, and ideas. Computers manipulate data in many ways, and this manipulation is called **processing**. The series of instructions that tell a computer how to carry out processing tasks is referred to as a **computer program**, or simply a "program." These programs form the **software** that sets up a computer to do a specific task. Some of the ways that a computer can process data include performing calculations, sorting lists of words or numbers, modifying documents and pictures, and drawing graphs. In a computer, most processing takes place in a component called the **central processing unit** (CPU), which is sometimes described as the computer's "brain."

TIP

When using the BookOnCD, click any boldface term to see its definition. You can also use the Glossary button at the top of the screen to locate a definition for any term that was introduced in an earlier chapter.

COMPUTER, INTERNET, WEB, AND E-MAIL BASICS

A computer stores data so that it will be available for processing. Most computers have more than one location for storing data, depending on how the data is being used. **Memory** is an area of a computer that temporarily holds data waiting to be processed, stored, or output. **Storage** is the area where data can be left on a permanent basis when it is not immediately needed for processing.

Output is the result produced by a computer. Some examples of computer output include reports, documents, music, graphs, and pictures. An output device displays, prints, or transmits the results of processing. Figure 1-1 helps you visualize the input, processing, storage, and output activities of a computer.

FIGURE 1-1
A computer can be defined by its ability to accept input, process data, store data, and produce output, all according to a set of instructions from a computer program.

A computer accepts input from an input device, such as a keyboard, mouse, scanner, or digital camera.

Data is processed in the CPU according to instructions that have been loaded into the computer's memory.

Computers produce output on devices such as screens and printers.

A computer uses disks, CDs, and DVDs to permanently store data.

What's so significant about a computer's ability to store instructions? Take a moment to think about the way you use a simple handheld calculator to balance your checkbook each month. You're forced to do the calculations in stages. Although you can store data from one stage and use it in the next stage, you cannot store the sequence of formulas—the program—required to balance your checkbook. Every month, therefore, you have to perform a similar set of calculations. The process would be much simpler if your calculator remembered the set of calculations you needed to perform, and simply asked you for this month's checkbook entries.

Early "computers" were really no more than calculating devices, designed to carry out a specific mathematical task. To use one of these devices for a different task, it was necessary to rewire its circuits—a job best left to an engineer. In a modern computer, the idea of a **stored program** means that a series of instructions for a computing task can be loaded into a computer's memory. These instructions can easily be replaced by a different set of instructions when it is time for the computer to perform another task.

The stored program concept allows you to use your computer for one task, such as word processing, and then easily switch to a different type of computing task, such as editing a photo or sending an e-mail message. It is the single most important characteristic that distinguishes a computer from other simpler and less versatile devices, such as calculators and pocket-sized electronic dictionaries.

COMPUTER CATEGORIES

Why is it useful to categorize computers? Computers are versatile machines that are able to perform a truly amazing assortment of tasks, but some types of computers are better suited to certain tasks than other types of computers. Categorizing computers is a way of grouping them according to criteria such as usage, cost, size, and capability. Knowing how a computer has been categorized provides an indication of its best potential use.

During the 1940s and 1950s, very few computers existed, and there was really no need to categorize them. Because the main circuitry was usually housed in a closet-sized metal frame, computer techies called these computers "mainframes." The term soon became synonymous with a category of large, expensive computers that were sold to big corporations and government agencies.

In 1968, the term "minicomputer" was used to describe a second computer category. These computers were smaller, less expensive, and less powerful than mainframes, but were, nevertheless, able to provide adequate computing power for small businesses. In 1971, the first microcomputer appeared. A **microcomputer** could be clearly differentiated from computers in other categories because its CPU consisted of a single "chip" called a **microprocessor**.

At one time, then, it was possible to define three distinct categories of computers: mainframes, minicomputers, and microcomputers. Technology has advanced rapidly since then. Today, just about every computer—no matter how large or small—uses one or more microprocessors as its CPU. Therefore, the use of a microprocessor is no longer a distinction between microcomputers and other computer categories. Furthermore, the term "minicomputer" has fallen into disuse. To reflect today's computer technology, the following categories might be more appropriate: personal computers, handheld computers, workstations, videogame consoles, mainframes, supercomputers, and servers.

What is a personal computer? A **personal computer** is a type of microcomputer designed to meet the computing needs of an individual. It typically provides access to a wide variety of computing applications, such as word processing, photo editing, e-mail, and Internet access. Personal computers are available as desktop computers, notebook computers, or tablet computers, as shown in Figure 1-2.

What are the characteristics of desktop computers? A **desktop computer** fits on a desk and runs on power from an electrical wall outlet. A desktop computer's keyboard is typically a separate component, connected to the main unit by a cable. The main unit can be housed in a vertical case (like the one shown in Figure 1-2, top) or a horizontal case. The vertical case is sometimes placed on the floor or in a cubbyhole beneath the desk. The horizontal case can be placed under the display screen to reduce the computer's "footprint" on the desk. The first personal computers were desktop models, and this style remains popular for offices, schools, and homes. Because their components can be manufactured economically, desktop computers typically provide the most computing power for your dollar. The price of an entry-level desktop computer starts at $500 or a bit less, but most consumers select more powerful models that cost between $1,000 and $1,200.

How do notebook computers differ from desktops? A **notebook computer** (also referred to as a "laptop"), is a small, lightweight personal

FIGURE 1-2
Personal computers are available in desktop, notebook, and tablet configurations.

A desktop computer fits on a desk and features a vertical case (like the one shown) or a horizontal case.

A notebook computer is small and lightweight, giving it the advantage of portability. It can be plugged into an electrical outlet, or it can run on battery power.

A tablet computer is similar in size to a notebook computer, but features a touch-sensitive screen that can be used for input instead of a keyboard.

computer that incorporates screen, keyboard, storage, and processing components into a single portable unit. Notebook computers can run on power supplied by an electrical outlet or a battery. These portable computers are ideal for mobile uses because they are easy to carry and can be used outdoors, in airports, and in classrooms without the need for a nearby electrical outlet. Notebook computers cost a bit more than a desktop computer with similar computing power and storage capacity. The price of an entry-level notebook computer starts at about $700, but consumers often spend between $1,000 and $1,500 to get the performance they want.

What is a tablet computer? A **tablet computer** is a portable computing device featuring a touch-sensitive screen that can be used as a writing or drawing pad. A "slate" tablet configuration, like the one in Figure 1-2, lacks a keyboard (although one can be attached) and resembles a high-tech clipboard. A "convertible" tablet computer is constructed like a notebook computer, but the screen folds face up over the keyboard to provide a horizontal writing surface. Tablet computers shine for applications that involve handwritten input, and many experts believe they might replace notebook computers when prices fall to equivalent levels. Since tablet computers were first introduced in 2002, their price has remained high, starting at about $1,200, but more typically costing $2,000 to $2,500.

What is a handheld? A **handheld computer**, such as a Palm, an iPAQ, or a PocketPC, features a small keyboard or touch-sensitive screen and is designed to fit into a pocket, run on batteries, and be used while you are holding it. Also called a **PDA** (personal digital assistant), a computer in this category can be used as an electronic appointment book, address book, calculator, and notepad. Inexpensive add-ons make it possible to send and receive e-mail, use maps and global positioning to get directions, and synchronize information with a personal computer.

PDAs and "smart" cell phones are converging into a single handheld technology that provides keypad input, color screen, digital camera, PDA software, voice communications, text messaging, Web browsing, and e-mail. PDA and smartphone prices start below $100 and range up to $700 for a model with a color screen and integrated cellular phone (Figure 1-3).

With its slow processing speed and small screen, a handheld computer is not powerful enough to handle many of the tasks that can be accomplished by desktop, notebook, or tablet personal computers. Yet handhelds provide important computing and communications functions in a mobile package.

TERMINOLOGY NOTE

The term "personal computer" is sometimes abbreviated as "PC." However, the abbreviation "PC" can also refer to a specific type of personal computer that descended from the original IBM PC and runs Windows software. In this book, "PC" refers to IBM PC descendants. It is not used as an abbreviation for the term "personal computer."

INFOWEBLINKS

Learn more about the latest PDA models, prices, software, and accessories by visiting the **PDA InfoWeb**.

www.course.com/np/concepts8/ch01

FIGURE 1-3
Many handheld computers feature a small keyboard, while others accept handwriting input.

What types of computers can be classified as workstations? The term "**workstation**" has two meanings. Computers advertised as workstations are usually powerful desktop computers designed for specialized tasks. A workstation can tackle tasks that require a lot of processing speed, such as medical imaging and computer-aided design. Some workstations contain more than one microprocessor, and most have circuitry specially designed for creating and displaying three-dimensional and animated graphics. Workstation prices range from $3,000 to $20,000. Because of its cost, a workstation, like the one in Figure 1-4, is often dedicated to design tasks, but is not used for typical microcomputer applications, such as word processing, photo editing, and accessing the Web.

A second meaning of the term "workstation" applies to an ordinary personal computer that is connected to a network. A **computer network** is two or more computers and other devices connected for the purpose of sharing data, programs, and hardware. A **LAN** (local area network) is simply a computer network located within a limited geographical area, such as a school computer lab or a small business.

FIGURE 1-4
A workstation resembles a desktop computer, but typically features more processing power and storage capacity.

Is a PlayStation a computer? A **videogame console**, such as Nintendo's GameCube, Sony's PlayStation, or Microsoft's Xbox, *is* a computer, but videogame consoles have not been considered a computer category because of their history as dedicated game devices that connect to a TV set and provide only a pair of joysticks for input. Today's videogame consoles, however, contain microprocessors that are equivalent to any found in a fast personal computer, and they are equipped to produce graphics that rival those on sophisticated workstations. Add-ons, such as keyboards, DVD players, and Internet access, make it possible to use a videogame console to watch DVD movies, send and receive e-mail, and participate in online activities, such as multiplayer games. As with handheld computers, videogame consoles like the one in Figure 1-5 fill a specialized niche and are not considered a replacement for a personal computer.

FIGURE 1-5
A videogame console includes circuitry similar to a personal computer's, but its input and output devices are optimized for gaming.

What's so special about a mainframe computer? A **mainframe computer** (or simply a "mainframe") is a large and expensive computer capable of simultaneously processing data for hundreds or thousands of users. Mainframes are generally used by businesses or governments to provide centralized storage, processing, and management for large amounts of data. Mainframes remain the computer of choice in situations where reliability, data security, and centralized control are necessary.

The price of a mainframe computer typically starts at several hundred thousand dollars and can easily exceed $1 million. Its main processing circuitry is housed in a closet-sized cabinet (Figure 1-6), but after large components are added for storage and output, a mainframe can fill a good-sized room.

FIGURE 1-6
This IBM S/390 zSeries 990 mainframe computer weighs about 1,400 pounds and is about 6.5 feet tall.

How powerful is a supercomputer? A computer falls into the **supercomputer** category if it is, at the time of construction, one of the fastest computers in the world. Because of their speed, supercomputers can tackle complex tasks that just would not be practical for other computers. Common uses for supercomputers include breaking codes, modeling worldwide weather systems, and simulating nuclear explosions. One impressive simulation designed to run on a supercomputer tracked the movement of thousands of dust particles as they were tossed about by a tornado.

COMPUTER, INTERNET, WEB, AND E-MAIL BASICS

At one time, supercomputer designers focused on building specialized, very fast, and very large CPUs. Today, a supercomputer CPU is constructed from thousands of microprocessors. Approximately 300 of the 500 fastest supercomputers in the world use microcomputer technology.

What makes a computer a "server"? In the computer industry, the term "server" has several meanings. It can refer to computer hardware, to a specific type of software, or to a combination of hardware and software. In any case, the purpose of a **server** is to "serve" computers on a network (such as the Internet or a LAN) by supplying them with data. A personal computer, workstation, or software that requests data from a server is referred to as a **client**. For example, on a network, a server might respond to a client's request for a Web page. Another server might handle the steady stream of e-mail that travels among clients from all over the Internet. A server might also allow clients within a LAN to share files or access a centralized printer.

Remarkably, just about any personal computer, workstation, mainframe, or supercomputer can be configured to perform the work of a server. That fact should emphasize the concept that a server does not require a specific type of hardware. Nonetheless, computer manufacturers categorize some of their computers as "servers" because they are especially suited for storing and distributing data on a network. Despite impressive performance on server-related tasks, these machines do not include features, such as sound cards, DVD players, and other fun accessories, that consumers expect on their desktop computers. Most consumers would not want to buy a server to replace a desktop computer.

PERSONAL COMPUTER SYSTEMS

What's a personal computer system? The term "computer system" usually refers to a computer and all the input, output, and storage devices that are connected to it. At the core of a personal computer system is a desktop, notebook, or tablet computer, which probably looks like one of those in Figure 1-7.

INFOWEBLINKS

What's the latest news about supercomputers? Visit the **Supercomputer InfoWeb** to learn more about these amazing machines.

www.course.com/np/concepts8/ch01

FIGURE 1-7

Personal computer designs run the gamut from drab gray boxes to colorful curvy cases.

Despite cosmetic differences among personal computers, a personal computer system usually includes the following equipment:

- **System unit.** The **system unit** is the case that holds the main circuit boards, microprocessor, power supply, and storage devices. The system unit for notebook computers holds a built-in keyboard and speakers, too.

- **Display device.** Most desktop computers use a separate **monitor** as a display device, whereas notebook computers use a flat panel **LCD screen** (liquid crystal display screen) attached to the system unit.

- **Keyboard.** Most computers are equipped with a keyboard as the primary input device.

- **Mouse.** A **mouse** is an input device designed to manipulate on-screen graphical objects and controls.

- **Hard disk drive.** A **hard disk drive** can store billions of characters of data. It is usually mounted inside the computer's system unit. A small external light indicates when the drive is reading or writing data.

- **CD and DVD drives.** A **CD drive** is a storage device that uses laser technology to work with data on computer or audio CDs. A **DVD drive** can work with data on computer CDs, audio CDs, computer DVDs, or DVD movie disks. Some CD and DVD drives are classified as "read only" devices that cannot be used to write data onto disks. They are typically used to access data from commercial software, music, and movie CDs or DVDs. "Writable" CD and DVD drives, however, can be used to store and access data.

- **Floppy disk drive.** A **floppy disk drive** is a storage device that reads and writes data on floppy disks.

- **Sound card and speakers.** Desktop computers have a rudimentary built-in speaker that's mostly limited to playing beeps. A small circuit board, called a **sound card**, is required for high-quality music, narration, and sound effects. A desktop computer's sound card sends signals to external speakers. A notebook's sound card sends signals to speakers that are built into the notebook system unit.

- **Modem and network cards.** Many personal computer systems include a built-in **modem** that can be used to establish an Internet connection using a standard telephone line. A **network card** is used to connect a computer to a network or cable Internet connection.

- **Printer.** A computer printer is an output device that produces computer-generated text or graphical images on paper.

FIGURE 1-8
Computer storage media include floppy disks, DVDs and CDs.

FIGURE 1-9
A typical personal computer system includes the system unit and a variety of storage, input, and output devices.

COMPUTER, INTERNET, WEB, AND E-MAIL BASICS

What's a peripheral device? The term **peripheral device** designates equipment that might be added to a computer system to enhance its functionality. Popular peripheral devices, such as those in Figure 1-10, include printers, digital cameras, scanners, joysticks, and graphics tablets.

Is a hard disk drive a peripheral device? The word "peripheral" is a relatively old part of computer jargon that dates back to the days of mainframes when the CPU was housed in a giant box and all input, output, and storage devices were housed separately. Technically, a peripheral is any device that is not housed within the CPU.

Although a hard disk drive seems to be an integral part of a computer, by the strictest technical definition, a hard disk drive would be classified as a peripheral device. The same goes for other storage devices and the keyboard, monitor, LCD screen, sound card, speakers, and modem. In the world of personal computers, however, the use of the term "peripheral" varies and is often used to refer to any components that are not housed inside the system unit.

DATA, INFORMATION, AND FILES

Is there a difference between data and information? In everyday conversation, people use the terms "data" and "information" interchangeably. Nevertheless, some computer professionals make a distinction between the two terms. They define data as the symbols that represent people, events, things, and ideas. Data becomes **information** when it is presented in a format that people can understand and use. Most computers store data in a **digital** format as a series of 1s and 0s. Each 1 or 0 is called a **bit**. Eight bits, called a **byte**, are used to represent one character—a letter, number, or punctuation mark.

As a rule of thumb, remember that (technically speaking) data is used by computers; information is used by humans. The bits and bytes that a computer stores are referred to as data. The words, numbers, and graphics displayed for people are referred to as information.

What is a file? A computer file, usually referred to simply as a **file**, is a named collection of data that exists on a storage medium, such as a hard disk, floppy disk, or CD. Although all files contain data, some files are classified as "data files," whereas other files are classified as "executable files." A **data file** contains data that can be processed—the text for a document, the numbers for a calculation, the specifications for a graph, the frames of a video, the contents of a Web page, or the notes of a musical passage. An **executable file** contains the programs or instructions that tell a computer how to perform a specific task. For example, the word processing program that tells your computer how to display and print text is stored as an executable file.

You can think of data files as passive—the data does not instruct the computer to do anything. Executable files, on the other hand, are active—the instructions stored in the file cause the computer to carry out some action.

How can I tell what's in a file? Every file has a **file name**, which often provides a clue to its contents. A file might also have a **file extension**—sometimes referred to as a "filename extension"—that further describes a file's contents. For example, in Pbrush.exe, "Pbrush" is the file name and "exe" is the file extension. As you can see, the file name is separated from the extension by a period called a "dot." To tell someone the name of the file Pbrush.exe, you would say, "Pbrush dot e-x-e."

FIGURE 1-10

Peripheral devices add to a computer's versatility.

Printer

Digital camera

Scanner

Graphics tablet

Executable files typically have .exe extensions. Data files have a variety of extensions, such as .bmp or .tif for a graphic, .mid for synthesized music, or .htm for a Web page. Chapter 4 provides additional information on file names and file types.

APPLICATION SOFTWARE AND OPERATING SYSTEM BASICS

What is application software? A computer can be "applied" to many tasks, such as writing, number crunching, video editing, and online shopping. **Application software** is a set of computer programs that helps a person carry out a task. Word processing software, for example, helps people create, edit, and print documents. Personal finance software helps people keep track of their money and investments. Video editing software helps people create and edit home movies—and even some professional films.

Is an operating system some type of application software? No. An **operating system** (OS) is essentially the master controller for all the activities that take place within a computer. Operating systems are classified as **system software**, not application software, because their primary purpose is to help the computer system monitor itself in order to function efficiently.

Unlike application software, an operating system does not directly help people perform application-specific tasks, such as word processing. People do, however, interact with the operating system for certain operational and storage tasks, such as starting programs and locating data files.

What are the most popular operating systems? Popular personal computer operating systems include Microsoft Windows and Mac OS. Microsoft Windows Mobile and Palm OS control most handheld computers. Linux and UNIX are popular operating systems for servers.

Microsoft Windows (usually referred to simply as "Windows") is the most widely used operating system for personal computers. As shown in Figure 1-11, the Windows operating system displays on-screen controls designed to be manipulated by a mouse.

FIGURE 1-11
The Windows operating system displays on-screen icons, menus, buttons, and other graphical controls designed to be manipulated by a mouse.

COMPUTER, INTERNET, WEB, AND E-MAIL BASICS

Is Windows software the same as the Windows operating system?
No. The term "Windows software" refers to any application software designed to run on computers that use the Microsoft Windows operating system. A program called Microsoft Word for Windows is an example of a word processing program—application software—that is referred to as "Windows software."

How does an operating system affect compatibility? Computers that operate in essentially the same way are said to be "compatible." Two of the most important factors that influence compatibility and define a computer's **platform** are the microprocessor and the operating system. Today, two of the most popular personal computer platforms are PCs and Macs.

PCs are based on the design for one of the first personal computer "superstars"—the IBM PC. The "great grandchildren" of the IBM PC are on computer store shelves today—a huge selection of personal computer brands and models manufactured by companies such as IBM, Hewlett-Packard, Toshiba, Dell, and Gateway. The Windows operating system was designed specifically for these personal computers and, therefore, the PC platform is sometimes called the "Windows platform." Most of the examples in this book pertain to PCs because they are so popular.

Macs are based on a proprietary design for a personal computer called the Macintosh, manufactured almost exclusively by Apple Computer, Inc. The stylish iMac is one of Apple's most popular computers, and like other computers in the Mac platform, it uses Mac OS as its operating system.

The PC and Mac platforms are not compatible because their microprocessors and operating systems differ. Consequently, application software designed for Macs does not typically work with PCs and vice versa. When shopping for new software, it is important to read the package to make sure it is designed to work with your computer platform.

INFOWEBLINKS

Apple Computer, Inc. is known for its innovative computer designs. You can learn about its newest computers by connecting to the **Apple Computers InfoWeb**.

www.course.com/np/concepts8/ch01

QUICKCHECK......SECTION A

1. A computer accepts input, processes data, stores data, and produces _____ according to a series of instructions.

2. The term "microprocessor" is a synonym for the term "microcomputer." True or false? _____

3. A(n) _____ computer is also referred to as a laptop.

4. Most computers include a network card designed to connect a computer to the Internet using standard telephone service. True or false? _____

5. Eight _____ form a byte.

6. PCs and Macs are not considered _____ because their microprocessors and operating systems differ.

CHECK ANSWERS

LAB 1-A
OPERATING A PERSONAL COMPUTER

In this lab, you'll learn:

- How to start a Windows computer
- What to do when a computer is in sleep mode
- How to deactivate a screen saver
- How to select a different screen saver
- The terminology used for the four sections of a computer keyboard
- How to use the Alt, Ctrl, Esc, Num Lock, Caps Lock, Windows, Fn, Backspace, Delete, and arrow keys
- The difference between forward and backward slashes
- The location of the tilde
- How to start and exit a program
- How to close a program that is not responding
- When to use the reset button
- How to shut down Windows

INTERACTIVE LAB

CLICK TO START THE LAB

LAB ASSIGNMENTS

1. Start the interactive part of the lab. Insert your Tracking Disk if you want to save your QuickCheck results. Perform each lab step as directed, and answer all the lab QuickCheck questions. When you exit the lab, your answers are automatically graded and your results are displayed.

2. Make a note of the brand and location of the computer you're using to complete these lab assignments.

3. Use the Start button to access your computer's Control Panel folder. Describe the status of your computer's power saver settings.

4. Preview the available screen savers on the computer you use most frequently. Select the screen saver you like the best and describe it in a few sentences.

5. What is the purpose of an Fn key? Does your computer keyboard include an Fn key? Explain why or why not.

6. In your own words, describe what happens when you (a) click the Close button, (b) hold down the Ctrl, Alt, and Del keys, (c) press the reset button, and (d) select the Shut Down option.

SECTION B
INTERNET BASICS

COMPUTER, INTERNET, WEB, AND E-MAIL BASICS

The Internet has changed society. E-mail and instant messaging have caused a major shift in the way people communicate. Online stores have changed our shopping habits. The ability to easily download music has stirred up controversy about intellectual property. The possibility of unauthorized access to online databases has made us more aware of our privacy and safety. Section B provides a basic overview of the Internet, with an emphasis on how you can connect to it and use it.

INTERNET RESOURCES

How does the Internet work? The **Internet** is a collection of local, regional, national, and international computer networks linked together to exchange data and distribute processing tasks. You can think of the Internet as a network of interconnected communications lines creating a sort of highway system for transporting data. The main routes of the Internet—analogous to interstate highways—are referred to as the **Internet backbone**. Constructed and maintained by major telecommunications companies, such as AT&T and Sprint, these telecommunications links can move huge amounts of data at incredible speeds. Data traveling from the United States can arrive in England in less than 60 ms—60 thousandths of a second.

In addition to the backbone, the Internet encompasses an intricate collection of regional and local communications links. These links can include local telephone systems, cable television lines, cellular telephone systems, and personal satellite dishes.

Internet communications links (Figure 1-12) transport data to and from millions of computers and other electronic devices. Amazingly, this data transport works seamlessly between all kinds of platforms—between PCs and Macs and even between personal computers and mainframes. Communication between all the different devices on the Internet is made possible by **TCP/IP** (Transmission Control Protocol/Internet Protocol), a standard set of rules for electronically addressing and transmitting data.

INFOWEBLINKS

Sometimes used as a synonym for the Internet, the term "cyberspace" was coined by science-fiction writer William Gibson. Visit the **Cyberspace InfoWeb** for additional background and links to books for sci-fi aficionados.

www.course.com/np/concepts8/ch01

FIGURE 1-12

The Internet backbone connects to regional and local communications links, which provide Internet access to individuals working at their personal computers.

Where is all the Internet data stored? The Internet provides access to an amazing volume of data, including corporate Web pages, merchandise catalogs, software, music, tutorials on all manner of subjects, school science projects, telephone directories, library card catalogs, and so on. Although difficult to pin down exact figures, it is estimated that the Internet provides access to more data than is stored in all the academic research libraries in the United States.

Most of the "stuff" that's accessible on the Internet is stored on servers, which are owned and maintained by government agencies, corporations, small businesses, schools, organizations, and even individuals. These servers use special server software to locate and distribute data requested by Internet users.

What kind of resources are available on the Internet? If you're looking for information, if you want to communicate with someone, or if you want to buy something, the Internet offers a good set of resources. Here is a quick overview of Internet resources:

- **Web sites.** Most people envision Web sites as various locations on the Internet that correspond to a corporation's headquarters, a store, a magazine, or a library. A Web site can provide information or access to other resources, such as search engines and e-mail.

- **Search engines.** Without search engines, using the Internet would be like trying to find a book in the Library of Congress by wandering around the stacks. Search engines, such as Google and Yahoo!, help catalog a huge portion of the data stored at Web sites.

- **Downloads and uploads.** Internet servers store all sorts of useful files containing documents, music, software, videos, animations, and photos. The process of transferring one of these files from a remote computer, such as a server, to a local computer, such as your personal computer, is called **downloading**. Sending a file from a local computer to a remote computer is called **uploading** (Figure 1-13).

INFOWEBLINKS

If you'd like to check out some of the resources described in this section, connect to the **Internet Resources InfoWeb**. There you'll find links to examples and to the software that you need to access these useful Internet resources.

www.course.com/np/concepts8/ch01

FIGURE 1-13
Many Web sites provide files that the public can download to personal computers. Uploads, on the other hand, are limited to people who have password access to the site.

For a demonstration of how to download a file, click the Start icon.

CLICK TO START

- **P2P file sharing.** A technology known as **peer-to-peer** (P2P) file sharing makes it possible to access files stored on another Internet user's hard disk—with permission, of course. This technology is the basis for popular music and file exchange Web sites, such as Morpheus and Kazaa.

COMPUTER, INTERNET, WEB, AND E-MAIL BASICS

- **E-mail.** Also known as "electronic mail," **e-mail** allows one person to send an electronic message to another person or to a group of people listed in a personal address book. A variation of e-mail called a **mailing list server**, or "listserv," maintains a public list of people who are interested in a particular topic. Messages sent to the list server are automatically distributed to everyone on the mailing list.

- **Bulletin boards. Usenet** is a worldwide bulletin board system that contains more than 15,000 discussion forums called **newsgroups**. Newsgroup members post messages to the bulletin board, which can be read and responded to by other group members.

- **Blogs.** The term **blog**, derived from the phrase "WeB LOG," refers to a personal journal posted on the Web for access by the general public. Blogs can focus on a single topic or cover a variety of issues. A typical blog includes commentary by the author as well as links to additional information. To find blogs, you can use a blog directory, like the one in Figure 1-14.

FIGURE 1-14
Blogs have become a popular way of disseminating information over the Internet. Blog directories, such as this one, provide links to blogs on all sorts of topics.

- **Chat groups and instant messaging.** A **chat group** consists of several people who connect to the Internet and communicate in a virtual "room" by typing comments to each other. A private version of a chat room, called **instant messaging**, allows two or more people to send typed messages back and forth.

- **Internet telephony.** Although it is not as simple as picking up the telephone, **Internet telephony** allows telephone-style conversations to travel over the Internet to virtually anywhere in the world. When using Internet telephony, the sound quality is sometimes worse than a cellular phone, but the cost is much less than conventional long distance service.

- **E-commerce.** The Internet is revolutionizing business by directly linking consumers with retailers, manufacturers, and distributors. **E-commerce**, or "electronic commerce," includes activities such as online shopping, electronic auctions, and online stock trading.

- **Broadcasting.** The Internet carries radio shows and teleconferences that can be broadcast worldwide. Internet radio is popular because broadcasts aren't limited to a small local region. Internet broadcasting technology, referred to as "multicasting," has the potential to increase the use and popularity of Internet broadcasts.

- **Remote access and control.** Using software, such as Telnet or SSH, and a valid password, it is possible to link two computers so that commands entered on one computer are executed remotely on the other computer. This capability of the Internet and other networks is handy, for example, when a technical support person located in a manufacturer's service center takes remote control of your computer to fix a problem.

INTERNET CONNECTIONS

What are my options for Internet connections? To take advantage of everything the Internet has to offer, you have to establish some sort of communications link between your computer and the Internet. Possibilities include using your existing telephone line, a cable television line, a personal satellite link, wireless or cell phone service, or special high-speed telephone services.

What's the easiest, cheapest way to access the Internet? Many people literally dial up the Internet using an existing telephone line. This type of connection—often referred to as a **dial-up connection**—is relatively simple and inexpensive because the necessary equipment and software are preinstalled on most new computers. A dial-up connection requires a device called a **voiceband modem** (often simply called a "modem"), which converts your computer's digital signals into a type of signal that can travel over telephone lines. Figure 1-15 can help you determine whether a computer has a modem.

FIGURE 1-15
The photo below shows three kinds of modems. An external modem (at the top left of this photo) connects to the computer with a cable. An internal modem (top right) is installed inside the computer's system unit. A PC card modem (bottom center) is typically used in notebook computers without built-in phone jacks.

CLICK TO START

To determine whether a computer has a modem, look for a place to plug in a standard phone cable.

Notebook computers without built-in modems require a PC card modem that slides into a small slot on the side of the case.

COMPUTER, INTERNET, WEB, AND E-MAIL BASICS

To establish a dial-up connection, your computer's modem dials a special access number, which is answered by an Internet modem. Once the connection is established, your computer is "on the Internet." When you complete an Internet session and log off, your modem "hangs up" and the connection is discontinued until the next time you dial in.

Theoretically, the top speed of a dial-up connection is 56 Kbps, meaning that 56,000 bits of data are transmitted per second. Actual speed is usually reduced by distance, interference, and other technical problems, however, so the speed of most 56 Kbps dial-up connections is more like 45 Kbps. This speed is usable for e-mail, e-commerce, and chat. It is not, however, optimal for applications that require large amounts of data to be quickly transferred over the Internet. Watching an Internet-based video or participating in a teleconference over a 56 Kbps dial-up connection can be like watching a badly organized parade—the sound can be out of sync with the image, and the "show" can be interrupted by lengthy pauses as your computer waits for the next set of video frames to arrive.

Does a cable modem provide a faster Internet connection? Many cable TV companies offer Internet access in addition to the traditional roster of movie channels, network television, and specialty channels. This type of Internet access, often referred to as "cable modem service," is offered to a cable company's customers for an additional monthly charge. Cable modem service usually requires two pieces of equipment: a network card and a cable modem. A network card is a device that's designed to connect a personal computer to a local area network—when you get cable modem service, this card allows you to join a computer network that provides Internet access. Many of today's computers come equipped with a preinstalled network card. If not, one can be added for less than $50. A **cable modem** (Figure 1-16) is a device that changes a computer's signals into a form that can travel over cable TV links. Cable modems can be installed by consumers or installed (sometimes for a fee) by the "cable guy" and typically remain the property of the cable company.

FIGURE 1-16
A cable modem can be a standalone device set up close to a computer, or it can be integrated with other electronic components in a "set-top box" on top of a television.

Cable modem service is referred to as an **always-on connection** because your computer is, in effect, always connected to the Internet, unlike a dial-up connection that is established only when the dialing sequence is completed. An always-on connection is convenient because you don't have to wait 30–40 seconds for the dial-answer sequence to be completed. A cable modem receives data at about 1.5 Mbps (1.5 million bits per second), which is more than 25 times faster than a dial-up connection. This speed is suitable for most Internet activities, including real-time video and teleconferencing.

What about access provided by a school or business network? The computers in a school lab or business are usually connected to a LAN that is linked to the Internet. These networked computers offer an always-on connection, similar to cable modem service. School and business networks do not, however, typically access the Internet via a cable company. Instead they use a high-speed telecommunications link dedicated solely to Internet access.

What other high-speed Internet access options are available? Many telephone and independent telecommunications companies offer high-speed Internet access over ISDN and DSL lines. **ISDN** (Integrated Services Digital Network) provides data transfer speeds of 64 Kbps or 128 Kbps. With substantial monthly fees and data transfer speeds that are only marginally better than a free 56 Kbps dial-up connection, ISDN ranks low on the list of high-speed Internet options for most consumers.

DSL (Digital Subscriber Line) is a generic name for a family of high-speed Internet links, including ADSL, SDSL, and DSL lite. Each type of DSL provides different maximum speeds—from twice as fast to approximately 125 times faster than a 56 Kbps dial-up connection. The faster types of DSL require professional installation, but DSL lite can be installed by consumers.

Both ISDN and DSL connections require proximity to a telephone switching station, which can be a problem for speed-hungry consumers in rural areas. Satellite dishes to the rescue! **DSS** (Digital Satellite Service) offers Internet access at an average speed of about 500 Kbps. Monthly fees for a DSS connection are typically more than DSL or cable modem service. DSS customers are also required to rent or purchase a satellite dish and pay for its installation.

INTERNET SERVICE PROVIDERS

What's an ISP? To access the Internet, you do not typically connect your computer directly to the backbone. Instead, you connect it to an ISP such as AOL (America Online), which in turn connects to the backbone. An **ISP** (Internet service provider) is a company that maintains Internet computers and telecommunications equipment in order to provide Internet access to businesses, organizations, and individuals. An ISP that offers dial-up connections, for example, maintains a bank of modems, which communicate with modems in customers' computers.

An ISP works in much the same way as a local telephone company. Just as a telephone company provides a point of access to telephones all over the world, an ISP is a point of access to the Internet. ISP customers arrange for service—in this case, for Internet access—for which they pay a monthly fee. In addition to a monthly fee, an ISP might also charge an installation fee. Dial-up subscribers might also be required to pay per-minute fees for long-distance access.

What's the difference between a local ISP and a national ISP? A local ISP usually supplies Internet access within a limited geographical area, such as within a particular city. Local ISPs typically provide dial-up service through a local telephone number.

A national ISP supplies access for customers spread throughout a large geographical area. AT&T WorldNet, for example, offers dial-up access numbers in more than 500 cities. Customers who live in or travel to any of these cities can use the access numbers without additional long-distance fees. Figure 1-17 lists some popular national ISPs.

FIGURE 1-17
Popular ISPs

ISP	SPECIALTY
AOL	Dial-up, cable
AOL Canada	Dial-up
AT&T WorldNet	Dial-up
AT&T Canada	Dial-up
Charter	Cable
Comcast	Cable
Cox	Cable
DirecWay	DSS
Earthlink	Dial-up, DSS
MSN	Dial-up, cable

COMPUTER, INTERNET, WEB, AND E-MAIL BASICS

How can I find a list of ISPs that provide service in my area? The Yellow Pages typically list ISPs under "Internet." Also, check newspaper ads for new services that are being offered in your area. Your computer might include a directory of national ISPs. Look for an Internet Connection icon on your desktop, or browse through the options on the Start menu to find the Internet Connection Wizard.

How do I choose an ISP? Selecting an ISP depends on a variety of factors, such as where service is provided; the speed of data transfer; and the cost of equipment, installation, and monthly service (Figure 1-18).

FIGURE 1-18
Choosing an ISP

Geographical Coverage	The ISP you select should provide service in the places that you typically use your computer. If your work takes you on the road a lot, you'll want to consider a national ISP that provides local access numbers in the cities you visit. Retirees and students who migrate between locations might also consider a national ISP. For homebodies, a local ISP is usually a very acceptable option. With cable modem or DSL service, your computer must remain tethered to your service provider's network, which does not provide Internet access while traveling.
Type of Service	Some ISPs specialize in one type of service. A company that offers dial-up connections might not also offer cable connections. If you want a particular type of service—cable modem service, for example—you might not have a choice of providers.
Quality of Service	The quality of dial-up and cable modem services tends to decrease as the number of customers increases. In the case of dial-up connections, too many customers clamoring for modem connections can result in busy signals when you try to connect to your ISP. Cable modem service works sort of like a lawn sprinkler system that's connected to a small water pump. With only one sprinkler, the water gushes out. Connect 100 sprinklers to the system and the gushing turns into a trickle. Because all the subscribers in your neighborhood use the same data "pipe," as more and more of your neighbors go online, the effective speed of your cable connection can deteriorate. Ask an ISP's current customers what they think of the access speed. Is it consistent, or does it deteriorate during peak usage hours?
Cost of Monthly Service	In the United States and Canada, monthly service fees vary from about $15–$20 per month for dial-up service to $50–$60 per month for basic cable service. ISP rate plans might offer unlimited access for a flat monthly fee. Other rate plans include a limited number of hours; if you're online for additional hours, you'll pay by the hour. Outside the United States and Canada, many ISPs charge by the minute for Internet access.
Cost of Equipment and Installation	When considering the cost of Internet service, it is important to factor in the cost of equipment and installation. Whereas a modem is relatively inexpensive, a satellite dish costs several hundred dollars. Installation can also be costly—sometimes exceeding $100.
Extra Services	An ISP typically provides a connection to the Internet and an e-mail account. It might also offer useful extra services, such as multiple e-mail accounts so that all members of your family can send and receive their own e-mail messages. Some ISPs, such as AOL, offer a host of proprietary services that are available only to subscribers. These services might include content channels with substantive articles on health, hobbies, investing, and sports; activities specially designed for kids and teens; online shops that comply with high standards for security and customer satisfaction; a variety of voice and text messaging services; and collections of free (and virus-free) software. To find out if proprietary features should influence your ISP choice, talk to subscribers who have similar computer experience; ask them if these features are useful.
Customer Service	Most ISPs are prepared to answer customers' questions over the phone or via e-mail. The critical customer service question is "How long will it take to get a response?" Some national ISPs are notorious for keeping customers on hold for hours, and an e-mail reply can take days. Given a choice, most customers prefer an ISP that can respond quickly. To get an idea of an ISP's response time and expertise, talk to current customers.

USER IDS AND PASSWORDS

Is access to the Internet restricted in any way? Although the Internet is a public network, access to the Internet, or to some parts of the Internet, can be restricted in various ways. For example, an ISP usually limits Internet access to its subscribers. Some parts of the Internet—such as military computers—are off limits to the general public. In addition, some parts of Web sites—such as the *New York Times* archives—limit access to paid members. Many parts of the Internet encourage memberships and offer additional perks if you sign up.

User IDs and passwords are designed to provide access for authorized users and to prevent unauthorized access. A **user ID** is a series of characters—letters and possibly numbers—that becomes a person's unique identifier, similar to a social security number. A **password** is a different series of characters that verifies the user ID, similar to the way a PIN (personal identification number) verifies your identity at an ATM machine. Typically, your ISP supplies a user ID and password that you use to connect to the Internet. You will accumulate additional user IDs and passwords from other sources for specific Internet activities, such as reading *New York Times* articles or participating in an online auction. The process of entering a user ID and password is usually referred to as "logging in" or "logging on" (Figure 1-19).

FIGURE 1-19
Typically, when you log in and enter your password, a series of asterisks appears on the screen to prevent someone from looking over your shoulder to discover your password.

Can I choose my own user ID? In some cases, you are allowed to select your user ID, but in other cases, it might be assigned by your service provider. Often a user ID is a variation of your name. Brunhilde Jefferson's user ID might be bjeffe, bjefferson, brunhilde_jefferson, or bjeff0918445.

The rules for creating a user ID are not consistent throughout the Internet, so it is important to read all the instructions carefully before finalizing your ID. For example, spaces might not be allowed in a user ID. Hence, the underline in brunhilde_jefferson is used instead of a space. There might be a length limitation, so Ms. Jefferson might have to choose a short user ID, such as bjeffe.

Some Internet computers don't differentiate between uppercase and lowercase letters, and would consider the user IDs B_Jefferson and b_jefferson to be the same. Other computers are **case sensitive** and differentiate between uppercase and lowercase. On such computers, if Ms. Jefferson selected Brun_Jeff as her user ID, she would not be able to gain access by typing brun_jeff. To avoid such problems, most people stick to lowercase letters for their user IDs.

How do I choose a secure password? Even when you are assigned a "starter" password, you should select a new password immediately, and then change it periodically. Don't share your password with anyone or write it down where it could be found. If your password is discovered, someone could log on and pretend to be you—sending inflammatory e-mail under your name and signing up for memberships at unsavory Web sites.

Your password should be a sequence of characters that is easy for you to remember, but would be difficult for someone else to guess. After all, your password provides protection only if it is secret (Figure 1-20).

Do select a password that is at least five characters long	**Don't** select a password that can be found in a dictionary
Do try to use both numbers and letters in your password	**Don't** use your name, nickname, social security number, birth date, or name of a close relative
Do select a password that you can remember	
Do consider making a password by combining two or more words or the first letters of a poem or phrase	**Don't** write your password where it is easy to find—under the keyboard is the first place that a password thief will look
Do change your password if you think that someone discovered it	**Don't** let anyone use your password "temporarily" to access Web sites or log on to your ISP

FIGURE 1-20
Use these tips to select a secure password.

How do I remember my passwords? When you use the Internet, you accumulate a batch of passwords—from your ISP, from online shopping sites, from your online travel agent, and maybe even from your favorite news and information sites. The problem is not remembering *one* password; it's remembering lots of different passwords and their corresponding user IDs.

Your passwords provide the most protection if they are unique, but if you want access to 40 different Internet sites that require passwords, you'll need a really good memory to remember 40 unique passwords and 40 user IDs. You can, of course, resort to writing them down. That practice, however, makes them much more susceptible to thievery.

Instead of using 40 different user IDs and passwords, you need some way to reduce the number of things you have to memorize. First, strive to select a unique user ID that you can use for more than one site. Remember that people with the same name who selected user IDs before you might have already taken the obvious user IDs. For example, when John Smith selects a user ID, you can bet that other people have already used johnsmith, jsmith, and john_smith. To keep his user ID unique, John might instead select jsl2wm (the first letters in "John Smith loves 2 watch movies").

Next, select two passwords—one for high security and one for low security. Use your high-security password to protect critical data—for online banking, for managing an online stock portfolio, or for your account at an online bookstore that stores a copy of your billing and credit card information. Change your high-security password periodically in all the places that you use it.

Use your low-security password in situations where you don't really care if your security is compromised. Some places on the Internet want you to establish an account with a user ID and password just to collect basic contact information and put your name on a mailing list. At other sites, your user ID and password provide access to information, but none of your own data (a credit card number, for example) is stored there. It is not necessary to change your low-security password very often.

QUICKCHECK......SECTION B

1. The main routes of the Internet are referred to as the Internet _____.

2. Communication between all the different devices on the Internet is made possible by TCP/_____.

3. The process of transferring a file from a remote computer to a local computer is referred to as _____.

4. A(n) _____ is a personal journal posted on the Web for access by the general public.

5. A(n) _____ modem converts your computer's digital data into signals that can travel over telephone lines.

6. Dial-up, cable modem, and DSL service are examples of always-on connections. True or false? _____

7. ISDN and _____ service require proximity to a telephone switching station, so they might not be available to rural customers.

8. Quality of _____ from an Internet service provider can deteriorate as the number of customers increases.

9. _____ sensitive computers distinguish between uppercase and lowercase letters.

10. When logging on to a computer or network, your _____ verifies your user ID.

CHECK ANSWERS

COMPUTER, INTERNET, WEB, AND E-MAIL BASICS

LAB 1-B
MAKING A DIAL-UP CONNECTION

In this lab, you'll learn:
- How to connect a computer to your telephone line
- How to connect your computer and your phone to the same wall plug
- The general procedure for subscribing to an ISP
- How to connect to the Internet using ISP-provided software
- Why you might need to manually create a dial-up connection
- What information is necessary to create a dial-up connection
- How to create your own customized dial-up icon
- How to use a dial-up icon to connect to your ISP
- How to disconnect at the end of an Internet session

INTERACTIVE LAB

CLICK TO START THE LAB

LAB ASSIGNMENTS

1. Start the interactive part of the lab. Insert your Tracking Disk if you want to save your QuickCheck results. Perform each lab step as directed, and answer all the lab QuickCheck questions. When you exit the lab, your answers are automatically graded and your results are displayed.

2. Make a list of at least five ISPs that are available in your area. If possible, include both local and national ISPs in your list.

3. Suppose that you intend to manually create a dial-up connection icon for AT&T WorldNet. What information do you need, in addition to the following, to create this dial-up connection?
    - AT&T's dial-in telephone number
    - AT&T's IP address
    - Your password

4. List the following information about the Internet connection you typically use: name of ISP, type of Internet connection (dial-up, DSL, cable modem, ISDN, DSS, school network, or business network), connection speed, and monthly fee. (If you don't currently have Internet access, describe the type of connection you would like to use.)

SECTION C
WEB BASICS

Once you have Internet access, you can begin to explore its many resources. The Web is one of the Internet's top attractions, used by millions of people every day. It is simple to use, yet provides access to a huge collection of information, including online stores, health information, stock quotes, genealogy data, dictionaries, online courses, music, photos, and videos.

Section C provides a basic introduction to the Web. If you're familiar with the Web, this section gives you a better understanding of how it works. For those of you just embarking onto the Web, this section describes the tools and techniques you need to get started. The Browsing and Searching lab at the end of this section provides hands-on experience with two important Web tools—browsers and search engines.

THE WORLD WIDE WEB

What is the Web? One of the Internet's most captivating attractions, the **Web** (short for "World Wide Web") is a collection of files that can be linked and accessed using HTTP. **HTTP** (Hypertext Transfer Protocol) is the communications standard that's instrumental in ferrying Web documents to all corners of the Internet.

Many Web-based files produce documents called **Web pages**. Other files contain photos, videos, animations, and sounds that can be incorporated into specific Web pages. Most Web pages contain **links** (sometimes called "hyperlinks") to related documents and media files (Figure 1-21).

FIGURE 1-21
On most Web pages, underlined text indicates a link, but other objects can serve as links. To activate a link, simply click it.

A graphic may or may not be a link. To discover if a graphic serves as a link, position the pointer on it and check to see if the arrow changes to a hand shape.

When the mouse pointer moved over this underlined link, it changed to a hand shape.

COMPUTER, INTERNET, WEB, AND E-MAIL BASICS

What is a Web site? A series of Web pages can be grouped into a **Web site**—a sort of virtual "place" in cyberspace. Every day, thousands of people shop at Nordstrom's Web site, an online department store featuring clothing, shoes, and jewelry. Thousands of people visit the Webopedia Web site to look up the meaning of computer terms. At the ABC News Web site, people not only read about the latest news, sports, and weather, but also discuss current issues with other readers. The Web encompasses these and hundreds of thousands of other sites.

Web sites are hosted by corporate, government, college, and private computers all over the world. The computers and software that store and distribute Web pages are called **Web servers**.

What is a URL? Every Web page has a unique address called a **URL** (Uniform Resource Locator, pronounced "You Are ELL"). For example, the URL for the Cable News Network Web site is *http://www.cnn.com*. Most URLs begin with http:// to indicate the Web's standard communications protocol. When typing a URL, the http:// can usually be omitted, so *www.cnn.com* works just as well as *http://www.cnn.com*.

Most Web sites have a main page that acts as a "doorway" to the rest of the pages at the site. This main page is sometimes referred to as a "home page," although this term has another meaning that's discussed later in this chapter. The URL for a Web site's main page is typically short and to the point, like *www.cnn.com*.

The pages for a Web site are typically stored in topic area folders, which are reflected in the URL. For example, the CNN site might include a weather center at *www.cnn.com/weather/* and an entertainment desk at *www.cnn.com/showbiz/*. A series of Web pages are then grouped under the appropriate topic. For example, you might find a page about hurricanes at the URL *www.cnn.com/weather/hurricanes.html,* and you could find a page about El Niño at *www.cnn.com/weather/elnino.html*. The file name of a specific Web page always appears last in the URL—*hurricanes.html* and *elnino.html* are the names of two Web pages. Web page file names usually have an .htm or .html extension, indicating that the page was created with **HTML** (Hypertext Markup Language), a standard format for Web documents. Figure 1-22 identifies the parts of a URL.

FIGURE 1-22
The URL for a Web page indicates the computer on which it is stored, its location on the Web server, its file name, and its extension.

http://www.cnn.com/showbiz/movies.htm

| Web protocol standard | Web server name | Folder name | Document name and file extension |

What are the rules for correctly typing a URL? A URL never contains a space, even after a punctuation mark, so do not type any spaces within a URL. An underline character is sometimes used to give the appearance of a space between words, as in the URL *www.detroit.com/top_10.html*. Be sure to use the correct type of slash—always a forward slash (/)—and duplicate the URL's capitalization exactly. The servers that run some Web sites are case sensitive, which means that an uppercase letter is not the same as a lowercase letter. On these servers, typing *www.cmu.edu/Overview.html* (with an uppercase "O") will not locate the page that's actually stored as *www.cmu.edu/overview.html* (with a lowercase "o").

BROWSERS

What is a browser? A Web browser—usually referred to simply as a **browser**—is a software program that runs on your computer and helps you access Web pages. Two of today's most popular browsers are Microsoft Internet Explorer (IE) and Netscape Navigator (Navigator). A browser window is typically divided into the sections shown in Figure 1-23.

INFOWEBLINKS

The best-selling browsers are updated on a regular basis, and occasionally new browsers challenge the old standbys. For up-to-the-minute information on these important Web tools, tune into the **Browser InfoWeb**.

www.course.com/np/concepts8/ch01

The title bar contains the name of the Web page that is currently displayed and the name of the browser.

The menu bar displays the titles of pull-down menus with options for commands such as saving, printing, copying, navigating, and configuring the browser's settings.

The toolbar contains a series of buttons for frequently used tasks.

The Address box provides a space for you to enter URLs.

If a Web page does not fit within the display area, scroll bars allow you to move the page up and down or right and left.

The status bar displays information about Web pages and links. For example, here it displays the URL of the link on which the pointer is positioned.

The display area shows the text, graphics, and links of Web pages.

FIGURE 1-23
A browser provides a sort of "window" in which it displays a Web page. The borders of the window contain a set of menus and controls to help you navigate from one Web page to another.

COMPUTER, INTERNET, WEB, AND E-MAIL BASICS

Which features are common to most browsers? Despite small cosmetic differences and some variations in terminology, Web browsers offer a remarkably similar set of features and capabilities. Figure 1-24 provides a quick overview of browser features, and Lab 1-C shows you how to use them.

FIGURE 1-24

Most browsers provide a standard set of features that allow you to work with Web pages.

Navigation buttons. After you look at a sequence of pages, the browser's Back button lets you retrace your steps to view pages you've seen previously. Most browsers also have a Forward button, which—contrary to what you might expect—does not take you to new pages you haven't yet viewed. Instead, the Forward button shows you the page you were viewing before you pressed the Back button.

Search. If you're looking for specific information on a "long" Web page, you can save yourself a lot of reading by using the Search or Find button.

History list. The Forward and Back buttons keep track of only the pages you have visited since you started your browser; however, they won't help you locate pages you visited in previous sessions. To help you revisit sites from previous sessions, your browser provides a History list. Many browsers allow you to specify how long a URL will remain in the History list. Two or three weeks is usually sufficient.

Print. Typically, a browser provides access to a print option from a button or a menu, allowing you to print the contents of a Web page.

URL box. Whether it's called a "URL box," an "Address box," a "Location box," or a "Netsite box," most browsers provide a space for entering URLs.

Favorites or Bookmarks. Suppose that you found a great Web site and you suspect you'll want to revisit it sometime in the future. Instead of writing down its URL, you can add the URL to a list, typically called "Favorites" or "Bookmarks." After adding a site to this list, you can simply click its URL to display it.

Stop button. Sometimes a Web page takes a long time to appear on your screen. If you don't want to wait for a page, click the Stop button.

Home button. Your browser lets you select a **home page**, which is the Web page that appears every time you start your browser. The idea is to select a home page that contains links or information you use often, such as a news site or a search engine. Whenever you click the Home button, your browser displays your home page, providing access to all the "goodies" it contains.

Exactly what does a browser do? A browser fetches and displays Web pages. Suppose that you want to view the Web page located at *www.e-course.com/boxer.html*. You enter the URL into a special Address box that's provided by your browser. When you press the Enter key, the browser contacts the Web server at *www.e-course.com* and requests the *boxer.html* page. The server sends your computer the data stored in *boxer.html*. This data includes two things: the information you want to view, and embedded codes, called **HTML tags**, that tell your browser how to display it. The tags specify details such as the background color, the text color and size, and the placement of graphics. Figure 1-25 shows that a browser assembles a document on your computer screen according to the specifications contained in HTML tags.

FIGURE 1-25
A browser uses HTML tags embedded in a document to correctly display text, titles, colors, headings, links, and graphics.

```
<html>
<head><title>Campus Sierra Club</title>
<body bgcolor="white">
<h1 align="center">
Picnic Island Expedition</h1>
<h2 align="center">
Brought to you by Frank Parker, Forestry Student</h2>
<p align="left">
Our next expedition heads out to Picnic Island in the Silver
Lakes Nature Preserve. We'll be collecting samples of ferns
and surveying ground cover density. If you're interested,
make sure that you attend the next meeting.
</p>
<hr>
<p align="center"> <img src="island.jpg">
</p>
<p align="center"> Web Resources:
<a href="http://www.usfs.gov/slnp">
</p>
Read more about th
</body>
```

An HTML document is basically a running string of text with embedded HTML tags, such as this tag that instructs the browser to center a line of text.

This tag specifies an image that is displayed on the Web page.

This tag defines a link to a Web page at the U.S. Forest Service Web site.

When the browser displays the Web page, the <align="center"> tag centers text.

The image specified by the <img src> tag is displayed.

The <a href> tag created this link to a Web page at the U.S. Forest Service site.

Can I copy and save information from a Web page? Most browsers provide a Copy command that allows you to copy a section of text from a Web page, which you can then paste into one of your own documents. To

COMPUTER, INTERNET, WEB, AND E-MAIL BASICS

keep track of the source for each text section, you can use the Copy command to record the Web page's URL from the Address box, and then paste the URL into your document (Figure 1-26).

FIGURE 1-26
To copy a passage of text from a Web page, highlight the text, click the Edit menu, then select Copy. Next, switch to your own document and use the Paste option.

For a demonstration of this process, click the Start icon.

CLICK TO START

SEARCH ENGINES

What is a search engine? The term **search engine** popularly refers to a Web site that provides a variety of tools to help you find information. Search engines such as Google and Yahoo! are indispensable tools when it comes to finding information on the Web. Depending on the search engine you use, you can find information by entering a description, filling out a form, or clicking a series of links to drill down through a list of topics and subtopics. Based on your input, the search engine displays a list of Web pages like the one shown in Figure 1-27.

FIGURE 1-27
In response to a query, a search engine produces a list of relevant Web pages, along with a brief description of each page and a link to it.

Search results are typically arranged in order of relevance so that the most promising Web pages should be at the top of the list. A brief description of the page helps you determine whether you want to view it.

Exactly what is a query? A **query** describes the information you want to find. It includes one or more keywords and can also include search operators. A **keyword** (sometimes called a "search term") is any word that describes the information you're trying to find. For example, *gorp* could be used as a keyword in a query for information about tasty trail mixes. You can enter more than one search term. Separate each term with a space or a search operator.

Search engines have a tendency to inundate you with possibilities—often finding thousands of potentially relevant Web pages. To receive a more manageable list of results, you need to formulate a more specific search. A **search operator** is a word or symbol that describes a relationship between keywords and thereby helps you create a more focused query. The search operators that you can use with each search engine vary slightly. To discover exactly how to formulate a query for a particular search engine, refer to its Help pages. Most search engines allow you to formulate queries with the search operators described in Figure 1-28.

INFOWEBLINKS

Search engines change at an astonishing rate. Visit the **Search Engine InfoWeb** for a list of popular search engines and their URLs, some comparative statistics, and tips on finding the search engine that's right for you.

www.course.com/np/concepts8/ch01

FIGURE 1-28
Search Operators

AND	When two search terms are joined by AND, both terms must appear on a Web page before it can be included in the search results. The query *railroad AND cars* will locate pages that contain both the words "railroad" and "cars." Your search results might include pages containing information about old railroad cars, about railroad car construction, and even about railroads that haul automobiles ("cars"). Some search engines use the plus symbol (+) instead of the word AND.
OR	When two search terms are joined by OR, either one or both of the search words could appear on a page. Entering the query *railroad OR cars* produces information about railroad fares, railroad routes, railroad cars, automobile safety records, and even car ferries.
NOT	The keyword following NOT must not appear on any of the pages found by the search engine. Entering *railroad NOT cars* would tell the search engine to look for pages that include "railroad" but not the keyword "cars." In some search engines, the minus sign (-) can be used instead of the word NOT.
Quotation Marks	Surrounding a series of keywords with quotation marks indicates that the search engine must treat the words as a phrase. The complete phrase must exist on a Web page for it to be included in the list of results. Entering *"green card"* would indicate that you are looking for information on immigration, not information on the color green, golf greens, or greeting cards.
NEAR	The NEAR operator tells a search engine that you want documents in which one of the keywords is located close to but not necessarily next to the other keyword. The query *library NEAR/15 congress* means that the words "library" and "congress" must appear within 15 words of each other. Successful searches could include documents containing phrases such as "Library of Congress" or "Congress funds special library research."
Wildcards	The asterisk (*) is sometimes referred to as a "wildcard character." It allows a search engine to find pages with any derivation of a basic word. For example, the query *medic** would not only produce pages containing the word "medic," but also "medics," "medicine," "medical," "medication," and "medicinal."
Field Searches	Some search engines allow you to search for a Web page by its title or by any part of its URL. The query *T:Backcountry Recipe Book* indicates that you want to find a specific Web page titled "Backcountry Recipe Book." In this search, the *T:* tells the search engine to look at Web page titles, and the information following the colon identifies the name of the title.

COMPUTER, INTERNET, WEB, AND E-MAIL BASICS 33

How do I use a topic directory? A **topic directory** is a list of topics and subtopics, such as Arts, Business, Computers, and so on, which are arranged in a hierarchy (Figure 1-29). The top level of the hierarchy contains general topics. Each successive level of the hierarchy contains increasingly specific subtopics. A topic directory might also be referred to as a "category list," an "index," or a "directory."

FIGURE 1-29
To use a topic directory, simply click a general topic. When a list of subtopics appears, click the one that's most relevant to the information you are trying to locate. If your selection results in another list of subtopics, continue to select the most relevant one until the search engine presents a list of Web pages. You can then link to these pages just as though you had used a keyword query.

CLICK TO START

Reproduced with permission of Yahoo! Inc. © 2004 by Yahoo! Inc. YAHOO! and the YAHOO! logo are trademarks of Yahoo! Inc.

How do I use a search form to find information? Many search engines provide an advanced search form that helps you formulate a very targeted search. A search form, like the one shown in Figure 1-30, helps you enter complex queries. It might also allow you to search for pages that are written in a particular language, located on a specific Web server, or created within a limited range of dates.

FIGURE 1-30
Many search engines provide forms that are designed to simplify the search process. These forms are usually accessible by clicking an Advanced Search link, which often is located on the main page of the search engine Web site.

Can't I just ask a simple question and get an answer? Instead of entering a cryptic query such as *movie+review+"The Producers"*, wouldn't it be nice to enter a more straightforward question like *Where can I find a review of The Producers?* A few search engines specialize in natural language queries, which accept questions written in plain English (Figure 1-31).

FIGURE 1-31
Some search engines accept natural language queries.

QUICKCHECK......SECTION C

1. HTTP (_____ Transfer Protocol) is the communications standard for the Web.

2. Every Web page has a unique address called a(n) _____. Hint: Use the abbreviation.

3. A browser assembles a Web page on your computer screen according to the specifications contained in _____ tags.

4. Google and Yahoo! are examples of _____ engines.

5. The _____ railroad AND cars will locate pages that contain both the words "railroad" and "cars."

6. Search _____, such as AND and OR, help you create targeted searches.

7. A natural _____ search engine accepts questions written in plain English.

CHECK ANSWERS

COMPUTER, INTERNET, WEB, AND E-MAIL BASICS

LAB LAB 1-C
BROWSING AND SEARCHING

In this lab, you'll learn:

- How to work with the URL box, site list, and History list
- How to use links and navigation buttons
- How to work with Bookmarks and Favorites lists
- What to do if you encounter a "page not found" message
- How to change your home page
- How to access a search engine
- Where to get help about using a search engine
- How to enter a keyword search query
- How to use a topic directory
- How to use the results list provided by a search engine

INTERACTIVE LAB

CLICK TO START THE LAB

LAB ASSIGNMENTS

1. Start the interactive part of the lab. Insert your Tracking Disk if you want to save your QuickCheck results. Perform each lab step as directed, and answer all the lab QuickCheck questions. When you exit the lab, your answers are automatically graded and your results are displayed.

2. Make a note of the brand and location of the computer you're using to complete these lab assignments.

3. Examine the Favorites or Bookmarks list. How many pages are included in this list? Link to three of the pages, indicate their URLs, and provide a brief description of their contents.

4. Suppose that you want to make your own trail mix, but you need a recipe. Enter the query *"trail mix" AND recipe* in three different search engines. (Refer to the Search Engine InfoWeb for a list of popular search engines.) Describe the similarities and differences in the results lists the three search engines produce.

5. Use the search engine of your choice to determine whether the query

    "Blue book price" Taurus -"used car"

    produces the same results as the query

    Blue book price Taurus -"used car"

    Make sure you enter each query exactly as specified, including the quotation marks (no space after the hyphen). Explain the similarities and differences in the query results.

SECTION D
E-MAIL BASICS

The Internet really took off when people discovered electronic mail. More than 15 billion e-mail messages speed over the Internet each year. E-mail, which is derived from the term "electronic mail," can refer to a single message or to the entire system of computers and software that transmits, receives, and stores e-mail messages. In this section of the chapter, you get some background information about how e-mail works—in particular, the difference between "free" Web-based e-mail and "traditional" store-and-forward e-mail. The lab for this section provides a hands-on overview of how to read, compose, send, and reply to e-mail messages.

E-MAIL OVERVIEW

Who can use e-mail? Any person with an e-mail account can send and receive e-mail. An **e-mail account** provides the rights to a storage area, or "mailbox," supplied by an e-mail provider, such as an ISP. Each mailbox has a unique address, which typically consists of a user ID, an @ symbol, and the name of the computer that maintains the mailbox. For example, suppose that a university student named Dee Greene has an electronic mailbox on a computer called rutgers.edu. If her user ID is "dee_greene," her e-mail address would be *dee_greene@rutgers.edu*.

Exactly what is an e-mail message? An **e-mail message** is a document that is composed on a computer and remains in digital, or "electronic," form so that it can be transmitted to another computer. The **message header** includes the recipient's e-mail address, message subject, and attachment file name. The body of the e-mail contains your message. The message header and body are usually displayed in a form, as shown in Figure 1-32.

FIGURE 1-32

When you compose an e-mail message, you can begin by entering the address of one or more recipients and the subject of the message. You can also specify one or more files to attach to the message. The body of the e-mail message contains the message itself.

When the message is sent, your e-mail software adds the date and your e-mail address to identify you as the sender.

What can I do with basic e-mail? Basic e-mail activities consist of writing, reading, replying to (Figure 1-33), and forwarding messages. Messages can be printed, kept for later reference, or deleted.

FIGURE 1-33
Your e-mail client's Reply button creates a new e-mail message and automatically addresses it to the person who sent the original message. Most e-mail systems also copy the text of the original message into the reply so that everyone has a complete transcript of the messages that were exchanged.

How does forwarding work? After you receive an e-mail message, you can use the Forward feature to pass it on to other people. You might, for example, forward a message that was sent to you but that should be handled by someone else. When you initiate the forwarding process, the original e-mail message is copied into a new message window, complete with the address of the original sender. You can then enter the address of the person to whom you are forwarding the message. You can also add a note about why you are passing the message along.

Some e-mail systems allow you to alter the text of the original message before you forward it. If you do so, include a note explaining your changes, especially if they alter the intent of the original message. You should not forward messages that were intended to be confidential. If you think that such a message needs to be shared with other people, obtain permission from the author of the original message.

What's an e-mail attachment? Originally, e-mail messages were stored in a plain and simple format called "ASCII text." No fancy formatting was allowed—no variation in font type or color, no underlining or boldface, and, of course, no pictures or sounds. Although you cannot insert a digital photo or sound file into a plain ASCII e-mail message, you can send these kinds of files as e-mail attachments. Any file that travels with an e-mail message is called an **e-mail attachment**. A conversion process called **MIME** (Multi-Purpose Internet Mail Extensions) provides a clever way of disguising digital photos, sounds, and other media as plain ASCII text that can travel over the Internet as e-mail attachments. An electronic message incorporated in the e-mail header provides your e-mail software with the information that allows it to reconstruct the attachment into its original form.

Suppose you want to e-mail a photo of your high school reunion to a friend. The photo is stored in a file called Reunion.gif. You can address an e-mail message to your friend, write a short note ("You missed a really fun reunion!"), and then use the Attachment option provided by your e-mail software to specify that the file Reunion.gif should accompany the e-mail. Your e-mail software converts Reunion.gif into a MIME format and sends it along with your message. When your friend receives the message, her e-mail software reconstitutes the file into your reunion photo. The way that the attachment is displayed on screen depends on your friend's e-mail software. The photo might appear at the end of the e-mail, or she might have to double-click an attachment icon to see it. With some e-mail systems, she might have to download the attachment file, and then open it using the same software with which it was created.

How does HTML relate to e-mail? Most e-mail software allows you to create e-mail messages in HTML format. Why use HTML format for your mail? HTML messages can contain lots of fancy formatting that's just not possible with plain ASCII text. By selecting your e-mail software's HTML option, you enter a world of colored, bold, italic, and underlined text; fancy fonts; embedded graphics; and various font sizes. The only limitation is that your e-mail recipients must have HTML-compliant e-mail software. Otherwise, your message will be delivered as plain, unformatted ASCII text.

What other e-mail features are available? In addition to attachments and HTML formatting, today's sophisticated e-mail systems typically offer features that help you perform the tasks listed in Figure 1-34.

FIGURE 1-34
E-mail features provide flexibility for sending and receiving messages.

- Maintain an address book and use it to select e-mail addresses instead of entering them every time you compose a message.
- Use the address book to send mail to a "group" that consists of several e-mail addresses.
- Send a "carbon copy" (Cc:) of a message to one or more recipients.
- Send a "blind carbon copy" (Bcc:), which hides the addresses in the Bcc: field from other recipients of the message.
- Assign a priority to a message—high priority is usually indicated by an exclamation point or red text.
- Find a particular message in your list of old mail.
- Enlarge text size for easier reading.
- Sort messages by date received, sender's name, subject, or priority.
- Refuse to accept messages that arrive from a particular e-mail address.
- Automate replies to messages that you receive while on vacation or when you will not be responding to e-mail messages for a few days.
- Automatically fetch mail at specified intervals.
- Check spelling before sending a message.

NETIQUETTE

Is e-mail different from other types of communication? In some respects, e-mail is similar to an old-fashioned letter because its message is conveyed without benefit of the facial expressions, voice inflections, and body gestures that accompany face-to-face conversations. When composing a message, it is important to carefully consider your audience and the message you want to convey.

COMPUTER, INTERNET, WEB, AND E-MAIL BASICS

For example, you might have gotten into the habit of using text messaging shorthand to write messages such as "thnq 4 spking w me 2day. c u 2moro at 10." (Translation: Thank you for speaking with me today. See you tomorrow at 10:00.) Text messaging shorthand recently emerged as a quick and convenient way to communicate when using e-mail, instant messaging, and cell phone text messaging. Although text messaging shorthand works among your friends, it would not be appropriate in other situations, such as confirming the time for a job interview.

By understanding netiquette, you can avoid some of the pitfalls and problems of e-mail communications. **Netiquette** is online jargon for "Internet etiquette." It is a series of customs or guidelines for maintaining civilized and effective communications in online discussions and e-mail exchanges.

- **Put a meaningful title on the subject line.** The subject line of your message should clearly describe the content of your e-mail message.

- **Use uppercase and lowercase letters.** An e-mail message that's typed in all uppercase means that you're "shouting."

- **Check spelling.** Most e-mail software offers a Check Spelling command. Use it.

- **Be careful what you send.** E-mail is not private, nor is it secure. Treat your messages as though they are postcards that can be read by anyone. Remember that all laws governing copyright, slander, and discrimination apply to e-mail.

- **Be polite.** Avoid wording that could sound inflammatory or argumentative. If you would not say it face-to-face, don't say it in e-mail.

- **Be cautious when using sarcasm and humor.** The words in your e-mail arrive without facial expressions or voice intonations, so a sarcastic comment can easily be misinterpreted.

- **Use smileys and text messaging shorthand cautiously.** Smileys are symbols that represent emotions (Figure 1-35). They can help convey the intent behind your words. Smileys and text messaging shorthand should be used only in correspondence with people who understand them.

- **Use the Bcc function for group mailings.** By placing your list of e-mail addresses in the Bcc box, the recipients of your message won't have to scroll through a long list of addresses before reaching the "meat" of your message.

- **Don't send replies to "all recipients."** Use the Reply All command only when there is a very specific need for everyone listed in the To, Cc, and Bcc boxes to receive the message.

- **Don't send huge attachments.** Try to limit the size of attachments to 50 KB or less. If necessary, use a compression program, such as WinZip, to shrink the attachment.

- **Explain all attachments.** Attachments can harbor computer viruses. To determine whether an attachment is legitimate, your correspondents will want to know the file name of the attachment, what the attachment contains, and the name of the software you used to create it.

- **Stay alert for viruses.** Because viruses can tag along with e-mail attachments, don't open an attachment unless it was sent from a reliable source, its purpose is clearly explained in the body of the e-mail, and it was scanned using antivirus software (see Chapter 4).

- **Notify recipients of viruses.** If you discover that your computer sent out infected attachments, use antivirus software to remove the virus, and then notify anyone to whom you recently sent mail.

INFOWEBLINKS

You can read more about netiquette, smileys, and text messaging shorthand at the **Netiquette InfoWeb**.

www.course.com/np/concepts8/ch01

FIGURE 1-35

Smileys, which are sometimes called "emoticons," are clever symbols that can be added to e-mail messages to convey emotions and take the edge off potentially inflammatory remarks.

:-)
"Don't take offense."

;-)
"Just kidding!"

:-(
"I'm not happy about that."

:-/
"I'm perplexed."

8-)
"I'm amazed."

SPAM

What is all this junk in my mailbox? One of e-mail's main disadvantages is **spam**—unwanted electronic junk mail about medical products, low-cost loans, and fake software upgrades that arrives in your online mailbox. Today's proliferation of spam is generated by marketing firms that harvest e-mail addresses from mailing lists, membership applications, and Web sites.

Globally, spam accounts for about 75% of all e-mail messages. Legislation to minimize spam has not met expectations. Although it is impossible to avoid spam, you can reduce it by following these guidelines:

- **Don't reply.** Never reply to spam when you receive it.

- **Guard your e-mail address.** Provide your e-mail address only to people from whom you want to receive e-mail. Be wary of providing your e-mail address at Web sites, entering it on application forms, or posting it in public places such as online discussion groups.

- **Use spam filters.** If your e-mail client offers a spam filter to block unwanted messages, put it to use. If your e-mail client does not provide a spam filter, you can download and install one from a shareware site on the Web. A **spam filter** automatically routes advertisements and other junk mail to the Deleted Items folder maintained by your e-mail client. Although spam filters can be effective for blocking spam and other unwanted e-mails, it sometimes blocks e-mail messages you want. After activating spam filters, periodically examine your Deleted Items folder to make sure the filters are not overly aggressive.

- **Report spam.** If your e-mail provider offers a way to report spam, use it.

- **Change your e-mail address.** When spam gets out of hand, you might have to consider changing your e-mail account so that you have a different e-mail address.

E-MAIL TECHNOLOGY

What is an e-mail system? An **e-mail system** is the equipment and software that carries and manipulates e-mail messages. It includes computers and software called **e-mail servers** that sort, store, and route mail. An e-mail system also includes the personal computers that belong to individuals who send and receive mail. E-mail is based on **store-and-forward technology**—a communications method in which data that cannot be sent directly to its destination is temporarily stored until transmission is possible. This technology allows e-mail messages to be routed to a server and held until they are forwarded to the next server or to a personal mailbox.

Three types of e-mail systems are widely used today: POP, IMAP, and Web-based mail. **POP** (Post Office Protocol) temporarily stores new messages in your mailbox on an e-mail server. When you connect to your ISP and request your mail, it is downloaded and stored on your computer. **IMAP** (Internet Messaging Access Protocol) is similar to POP, except that you have the option of downloading your mail or leaving it on the server. **Web-based e-mail** keeps your mail at a Web site, instead of transferring it to your computer.

How do I use Web-based e-mail? Before you can use Web-based e-mail, you need an e-mail account with a Web-based e-mail provider. To obtain one, simply connect to the Web-based e-mail provider's Web site and enter the information required to obtain an e-mail address, a user ID, and a password. Armed with these identifiers, you can connect to the

---

INFOWEBLINKS

U.S. lawmakers enacted the CAN-SPAM Act in an attempt to control the flood of unwanted e-mail. The act allows spam, but requires messages to be labeled so they can be easily filtered out by ISPs or users. For an update on efforts to control spam, connect to the **Spam InfoWeb**.

www.course.com/np/concepts8/ch01

INFOWEBLINKS

One of the biggest advantages of a Web-based e-mail account is that it's free. For descriptions and addresses of the most popular e-mail Web sites, hop over to the **Web-based E-mail InfoWeb**.

www.course.com/np/concepts8/ch01

COMPUTER, INTERNET, WEB, AND E-MAIL BASICS   41

e-mail Web site from any computer that has access to the Internet (Figure 1-36). At the Web site, you can write, read, reply to, and delete e-mail messages. Because most Web-based e-mail providers allocate a limited amount of space to each account, it is important to delete messages when you no longer need them. You don't want your electronic mailbox to overflow and cause some messages to be returned to the senders.

FIGURE 1-36

If you have a Web-based e-mail account, you can use a browser to access your e-mail messages. Writing, reading, replying to, forwarding, and deleting messages can be accomplished by interacting with a series of Web pages that lists your mail.

Reproduced with permission of Yahoo! Inc. © 2004 by Yahoo! Inc. YAHOO! and the YAHOO! logo are trademarks of Yahoo! Inc.

How do POP and IMAP work? Although you can choose to use Web-based mail, you usually don't have much choice about whether you'll use POP or IMAP—you use the one offered by your ISP. Of the two, POP is currently the most typical. Most people who use POP have obtained an e-mail account from an ISP. Such an account provides a mailbox on the ISP's **POP server**—a computer that stores your incoming messages until they can be transferred to your hard disk. Using POP requires **e-mail client software**, such as Microsoft Outlook or QUALCOMM Eudora. This software, which is installed on your computer, provides an Inbox and an Outbox that allow you to work with your mail, even when your computer is not online.

An Inbox holds incoming messages. When you ask the e-mail server to deliver your mail, all messages stored in your mailbox on the server are transferred to your computer, stored on your computer's disk drive, and listed as new mail in your Inbox. You can then disconnect from the Internet, if you like, and read the new mail at your leisure.

As shown in Figure 1-37, an Outbox temporarily holds messages you have composed and completed, but haven't transmitted over the Internet. Suppose you want to compose several e-mail messages. You can fire up your e-mail client software, but remain offline while you work on the messages. The ability to compose mail offline is especially useful if you access the Internet over a dial-up connection because the phone line isn't tied up while you compose mail. As you complete a message, it is stored on your computer and listed in the Outbox. When you go online, you

FIGURE 1-37

Outgoing mail can be stored in your Outbox until you connect to the Internet and send it. Incoming mail can be stored on a POP server until it is downloaded to the Inbox on your hard disk.

can send all the mail being held in your Outbox. Outgoing mail is routed by an **SMTP server** (Simple Mail Transfer Protocol server) instead of a POP server, as Figure 1-37 illustrates.

Does e-mail client software work only for offline e-mail tasks? No. Although you can use your e-mail client software to compose, read, and reply to messages while you're offline, you can also use it while you are online. In fact, this software often provides a setting that bypasses the Outbox and immediately sends messages out over the Internet.

Is POP mail better than Web-based e-mail? Before answering this question, let's review the important distinctions between the two types of e-mail. First, POP mail requires you to install and use e-mail client software, whereas Web-based e-mail allows you to use a browser as e-mail client software. Second, POP transfers messages to your computer's hard disk, whereas a Web-based e-mail system retains your messages on its server. Both e-mail systems have similar features, allowing you to read, compose, reply to, delete, and forward e-mail messages; maintain an address book; and send attachments. Each system does, however, have unique advantages. Your needs determine which system is better.

- **Control.** POP mail gives you more control over your messages because they are transferred to your computer's hard disk, where you can control access to them. Web-based e-mail maintains your messages on its server, where you have less control over who can access them.

- **Security.** When messages are stored on your computer, a hard disk drive malfunction could wipe out all your correspondence (along with the rest of your files). Your Web-based e-mail provider is rigorous about safeguarding its data, so your mail might be safer than if it was stored on your hard disk.

- **Travel.** The major advantage of Web-based e-mail is that you can access your messages from any computer connected to the Internet. Therefore, you can get your e-mail when you travel without taking your computer. In contrast, with POP, your computer contains your old mail, your address book, and your e-mail software. Therefore, to use your familiar e-mail tools on the road, you really have to carry your computer with you.

INFOWEBLINKS

What's the latest news about e-mail client software? You'll find descriptions, reviews, and links at the **E-mail Client Software InfoWeb**.

www.course.com/np/concepts8/ch01

QUICKCHECK......SECTION D

1. In an e-mail address, the ☐ symbol separates the user ID from the name of the e-mail server.

2. E-mail attachments are typically converted using ☐, which disguises media and other files as plain ASCII text. Hint: Use the abbreviation.

3. Unwanted e-mail messages are called ☐.

4. Store-and-☐ technology stores messages on an e-mail server until they are forwarded to an individual's computer.

5. For many e-mail systems, a(n) ☐ server handles outgoing mail, and a(n) ☐ server handles incoming mail.

CHECK ANSWERS

COMPUTER, INTERNET, WEB, AND E-MAIL BASICS

LAB LAB 1-D
USING E-MAIL

In this lab, you'll learn:
- How to open a Web-based e-mail account
- How to compose an e-mail message
- How to reply to a message
- How to intersperse your reply within the text of the original message
- How to delete a message
- How to print a message
- How to add a name to your address book
- How to create a group in your address book
- How to use your address book
- How to add an attachment to an e-mail message
- How to view an e-mail attachment

INTERACTIVE LAB

CLICK TO START THE LAB

LAB ASSIGNMENTS

1. Start the interactive part of the lab. Insert your Tracking Disk if you want to save your QuickCheck results. Perform each lab step as directed, and answer all the lab QuickCheck questions. When you exit the lab, your answers are automatically graded and your results are displayed.

2. Using the e-mail software of your choice, send an e-mail message to *kendra_hill@cciw.com*. In the body of your message, ask for a copy of the "Most Influential Person Survey."

3. Wait a few minutes after sending the message to Kendra Hill, and then check your mail. You should receive a survey from Kendra Hill. Reply to this message and Cc: your instructor. In your reply, answer each question in the survey, interspersing your answers with the original text. Send the reply, following the procedures required by your e-mail provider.

4. Examine the address book offered by your e-mail software. Describe how much information (name, home address, business address, birth date, telephone number, fax number, and so on) you can enter for each person. In your opinion, would this address book be suitable for a business person to use for storing contact information? Why or why not? Send the descriptions and answers to these questions to your instructor in an e-mail.

TECHTALK
THE BOOT PROCESS

The sequence of events that occurs between the time that you turn on a computer and the time that it is ready for you to issue commands is referred to as the boot process or "booting" your computer. The term "boot" comes from the word "bootstrap," which describes a small loop on the back of a boot. Just as you can pull on a big boot using a small bootstrap, your computer boots up by first loading a small program into memory, and then it uses that small program to load a large operating system. Your computer's small bootstrap program is built into special ROM (read-only memory) circuitry housed in the computer's system unit. When you turn on a computer, the ROM circuitry receives power and begins the boot process.

With a Windows computer, the boot process usually proceeds smoothly and, in a short time, you can begin working with your application software. Sometimes, however, the boot process encounters a problem that must be fixed before you can begin a computing session. You can fix many of the problems a computer might encounter during the boot process. Make sure, however, that you follow the guidelines provided by your school or employer if you encounter equipment problems with computers in school labs or your workplace.

What's the purpose of the boot process? The **boot process** involves a lot of flashing lights, whirring noises, and beeping as your computer performs a set of diagnostic tests called the **power-on self-test** (POST). The good news is that these tests can warn you if certain crucial components of your computer system are out of whack. The bad news is that these tests cannot warn you of impending failures. Also, problems identified during the boot process usually must be fixed before you can start a computing session.

The boot process serves an additional purpose—loading the operating system from the hard disk into memory. Without the operating system, a computer's CPU is pretty much unable to communicate with any input, output, or storage devices. It can't display information, accept commands, store data, or run any application software. Therefore, loading the operating system is a crucial step in the boot process.

Why doesn't a computer simply leave the operating system in memory? Most of a computer's memory is "volatile" random access memory (RAM), which cannot hold any data when the power is off. Although a copy of the operating system is housed in RAM while the computer is in operation, this copy is erased as soon as the power is turned off.

In addition to RAM, computers have non-volatile memory circuitry, such as ROM and CMOS, which can store data even when the power is off. Typically, ROM and CMOS are not nearly large enough to store an entire operating system.

Given the volatility of RAM and the insufficient size of ROM and CMOS, computer designers decided to store the operating system on a computer's hard disk. During the boot process, a copy of the operating system is copied into RAM where it can be accessed quickly whenever the computer needs to carry out an input, output, or storage operation. The operating system remains in RAM until the computer is turned off (Figure 1-38).

FIGURE 1-38
The bootstrap program copies the operating system into RAM, where it can be directly accessed by the processor to carry out input, output, or storage operations.

Instructions in ROM tell the computer to copy the operating system from disk to RAM.

Hard disk ROM

RAM   Operating system is available to the processor as needed.

Processor

COMPUTER, INTERNET, WEB, AND E-MAIL BASICS

What is the order of events during the boot process? Six major events happen during the boot process:

1. Power up. When you turn on the power switch, the power light is illuminated, and power is distributed to the computer circuitry.

2. Start boot program. The microprocessor begins to execute the bootstrap program that is stored in ROM.

3. Power-on self-test. The computer performs diagnostic tests of several crucial system components.

4. Identify peripheral devices. The operating system identifies the peripheral devices that are connected to the computer and checks their settings.

5. Load operating system. The operating system is copied from the hard disk to RAM.

6. Check configuration and customization. The microprocessor reads configuration data and executes any customized startup routines specified by the user.

What if I turn on a computer and nothing happens? The first step in the boot process is the power-up stage. Power from a wall outlet or battery activates a small power light. If the power light does not come on when you flip the "on" switch, refer to the checklist in Figure 1-39.

What problems are likely to show up during the power-on self-test? The POST checks your computer's main circuitry, screen display, memory, and keyboard. It can identify when one of these devices has failed, but it cannot identify intermittent problems or impending failures.

The POST notifies you of a hardware problem by displaying an error message on the screen or by emitting a series of beeps. These error messages can help you pinpoint the source of a problem. Unfortunately, many computers display these error messages as numeric codes, such as "1790 Disk 0 Error." You can check the documentation or Web site for your computer to find the specific meaning of numeric error codes.

A **beep code** provides your computer with a way to signal a problem, even if the screen is not functioning. Two short beeps might mean a problem with the keyboard. Three long beeps might mean a problem with the screen display. Beep codes differ from one computer to another, depending on the ROM bootstrap program. The printed or online reference manual for a computer usually explains the meaning of each beep code.

Should I try to fix these problems myself? If a computer displays error messages, emits beep codes, or seems to "freeze up" during the boot process, you can take some simple steps that might fix it. First, turn the computer off. After the computer has powered off, wait five seconds, and then try to start the computer again and hope that the boot process proceeds smoothly. If the boot problem reoccurs, turn the computer off again and check all the cables that run between your computer and peripheral devices, such as the keyboard, mouse, and monitor. After checking the cables, try to boot again. If you still encounter a boot error, contact a technical support person.

FIGURE 1-39
Power-up Checklist

Make sure the power cable is plugged into the wall and into the back of the computer.

If you're using a notebook or tablet computer, check batteries or plug into a wall outlet.

Make sure the wall outlet is supplying power (plug in a lamp and make sure you can turn it on).

If the computer is plugged into a surge strip, extension cord, or uninterruptible power supply, make sure it is turned on and functioning correctly.

Can you hear the fan in your desktop computer? If not, the computer's power supply mechanism might have failed.

What's the long list of stuff that appears on my screen during the boot process? After the POST, the bootstrap program tries to identify all devices connected to the computer. On some computers, the settings for each device appear on the screen during the boot process, creating a list of rather esoteric information, as shown in Figure 1-40.

```
Award Medallion BIOS v6.0
Copyright (C) 2002-03, Award Software, Inc.

Copyright 2002 by Hewlett Packard, Inc
    Rev. 1.01

Intel(R) Pentium(R) III 500MHz Processor
Memory Test : 1310725 OK

Award Plug and Play BIOS Extension v1.0A
Initialize Plug and Play Cards . . .
PNP Init Completed

Detecting Primary Master        Maxtor 53073H6
Detecting Primary Slave         IOMEGA ZIP 100    ATAPI
Detecting Secondary Master      R/RW 4x4x24
Detecting Secondary Slave       FX482IT
```

FIGURE 1-40
During the boot process, a computer attempts to identify storage devices, display devices, and other peripheral devices.

On occasion, a device gets skipped or misidentified during the boot process. An error message is not produced, but the device won't seem to work properly. To solve this problem, shut down the computer and reboot. If a device causes persistent problems, check the manufacturer's Web site to see if a new software "patch" will improve its operation.

Do computers have trouble loading the operating system? Problems during the last stages of the boot process are rare, except when a disk has been inadvertently left in the floppy disk drive. Before computers were equipped with hard disk drives, floppy disks were used to store the operating system and application software. As a legacy from these early machines, today's computers first check the floppy disk drive for a disk containing the operating system. If it doesn't find a disk in the drive, it merrily proceeds to look for the operating system on the hard disk. However, if a floppy disk happens to be hanging around in drive A, the computer assumes that you want to boot from it and looks for the operating system on that disk. The error message "Non-system disk or disk error" is the clue to this problem. Remove the floppy disk and press any key to resume the boot process.

How do I know when the boot process is finished? The boot process is complete when the computer is ready to accept your commands. Usually, the computer displays an operating system prompt or a main screen. The Windows operating system, for example, displays the Windows desktop when the boot process is complete.

If Windows cannot complete the boot process, you are likely to see a menu with an option for Safe Mode. **Safe Mode** is a limited version of Windows that allows you to use your mouse, monitor, and keyboard, but no other peripheral devices (Figure 1-41). This mode is designed for troubleshooting, not real computing tasks. If your computer enters Safe Mode at the end of the boot process, use the Shut Down command on the Start menu to

COMPUTER, INTERNET, WEB, AND E-MAIL BASICS

properly shut down and turn off your computer. You can then turn on your computer again. It should complete the boot process in regular Windows mode. If your computer enters Safe Mode again, consult a technician.

FIGURE 1-41
Windows enters Safe Mode as a response to a problem—usually caused by the device driver software that controls a piece of peripheral equipment. You can also force a computer into Safe Mode by pressing the F8 key during the boot sequence.

When a computer is behaving erratically, does rebooting help?
Under some circumstances—such as when a computer has been left on for a few weeks straight—the operating system seems to forget how to handle part of its job. Such problems can be caused by transient "soft errors" in the memory circuits that are supposed to hold the operating system instructions. In other cases, areas of memory that are supposed to be reserved for the operating system somehow get overwritten by snippets of application programs. The end effect is the same—parts of the operating system are missing and can't control a particular input, output, or storage function. As a result, a computer might begin to behave erratically. The remedy for this problem is to restore the operating system back to full functionality. Usually, rebooting does the trick. If not, consider the possibility that your computer might have contracted a virus. (More information on viruses can be found in Chapter 4.)

INFOWEBLINKS

Safe Mode can help technically savvy computer owners identify and fix a number of problems caused by installing new hardware devices. To learn more, check out the **Safe Mode InfoWeb**.

www.course.com/np/concepts8/ch01

QUICKCHECK........TECHTALK

1. The boot process loads the [   ] system from the hard disk into memory.

2. During the boot process, the [   ] checks your computer's main circuitry, screen display, memory, and keyboard.

3. Windows [   ] Mode provides a limited version of Windows that allows you to troubleshoot, but not use most peripheral devices.

4. If a computer is behaving erratically, rebooting might restore functionality. True or false? [   ]

CHECK ANSWERS

ISSUE
E-MAIL PRIVACY

When you drop an envelope into the corner mailbox, you probably expect it to arrive at its destination unopened, with its contents kept safe from prying eyes. When you make a phone call, you might assume that your conversation will proceed unmonitored by wiretaps or other listening devices. Can you also expect an e-mail message to be read only by the person to whom it is addressed?

In the United States, the Electronic Communications Privacy Act of 2000 prohibits the use of intercepted e-mail as evidence unless a judge approved a search warrant. That doesn't mean the government isn't reading your mail. Heightened security concerns after the September 11, 2001 terrorist attacks resulted in the rapid passage of the Patriot Act, which became law on October 26, 2001. In an effort to assist law enforcement officials, the "Patriot Act" relaxes the rules for obtaining and implementing search warrants and lowers the Fourth Amendment standard for obtaining a court order to compel an ISP to produce e-mail logs and addresses.

To eavesdrop on e-mail from suspected terrorists and other criminals, the FBI developed a technology called Carnivore, which scans through messages entering and leaving an ISP's e-mail system to find e-mail associated with a person who is under investigation. Privacy advocates are concerned because Carnivore scans all messages that pass through an ISP, not just those messages sent to or received by a particular individual.

Although law enforcement agencies are required to obtain a court order before intercepting e-mail, no such restriction exists for employers who want to monitor employee e-mail. According to the American Management Association, 27% of U.S. businesses monitor employee e-mail. But this intentional eavesdropping is only one way in which the contents of your e-mail messages might become public. The recipient of your e-mail can forward it to one or more people—people you never intended for it to reach. Your e-mail messages could pop up on a technician's screen in the course of system maintenance, updates, or repairs. Also, keep in mind that e-mail messages—including those you delete from your own computer—can be stored on backups of your ISP's e-mail server. You might wonder if such open access to your e-mail is legal. The answer in most cases is yes.

The United States Omnibus Crime Control and Safe Streets Act of 1968 and the Electronic Communications Privacy Act of 1986 prohibit public and private employers from engaging in surreptitious surveillance of employee activity through the use of electronic devices. However, two exceptions to these privacy statutes exist. The first exception permits an employer to monitor e-mail if one party to the communication consents to the monitoring. An employer must inform employees of this policy before undertaking any monitoring. The second exception permits employers to monitor employees' e-mail if a legitimate business need exists, and the monitoring takes place within the business-owned e-mail system.

Employees generally have not been successful in defending their rights to e-mail privacy because courts have ruled that an employee's right to privacy does not outweigh a company's rights and interests. Courts seem to agree that because a company owns and maintains its e-mail system, it has the right to monitor the messages it carries.

Like employees of a business, students who use a school's e-mail system cannot be assured of e-mail privacy. When a CalTech student was accused of

COMPUTER, INTERNET, WEB, AND E-MAIL BASICS

sexually harassing a female student by sending lewd e-mail to her and her boyfriend, investigators retrieved all the student's e-mail from the archives of the e-mail server. The student was expelled from the university even though he claimed that the e-mail had been "spoofed" to make it look as though he had sent it, when it had actually been sent by someone else.

Why would an employer want to know the contents of employee e-mail? Why would a school be concerned with the correspondence of its students? It is probably true that some organizations simply snoop on the off chance that important information might be discovered. Other organizations have more legitimate reasons for monitoring e-mail. An organization that owns an e-mail system can be held responsible for the consequences of actions related to the contents of e-mail messages on that system. For example, a school has a responsibility to protect students from harassment. If it fails to do so, it can be sued along with the author of the offending e-mail message. Organizations also recognize a need to protect themselves from false rumors and industrial espionage. For example, a business wants to know if an employee is supplying its competitor with information on product research and development.

Many schools and businesses have established e-mail privacy policies, which explain the conditions under which you can and cannot expect your e-mail to remain private. These policies are sometimes displayed when the computer boots or a new user logs in. Court decisions, however, seem to support the notion that because an organization owns and operates an e-mail system, the e-mail messages on that system are also the property of the organization. The individual who authors an e-mail message does not own all rights related to it. The company, school, or organization that supplies your e-mail account can, therefore, legally monitor your messages. You should use your e-mail account with the expectation that some of your mail will be read from time to time. Think of your e-mail as a postcard, rather than a letter, and save your controversial comments for face-to-face conversations.

INFOWEBLINKS

You'll find lots more information about e-mail privacy (and lack of it) at the **E-mail Privacy InfoWeb**.

www.course.com/np/concepts8/ch01

WHAT DO YOU THINK?

1. Do you think most people believe that their e-mail is private?   ◯ Yes   ◯ No   ◯ Not sure

2. Do you agree with CalTech's decision to expel the student who was accused of sending harassing e-mail to another student?   ◯ Yes   ◯ No   ◯ Not sure

3. Should the laws be changed to make it illegal for employers to monitor e-mail without court approval?   ◯ Yes   ◯ No   ◯ Not sure

4. Would you have different privacy expectations regarding an e-mail account at your place of work as opposed to an account you purchase from an e-mail service provider?   ◯ Yes   ◯ No   ◯ Not sure

SAVE RESPONSES

COMPUTERS IN CONTEXT
HOMELAND SECURITY

Once a localized problem affecting the Middle East and South Asia, terrorism is now spreading around the globe. Governments in many countries are devoting significant resources to combat this growing threat. In the United States, the Department of Homeland Security (DHS) is responsible for reducing America's vulnerability to terrorism and leading a unified national effort to prevent terrorist attacks on American citizens and assets.

Highly publicized efforts of the DHS include rigorous passenger and baggage screening, stepped up border patrols, smallpox vaccinations for military personnel, and a color-coded Homeland Security Advisory System that specifies the current threat level.

Technology is a key component of the DHS strategy. Electronic sniffing devices in airports detect explosives. The PROTECT system, designed to be deployed in subways, uses chemical detectors to sense toxic fumes, video surveillance cameras to monitor subway-train and passenger status, a computer program to predict the dispersion of toxic materials, and a wireless communications system to coordinate emergency responders.

Computer systems assist efforts to identify terrorists among the millions of people who travel into and within U.S. borders. US-VISIT is a system designed to verify the identities of foreign visitors. An inkless fingerprinting system and digital camera collect fingerprints and photographs of visitors, which are compared to travel documents and databases containing terrorist watchlists. US-VISIT integrates data from more than 20 systems, including the Student Exchange Visitor Information System, the National Crime Information Center, and Interpol.

A complex system of watchlists and security triggers (such as buying a one-way ticket or paying with cash) is used to monitor passengers on domestic flights. According to one source, of the more than 600 million passengers who fly during a year, approximately 15% are flagged for closer scrutiny. The DHS hopes a computer system called CAPPS II can reduce flagged passengers to only 5%.

The Multistate Anti-terrorism Information Exchange System (MATRIX) provides the capability to collect, store, analyze, and exchange sensitive terrorist and other criminal intelligence data among state and federal agencies. MATRIX accesses databases containing information about criminal history, driver's licenses, vehicle registrations, and digitized photographs.

Terrorists might use cell phones or e-mail to communicate and plan attacks. The National Security Agency (NSA) uses electronic intercepts to monitor worldwide "chatter." Computerized language translation programs help English-speaking agents sift through communications in other languages. Arabic, for example, presents a fairly complex computer translation problem. The written language uses a script that reads from right to left in which punctuation and vowels are often omitted. The meaning of a particular word can only be interpreted in context. To grasp the problem, imagine that English has no vowels. Does "plc" mean "police" or "place"? The difference could be important in a communication such as "th plns r n plc."

According to the NSA's Web site, "The old adage that 'knowledge is power' has perhaps never been truer than when applied to today's threats against our nation..." The intelligence community's prevailing strategy is to collect as much data as possible—leaving no stone unturned for fear that it might contain a key clue to the next big attack. Electronic surveillance generates mountains of data. NSA is constructing a data center in Colorado designed to collect and store 10 terabytes of data every day—that's about as much data as is stored in the entire Library of Congress with its 29 million books and 530 miles of bookshelves!

But data is not necessarily knowledge. According to one expert, "The billions of dollars spent on homeland defense will inundate intelligence analysts with information: photos from satellites, intercepted e-mails, banking records. Someone—or something—has to separate the information from the noise."

Efforts are underway to analyze and cross-check data to uncover patterns that can signal terrorist activity, but these activities have generated controversy. Privacy advocates worry that data might be used to spy on law-abiding citizens. Civil liberties advocates wonder if honest citizens might be mistakenly flagged as terrorists and have no way to correct their status. Computer experts worry about the security of government databases and their vulnerability to hackers.

On the positive side, homeland security agencies are taking steps to secure the national computer and communications infrastructure with programs that target individual computer owners, corporate computer networks, Internet service providers, and communications carriers.

A DHS division called US-CERT is responsible for analyzing and reducing computer system vulnerabilities, disseminating cyber-threat warning information, and coordinating incident response activities. A terrorist attack on the computer and communications infrastructure is likely to take the form of a virus or worm, so US-CERT monitors malicious code spread by garden-variety hackers, and has been effective in reducing the damage from the Blaster worm, the SoBig virus, and vulnerabilities in the Microsoft Windows operating system.

Individuals can subscribe to US-CERT's Cyber Security Alerts to receive e-mail when threats and vulnerabilities are discovered. US-CERT also offers a biweekly Cyber Security Tips newsletter with information on how to keep your computer and home network secure. US-CERT's National Cyber Alert System also provides bulletins for technicians about network threats and risk management at the corporate level.

Homeland security efforts are producing job opportunities in government agencies and the private sector. Degree programs at George Washington University, San Diego State University, and several community colleges are preparing graduates for challenging security careers. The Naval Postgraduate School course catalog includes basics, such as Introduction to Homeland Security, and advanced courses in asymmetric conflict and vulnerability analysis.

INFOWEBLINKS

You'll find additional information about this Computers in Context topic by visiting the **Computers and Homeland Security InfoWeb**.

www.course.com/np/concepts8/ch01

INTERACTIVE SUMMARY

To review important concepts from this chapter, fill in the blanks to best complete each sentence. When using the NP8 BookOnCD, click the Check Answers buttons to automatically score your answers. Place your Tracking Disk in the floppy disk drive if you want to save your scores.

A computer is a device that accepts input, _____ data, stores data, and produces output according to a series of stored instructions. Before a computer processes data, it is temporarily held in _____. This data is then processed in the _____ (CPU). The idea of a _____ program means that a series of instructions for a computing task can be loaded into a computer's memory.

Computers are grouped into categories, such as personal computers, handhelds, mainframes, supercomputers, servers, workstations, and videogame consoles. A _____ computer is a type of microcomputer designed to meet the needs of an individual. Computers process, store, and transmit data in _____ format as a series of 1s and 0s. Each 1 or 0 is called a _____. Eight bits, called a _____, represent one character—a letter, number, or punctuation mark. Data becomes _____ when it is presented in a format that people can understand and use.

An _____ system, such as Windows, UNIX, or Mac OS, is essentially the master controller for all activities that take place within a computer. _____ software is any set of computer programs that helps a person carry out a task. Although "Windows" is the name of an operating system, the term "Windows software" refers to application software designed for computers that run the Windows operating system.

CHECK ANSWERS

The Internet is a collection of local, regional, national, and international computer _____ that are linked together to exchange data and distribute processing tasks. The main routes of the Internet are referred to as the Internet _____. Communication between all the devices on the Internet is made possible by a standard set of rules called _____. The Internet hosts a wide variety of activities, such as Web browsing, e-commerce, e-mail, bulletin boards, chat groups, instant messaging, Internet telephony, digital broadcasts, remote access, downloads, uploads, and peer-to-peer file sharing.

Many people access the Internet using a dial-up connection that simply requires a telephone line and a _____. Faster access methods include cable modem service, ISDN, DSL, and satellite service. Regardless of the access method, individuals cannot typically connect directly to the Internet backbone and, therefore, need to use an _____ as an intermediary. Both national ISPs and local ISPs have advantages that cater to different computing lifestyles.

Access to the Internet is not restricted, but access to some areas requires a _____ and password. Passwords are most secure when they consist of two non-related words or a word and a number. Managing multiple passwords can be simplified by selecting a low-security password and a high-security password, and then applying them as necessary.

CHECK ANSWERS

COMPUTER, INTERNET, WEB, AND E-MAIL BASICS

Composed of millions of files stored on Web _____ all over the world, the Web is one of the most popular aspects of the Internet. Many of these Web-based files are documents that a browser displays as Web _____. Other files contain photos, videos, animations, and sound clips that can be incorporated into specific Web pages. Web pages also contain _____ to related documents and media files. Every Web page has a unique address called a _____. Most of them begin with "http", which stands for Hypertext _____ Protocol, the communications standard that's instrumental in ferrying Web documents to all corners of the Internet. A group of Web pages is usually referred to as a Web _____.

A _____ is a software program that runs on your computer and helps you access Web pages. It fetches Web pages and interprets HTML _____ to properly display the page on your computer screen. Current browsers simply fetch information from a given URL, but they do not have the capability to search for information based on your search specifications. A search _____ provides the tools you need to search for specific information on the Web. These tools include keyword search input areas, advanced search forms, topic directories, and "agents" that understand queries entered as simple questions.

CHECK ANSWERS

E-mail, short for "electronic mail," can refer to a single electronic message or to the entire system of computers and software that transmits, receives, and stores digital e-mail messages. Any person with an e-mail _____ can send and receive electronic mail. Basic e-mail activities include composing, reading, replying to, sending, forwarding, and deleting messages. More advanced activities include adding attachments, using HTML format, and maintaining an address book. Most e-mail messages are created in a plain and simple format called _____ text. It is also possible to create messages in _____ format, which includes underlining, fancy fonts, colored text, and embedded graphics.

E-mail has similarities with and differences from other forms of communications, but it is the differences that spawned a collection of online communications guidelines called _____.

An e-mail system consists of e-mail servers, which are accessible to e-mail account holders. Today, consumers can choose between three types of e-mail. _____ mail holds your incoming mail on an e-mail server until you download it to your computer using e-mail _____ software. _____ mail gives you the option of downloading your mail or storing it on the e-mail server. _____-based mail allows you to use a browser as e-mail client software.

CHECK ANSWERS

INTERACTIVE KEY TERMS

Make sure you understand all the boldfaced key terms presented in this chapter. If you're using the NP8 BookOnCD, you can use this list of terms as an interactive study activity. First, try to define a term in your own words, and then click the term to compare your definition with the definition presented in the chapter.

Always-on connection, 19	Instant messaging, 17	Spam filter, 40
Application software, 12	Internet, 15	Storage, 5
Beep code, 45	Internet backbone, 15	Store-and-forward technology, 40
Bit, 11	Internet telephony, 17	Stored program, 5
Blog, 17	ISDN, 20	Supercomputer, 8
Boot process, 44	ISP, 20	System software, 12
Browser, 28	Keyword, 32	System unit, 10
Byte, 11	LAN, 8	Tablet computer, 7
Cable modem, 19	LCD screen, 10	TCP/IP, 15
Case sensitive, 22	Links, 26	Topic directory, 33
CD drive, 10	Macs, 13	Uploading, 16
Central processing unit (CPU), 4	Mailing list server, 17	URL, 27
Chat group, 17	Mainframe computer, 8	Usenet, 17
Client, 9	Memory, 5	User ID, 22
Computer, 4	Message header, 36	Videogame console, 8
Computer network, 8	Microcomputer, 6	Voiceband modem, 18
Computer program, 4	Microprocessor, 6	Web, 26
Data, 4	MIME, 37	Web pages, 26
Data file, 11	Modem, 10	Web servers, 27
Desktop computer, 6	Monitor, 10	Web site, 27
Dial-up connection, 18	Mouse, 10	Web-based e-mail, 40
Digital, 11	Netiquette, 39	Workstation, 8
Downloading, 16	Network card, 10	
DSL, 20	Newsgroups, 17	
DSS, 20	Notebook computer, 6	
DVD drive, 10	Operating system, 12	
E-commerce, 17	Output, 5	
E-mail, 17	Password, 22	
E-mail account, 36	PCs, 13	
E-mail attachment, 37	PDA, 7	
E-mail client software, 41	Peer-to-peer, 16	
E-mail message, 36	Peripheral device, 11	
E-mail servers, 40	Personal computer, 6	
E-mail system, 40	Platform, 13	
Executable file, 11	POP, 40	
File, 11	POP server, 41	
File extension, 11	Power-on self-test (POST), 44	
File name, 11	Processing, 4	
Floppy disk drive, 10	Query, 32	
Handheld computer, 7	Safe Mode, 46	
Hard disk drive, 10	Search engine, 31	
Home page, 29	Search operator, 32	
HTML, 27	Server, 9	
HTML tags, 30	Smileys, 39	
HTTP, 26	SMTP server, 42	
IMAP, 40	Software, 4	
Information, 11	Sound card, 10	
Input, 4	Spam, 40	

COMPUTER, INTERNET, WEB, AND E-MAIL BASICS

INTERACTIVE SITUATION QUESTIONS

Apply what you've learned to some typical computing situations. When using the NP8 BookOnCD, you can type your answers, and then use the Check Answers button to automatically score your responses. Place your Tracking Disk in the floppy disk drive if you want to save your scores.

1. Suppose that you walk into an office and see the devices pictured to the right. You would probably assume that they are the screen and keyboard for a _____ personal computer, _____, or server.

2. You receive a CD from a friend. It contains a file called EverQuest.exe. Because of the file extension, you assume that the disk contains a(n) _____ file that is some type of computer program, rather than a data file.

3. You are a musician and you use your Gateway PC to compose music. Your friend, who has an iMac computer, wants you to try the software she uses. If she loans you her composition software, can you use it on your PC? Yes or no? _____

4. You are a computer technician hired by Ben and Jerry's Ice Cream to set up a Web site. You know that your site requires a unique _____ that pinpoints its location on the Internet, and your server will have to use _____, the standard Internet protocol that transports data between all sorts of computer platforms over the Internet.

5. You want the cheapest Internet connection. You don't mind if the connection is limited to speeds under 56 Kbps and doesn't provide very good video performance. You would probably select an ISP that provides a(n) _____ connection.

6. You need to select a password for your online bank account. Which of the following passwords would be the LEAST secure: jeff683, hddtmrutc, gargantuan, brickcloset, fanhotshot, or high348? _____

7. You want to look at the latest Nike athletic shoes. The URL that will probably get you to Nike's home page is _____.

8. You want to find some Web pages that contain information about snowboarding competitions. You know that your _____ can only fetch and display Web pages, so you'll need to connect to a(n) _____ and enter a query, such as "snowboard competition."

9. If your ISP does not supply you with an e-mail account, you can get a free _____ e-mail account from a site such as Hotmail or Yahoo!.

10. You receive an e-mail message that contains colored text and underlining. You assume that the person who sent the message had his mail software set for _____ format.

CHECK ANSWERS

INTERACTIVE PRACTICE TESTS

Practice tests that consist of 10 multiple-choice, true/false, and fill-in-the-blank questions are available on both the NP8 BookOnCD and the NP8 Web site. The questions are selected at random from a large test bank, so each time you take a test, you'll receive a different set of questions. Your tests are scored immediately, and you can print study guides that help you find the correct answers for any questions that you missed.

www.course.com/np/concepts8/ch01

CLICK TO START

REVIEW
ON THE WEB

PROJECTS

An NP8 Project is an open-ended activity that helps you apply the concepts you have learned. Many projects require resources in addition to your textbook, such as current magazines, library materials, or Web access. When you tackle a project, be prepared to use your critical thinking skills, logical analysis, and creativity. Projects for this chapter include:

- Issue Research: E-mail Privacy
- Who Wants to be a Millionaire
- Computers in Homeland Security
- Micros, Minis, Mainframes, and Supercomputers
- Anonymous E-mail?
- Get Creative
- Describe Your Personal Computer Using Key Terms

To work with the Projects for this chapter, connect to the **New Perspectives NP8 Web Site**.

www.course.com/np/concepts8/ch01

TECHTV VIDEO PROJECT

The TechTV segment *Predicting Big Surf* highlights one of many unique ways to use the Web. After you watch this video, write a short description of it. Then, browse around the Web to look for other unique applications. Write a short description of at least three applications you found and then explain whether in your opinion they offer good, solid services or are simply gimmicks.

To work with the Video Projects for this chapter, connect to the **New Perspectives NP8 Web Site**.

www.course.com/np/concepts8/ch01

STUDY TIPS

Study Tips help you to organize and consolidate the information in a chapter by making lists, outlines, charts, and sketches. You can use paper and pencil or word processing software to complete most of the Study Tips.

To work with the Study Tips for this chapter, connect to the **New Perspectives NP8 Web Site**.

www.course.com/np/concepts8/ch01

ONLINE GAMES

Test your comprehension of the concepts introduced in Chapter 1 by playing the NP8 Online Games. At the end of each game, you have three options:

- Print a comprehensive study guide complete with page references
- Print your results to be submitted to your instructor
- Save your results to be submitted to your instructor via e-mail

To work with the Online Games for this chapter, connect to the **New Perspectives NP8 Web Site**.

www.course.com/np/concepts8/ch01

COMPUTER, INTERNET, WEB, AND E-MAIL BASICS

57

STUDENT EDITION LABS

Extend your knowledge of computer basics with the Chapter 1 Student Edition Lab.

The following Student Edition Lab is offered with Chapter 1:

- E-mail

To work Chapter 1
Student E correspond ab and its
ment, conne assign-
Perspectives e New
Site.
www.course.com/np

Go to the NP8 New Perspectives Web site for specific lab topics.

Work hands-on in structured simulations practicing important skills and concepts

Test your comprehension of the lab topics through a series of objective-based questions

Track Your Progress with the Student Edition Labs

- Student Edition Labs test your comprehension of the lab topics through a series of trackable objective-based questions. Your instructor will direct you to either print your results or submit them via e-mail.

- Student Edition Lab Assignments, available on the New Perspectives NP8 Web site, require you to apply the skills learned through the lab in a live environment. Go to the New Perspectives NP8 Web site for detailed instruction on individual Student Edition Lab Assignments.

If you have a SAM user profile, you have access to even more interactive content. Log in to your SAM account and go to your assignments page to see what your instructor has assigned for this chapter.

SECTION A, CHAPTER 2

COMPUTER HARDWARE

CONTENTS

SECTION A:
DATA REPRESENTATION AND DIGITAL ELECTRONICS

Data Representation
Quantifying Bits and Bytes
Digital Electronics

❋ **SECTION B:**
MICROPROCESSORS AND MEMORY

Microprocessor Basics
Microprocessor Performance Factors
Today's Microprocessors
Random Access Memory
Read-only Memory
CMOS Memory
Buying a Computer

❋ **SECTION C: STORAGE DEVICES**

Storage Basics
Floppy Disk Technology
Hard Disk Technology
Tape Storage
CD and DVD Technology
Solid State Storage

❋ **SECTION D:**
INPUT AND OUTPUT DEVICES

Basic Input Devices
Display Devices
Printers
Installing Peripheral Devices

❋ **TECHTALK: HOW A MICROPROCESSOR EXECUTES INSTRUCTIONS**

❋ **ISSUE: COMPUTERS AND THE ENVIRONMENT**

❋ **COMPUTERS IN CONTEXT: MILITARY**

❋ **REVIEW ACTIVITIES**

Interactive Summary
Interactive Key Terms
Interactive Situation Questions
Interactive Practice Tests
Review on the Web

LABS

❋ Working with Binary Numbers
❋ Benchmarking

TIP

When using the BookOnCD, the ❋ icons are "clickable" to access resources on the CD. The ✚ icons are clickable to access resources on the Web. You can also access Web resources by using your browser to connect directly to the NP8 New Perspectives Web site at:

www.course.com/np/concepts8/ch02

COMPUTER HARDWARE

CHAPTER PREVIEW

Before you begin Chapter 2, you can use the Web-based preview activities to hear an overview of the chapter, check your current level of expertise about key concepts, and look through a list of learning objectives. You can access the preview activities by clicking the ✦ icon when using the BookOnCD or going to the New Perspectives NP8 Web site.

CHAPTER OVERVIEW
Whether you are shopping for a new computer, using your trusty laptop, or troubleshooting a problem, it is useful to have some background in hardware terminology. Get your book and highlighter ready, then connect to the New Perspectives NP8 Web site where you can listen to an overview that points out the most important concepts for this chapter.

www.course.com/np/concepts8/ch02 ✦

CHAPTER PRE-ASSESSMENT
How much do you know about bits and bytes, RAM and ROM, processors and storage, printers and monitors? To gauge your level of knowledge before beginning the chapter, take the pre-assessment quiz at the New Perspectives NP8 Web site. Armed with your results from this quiz, you can focus your study time on concepts that will round out your knowledge of computer hardware and improve your test scores.

www.course.com/np/concepts8/ch02 ✦

LEARNING OBJECTIVES
When you complete this chapter you should be able to:

- Explain why most computers are digital and how that relates to representing numbers by using 0 and 1 bits
- Describe the role of a microprocessor's ALU, control unit, registers, and instruction set
- List the factors that affect microprocessor performance
- Explain how RAM works and how it differs from disk storage
- List facts about RAM that are important to computer buyers and owners
- Describe the difference between magnetic, optical, and solid state storage
- Use criteria such as versatility, durability, capacity, access time, and data transfer rate to compare storage technologies: floppy disks, hard disks, tapes, CDs, DVDs, and USB Flash drives

- Explain the factors that might help a shopper decide whether to purchase a CRT, LCD, or plasma monitor
- Compare and contrast the technologies and applications for ink jet, solid ink, thermal, dye sublimation, laser, and dot matrix printers
- Describe the components of a computer's expansion bus, including various types of expansion slots and cables
- Explain the hardware compatibility considerations, device drivers, and procedures involved in installing a peripheral device

A detailed list of learning objectives is provided at the New Perspectives NP8 Web site

www.course.com/np/concepts8/ch02 ✦

SECTION A, CHAPTER 2

DATA REPRESENTATION AND DIGITAL ELECTRONICS

Understanding what makes a computer "tick" can come in handy in today's information age. It helps you decipher computer ads, troubleshoot equipment problems, and make software work. Although scientists are tinkering with exotic technologies such as quantum computers and molecular computers, just about every computer today is an electronic, digital device based on a concept that's as simple as a basic light switch.

DATA REPRESENTATION

What is data representation? People use computers to work with many kinds of data, including numbers, text, music, photos, and videos. **Data representation** is the process of transforming this diverse data into a form that computers can use for processing. Today, computers typically represent data digitally.

How do computers represent data digitally? Most computers are digital devices. A **digital device** works with discrete—distinct and separate—data, such as the digits 1 and 0. In contrast, an **analog device** works with continuous data. As an analogy, a traditional light switch has two discrete states—on and off—so it is a digital device. A dimmer switch, on the other hand, has a rotating dial that controls a continuous range of brightness. It is, therefore, an analog device (Figure 2-1).

Most computers use the simplest type of digital technology—their circuits have only two possible states. For convenience, let's say that one of those states is "on" and the other state is "off." When discussing these states, we usually indicate the "on" state with 1 and the "off" state with 0. So the sequence "on" "on" "off" "off" would be written 1100. These 1s and 0s are referred to as **binary digits**. It is from this term that we get the word "bit"—*bi*nary digi*t*. Computers use sequences of bits to digitally represent numbers, letters, punctuation marks, music, pictures, and videos.

How does a computer represent numbers? **Numeric data** consists of numbers that might be used in arithmetic operations. For example, your annual income is numeric data, as is your age. The price of a bicycle is numeric data. So is the average gas mileage for a vehicle, such as a car or SUV. Computers represent numeric data using the binary number system, also called "base 2."

The **binary number system** has only two digits: 0 and 1. No numeral like "2" exists in this system, so the number "two" is represented in binary as "10" (pronounced "one zero"). You'll recognize the similarity to what happens when you're counting from 1 to 10 in the familiar decimal system. After you reach 9, you run out of digits. For "ten," you have to use "10"—zero is a placeholder and the "1" indicates "one group of tens."

In binary, you just run out of digits sooner—right after you count to 1. To get to the next number, you have to use the zero as a placeholder and the "1" indicates "one group of 2s." In binary then, you count 0 ("zero"), 1 ("one"), 10 ("one zero"), instead of counting 0, 1, 2 in decimal. If you need to brush up on binary numbers, refer to Figure 2-2 on the next page and to the lab at the end of Section A.

FIGURE 2-1
A computer is a digital device, more like a standard light switch than a dimmer switch.

COMPUTER HARDWARE

Decimal (Base 10)	Binary (Base 2)
0	0
1	1
2	10
3	11
4	100
5	101
6	110
7	111
8	1000
9	1001
10	1010
11	1011
1000	1111101000

FIGURE 2-2
The decimal system uses ten symbols to represent numbers: 0, 1, 2, 3, 4, 5, 6, 7, 8, and 9. The binary number system uses only two symbols: 0 and 1.

The important point to understand is that the binary number system allows computers to represent virtually any number simply by using 0s and 1s, which conveniently translate into electrical "on" and "off" signals. The average gas mileage for an SUV (11) is 1011 in binary, and can be represented by "on" "off" "on" "on."

How can a computer represent words and letters using bits?

Character data is composed of letters, symbols, and numerals that are not used in arithmetic operations. Examples of character data include your name, address, and hair color. Just as Morse code uses dashes and dots to represent the letters of the alphabet, a digital computer uses a series of bits to represent letters, characters, and numerals. Figure 2-3 illustrates how a computer can use 0s and 1s to represent the letters and symbols in the text "HI!"

Computers employ several types of codes to represent character data, including ASCII, EBCDIC, and Unicode. **ASCII** (American Standard Code for Information Interchange, pronounced "ASK ee") requires only seven bits for each character. For example, the ASCII code for an uppercase "A" is 1000001. ASCII provides codes for 128 characters, including uppercase letters, lowercase letters, punctuation symbols, and numerals.

A superset of ASCII, called **Extended ASCII**, uses eight bits to represent each character. For example, Extended ASCII represents the letter "A" as 01000001. Using eight bits instead of seven bits allows Extended ASCII to provide codes for 128 more characters than plain ASCII. The additional Extended ASCII characters include boxes, circles, and other graphical symbols. An alternative to the 8-bit Extended ASCII code, called **EBCDIC** (Extended Binary-Coded Decimal Interchange Code, pronounced "EB seh dick"), is usually used only by older, IBM mainframe computers.

Unicode (pronounced "YOU ni code") uses sixteen bits and provides codes for 65,000 characters—a real bonus for representing the alphabets of multiple languages. For example, Unicode represents an uppercase "A" in the Russian Cyrillic alphabet as 0000010000010000.

FIGURE 2-3
A computer treats the letters and symbols in the word "HI!" as character data, which can be represented by a string of 0s and 1s.

H I !
01001000 01001001 00100001

Why do ASCII and Extended ASCII provide codes for 0, 1, 2, 3, 4, 5, 6, 7, 8, and 9? The table in Figure 2-4 illustrates the variety of letters and symbols represented by Extended ASCII. You might wonder why the table contains codes for 0, 1, 2, 3, and so on. Aren't these numbers represented by the binary number system? A computer uses Extended ASCII character codes for 0, 1, 2, 3 to represent numerals that are not used for calculations. For example, you don't typically use your social security "number" in calculations, so it is considered character data and represented using Extended ASCII. Likewise, the "numbers" in your street address can be represented by character codes rather than binary numbers.

FIGURE 2-4
The Extended ASCII code uses a series of eight 1s and 0s to represent 256 characters, including lowercase letters, uppercase letters, symbols, and numerals. The first 32 ASCII characters are not shown in this table because they represent special control sequences that cannot be printed. The two "blank" entries are space characters.

How does a computer convert music and pictures into codes? Music and pictures are not small, discrete objects like numbers or the letters of the alphabet. To work with music and pictures, they must be digitized. The term **digitize** means to convert raw, analog data into digital format represented by 0s and 1s.

A photograph or drawing can be digitized by treating it as a series of colored dots. Each dot is assigned a binary number according to its color. For example, a green dot might be represented by 0010 and a red dot by 1100, as shown in Figure 2-5. A digital image is simply a list of color numbers for all the dots it contains. In a similar way, music can be digitized by assigning binary codes to notes.

FIGURE 2-5
An image can be digitized by assigning a binary number to each dot.

A red dot might be digitized as 1100.

COMPUTER HARDWARE

When a computer works with a series of 1s and 0s, how does it know which code to use? All the "stuff" that your computer works with is stored in files as a long—make that really long—series of 1s and 0s. Your computer needs to know whether to interpret those 1s and 0s as ASCII code, binary numbers, or the code for a picture or sound. Imagine the mess if your computer thought that your term paper, stored as ASCII, was an accounting file that contained a series of numbers stored in binary format. It would never be able to reconstruct the words and sentences of your term paper.

To avoid confusion, most computer files contain a **file header** with information on the code used to represent the file data. A file header is stored along with the file and can be read by the computer, but never appears on the screen. By reading the header information, a computer can tell how a file's contents were coded.

QUANTIFYING BITS AND BYTES

How can I tell the difference between bits and bytes? Computer ads include lots of abbreviations relating to bits and bytes. A few key concepts can help you understand what these abbreviations mean. Even though the word "bit" is an abbreviation for "binary digit," it can be further abbreviated, usually as a lowercase "b." A byte, on the other hand, is composed of eight bits and usually abbreviated as an uppercase "B."

Transmission speeds are typically expressed in bits, whereas storage space is typically expressed in bytes. In Chapter 1, for example, you learned that the speed of most voice band modems is 56 Kbps—56 kilobits per second. In a computer ad, you might see the capacity of a hard disk drive described as 40 GB—40 gigabytes.

What do the prefixes kilo-, mega-, and giga- mean? When working with computers, you'll frequently encounter references such as "50 kilobits per second," "1.44 megabytes," and "2.8 gigahertz." Kilo, mega, giga, and similar terms are used to quantify computer data.

In common usage, "kilo," abbreviated as "K," means 1,000. For example, $50 K means $50,000. In the decimal number system we use on a daily basis, the number 1,000 is 10 to the 3rd power, or 10^3. In the world of computers where base 2 is the norm, a "kilo" is precisely 1,024, or 2^{10}. A **kilobit** (abbreviated Kb or Kbit) is 1,024 bits. A **kilobyte** (abbreviated KB or Kbyte) is 1,024 bytes. Kilobytes are often used when referring to the size of small computer files.

The prefix "mega" means a million, or in the context of bits and bytes, precisely 1,048,576 (the equivalent of 2^{20}). A **megabit** (Mb or Mbit) is 1,048,576 bits. A **megabyte** (MB or MByte) is 1,048,576 bytes. Megabytes are often used when referring to the size of medium to large computer files or to floppy disk capacity.

In computer lingo, the prefix "giga" refers to a billion, or precisely 1,073,741,824. As you might expect, a **gigabit** (Gb or Gbit) is approximately one billion bits. A **gigabyte** (GB or GByte) is one billion bytes. Gigabytes are typically used to refer to RAM and hard disk capacity.

Computers—especially mainframes and supercomputers—sometimes work with huge amounts of data, and so terms such as tera- (trillion), peta- (thousand trillion), and exa- (quintillion) are also handy. Figure 2-6 summarizes the terms commonly used to quantify computer data.

FIGURE 2-6
Quantifying Digital Data

Bit	One binary digit
Byte	8 bits
Kilobit	1,024 or 2^{10} bits
Kilobyte	1,024 or 2^{10} bytes
Megabit	1,048,576 or 2^{20} bits
Megabyte	1,048,576 or 2^{20} bytes
Gigabit	2^{30} bits
Gigabyte	2^{30} bytes
Terabyte	2^{40} bytes
Petabyte	2^{50} bytes
Exabyte	2^{60} bytes

SECTION A, CHAPTER 2

DIGITAL ELECTRONICS

How does a computer store and transport all those bits? Because most computers are electronic devices, bits take the form of electrical pulses that can travel over circuits, in much the same way that electricity flows over a wire when you turn on a light switch. All the circuits, chips, and mechanical components that form a computer are designed to work with bits. Most of these essential components are housed within the computer's system unit.

What's inside the system unit? If it weren't for the miniaturization made possible by digital electronic technology, computers would be huge, and the inside of a computer's system unit would contain a complex jumble of wires and other electronic gizmos. Instead, today's computers contain relatively few parts. Desktop computers with large system units are designed so that owners can easily upgrade audio, visual, and storage components. Small desktop and notebook computers, on the other hand, usually provide access for expansion and replacement from outside of the case. In Figure 2-7, you can see what's inside a typical desktop computer.

FIGURE 2-7
A computer's system unit typically contains circuit boards, storage devices, and a power supply that converts current from an AC wall outlet into the DC current used by computer circuitry.

- Power supply and fan
- Microprocessor located under cooling fan
- Expansion cards
- CD drive
- Floppy disk drive
- Hard disk drive
- Cables that transfer data from storage devices to system board
- Main circuit board (system board)

FIGURE 2-8
A computer chip is classified by the number of miniaturized components it contains—from small-scale integration (SSI) of less than 100 components per chip to ultra large-scale integration (ULSI) of more than 1 million components per chip.

What's a computer chip? The terms "computer chip," "microchip," and "chip" originated as technical jargon for "integrated circuit." An **integrated circuit** (IC), such as the one pictured in Figure 2-8, is a super-thin slice of semiconducting material packed with microscopic circuit elements, such as wires, transistors, capacitors, logic gates, and resistors.

Semiconducting materials (or "semiconductors"), such as silicon and germanium, are substances with properties between those of a conductor (like copper) and an insulator (like wood). To fabricate a chip, the conductive properties of selective parts of the semiconducting material can be enhanced to essentially create miniature electronic pathways and components, such as transistors.

COMPUTER HARDWARE

The assortment of chips inside a computer includes the microprocessor, memory modules, and support circuitry. These chips are packaged in a protective carrier that also provides connectors to other computer components. Chip carriers vary in shape and size—including small rectangular **DIPs** (dual in-line package) with caterpillar-like legs protruding from a black, rectangular "body"; long, slim **DIMMs** (dual in-line memory modules); pincushion-like **PGAs** (pin-grid arrays); and cassette-like **SEC cartridges** (single edge contact cartridges). Terms like DIMM and PGA frequently appear in computer ads. Figure 2-9 helps you visualize these components.

INFOWEBLINKS

Find out how thousands of miles of wires and millions of components can be miniaturized to the size of a baby's fingernail by connecting to the **Integrated Circuits InfoWeb**.

www.course.com/np/concepts8/ch02

FIGURE 2-9

Integrated circuits can be used for microprocessors, memory, and support circuitry. They are housed within a ceramic carrier. These carriers exist in several configurations, or "chip packages," such as DIPs, DIMMs, PGAs, and SECs.

A DIP has two rows of pins that connect the IC circuitry to a circuit board.

A DIMM is a small circuit board containing several chips, typically used for memory.

A PGA is a square chip package with pins arranged in concentric squares, typically used for microprocessors.

An SEC cartridge was pioneered by Intel to house Pentium III microprocessors.

How do chips fit together to make a computer? The computer's main circuit board, called a **system board**, "motherboard," or "main board," houses all essential chips and provides connecting circuitry between them. If you look carefully at a system board, you'll see that some chips are permanently soldered in place. Other chips are plugged into special sockets and connectors, which allow chips to be removed for repairs or upgrades. When multiple chips are required for a single function, such as generating stereo-quality sound, the chips might be gathered together on a separate small circuit board, which can then be plugged into a special slot-like connector. Figure 2-10 on the next page provides a handy guide that can help you identify the components on your computer's system board.

FIGURE 2-10
A computer system board provides sockets for chips, slots for small circuit boards, and the circuitry that connects all these components.

- Expansion card
- Connectors for storage device cables
- Battery that powers the computer's real-time clock
- DIMM module containing memory chips
- Expansion slots hold additional expansion cards, such as a modem or sound card
- SEC-style microprocessor
- Connector for power supply
- Circuitry that transports data from one component to another
- DIP holding a ROM chip

QUICKCHECK......SECTION A

1. Most computers are _____ devices that work with discrete numbers, such as 1s and 0s.

2. The _____ number system represents numeric data as a series of 0s and 1s.

3. Extended _____ uses eight bits to represent each letter of the alphabet.

4. A computer uses _____ codes to represent the numerals in your social security number and street address, whereas it uses _____ numbers to code numeric data such as your age.

5. A(n) _____ is approximately one billion bytes.

6. A(n) _____ circuit contains microscopic elements, such as wires, transistors, and capacitors, that are packed onto a very small square of semiconducting material.

7. A computer's _____ board is also called a "motherboard" or "main board."

CHECK ANSWERS

COMPUTER HARDWARE

LAB
LAB 2-A
WORKING WITH BINARY NUMBERS

In this lab, you'll learn:
- The difference between the binary number system and the decimal number system
- How to count in binary
- How to convert decimal numbers into binary numbers
- How to convert binary numbers into decimal numbers
- How to use the Windows Calculator to convert numbers
- How to work with "powers of two"

INTERACTIVE LAB

CLICK TO START THE LAB

LAB ASSIGNMENTS

1. Start the interactive part of the lab. Insert your Tracking Disk if you want to save your QuickCheck results. Perform each lab step as directed, and answer all the lab QuickCheck questions. When you exit the lab, your answers are automatically graded and your results are displayed.

2. Using paper and pencil, manually convert the following decimal numbers into binary numbers. Your instructor might ask you to show the process that you used for each conversion.

   a. 100   b. 1,000   c. 256   d. 27
   e. 48   f. 112   g. 96   h. 1,024

3. Using paper and pencil, manually convert the following binary numbers into decimal numbers. Your instructor might ask you to show the process that you used for each conversion.

   a. 100   b. 101   c. 1100   d. 10101
   e. 1111 f. 10000   g. 1111000 h. 110110

4. Describe what is wrong with the following sequence:

   10 100 110 1000 1001 1100 1110 10000

5. What is the decimal equivalent of 2^0? 2^1? 2^8?

SECTION B
MICROPROCESSORS AND MEMORY

A typical computer ad contains a long list of specifications that describe a computer's components and capabilities. Savvy shoppers understand how these specifications affect computer performance and price. Most computer specifications begin with the microprocessor type and speed. Computer manufacturers want consumers to think that faster is better, but is there a point at which you can pay for speed you won't need? Computer ads also contain information about a computer's memory capacity. Lots of memory can add hundreds of dollars to the cost of a computer. Consumers are right to ask "How much RAM is enough?"

Section B explains how the microprocessor and memory work, and how they affect computer performance and price.

MICROPROCESSOR BASICS

What exactly is a microprocessor? A **microprocessor** (sometimes simply referred to as a "processor") is an integrated circuit designed to process instructions. It is the most important, and usually the most expensive, component of a computer. Although a microprocessor is sometimes mistakenly referred to as "a computer on a chip," it can be more accurately described as "a CPU on a chip" because it contains—on a single chip—circuitry that performs essentially the same tasks as the central processing unit (CPU) of a classic mainframe computer.

What does it look like? Looking inside a computer, you can usually identify the microprocessor because it is the largest chip on the system board, although it might be hidden under a cooling fan. Most of today's microprocessors are housed in a PGA (pin grid array) chip package, as shown in Figure 2-11.

FIGURE 2-11
Today's microprocessors are typically housed in a PGA chip package.

How does a microprocessor work? Inside the chip carrier, a microprocessor is a very complex integrated circuit, containing as many as 300 million miniaturized electronic components. The miniaturized circuitry in a microprocessor is grouped into important functional areas, such as the ALU and the control unit.

The **ALU** (arithmetic logic unit) performs arithmetic operations, such as addition and subtraction. It also performs logical operations, such as comparing two numbers to see if they are the same. The ALU uses **registers** to hold data that is being processed, just as you use a mixing bowl to hold the ingredients for a batch of brownies. The microprocessor's **control unit** fetches each instruction, just as you get each ingredient out of a cupboard or the refrigerator. The computer loads data into the ALU's registers, just as you add all the ingredients to the mixing bowl. Finally, the control unit gives the ALU the green light to begin processing, just as you flip the switch to your electric mixer to begin

COMPUTER HARDWARE

blending the brownie ingredients. Figure 2-12 illustrates a microprocessor control unit and ALU preparing to add 2 + 3.

Where does the microprocessor get its instructions? The simple answer is that a microprocessor executes instructions provided by a computer program. However, a microprocessor can't follow just any instructions. A program that contains an instruction to "self destruct" won't have much effect because a microprocessor can perform only a limited list of instructions—"self destruct" isn't one of them.

The list of instructions that a microprocessor can perform is called its **instruction set**. These instructions are hard-wired into the processor's circuitry and include basic arithmetic and logical operations, fetching data, and clearing registers. A computer can perform very complex tasks, but it does so by performing a combination of simple tasks from its instruction set.

MICROPROCESSOR PERFORMANCE FACTORS

What makes one microprocessor perform better than another? Computer ads like the one in Figure 2-13 include microprocessor specifications related to its performance. A microprocessor's performance is affected by several factors, including clock speed, word size, cache size, instruction set, and processing techniques.

What do MHz and GHz have to do with computer performance? The speed specifications that you see in a computer ad indicate the speed of the **microprocessor clock**—a timing device that sets the pace for executing instructions. Most computer ads specify the speed of a microprocessor in megahertz or gigahertz. **Megahertz** (MHz) means a million cycles per second. **Gigahertz** (GHz) means a billion cycles per second.

A cycle is the smallest unit of time in a microprocessor's universe. Every action a processor performs is measured by these cycles. It is important, however, to understand that the clock speed is not equal to the number of instructions a processor can execute in one second. In many computers, some instructions occur within one cycle, but other instructions might require multiple cycles. Some processors can even execute several instructions in a single clock cycle.

A specification such as 3.6 GHz means that the microprocessor's clock operates at a speed of 3.6 billion cycles per second. All other things being equal, a computer with a 2.8 GHz processor is faster than a computer with a 1.5 GHz processor or a 933 MHz processor.

In 2004, a major chip maker began to phase in the use of "processor numbers" (PN) as a replacement for clock speeds. The Pentium 4 3.6 GHz processor became the Pentium 4 560, for example. Processor numbers do not indicate clock speed. They can indicate speed relative to other processors within the same family, but not between different families. For example, the Pentium 4 560 is faster than the Pentium 4 540. However, an Intel M processor 755 is not faster than the Pentium 4 560. Even though 755 is a larger number than 560, the M processor and Pentium 4 are indifferent processor families. Their processor numbers cannot be compared to each other.

FIGURE 2-12

The control unit fetches the ADD instruction, then loads data into the ALU's registers where it is processed.

| Control Unit |
| ADD |

| ALU |
| Register 2 |
| Register 3 |

FIGURE 2-13

A typical computer ad provides specifications, like those highlighted in yellow, for processor performance.

- **Intel Pentium 4 560 32-bit processor 3.6 GHz with Hyper-Threading**
- **1 MB L2 cache**
- 2 GB 533 MHz SDRAM (max. 4 GB)
- 160 GB SATA HD (7200 rpm)
- 48X CD-RW + 12X DVD+RW/+R with double-layer write capable
- 3.5" 1.44 MB floppy disk drive
- 17" LCD TV
- 256 MB AGP graphics card
- Sound Blaster PCI sound card
- Altec Lansing speakers
- U.S. Robotics 56 Kbps modem
- Mouse & keyboard
- External drive bays: 2 5.25" bays for disk, tape, or CD drives; 1 3.5" bay for a floppy drive
- Internal drive bays: 1 HDD bay
- 8 USB ports: 2 front, 6 back
- 2 serial, 1 parallel, and 1 video port
- 1 network port (RJ45 connector)
- 4 PCI slots and 1 AGP slot
- Windows XP Home Edition
- Home/small business software bundle
- 3-year limited warranty

Which is faster, a 32-bit processor or a 64-bit processor? **Word size** refers to the number of bits that a microprocessor can manipulate at one time. Word size is based on the size of registers in the ALU and the capacity of circuits that lead to those registers. A processor with a 32-bit word size, for example, has 32-bit registers, processes thirty-two bits at a time, and is referred to as a "32-bit processor." Processors with a larger word size can process more data during each processor cycle—a factor that leads to increased computer performance. Today's personal computers typically contain 32-bit or 64-bit processors.

How does the cache size affect performance? **Cache** (pronounced "cash") is sometimes called "RAM cache" or "cache memory." It is special high-speed memory that allows a microprocessor to access data more rapidly than from memory located elsewhere on the system board. Some computer ads specify cache type and capacity. A **Level 1 cache** (L1) is built into the processor chip, whereas a **Level 2 cache** (L2) is located on a separate chip and takes a little more time to get data to the processor. Cache capacity is usually measured in kilobytes.

In theory, a large cache increases processing speed. In today's computers, however, cache size is usually tied to a particular processor brand and model. Cache size is not of particular significance to consumers because it is not configurable. For example, you can't add more L1 cache to your computer without replacing the microprocessor.

How does the instruction set affect performance? As chip designers developed various instruction sets for microprocessors, they tended to add increasingly more complex instructions, each requiring several clock cycles for execution. A microprocessor with such an instruction set uses **CISC** (complex instruction set computer) technology. A microprocessor with a limited set of simple instructions uses **RISC** (reduced instruction set computer) technology. A RISC processor performs most instructions faster than a CISC processor. It might, however, require more of these simple instructions to complete a task than a CISC processor requires for the same task. Most processors in today's Macs use RISC technology; most PCs use CISC technology.

A processor's ability to handle graphics can be enhanced by adding specialized graphics and multimedia instructions to a processor's instruction set. 3DNow!, MMX, and SSE-2 are examples of instruction set enhancements sometimes mentioned in computer ads. Although instruction set enhancements have the potential to speed up games, graphics software, and video editing, they work only with software designed to utilize these specialized instructions.

Can a microprocessor execute more than one instruction at a time? Some processors execute instructions "serially"—that is, one instruction at a time. With **serial processing**, the processor must complete all steps in the instruction cycle before it begins to execute the next instruction. However, using a technology called **pipelining**, a processor can begin executing an instruction before it completes the previous instruction. Many of today's microprocessors also perform **parallel processing**, in which multiple instructions are executed at the same time. Pipelining and parallel processing enhance processor performance.

To get a clearer picture of serial, pipelining, and parallel processing techniques (Figure 2-14), consider an analogy in which computer instructions are pizzas. Serial processing executes only one instruction at a time, just like a pizzeria with one oven that holds only one pizza. Pipelining is similar

FIGURE 2-14
Microprocessor designers have developed techniques for serial, pipelining, and parallel processing.

In serial processing, one instruction is processed at a time.

In pipelining, an instruction can begin to be processed before the previous instruction's processing is complete.

In parallel processing, multiple instructions can be processed at the same time.

TERMINOLOGY NOTE

The term Hyper-Threading, which appears in many computer ads, refers to a technology that enables processors to execute multiple instructions in parallel.

COMPUTER HARDWARE

to a pizza conveyor belt. A pizza (instruction) starts moving along the conveyor belt into the oven, but before it reaches the end, another pizza starts moving along the belt. Parallel processing is similar to a pizzeria with many ovens. Just as these ovens can bake more than one pizza at a time, a parallel processor can execute more than one instruction at a time.

With so many factors to consider, how can I compare microprocessor performance? Various testing laboratories run a series of tests to gauge the overall speed of a microprocessor. The results of these tests—called **benchmarks**—can then be compared to the results for other microprocessors. The results of benchmark tests are usually available on the Web and published in computer magazine articles.

TODAY'S MICROPROCESSORS

Which companies produce most of today's popular microprocessors? Intel is the world's largest chipmaker and supplies a sizeable percentage of the microprocessors that power PCs. In 1971, Intel introduced the world's first microprocessor—the 4004. The company has produced a steady stream of new processor models, including the 8088 processor that powered the original IBM PC.

AMD (Advanced Micro Devices) is Intel's chief rival in the PC chip market. Motorola is the main chip supplier for Apple computers. Transmeta Corporation specializes in chips for mobile computing devices, such as tablet computers.

Which microprocessor is best for my PC? Microprocessor models and enhancements seem to appear more frequently than new car models. Intel is continually upgrading its line of Pentium processors. After introducing the original Pentium in 1993, the Pentium II was unveiled in 1997, the Pentium III in 1999, the Pentium 4 in 2000, the Itanium in 2001, and the Itanium2 in 2002. Intel's "budget" Celeron processors are not quite as powerful as the Pentiums, but they do a fine job of running software, and might mean a savings of $100 to $300 on the price of a computer.

AMD's Athlon and Opteron processors are direct competitors to Intel's Pentium and Itanium lines. AMD processors are less expensive than comparable Intel models and have a slight performance advantage according to some benchmarks.

The microprocessor that's "best" for you depends on your budget and the type of work and play you plan to do. The microprocessors marketed with the current crop of computers can handle most business, educational, and entertainment applications (Figure 2-15). You'll want to consider the fastest processor offerings from Intel or AMD if you typically engage in processing-hungry activities, such as 3-D animated computer games, desktop publishing, or video editing.

Can I replace my computer's microprocessor with a faster one? It is technically possible to upgrade your computer's microprocessor, but computer owners rarely do so. The price of the latest, greatest microprocessor can often get you more than halfway to buying an entirely new computer system. Technical factors also discourage microprocessor upgrades. A microprocessor can operate at full efficiency only if all components in the computer can also handle the faster speeds. In many cases, installing a new processor in an old computer can be like attaching a huge outboard engine to a canoe. Safety issues aside, a canoe is not designed to handle all that power, so you can't expect it to go as fast as a high-performance speedboat.

FIGURE 2-15
Today's popular personal computer, server, and workstation microprocessors.

Intel Pentium 4
32-bit processor
PN: 5xx 2.8–3.6 GHz
CISC instruction set Hyper-Threading technology
Popular for desktop computers and servers

Intel Itanium 2
64-bit processor
1.0–1.6 GHz
Popular for workstations and servers

Intel Pentium M
32-bit processor
PN 7xx 1.7–2.6 GHz
Popular for mobile computing devices, such as notebook and tablet computers

Intel Celeron
32-bit processor
PN 3xx 950MHz–2.8 GHz
Popular for low-cost computers

AMD Athlon
32-bit processor
2.0–2.4 GHz
Popular alternative to Intel Pentium processors

Transmeta Crusoe
32-bit processor
500 MHz–1.6 GHz
Used in mobile computing devices, such as tablet computers

Motorola PowerPC
32-bit RISC processor
1.8–2.5 GHz
Used in Apple Power Mac, iMac, and PowerBook computers

INFOWEBLINKS

For updates on popular microprocessors, you can connect to the **Microprocessor Update InfoWeb**.

www.course.com/np/concepts8/ch02

RANDOM ACCESS MEMORY

What is RAM? RAM (random access memory) is a temporary holding area for data, application program instructions, and the operating system. In a personal computer, RAM is usually several chips or small circuit boards that plug into the system board within the computer's system unit.

A computer's RAM capacity is invariably included in the list of specifications in a computer ad (Figure 2-16). The amount of RAM in a computer can affect the overall price of a computer system. To understand how much RAM your computer needs and to understand computer ad terminology, it is handy to have a little background on how RAM works and what it does.

Why is RAM so important? RAM is the "waiting room" for the computer's processor. It holds raw data waiting to be processed as well as the program instructions for processing that data. In addition, RAM holds the results of processing until they can be stored more permanently on disk or tape. Let's look at an example. When you use personal finance software to balance your checkbook, you enter raw data for check amounts, which is held in RAM. The personal finance software sends the instructions for processing this data to RAM. The processor uses these instructions to calculate your checkbook balance and sends the results back to RAM. From RAM, your checkbook balance can be stored on disk, displayed, or printed (Figure 2-17).

FIGURE 2-16
A computer ad typically specifies the amount and type of RAM.

- Intel Pentium 4 560 32-bit processor 3.6 GHz with Hyper-Threading
- 1 MB L2 cache
- 1 GB 533 MHz SDRAM (max. 4 GB)
- 160 GB SATA HD (7600 rpm)
- 48 X CD-RW + 12 X DVD+RW/+R with double-layer write capable
- 3.5" 1.44 MB floppy disk drive

FIGURE 2-17
RAM is the computer equivalent of the waiting room at an airport or a train station. It holds data waiting to be processed, stored, displayed, or printed.

In addition to data and application software instructions, RAM also holds operating system instructions that control the basic functions of a computer system. These instructions are loaded into RAM every time you start your computer, and they remain there until you turn off your computer.

How does RAM differ from hard-disk storage? People who are new to computers sometimes tend to confuse RAM and hard-disk storage, maybe because both components hold data, because they typically are "hidden" inside the system unit, or because they can both be measured in gigabytes. To differentiate between RAM and hard-disk storage, remember that RAM holds data in circuitry that's directly connected to the system board, whereas hard-disk storage places data on magnetic media. RAM is temporary storage; hard-disk storage is more permanent. In addition, RAM usually has less storage capacity than that of hard-disk storage.

COMPUTER HARDWARE

CMOS MEMORY

Where does a computer store its basic hardware settings? To operate correctly, a computer must have some basic information about storage, memory, and display configurations. For example, your computer needs to know how much memory is available so that it can allocate space for all the programs you want to run. RAM goes blank when the computer power is turned off, so configuration information cannot be stored there. ROM would not be a good place for this information, either, because it holds data on a permanent basis. If, for example, your computer stored the memory size in ROM, you could never add more memory—well, you might be able to add it, but you couldn't change the size specification in ROM. To store some basic system information, your computer needs a type of memory that's more permanent than RAM, but less permanent than ROM. CMOS is just the ticket.

CMOS memory (complementary metal oxide semiconductor memory), pronounced "SEE moss," is a type of chip that requires very little power to hold data. It can be powered by a small battery that's integrated into the system board and automatically recharges while your computer power is on. The battery trickles power to the CMOS chip so that it can retain vital data about your computer system configuration even when your computer is turned off.

When you change the configuration of your computer system—by adding RAM, for example—the data in CMOS must be updated. Some operating systems recognize such changes and automatically perform the update. You can manually change CMOS settings by running the CMOS setup program, as described in Figure 2-21.

FIGURE 2-21
CMOS holds computer configuration settings, such as the date and time, hard disk capacity, number of floppy disk drives, and RAM capacity. To access the CMOS setup program, hold down the F1 key as your computer boots. But be careful! If you make a mistake with these settings, your computer might not be able to start.

If you mistakenly enter the Setup program, follow the on-screen instructions to exit and proceed with the boot process. In Figure 2-21, the Esc (Escape) key allows you to exit the Setup program without making any changes to the CMOS settings.

What information about memory in computer ads is most important? Even though ROM and CMOS have important roles in the operation of a computer, RAM capacity really makes a difference you can notice. The more data and programs that can fit into RAM, the less time your computer will spend moving data to and from virtual memory. With lots of RAM, you'll find that documents scroll faster, games respond more quickly, and many graphics operations take less time than with a computer that has a skimpy RAM capacity.

Most ads specify RAM capacity, speed, and type. Now when you see the specification "512 MB 400 MHz SDRAM (max. 2 GB)" in a computer ad, you'll know that the computer's RAM capacity is 512 megabytes (plenty to run most of today's software), that it operates at 400 megahertz (fairly fast), and that it uses SDRAM (a little slower and less expensive than RDRAM). You'll also have important information about the maximum amount of RAM that can be installed in the computer—2 GB, which is more than enough for the typical computer owner who does a bit of word processing, surfs the Web, and plays computer games.

BUYING A COMPUTER

How do I get the best computer for my money? Different buyers have different needs, so your first step in buying a computer is to assess your budget and think about how you plan to use your computer. Armed with an understanding of the terminology you learned in Sections A and B, you can begin to look at ads and visit online computer stores. The Computer Buyer's Guide InfoWeb is designed to help you get started. Sections C and D provide information about storage and add-on devices that you'll also find useful when shopping for a new computer.

INFOWEBLINKS

The **Computer Buyer's Guide InfoWeb** contains all kinds of tips about how to be a savvy computer shopper. Plus, you'll find worksheets to help assess your needs, compare different computers, and shop for fun accessories.

www.course.com/np/concepts8/ch02

QUICKCHECK......SECTION B

1. The ALU uses _____ to hold data as the microprocessor performs arithmetic and logical operations.

2. The _____ unit in the CPU fetches instructions and coordinates the operation of the entire computer system.

3. Microprocessor _____ sets can be classified as CISC or RISC.

4. A microprocessor's _____ speed is provided in a specification such as 3.6 GHz.

5. Some chip makers use a _____ number, such as 560, to differentiate microprocessors.

6. RAM is _____, which means that it cannot hold data when the computer power is off.

7. A computer does not usually run out of RAM because it can use an area of the hard disk called _____ memory.

8. The instructions for loading the operating system into RAM when a computer is first turned on are stored in _____ memory.

CHECK ANSWERS

COMPUTER HARDWARE

LAB 2-B
BENCHMARKING

In this lab, you'll learn:

- Which computer performance factors can be measured by benchmark tests
- How to run a test that identifies a computer's processor type, RAM capacity, and graphics card type
- How to run benchmarking software that analyzes a computer's processor speed and graphics processing speed
- How to interpret the results of a benchmark test
- How to compare the results from benchmark tests that were performed on different system configurations
- When benchmark tests might not provide accurate information on computer performance

INTERACTIVE LAB

CLICK TO START THE LAB

LAB ASSIGNMENTS

1. Start the interactive part of the lab. Insert your Tracking Disk if you want to save your QuickCheck results. Perform each lab step as directed, and answer all the lab QuickCheck questions. When you exit the lab, your answers are automatically graded and your results are displayed.

2. If Microsoft Word is available, use the System Info button to analyze the computer you typically use. Provide the results of the analysis along with a brief description of the computer you tested and its location (at home, at work, in a computer lab, and so on).

PROCESSOR BENCHMARKS

Processor	Quake 3 Arena	Sysmark2000
Athlon 1.466 MHz	204.7	267
Pentium 4 1.5 GHz	219.5	210

3. From the Processor Benchmarks table above, which processor appears to be faster at graphics processing? Which processor appears to be better at overall processing tasks?

4. Explain why you might perform a benchmark test on your own computer, but get different results from those stated in a computer magazine, which tested the same computer with the same benchmark test.

5. Use a search engine on the Web to find benchmark ratings for Intel's Pentium 4 processors. What do these ratings show about the relative performance for 1.5 GHz, 2.4 GHz, and 3.0 GHz Pentium 4s?

SECTION C
STORAGE DEVICES

Computer manufacturers typically try to entice consumers by configuring computers with a variety of storage devices, such as a floppy disk drive, hard disk drive, and some sort of CD or DVD drive. What's the point of having so many storage devices? As it turns out, none of today's storage technologies is perfect. One technology might provide fast access to data, but it might also be susceptible to problems that could potentially wipe out all your data. A different technology might be more dependable, but it might have the disadvantage of relatively slow access to data.

Smart shoppers make sure their new computers are equipped with a variety of storage devices. Informed computer owners understand the strengths and weaknesses of each storage technology so that they can use these devices with maximum effectiveness. In this section, you'll learn many secrets that can make you a smart storage technology buyer and owner. The storage technologies you'll learn about are now used in a variety of devices—from digital cameras to player pianos—so an understanding of storage technology can be useful outside the boundaries of personal computing.

STORAGE BASICS

What are the basic components of a data storage system? A data storage system has two main components: a storage medium and a storage device. A **storage medium** (storage media is the plural) is the disk, tape, CD, DVD, paper, or other substance that contains data. A **storage device** is the mechanical apparatus that records and retrieves data from a storage medium. Storage devices include floppy disk drives, Zip drives, hard disk drives, tape drives, CD drives, and DVD drives. The term "storage technology" refers to a storage device and the media it uses.

How does a storage system interact with other computer components? You can think of your computer's storage devices as having a direct pipeline to RAM. Data gets copied from a storage device into RAM, where it waits to be processed. After data is processed, it is held temporarily in RAM, but it is usually copied to a storage medium for more permanent safekeeping.

As you know, a computer works with data that has been coded into bits that can be represented by 1s and 0s. When data is stored, these 1s and 0s must be converted into some kind of signal or mark that's fairly permanent, but can be changed when necessary.

Obviously, the data is not literally written as "1" or "0." Instead, the 1s and 0s must be transformed into changes in the surface of a storage medium. Exactly how this transformation happens depends on the storage technology. For example, floppy disks store data in a different way than CD-ROMs. Three types of storage technologies are commonly used for personal computers: magnetic, optical, and solid state.

INFOWEBLINKS

For a table that compares the speeds, costs, and capacities of popular storage devices, and to get an update on the latest computer storage technologies, connect to the **Storage Frontiers InfoWeb**.

www.course.com/np/concepts8/ch02

TERMINOLOGY NOTE

The process of storing data is often referred to as "writing data" or "saving a file" because the storage device writes the data on the storage medium to save it for later use.

The process of retrieving data is often referred to as "reading data," "loading data," or "opening a file."

COMPUTER HARDWARE

How does magnetic storage work? Hard disk, floppy disk, and tape storage technologies can be classified as **magnetic storage**, which stores data by magnetizing microscopic particles on the disk or tape surface. The particles retain their magnetic orientation until that orientation is changed, thereby making disks and tapes fairly permanent but modifiable storage media. A **read-write head** mechanism in the disk drive reads and writes the magnetized particles that represent data. Figure 2-22 shows how a computer stores data on magnetic media.

FIGURE 2-22

Before data is stored, particles on the surface of the disk are scattered in random patterns. The disk drive's read-write head magnetizes the particles, and orients them in a positive (north) or negative (south) direction. These patterns of magnetized particles represent 0 and 1 bits.

Data stored magnetically can be easily changed or deleted simply by changing the magnetic orientation of the appropriate particles on the disk surface. This feature of magnetic storage provides lots of flexibility for editing data and reusing areas of a storage medium containing unneeded data.

Data stored on magnetic media such as floppy disks can be altered by magnetic fields, dust, mold, smoke particles, heat, and mechanical problems with a storage device. Placing a magnet on a floppy disk, for example, is a sure way of losing data.

Magnetic media gradually lose their magnetic charge, resulting in lost data. Some experts estimate that the reliable life span of data stored on magnetic media is about three years. They recommend that you refresh your data every two years by recopying it.

How does optical storage work? CD and DVD storage technologies can be classified as **optical storage**, which stores data as microscopic light and dark spots on the disk surface. The dark spots, shown in Figure 2-23, are called **pits**. The lighter, non-pitted surface areas of the disk are called **lands**.

Optical storage gets its name because data is read using a laser light, and it is possible to see the data using a high-powered microscope. The transition between pits and lands is interpreted as the 1s and 0s that represent data. An optical storage device uses a low-power laser light to read the data stored on an optical disk.

The surface of an optical disk is coated with clear plastic, making the disk quite durable and less susceptible to environmental damage than data recorded on magnetic media. An optical disk, such as a CD, is not susceptible to humidity, fingerprints, dust, magnets, or spilled soft drinks, and its useful life is estimated at more than 200 years.

FIGURE 2-23

As seen through an electron microscope, the pits on an optical storage disk look like small craters. Each pit is less than 1 micron (one millionth of a meter) in diameter—1,500 pits lined up side by side are about as wide as the head of a pin.

How does solid state storage work? A variety of compact storage cards can be classified as **solid state storage**, which stores data in a non-volatile, erasable, low-power chip. The chip's circuitry is arranged as a grid (Figure 2-24), and each cell in the grid contains two transistors that act as gates. When the gates are open, current can flow and the cell has a value that represents a "1" bit. When the gates are closed by a process called Fowler-Nordheim tunneling, the cell has a value that represents a "0" bit. Very little power is required to open or close the gates, which makes solid state storage ideal for battery-operated devices, such as digital cameras. Once the data is stored, it is non-volatile—the chip retains the data without the need for an external power source.

Some solid state storage requires a device called a **card reader** to transfer data to or from a computer. Other solid state storage plugs directly into a USB port on a computer's system unit.

Solid state storage provides faster access to data than magnetic or optical storage technology because it includes no moving parts. Solid state storage is very durable—it is virtually impervious to vibration, magnetic fields, or extreme temperature fluctuations. On the downside, the capacity of solid state storage does not currently match that of hard disks, or DVDs. The cost per megabyte of storage—about 25¢—is significantly higher than for magnetic or optical storage.

Can I add storage devices to my computer? Many storage devices—especially those for solid state storage media—simply plug into connectors built into your computer's system unit. You'll learn more about these connectors, including USB, in Section D.

As an alternative, you can install storage devices inside your computer's system unit case in "parking spaces" called **drive bays**. An external drive bay provides access from outside the system unit—a necessity for a storage device with removable media, such as floppy disks, CDs, tapes, and DVDs. Internal drive bays are located deep inside the system unit and are designed for hard disk drives, which don't use removable storage media (Figure 2-25).

FIGURE 2-24
A solid state storage medium stores data in a microscopic grid of cells. A card reader transfers data between the card and a computer.

FIGURE 2-25
Most notebook computers provide bays for one floppy disk drive, one hard disk drive, and one CD or DVD drive.

An empty drive bay located on the side of a notebook computer

An empty 5.25" drive bay can hold CD, DVD, tape, or multifunction solid state drives

An empty 3.5" drive bay can hold a floppy disk drive

Most desktop computers have several drive bays, some accessible from outside the case, and others—designed for hard disk drives—without any external access.

Empty drive bays are typically hidden from view with a face plate.

CLICK TO START

COMPUTER HARDWARE

Which storage technology is best? Each storage technology has its advantages and disadvantages. If one storage system was perfect, we wouldn't need so many disk and tape drives connected to our computers! To compare storage devices, it is useful to apply the criteria of versatility, durability, speed, and capacity:

- **Versatility.** Some storage devices can access data from only one type of medium. More versatile devices can access data from several different media. A floppy disk drive, for example, can access only floppy disks, whereas a DVD drive can access computer DVDs, DVD movies, audio CDs, computer CDs, and CD-Rs.

- **Durability.** Most storage technologies are susceptible to damage from mishandling or other environmental factors, such as heat and moisture. Some technologies are more susceptible than others to damage that could cause data loss. Optical and solid state technologies tend to be less susceptible than magnetic technologies.

- **Speed.** Quick access to data is important, so fast storage devices are preferred over slower devices. **Access time** is the average time it takes a computer to locate data on the storage medium and read it. Access time for a personal computer storage device, such as a disk drive, is measured in milliseconds (thousandths of a second). One millisecond (ms) is one-thousandth of a second. Lower numbers indicate faster access times. For example, a drive with a 6 ms access time is faster than a drive with an access time of 11 ms.

    Access time is best for random-access devices. **Random access** (also called "direct access") is the ability of a device to "jump" directly to the requested data. Floppy disk, hard disk, CD, and DVD drives are random-access devices, as is solid state storage. A tape drive, on the other hand, must use slower **sequential access** by reading through the data from the beginning of the tape. The advantage of random access becomes clear when you consider how much faster and easier it is to locate a song on a CD (random access) than on a cassette tape (sequential access).

    Data transfer rate is the amount of data a storage device can move per second from the storage medium to the computer. Higher numbers indicate faster transfer rates. For example, a CD-ROM drive with a 600 KBps (kilobytes per second) data transfer rate is faster than one with a 300 KBps transfer rate.

- **Capacity.** In today's computing environment, higher capacity is almost always preferred. Storage capacity is the maximum amount of data that can be stored on a storage medium, and it is measured in kilobytes, megabytes, gigabytes, or terabytes.

FLOPPY DISK TECHNOLOGY

What is floppy disk technology? One of the oldest storage technologies, floppy disks are classified as magnetic storage because data is stored by magnetizing microscopic particles on the disk surface. A **floppy disk** is a round piece of flexible mylar plastic covered with a thin layer of magnetic oxide and sealed inside a protective casing. If you break open the disk casing (something you should never do unless you want to ruin the disk), you would see that the mylar disk inside is thin and literally floppy. Floppy disk technology is used for standard HD DS disks as well as Zip disks.

What is a standard HD DS disk? At one time, just about every personal computer included a floppy disk drive designed for high-density (HD) double-sided (DS) disks. These "standard" floppy disks (Figure 2-26) are still in use. They have a capacity of 1.44 MB—enough space for a 300-page

FIGURE 2-26
A standard floppy disk drive, reads and writes data on a 3.5" HD DS floppy disk.

document or one medium-resolution photograph. Floppy disks are also referred to as "floppies" or "diskettes." It is not correct to call them "hard disks" even though they seem to have a "hard" or rigid plastic casing. The term "hard disk" refers to an entirely different storage technology.

What are the advantages and disadvantages of HD DS floppy disks?
When just about every computer had a floppy disk drive, files could be easily transferred from one computer to another using a floppy disk. Floppies are still used in some school computer labs so that students can transport their data to different lab machines or their personal computers. Today, however, many computers do not have a standard floppy disk drive. File transfers tend to take place using other technologies. Solid state storage media is smaller and more durable for mobile applications. Local computer networks and the Internet have made it easy to share data files without physically transporting them from one place to another.

A standard floppy disk's 1.44 MB capacity is not really sufficient for today's media-intensive applications. Many MP3 music files and photos are too large to fit on a floppy. In the past, floppy disks were extensively used to distribute software. CDs and DVDs offer more capacity for distributing the huge files for today's software applications. Web downloads offer more convenience for smaller files.

Can I protect the data on a HD DS floppy disk? An HD DS floppy disk features a **write-protect window** (Figure 2-27). When you open the window, the disk is "write-protected," which means that a computer cannot write data on the disk. Although it sounds like a useful feature, the write-protect window doesn't do much to protect your data from accidental erasures or changes. Typically when you use a disk, you want to save a new file or modify the data in an existing file. To do so, you must close the write-protect window and the disk is no longer protected. Therefore, when you use a disk and the chance of mistakenly deleting data is highest, you're not likely to have the write-protect feature on.

What is a Zip disk? A Zip disk is a special high-capacity floppy disk, available in 100 MB, 250 MB, and 750 MB versions. Zip disks and their drives, shown in Figure 2-28, are manufactured by Iomega. A Zip drive does not read standard HD DS floppy disks and Zip disks cannot be read by a standard floppy disk drive.

What are the advantages and disadvantages of Zip disks? Zip disks offer portability, simplicity, speed, and security. The storage capacity of Zip disks makes them more useful than standard HD DS floppy disks for storing large music and photo files. The process of reading and writing data is relatively fast and easy. Files on a Zip disk can even be password protected to ensure the security of important data.

Even the highest capacity Zip disks have far less capacity than DVDs or hard disks, however. They cannot substitute for a hard disk as primary storage, nor can they substitute for DVDs for video applications.

How can Zip disks store more data than a standard floppy disk? The amount of data that a disk stores depends on its density. **Disk density** refers to the closeness and size of the magnetic particles on the disk surface. The higher the disk density, the smaller the magnetic particles on the disk surface, and the more data it can store. Think of it this way: Just as you can put more lemons than grapefruit in a basket, you can store more data on a disk coated with smaller particles than one with larger particles. Zip disks store data at a higher density than a standard 3.5" floppy disk.

FIGURE 2-27
When the write-protect window is open, the disk drive cannot add, modify, or delete data from a disk.

FIGURE 2-28
A Zip disk requires a special disk drive, but is transportable and provides more storage capacity than a standard floppy disk.

COMPUTER HARDWARE 83

HARD DISK TECHNOLOGY

Why are hard disk drives so popular? Hard disk technology is the preferred type of main storage for most computer systems for three reasons. First, it provides lots of storage capacity. Second, it provides fast access to files. Third, a hard disk is economical. Incredibly, a hard disk typically stores millions of times more data than a floppy disk, but a hard disk drive might cost only three times as much as a floppy disk drive.

How does a hard disk work? A hard disk is one or more platters and their associated read-write heads. A **hard disk platter** is a flat, rigid disk made of aluminum or glass and coated with magnetic iron oxide particles. Each platter has a read-write head that hovers over the surface to read data, as shown in Figure 2-29.

The drive spindle supports one or more hard disk platters. Both sides of the platter are used for data storage. More platters mean more data storage capacity. Hard disk platters rotate as a unit on the spindle to position read-write heads over specific data. The platters spin continuously, making thousands of rotations per minute.

FIGURE 2-29
Hard disk platters are sealed inside the drive case or cartridge to prevent dust and other contaminants from interfering with the read-write heads.

CLICK TO START

Each data storage surface has its own read-write head, which moves in and out from the center of the disk to locate data. The head hovers only a few microinches above the disk surface, so the magnetic field is more compact than on a floppy disk. As a result, more data is packed into a smaller area on a hard disk platter.

Personal computer hard disk platters are typically 3.5" in diameter with storage capacities ranging from 40 to160 GB. Miniature hard drives, such as the 1.8" drive featured on Apple's iPod digital music player, store 20 to 40 GB. The density of particles on the disk surface provide hard disks with capacities far greater than floppy disks. Also, the access time for a hard disk is significantly faster than for a floppy disk. Hard disk access times of 6 to 11 ms are not uncommon, whereas a floppy takes about half a second to spin up to speed and find data. Hard disk drive speed is sometimes measured in revolutions per minute (rpm). The faster a drive spins, the more rapidly it can position the read-write head over specific data. For example, a 7,200 rpm drive is able to access data faster than a 5,400 rpm drive.

Computer ads typically specify the capacity, access time, and speed of a hard disk drive. So "160 GB 8 ms 7200 RPM HD" means a hard disk drive with 160 gigabyte capacity, access time of 8 milliseconds, and speed of 7,200 revolutions per minute.

You might guess that a hard disk drive would fill one platter before storing data on a second platter. However, it is more efficient to store data at the same locations on all platters before moving the read-write heads to the next location. A vertical stack of storage locations is called a "cylinder"—the basic storage bin for a hard disk drive.

What's all this business about Ultra ATA, EIDE, SCSI, and DMA? Computer ads use these acronyms to describe hard disk drive technology. A hard drive mechanism includes a circuit board called a **controller** that

TERMINOLOGY NOTE

You often see the terms "hard disk" and "hard disk drive" used interchangeably. You might also hear the term "fixed disk" used to refer to hard disks.

positions the disk and read-write heads to locate data. Disk drives are classified according to their controllers. Popular drive controllers include SATA, Ultra ATA, EIDE, and SCSI. Although computer ads often specify the hard drive controller type, consumers don't really have much choice. If you want a 160 GB drive, for example, your hardware vendor is likely to offer only one brand of drive with one type of controller. Figure 2-30 shows a typical controller mounted on a hard disk drive.

FIGURE 2-30
A hard disk controller circuit board is typically mounted in the hard disk drive case.

The storage technology used on many PCs transfers data from a disk, through the controller, to the processor, and finally to RAM before it is actually processed. Computer ads sometimes specify this technology. For example, DMA (direct memory access) technology allows a computer to transfer data directly from a drive into RAM, without intervention from the processor. This architecture relieves the processor of data-transfer duties and frees up processing cycles for other tasks. UDMA (ultra DMA) is a faster version of DMA technology.

What's the downside of hard disk storage? Hard disks are not as durable as many other storage technologies. The read-write heads in a hard disk hover a microscopic distance above the disk surface. If a read-write head runs into a dust particle or some other contaminant on the disk, it might cause a **head crash**, which damages some of the data on the disk. To help prevent contaminants from contacting the platters and causing head crashes, a hard disk is sealed in its case. A head crash can also be triggered by jarring the hard disk while it is in use. Although hard disks have become considerably more rugged in recent years, you should still handle and transport them with care. You should also make sure that you make a backup copy of the data stored on your hard disk in case of a head crash.

Can I use a second hard disk drive to increase storage space? You can increase the storage capacity of your computer by adding a second hard disk drive. A second hard disk drive can also provide backup for your primary drive. Hard disk drives are available as internal or external units. Internal drives are inexpensive and can be easily installed in a desktop computer's system unit. External drives are slightly more expensive and connect to a desktop or notebook computer using a cable.

Removable hard disks or hard disk cartridges offer even more options. They contain platters and read-write heads that can be inserted and removed from the drive much like a floppy disk. Removable hard disks, such as Iomega's REV drive, provide security for data by allowing you to remove the hard disk cartridge and store it separately from the computer.

COMPUTER HARDWARE

TAPE STORAGE

What's the purpose of a tape drive? As you have learned, a head crash can easily destroy hard disk data. Protecting data on the hard disk is of particular concern because it contains so much data that would be difficult and time-consuming to reconstruct. A **tape backup** is a copy of the data on a hard disk, which is stored on magnetic tape and used to restore lost data. Tape drive manufacturers produce several types of drives and each requires a specific type of tape. Figure 2-31 shows some of the most popular tape formats for personal computer tape drives.

FIGURE 2-31
A tape cartridge is a removable magnetic tape module similar to a cassette tape. Popular tape drives for personal computers use tape cartridges, but there are several specifications and cartridge sizes, including (from top to bottom) ADR (advanced digital recording), Ditto, Travan, and DDS (digital data storage). Check the tape drive manual to make sure you purchase the correct type of tape for your tape drive.

A tape backup device is relatively inexpensive and can simplify the task of reconstructing lost data. A backup tape can hold the entire contents of a hard disk. If the hard drive fails, that data can be copied from the tape to any functional hard disk.

Tape drives are primarily used on business computers. Unlike CDs and DVDs, a tape backup device is not suitable for everyday storage tasks. To find out why, you need to understand how a tape drive works.

How does a tape drive work? A tape is a sequential, rather than a random-access, storage medium. Essentially, data is arranged as a long sequence of bits that begins at one end of the tape and stretches to the other end. The beginning and end of each file are marked with special "header labels." To locate a file, the tape drive must start at one end of the tape and read through all the data until it finds the right header label. A tape can contain hundreds or—in the case of a mainframe—thousands of feet of tape. Access time is measured in seconds, not in milliseconds as for a hard disk drive.

Tape is simply too slow to be practical as your computer's main storage device. Its pokey nature doesn't, however, diminish its effectiveness as a backup device. When you make a backup, you're simply streaming lots of data onto the tape. You don't need to locate specific data or jump back and forth between different files. A sequential device is just fine for this sort of work.

When backing up data, access time is less important than the time it takes to copy data from your hard disk to tape. Manufacturers do not always supply such performance specifications, but most users can expect a tape drive to back up 1 GB in 15-20 minutes. Chapter 4 provides more details on the process and equipment for making backups.

CD AND DVD TECHNOLOGY

Is there a difference between CD and DVD technology? Today, most computers come equipped with some type of optical drive—a CD drive or a DVD drive. The underlying technology for CD and DVD drives is similar, but storage capacities differ.

A computer CD drive is based on the same technology as an audio CD player. A **CD** (compact disc) was originally designed to hold 74 minutes of recorded music. This capacity provides 650 MB of storage space for computer data. Later improvements in CD standards increased the capacity to 80 minutes of music or 700 MB of data.

DVD ("digital video disc" or "digital versatile disk") is a variation of CD technology that was originally designed as an alternative to VCRs, but was quickly adopted by the computer industry to store data. A computer's DVD drive can read disks that contain computer data as well as disks that contain DVD movies.

Originally designed to provide enough storage capacity for a full-length movie, a DVD holds much more data than a CD. The capacity of a DVD is about 4.7 GB (4,700 MB), compared with 650-700 MB on a CD. A **double layer DVD** has two recordable layers on the same side and can store 8.5 GB of data.

How do CD and DVD drives work? CD and DVD drives contain a spindle that rotates the disk over a laser lens. The laser directs a beam of light toward the underside of the disk. Dark "pits" and light "lands" on the disk surface reflect the light differently. As the drive reads the disk, these differences are translated into the 0s and 1s that represent data (Figure 2-32).

FIGURE 2-32
CD and DVD drives use a laser to read data from the underside of a disk.

- Drive spindle spins disk
- Laser lens directs a beam of light to the underside of the CD-ROM disk
- Laser pickup assembly senses the reflectivity of pits and lands
- Tracking mechanism positions a disk track over the laser lens

Optical drives use several technologies to write data on CD and DVD disks. **Recordable technology** (R) uses a laser to change the color in a dye layer sandwiched beneath the clear plastic disk surface. The laser creates dark spots in the dye that are read as pits. The change in the dye is permanent, so data cannot be changed once it has been recorded.

Rewritable technology (RW) uses "phase change" technology to alter a crystal structure on the disk surface. Altering the crystal structure creates patterns of light and dark spots similar to the pits and lands on a CD. The crystal structure can be changed from light to dark and back again many times, making it possible to record and modify data much like on a hard disk.

The suffixes "R" and "RW" denote specific CD and DVD technologies. For example, CD-R specifies "CD recordable" technology. CD-RW specifies "CD rewritable" technology.

TERMINOLOGY NOTE

DVDs have two types of recordable and two types of rewritable formats. The recordable formats are designated as DVD-R and DVD+R. The rewritable formats are designated as DVD-RW and DVD+RW.

COMPUTER HARDWARE

What are my choices for CD and DVD media? Several CD and DVD formats are currently popular for use in personal computers:

- **CD-DA** (compact disc digital audio), more commonly known as "audio CD," is the format for commercial music CDs. Music is typically recorded on audio CDs by the manufacturer, but can't be changed by the consumer.
- **DVD-Video** (digital versatile disc video) is the format for commercial DVDs that contain feature-length films.
- **CD-ROM** (compact disc read-only memory, pronounced "cee dee rom") was the original format for storing computer data. Data is stamped on the disk at the time it is manufactured. Data cannot be added, changed, or deleted from these disks.
- **DVD-ROM** (digital versatile disk read-only memory) contains data stamped onto the disk surface at the time of manufacture. Like CD-ROMs, the data on these disks is permanent, so you cannot add or change data.
- **CD-R** (compact disc recordable) disks store data using recordable technology. The data on a CD-R cannot be erased or modified once you record it. However, most CD-R drives allow you to record your data in multiple sessions. For example, you can store two files on a CD-R disk today, and add data for a few more files to the disk tomorrow.
- **DVD+R** (digital versatile disk recordable) disks store data using recordable technology similar to a CD-R, but with DVD storage capacity.
- **CD-RW** (compact disc rewritable) disks store data using rewritable technology. Stored data can be recorded and erased multiple times, making it a very flexible storage option.
- **DVD+RW** (digital versatile disk rewritable) disks store data using rewritable technology similar to CD-RW, but with DVD storage capacity.

Can I use a single drive to work with any CD or DVD media? Most CD drives can read CD-ROM, CD-R, and CD-RW disks. Most DVD drives can read CD and DVD formats. Storing computer data and creating music CDs requires a recordable or rewritable device. As you can see from the table in Figure 2-33, the most versatile optical storage device is a DVD+R/+RW/CD-RW combo.

INFOWEBLINKS

For more information about current CD and DVD technology, plus tips on how to handle and clean your CDs, connect to the **CD & DVD InfoWeb**.

www.course.com/np/concepts8/ch02

TERMINOLOGY NOTE

Even though CD-ROM and ROM-BIOS both contain the word "ROM," they refer to quite different technologies. ROM BIOS refers to a chip on the system board that contains permanent instructions for the computer's boot sequence. A CD-ROM drive is an optical storage device that's usually installed in one of the system unit's drive bays.

FIGURE 2-33
CD and DVD Capabilities

	Play Audio CDs	Play DVD Movies	Read CD Data	Read DVD Data	Create Music CDs	Store Data on CDs	Store Data on DVDs
CD-ROM Drive	✔		✔				
CD-R Drive	✔		✔		✔	✔	
CD-RW Drive	✔		✔		✔	✔	
DVD/CD-RW Drive	✔	✔	✔	✔	✔	✔	
DVD+R/+RW/CD-RW Drive	✔	✔	✔	✔	✔	✔	✔

Are rewritable CD or DVD drives an acceptable replacement for a hard disk? A rewritable CD or DVD drive is a fine addition to a computer system, but is not a good replacement for a hard disk drive. Unfortunately, the process of accessing, saving, and modifying data on a rewritable disk is relatively slow compared to the speed of hard disk access.

The original CD drives could access 150 KB of data per second. The next generation of drives doubled the data transfer rate and were consequently dubbed "2X" drives. Transfer rates seem to be continually increasing. A 46X CD drive, for example, transfers data at 55.40 Mbps, which is still relatively slow compared to a hard disk drive's transfer rate of 2,560 Mbps.

The speed of a DVD drive is measured on a different scale than a CD drive. A 1X DVD drive is about the same speed as a 9X CD drive. Today's DVD drives typically have 16X speeds for a data transfer rate of 177.28 Mbps.

Is my computer DVD drive the same as the one connected to my TV? Not exactly. Even with the large storage capacity of a DVD, movie files are much too large to fit on a disk unless they are compressed, or shrunk, using a special type of data coding called MPEG-2. The DVD player you connect to your television includes MPEG decoding circuitry, which is not included on your computer's DVD drive. When you play DVD movies on your computer, it uses the CPU as an MPEG decoder. The necessary decoder software is included with Windows or can be located on the DVD itself.

SOLID STATE STORAGE

When would I use solid state storage? Solid state storage is portable, provides fast access to data, and uses very little power, so it is an ideal solution for storing data on mobile devices and transporting data from one device to another. It is widely used in consumer devices, such as digital cameras, MP3 music players, notebook computers, PDAs, and cell phones.

A solid state memory card in a digital camera can hold data for hundreds of snapshots. The card can be removed from the camera and inserted into a card reader that's connected to a computer. Once the data is downloaded, the photos can be edited using the computer's graphics software and transmitted via the computer's Internet connection.

Moving data in the other direction, a computer can download MP3 music files and store them on a solid state memory card. That card can be removed from the computer and inserted into a portable MP3 player, so you can hear your favorite tunes while you're on the go.

You can even use solid state storage as you would a floppy disk to transport data from one computer to another—say from your home computer to a computer in your school lab or your workplace.

What are my options for solid state storage? Several types of solid state storage are available to today's consumers (Figure 2-34). A **USB flash drive**, such as Sony's MicroVault, is a portable storage device featuring a built-in connector that plugs directly into a computer's USB port. A USB flash drive requires no card reader, making it easily transportable from one computer to another. Nicknamed "pen drives" or "keychain drives," USB flash drives are about the size of a highlighter pen and so durable that you can literally carry them on your key ring. You can open, edit, delete, and run files stored on a USB flash drive just as though those files were stored on your computer's hard disk.

FIGURE 2-34
Popular Solid State Storage Options

USB flash drive: 32 MB–4 GB capacities

CompactFlash card: 8 MB–2 GB capacities

COMPUTER HARDWARE

CompactFlash (CF) cards are about the size of a matchbook and provide high storage capacities and access speeds. CompactFlash cards include a built-in controller that reads and writes data within the solid state grid. The built-in controller removes the need for control electronics on the card reader, so the device that connects to your computer to read the card's data is simply an adapter that collects data from the card and shuttles it to the computer's system unit. With their high storage capacities and access speeds, CompactFlash cards are idea for use on high-end digital cameras that require megabytes of storage for each photo.

MultiMedia cards (MMC) offer solid state storage in a package about the size of a postage stamp. Initially used in mobile phones and pages, use of MultiMedia cards has spread to digital cameras and MP3 players. Like CompactFlash cards, MultiMedia cards include a built-in controller, so MMC readers are electronically simple and very inexpensive.

SecureDigital (SD) cards are based on MultiMedia card technology, but feature significantly faster data transfer rates and include cryptographic security protection for copyrighted data and music. SecureDigital cards are popular for storage on digital music players and digital cameras.

SmartMedia cards were originally called "solid state floppy disk cards" because they look much like a miniature floppy disk. Unlike other popular solid state storage, SmartMedia cards do not include a built-in controller, which means that the SmartMedia reader manages the read/write process. These cards are the least durable of the solid state storage media and should be handled with care.

MultiMedia card: 32–512 MB capacities

SecureDigital card: 32 MB–1 GB capacities

SmartMedia card: 32–128 MB capacities

QUICKCHECK......SECTION C

1. A magnetic storage device uses a read-write [   ] to magnetize particles that represent data.

2. Data on an optical storage medium, such as a DVD, is stored as pits and [   ].

3. [   ] time is the average time it takes a computer to locate data on a storage medium and read it.

4. A disk drive is a(n) [   ] access device, whereas a tape drive is a(n) [   ] access device.

5. Higher disk [   ] provides increased storage capacity.

6. Hard disks are susceptible to head [   ], so it is important to make backup copies.

7. CD-RW technology allows you to write data on a disk, and then change that data. True or false? [   ]

8. A(n) [   ] DVD has a capacity of 8.5 GB.

CHECK ANSWERS

SECTION D
INPUT AND OUTPUT DEVICES

This section provides an overview of the most popular input and output devices for personal computers. It begins with input devices, including keyboards, mice, trackpads, and joysticks. Next, a survey of computer display devices helps you sort out the differences among CRT, LCD, and plasma displays. A guide to printers describes today's most popular printer technologies and provides a handy comparison chart. You'll learn about other peripheral devices in later chapters.

You'll also take a look at the computer's expansion bus—the components that carry data to peripheral devices. With an understanding of how the expansion bus works, you'll be able to select, install, and use all kinds of peripherals.

BASIC INPUT DEVICES

What devices can I use to get data into a computer? Most computer systems include a keyboard and pointing device for basic data input. Additional input devices, such as scanners, digital cameras, and graphics tablets, are handy for working with graphical input. Microphones and electronic instruments provide input capabilities for sound and music.

What's special about a computer keyboard's design? The design of most computer keyboards is based on the typewriter's QWERTY layout, which was engineered to keep the typewriter's mechanical keys from jamming. In addition to the basic typing keypad, desktop and notebook computer keyboards include an editing keypad to efficiently move the screen-based insertion point and a collection of function keys designed for computer-specific tasks. Most desktop computer keyboards also include a calculator-style numeric keypad. You can even find tiny keyboards on handheld devices—entering text and numbers is an important part of most computing tasks. Figure 2-35 illustrates a variety of keyboards you might encounter on various computing devices.

FIGURE 2-35
Computer keyboards come in a variety of sizes and styles.

COMPUTER HARDWARE

What does a pointing device do? A **pointing device** allows you to manipulate an on-screen pointer and other screen-based graphical controls. The most popular pointing devices for personal computers include mice, trackballs, pointing sticks, trackpads, and joysticks.

How does a mouse work? A standard desktop computer includes a mouse as its primary pointing device. Many computer owners also add a mouse to their notebook computers. A mouse includes one or more buttons that can be "clicked" to input command selections, such as "Start" and "Shut down." To track its position, a computer mouse uses one of two technologies: mechanical or optical (Figure 2-36). Most computer owners prefer the performance of an optical mouse because it provides more precise tracking, greater durability, less maintenance, and more flexibility to use the mouse on a wide variety of surfaces without a mouse pad.

FIGURE 2-36
A mechanical mouse (left) reads its position based on the movement of a ball that rolls over a mouse pad placed on a desk.

An optical mouse uses an onboard chip to track a light beam as it bounces off a surface, such as a desk, clipboard, or mouse pad.

When would I use other pointing devices? A **pointing stick**, or "TrackPoint," looks like the tip of an eraser embedded in the keyboard of a notebook computer. It is a space-saving device that you can push up, down, or sideways to move the on-screen pointer. A **trackpad** is a touch-sensitive surface on which you can slide your fingers to move the on-screen pointer. A **trackball** looks like a mechanical mouse turned upside down. You use your fingers or palm to roll the ball and move the pointer. Pointing sticks, trackpads, and trackballs (Figure 2-37) are typically used with notebook computers as an alternative to a mouse.

A **joystick** looks like a small version of a car's stick shift. Moving the stick provides input to on-screen objects, such as a pointer or an action figure in a computer game. Joysticks, like the one pictured in Figure 2-37, can include several sticks and buttons for arcade-like control when playing computer games.

FIGURE 2-37
Alternative Pointing Devices

Pointing stick   Trackpad   Trackball   Joystick

DISPLAY DEVICES

What are my options for display devices? A computer display screen is usually classified as an output device because it typically shows the results of a processing task. Some screens, however, can be classified as both input and output devices because they include touch-sensitive technology that accepts input. Display devices used for output offer three technology options: CRT, LCD, and plasma (Figure 2-38).

A **CRT** (cathode ray tube) display device uses the same sort of bulky glass tube as a standard television. Gun-like mechanisms in the tube spray beams of electrons toward the screen and activate individual dots of color that form an image. CRT display devices, often simply called "monitors," offer an inexpensive and dependable computer display. They are bulky, however, and consume a fair amount of power.

An **LCD** (liquid crystal display) produces an image by manipulating light within a layer of liquid crystal cells. Modern LCD technology is compact in size and lightweight, and provides an easy-to-read display. LCDs are standard equipment on notebook computers. Standalone LCDs, referred to as "LCD monitors" or "flat panel displays," have also become available for desktop computers as a replacement for CRT monitors. The advantages of LCD monitors include display clarity, low radiation emission, portability, and compactness. They are, however, more expensive than CRT monitors.

Plasma screen technology creates an on-screen image by illuminating miniature colored fluorescent lights arrayed in a panel-like screen. The name "plasma" comes from the type of gas that fills fluorescent lights and gives them their luminescence. Like LCD screens, plasma screens are compact, lightweight, and more expensive than CRT monitors.

CRT, LCD, and plasma screens can be equipped with NTSC (standard American television) or HDTV (high-definition television) circuitry so they accept television signals from an antenna or cable. This technology lets you view computer data and television on the same display device using split-screen or picture-in-picture format.

Which display technology produces the best image? Image quality is a factor of screen size, dot pitch, width of viewing angle, refresh rate, resolution, and color depth. Screen size is the measurement in inches from one corner of the screen diagonally across to the opposite corner. Typical monitor screen sizes range from 13" to 21". On most monitors, the viewable image does not stretch to the edge of the screen. Instead, a black border makes the image smaller than the size specified. Many computer ads now include a measurement of the **viewable image size** (vis).

Dot pitch (dp) is a measure of image clarity. A smaller dot pitch means a crisper image. Technically, dot pitch is the distance in millimeters between like-colored **pixels**—the small dots of light that form an image. A dot pitch between .26 and .23 is typical for today's monitors.

A monitor's **viewing angle width** indicates how far to the side you can still clearly see the screen image. A wide viewing angle indicates that you can view the screen from various positions without compromising image quality. CRT and plasma screens offer the widest viewing angles. Graphics artists tend to prefer CRT screens, which display uniform color from any angle.

In the context of computer displays, **refresh rate** (also referred to as "vertical scan rate") is the speed at which the screen is repainted. Typically, CRT monitors are refreshed 60 times per second (60 Hz) or 75 times per second (75 Hz). The faster the refresh rate, the less the monitor flickers.

FIGURE 2-38
Display Device Technology

CRT

LCD

Gas plasma

INFOWEBLINKS

For up-to-the-minute information on the latest and greatest graphics cards, monitors, and LCD displays, check out the **Display Devices InfoWeb.**

www.course.com/np/concepts8/ch02

COMPUTER HARDWARE

The number of colors a monitor can display is referred to as **color depth** or "bit depth." Most PC display devices have the capability to display millions of colors. When set at 24-bit color depth (sometimes called "True Color"), your PC can display more than 16 million colors—and produce what are considered photographic-quality images. Windows allows you to select resolution and color depth. Most desktop owners choose 24-bit color at 1024 x 768 resolution.

The number of horizontal and vertical pixels that a device displays on a screen is referred to as its **resolution**. The resolution for many early PC displays was referred to **VGA** (Video Graphics Array). Higher resolutions were later provided by **SVGA** (Super VGA), **XGA** (eXtended Graphics Array), **SXGA** (Super XGA), and **UXGA** (Ultra XGA) (Figure 2-39).

At higher resolutions, text and other objects appear smaller, but the computer can display a larger work area, such as an entire page of a document. The two screen shots in Figure 2-40 help you compare a display set at 640 x 480 resolution with a display set at 1024 x 768 resolution.

FIGURE 2-39
Common PC Resolutions

Standard	Resolution
VGA	640 x 480
SVGA	800 x 600
XGA	1024 x 768
SXGA	1280 x 1024
UXGA	1600 x 1200

FIGURE 2-40
The screen on the left shows 1024 x 768 resolution. Notice the size of text and other screen-based objects. The screen on the right shows 640 x 480 resolution. Text and other objects appear larger on the low-resolution screen, but you see a smaller portion of the screen desktop.

What are the components of a typical computer display system? In addition to a display device, such as a monitor, a computer display system also requires graphics circuitry that generates the signals for displaying an image on the screen. Graphics circuitry, referred to as "integrated graphics", is built into a computer's system board. Graphics circuitry can also be supplied by a small circuit board called a **graphics card** ("graphics board" or "video card"), like the one in Figure 2-41. Today's fastest graphics cards fit into an AGP expansion slot, which you'll learn about later in this section.

A graphics card typically contains a graphics processing unit (GPU) and special video memory, which stores screen images as they are processed, but before they are displayed. Lots of video memory is the key to lightning-fast screen updating for fast action games, 3-D modeling, and graphics-intensive desktop publishing. In addition to video memory, most graphics cards contain special graphics accelerator technology to further boost performance.

FIGURE 2-41
A graphics card is a small circuit board that plugs into the system board.

PRINTERS

What printer technologies are available for personal computers? Printers are one of the most popular output devices available for personal computers. Today's best-selling printers typically use ink jet or laser technology. Printer technologies for specialized applications include dot matrix, solid ink, thermal transfer, and dye sublimation.

How does an ink jet printer work? An **ink jet printer** has a nozzle-like print head that sprays ink onto paper to form characters and graphics. The print head in a color ink jet printer consists of a series of nozzles, each with its own ink cartridge. Most ink jet printers use CMYK color, which requires only cyan (blue), magenta (pink), yellow, and black inks to create a printout that appears to have thousands of colors. Alternatively, some printers use six ink colors to print midtone shades that create slightly more realistic photographic images.

Ink jet printers, such as the one in Figure 2-42, outsell all other types of printers because they are inexpensive and produce both color and black-and-white printouts. They work well for most home and small business applications. Small, portable ink jet printers meet the needs of many mobile computer owners. Ink jet technology also powers many photo printers, which are optimized to print high-quality images produced by digital cameras and scanners.

How do laser printers compare to ink jet printers? A **laser printer**, such as the one in Figure 2-43, uses the same technology as a photocopier to paint dots of light on a light-sensitive drum. Electrostatically charged ink is applied to the drum and then transferred to paper. Laser technology is more complex than ink jet technology, which accounts for the higher price of laser printers.

A basic laser printer produces only black-and-white printouts. Color laser printers are available, but are somewhat more costly than basic black-and-white models. Laser printers are often the choice for business printers, particularly for applications that produce a high volume of printed material.

FIGURE 2-42
Most ink jet printers are small, lightweight, and inexpensive, yet produce very good-quality color output.

FIGURE 2-43
Laser printers are a popular technology when high-volume output or good-quality printouts are required.

CLICK TO START

What is a dot matrix printer? When PCs first appeared in the late 1970s, dot matrix printers were the technology of choice, and they are still available today. A **dot matrix printer** produces characters and graphics by using a grid of fine wires. As the print head noisily clatters across the paper, the wires strike a ribbon and paper in a pattern prescribed by your PC. Dot

COMPUTER HARDWARE

matrix printers can print text and graphics—some even print in color using a multicolored ribbon.

Today, dot matrix printers, like the one in Figure 2-44, are used primarily for "back-office" applications that demand low operating cost and dependability, but not high print quality.

FIGURE 2-44
Unlike laser and ink jet technologies, a dot matrix printer actually strikes the paper and, therefore, can print multipart carbon forms.

Print head contains a matrix of thin wires

Characters are formed from a pattern of dots created as the wires strike an inked ribbon.

What other printer technologies are available? A **solid ink printer** melts sticks of crayon-like ink and then sprays the liquefied ink through the print head's tiny nozzles. A solid ink printer produces vibrant colors and is sometimes used for professional graphics applications.

A **thermal transfer printer** uses thousands of tiny heating elements to melt the wax from a page-sized ribbon onto specially coated paper or transparency film (the kind used for overhead projectors). This type of printer excels at printing colorful transparencies for presentations, but the fairly expensive per-page costs and the requirement for special paper make it a niche market printer used mainly by businesses.

A **dye sublimation printer** uses technology similar to thermal transfer, but the page-sized ribbon contains dye instead of colored wax. Dye sublimation printers produce excellent color quality—perhaps the best of any printer technology. At $3 to $4 per page, however, these printers are a bit pricey for most personal computer owners.

What features should I look for in a printer? Printers differ in resolution, speed, duty cycle, operating costs, duplex capability, and memory.

- **Resolution.** The quality or sharpness of printed images and text depends on the printer's resolution—the density of the gridwork of dots that create an image. Printer resolution is measured by the number of dots printed per linear inch, abbreviated as dpi. At normal reading distance, a resolution of about 900 dpi appears solid to the human eye, but a close examination reveals a dot pattern. If you want magazine-quality printouts, 900 dpi is sufficient resolution. If you are aiming for resolution similar to expensive coffee-table books, look for printer resolution of 2,400 dpi or higher.

- **Print speed.** Printer speeds are measured either by pages per minute (ppm) or characters per second (cps). Color printouts typically take longer than black-and-white printouts. Pages that contain mostly text tend to print more rapidly than pages that contain graphics. Six to ten pages per minute is a typical speed for a personal computer printer.

- **Duty cycle.** In addition to printer speed, a printer's **duty cycle** determines how many pages a printer is able to churn out. Printer duty cycle is usually measured in pages per month. For example, a personal laser printer has a duty cycle of about 3,000 pages per month (ppm)—that means roughly 100 pages per day. You wouldn't want to use it to produce 5,000 campaign brochures for next Monday, but you would find it quite suitable for printing 10 copies of a five-page outline for a meeting tomorrow.

- **Operating costs.** The initial cost of a printer is only one of the expenses associated with printed output. Ink jet printers require frequent replacements of relatively expensive print heads. Laser printers require toner cartridge refills. Dot matrix printers require replacement ribbons. When shopping for a printer, you can check online resources to determine how often you'll need to replace printer supplies and how much they are likely to cost.

- **Duplex capability.** A printer with duplex capability can print on both sides of the paper. This environment-friendly option saves paper but can slow down the print process, especially on ink-jet printers that pause to let the ink dry before printing the second side.

- **Memory.** A computer sends data for a printout to the printer along with a set of instructions on how to print that data. **Printer Control Language** (PCL) is the most widely used language for communication between computers and printers, but **PostScript** is an alternative printer language that many publishing professionals prefer. The data that arrives at a printer along with its printer language instructions require memory. A large memory capacity is required to print color images and graphics-intensive documents. Some printers accept additional memory, if you find that your printer requires more memory for the types of document you typically print.

Figure 2-45 provides comparative information for ink jet, laser, and dot matrix printers. For specific information on a particular brand and model of printer, check the manufacturer's Web site.

INFOWEBLINKS

Before you shop for a printer, take a look at the buying tips in the **Printer Buyer's Guide InfoWeb**.

www.course.com/np/concepts8/ch02

FIGURE 2-45
Printer Comparison

PRINTER TYPE	MAX. RESOLUTION	SPEED	DUTY CYCLE	OPERATING COST	MEMORY
Ink Jet (B&W) (color)	2400 x 1200	6–12 ppm 1–2 ppm	3,000 ppm	2–4¢ /page 8–20¢/page	256 KB–2 MB
Laser (B&W) (color)	2400 dpi	17 ppm 2–4 ppm	150,000 ppm	1–2¢/page	8–32 MB
Dot Matrix (B&W)	72–360 dpi	5–6 ppm	6,000-60,000 ppm	1.5–.2¢/page	2–128 KB

INSTALLING PERIPHERAL DEVICES

Is it difficult to install a new peripheral device? At one time, installing computer peripherals required a screw driver and extensive knowledge of ports, slots, boards, and device drivers. Today, many peripheral devices connect to an external USB (universal serial bus) port and Windows automatically loads their device drivers, making installation as simple as plugging in a table lamp. USB is currently the most popular technology for connecting peripherals.

On most new computer models, USB ports are conveniently located on the front of the system unit for easy access. Many kinds of peripheral devices—including mice, scanners, and joysticks—are available with USB connections. Several types of storage devices, such as USB Flash drives, also use USB connections.

There are still occasions, however, when a simple USB connection is not available. Installing high-end graphics and sound cards for a multimedia or serious gaming computer typically requires you to open the system unit.

COMPUTER HARDWARE

Whether you are working with a simple USB connection or more complex equipment, a little information about the computer's data bus will arm you with the information you need to negotiate the steps for installing most peripheral devices.

How does a computer move data to and from peripheral devices? When you install a peripheral device, you are basically creating a connection for data to flow between the device and the computer. Within a computer, data travels from one component to another over circuits called a **data bus**. One part of the data bus runs between RAM and the microprocessor. Other parts of the data bus connect RAM to various storage and peripheral devices. The segment of the data bus that extends between RAM and peripheral devices is called the **expansion bus**. As data moves along the expansion bus, it can travel through expansion slots, cards, ports, and cables.

What's an expansion slot? An **expansion slot** is a long, narrow socket on the system board into which you can plug an expansion card. An **expansion card** is a small circuit board that gives a computer the capability to control a storage device, an input device, or an output device. Expansion cards are also called "expansion boards," "controller cards," or "adapters." Figure 2-46 shows how to plug an expansion card into an expansion slot.

FIGURE 2-46
An expansion card simply slides into an expansion slot and is secured with a small screw. Before you open the case, make sure you unplug the computer and ground yourself—that's technical jargon for releasing static electricity by using a special grounding wristband or by touching both hands to a metal object.

CLICK TO START

Expansion cards are built for only one type of slot. If you plan to add or upgrade a card in your computer, you must make sure the right type of slot is available on the system board. Most desktop computers provide four to eight expansion slots, some containing factory-installed expansion cards, such as those listed in Figure 2-47.

Expansion slots are classified as these types:

- **ISA** (Industry Standard Architecture) slots are an old technology, used today only for some modems and other relatively slow devices. Many new computers have few or no ISA slots.
- **PCI** (Peripheral Component Interconnect) slots offer fast transfer speeds and a 32-bit or 64-bit data bus. These slots typically house a graphics card, sound card, video capture card, modem, or network interface card.
- **AGP** (Accelerated Graphics Port) slots provide a high-speed data pathway primarily used for graphics cards.

Do notebook computers contain expansion slots? Most notebook computers are equipped with a special type of external slot called a **PCMCIA slot** (Personal Computer Memory Card International Association).

FIGURE 2-47
Factory-Installed Expansion Cards

Graphics card provides a path for data traveling to the monitor.

Modem provides a way to transmit data over phone lines or cable television lines.

Sound card carries data out to speakers and headphones or back from a microphone.

Network card allows you to connect your computer to a local area network.

Typically, a notebook computer has only one of these slots, but the slot can hold more than one **PC card** (also called "PCMCIA expansion cards" or "Card Bus cards").

What is an expansion port? An **expansion port** is any connector that passes data in and out of a computer or peripheral device. Ports are sometimes called "jacks" or "connectors"—the terminology is inconsistent.

An expansion port is often housed on an expansion card so that it is accessible through an opening in the back of the computer's system unit. A port might also be built into the system unit case of a desktop or notebook computer. The built-in ports supplied with a computer usually include a mouse port, keyboard port, serial port, and USB port. Ports that have been added with expansion cards usually protrude through rectangular cutouts in the back of the case. Figure 2-48 illustrates the major types of expansion ports on a typical desktop computer.

FIGURE 2-48
Expansion Ports

How do I know which cable to use? With so many types of ports, you can expect a corresponding variety of cables. If a cable is supplied with a peripheral device, you can usually figure out where to plug it in by matching the shape of the cable connector to the port. Some manufacturers also color code ports and plugs to make them easy to match. Figure 2-49 on the next page provides information about the computer cables you're most likely to encounter.

Why do some peripheral devices include a disk or CD? Some devices require software, called a **device driver**, to set up communication between your computer and the device. The directions supplied with your peripheral device include instructions on how to install the device driver. Typically, you use the device driver disk or CD one time to get everything set up, and then you can put the disk away in a safe place.

Long-time computer techies probably remember the days when installing a peripheral device meant messing around with little electronic components called dip switches and a host of complex software settings called IRQs. Fortunately, today's PCs include a feature called **Plug and Play** (PnP) that automatically takes care of these technical details. Although it took several years to refine Plug and Play technology, it works quite well for just about every popular peripheral device. If PnP doesn't work, your computer simply won't recognize the device and won't be able to transmit data to it or receive data from it. If you've got a stubborn peripheral device, check the manufacturer's Web site for a device driver update, or call the manufacturer's technical support department.

What's the most important thing to remember about installing peripherals? Installing a peripheral device is not difficult when you remember that it's all about using the expansion bus to make a connection between the system board and a peripheral device. The cable you use must match the peripheral device and a port on the computer. If the right type of port is not available, you might have to add an expansion card. Once the connection is made, PnP should recognize the new device. If not, you'll probably have to install driver software.

COMPUTER HARDWARE   99

FIGURE 2-49
Personal Computer Cables and Connectors

CONNECTOR	DESCRIPTION	DEVICES
Serial DB-9	Connects to serial port, which sends data over a single data line one bit at a time at speeds of 56 Kbps.	Mouse or modem
Parallel DB-25M	Connects to parallel port, which sends data simultaneously over eight data lines at speeds of 12,000 Kbps.	Printer, external CD drive, Zip drive, external hard disk drive, or tape backup device
USB	Connects to USB port, which sends data over a single data line and can support up to 127 devices. USB-1 carries data at speeds up to 12,000 Kbps; USB-2, at 480,000 Kbps.	Modem, keyboard, joystick, scanner, mouse, external hard disk drive, MP3 player, digital camera
SCSI C-50F	Connects to SCSI port, which sends data simultaneously over 8 or 16 data lines at speeds between 40,000 Kbps and 640,000 Kbps; supports up to 16 devices.	Internal or external hard disk drive, scanner, CD drive, tape backup device
IEEE 1394	Connects to the FireWire port, which sends data at 400,000 Kbps.	Video camera, DVD player
VGA HDB-15	Connects to the video port.	Monitor

QUICKCHECK......SECTION D

1. Computer _____ devices include mice, trackpads, trackballs, and joysticks.
2. In the context of computer displays, _____ rate refers to the speed at which the screen image is repainted.
3. The number of dots that form an image on a monitor or printer is referred to as _____.
4. A printer with _____ capability can print on both sides of the paper.
5. AGP, PCI, and ISA are types of expansion _____.
6. A(n) _____ port provides one of the fastest, simplest ways to connect peripherals.
7. Many peripheral devices come packaged with _____ driver software.

CHECK ANSWERS

TECHTALK
HOW A MICROPROCESSOR EXECUTES INSTRUCTIONS

Remarkable advances in microprocessor technology have produced exponential increases in computer speed and power. In 1965, Gordon Moore, co-founder of chipmaker giant Intel Corporation, predicted that the number of transistors on a chip would double every year. Much to the surprise of engineers and Moore himself, "Moore's law" accurately predicted 30 years of chip development. In 1958, the first integrated circuit contained two transistors. Today's processors feature millions of transistors.

What's really fascinating, though, is how these chips perform complex tasks simply by manipulating those ubiquitous bits. How can pushing around 1s and 0s result in professional-quality documents, exciting action games, animated graphics, cool music, e-commerce Web sites, and street maps? To satisfy your curiosity about what happens deep in the heart of a microprocessor, you'll need to venture into the realm of instruction sets, fetch cycles, accumulators, and pointers.

What kind of instructions does a computer execute? A computer accomplishes a complex task by performing a series of very simple steps, referred to as instructions. An instruction tells the computer to perform a specific arithmetic, logical, or control operation.

To be executed by a computer, an instruction must be in the form of electrical signals—those now familiar 1s and 0s that represent "ons" and "offs." In this form, instructions are referred to as **machine code**. They are, of course, very difficult for people to read, so typically when discussing them, we use more understandable mnemonics, such as JMP, M1, and REG1.

An instruction has two parts: the op code and the operands. An **op code**, which is short for "operation code," is a command word for an operation such as add, compare, or jump. The **operands** for an instruction specify the data, or the address of the data, for the operation. Let's look at an example of an instruction from a hypothetical instruction set:

| Op code | → | JMP M1 | ← | Operand |

In the instruction JMP M1, the op code is JMP and the operand is M1. The op code JMP means jump or go to a different instruction. The operand M1 stands for the RAM address of the instruction to which the computer is supposed to go. The instruction JMP M1 has only one operand, but some instructions have more than one operand. For example, the instruction ADD REG1 REG2 has two operands: REG1 and REG2.

The list of instructions that a microprocessor is able to execute is known as its instruction set. This instruction set is built into the microprocessor when it is manufactured. Every task that a computer performs is determined by the list of instructions in its instruction set. As you look at the instruction set in Figure 2-50 on the next page, consider that the computer must use instructions such as these for all the tasks it helps you perform—from database management to word processing.

COMPUTER HARDWARE

FIGURE 2-50
A Simple Microprocessor Instruction Set

Op Code	Operation	Example
INP	Input the given value into the specified memory address	INP 7 M1
CLA	Clear the accumulator to 0	CLA
MAM	Move the value from the accumulator to the specified memory location	MAM M1
MMR	Move the value from the specified memory location to the specified register	MMR M1 REG1
MRA	Move the value from the specified register to the accumulator	MRA REG1
MAR	Move the value from the accumulator to the specified register	MAR REG1
ADD	Add the values in two registers; place the result in the accumulator	ADD REG1 REG2
SUB	Subtract the value in the second register from the value in the first register; place the result in the accumulator	SUB REG1 REG2
MUL	Multiply values in two registers; place the result in the accumulator	MUL REG1 REG2
DIV	Divide the value in the first register by the value in the second register; place the result in the accumulator	DIV REG 1 REG2
INC	Increment (increase) the value in the register by 1	INC REG1
DEC	Decrement (decrease) the value in the register by 1	DEC REG1
CMP	Compare the values in two registers. If values are equal, put 1 in the accumulator; otherwise, put 0 in the accumulator	CMP REG1 REG2
JMP	Jump to the instruction at the specified memory address	JMP P2
JPZ	Jump to the specified address if the accumulator holds 0	JPZ P3
JPN	Jump to the specified address if the accumulator does not hold 0	JPN P2
HLT	Halt program execution	HLT

What happens when a computer executes an instruction? The term **instruction cycle** refers to the process in which a computer executes a single instruction. Some parts of the instruction cycle are performed by the microprocessor's control unit; other parts of the cycle are performed by the ALU. The steps in this cycle are summarized in Figure 2-51.

FIGURE 2-51
The instruction cycle includes four activities.

1. Fetch instruction
2. Interpret instruction
3. Execute instruction
4. Increment pointer to the next instruction

What role does the control unit play? The instructions that a computer is supposed to process for a particular program are held in RAM. When the program begins, the RAM address of the first instruction is placed in a part of the microprocessor's control unit called an instruction pointer. The control unit can then fetch the instruction by copying data from that address into its instruction register. From there, the control unit can interpret the instruction, gather the specified data, or tell the ALU to begin processing. Figure 2-52 helps you visualize the control unit's role in processing an instruction.

FIGURE 2-52
The control unit fetches instructions, interprets them, fetches data, and tells the ALU which processing operations to perform.

When does the ALU swing into action? The ALU is responsible for performing arithmetic and logical operations. It uses registers to hold data ready to be processed. When it gets the go-ahead signal from the control unit, the ALU processes the data and places the result in an accumulator. From the accumulator, the data can be sent to RAM or used for further processing. Figure 2-53 helps you visualize what happens in the ALU as the computer processes data.

FIGURE 2-53
The ALU uses data from its registers to perform arithmetic and logical operations. The results are placed in another register, called the accumulator.

What happens after an instruction is executed? When the computer completes an instruction, the control unit "increments" the instruction pointer to the RAM address of the next instruction and the instruction cycle begins again. So how does this all fit together? Figure 2-54 on the next page explains how the ALU, control unit, and RAM work together to process instructions.

COMPUTER HARDWARE

FIGURE 2-54
The ALU, control unit, and RAM all have a part to play in processing instructions.

1. The instruction pointer indicates the memory location that holds the first instruction (M1).

   M1 MMR M6 R1
   M2 MMR M7 R2
   M3 ADD
   M4
   M5
   M6 100
   M7 200

   Control Unit — Instruction Pointer: M1
   ALU — Accumulator, R1, R2
   Instruction Register

2. The computer fetches the instruction and puts it into the instruction register.

   M1 MMR M6 R1
   M2 MMR M7 R2
   M3 ADD
   M4
   M5
   M6 100
   M7 200

   Control Unit — Instruction Pointer: M1
   Instruction Register: MMR M6 R1
   ALU — Accumulator, R1, R2

3. The computer executes the instruction that is in the instruction register; it moves the contents of M6 into register 1 of the ALU.

   M1 MMR M6 R1
   M2 MMR M7 R2
   M3 ADD
   M4
   M5
   M6 100
   M7 200

   Control Unit — Instruction Pointer: M1
   Instruction Register: MMR M6 R1
   ALU — Accumulator, R1: 100, R2

4. The instruction pointer changes to point to the memory location that holds the next instruction.

   M1 MMR M6 R1
   M2 MMR M7 R2
   M3 ADD
   M4
   M5
   M6 100
   M7 200

   Control Unit — Instruction Pointer: M2
   Instruction Register
   ALU — Accumulator, R1: 100, R2

5. The computer fetches the instruction and puts it in the instruction register.

   M1 MMR M6 R1
   M2 MMR M7 R2
   M3 ADD
   M4
   M5
   M6 100
   M7 200

   Control Unit — Instruction Pointer: M2
   Instruction Register: MMR M7 R2
   ALU — Accumulator, R1: 100, R2

6. The computer executes the instruction; it moves the contents of M7 into register 2 of the ALU.

   M1 MMR M6 R1
   M2 MMR M7 R2
   M3 ADD
   M4
   M5
   M6 100
   M7 200

   Control Unit — Instruction Pointer: M2
   Instruction Register: MMR M7 R2
   ALU — Accumulator, R1: 100, R2: 200

7. The computer fetches the instruction and puts it in the instruction register.

   M1 MMR M6 R1
   M2 MMR M7 R2
   M3 ADD
   M4
   M5
   M6 100
   M7 200

   Control Unit — Instruction Pointer: M3
   Instruction Register: ADD
   ALU — Accumulator, R1: 100, R2: 200

8. The computer executes the instruction. The result is put in the accumulator.

   M1 MMR M6 R1
   M2 MMR M7 R2
   M3 ADD
   M4
   M5
   M6 100
   M7 200

   Control Unit — Instruction Pointer: M3
   Instruction Register: ADD
   ALU — Accumulator: 300, R1: 100, R2: 200

QUICKCHECK........TECHTALK

1. _____ code instructions are in the form of 0s and 1s.
2. JMP is an example of a(n) _____ code.
3. An instruction _____ indicates the instruction to be executed.
4. The results of processing are held in a(n) _____.

CHECK ANSWERS

ISSUE
COMPUTERS AND THE ENVIRONMENT

Manufacturing an average desktop computer with a CRT monitor requires 48 pounds of chemicals and 529 pounds of fossil fuels, according to a United Nations study. That makes producing a computer more materials-intensive than manufacturing an automobile. Extending the lifespan of your computer might be environmentally friendly, but keeping up with technology probably means replacing your computer every few years.

When it is time to replace your computer, is there a way to do it in an environmentally safe way? According to the National Safety Council, an estimated 300 million computers will be discarded by the year 2007. A recycling company called Back Thru the Future Micro Computer, Inc. (BTTF) estimates that 63 million computers will be retired in 2005 alone, compared with just 20 million that became obsolete in 1998. BTTF also estimates that printer ink cartridges are discarded at the rate of almost eight cartridges every second in the United States alone. A recycling company called GreenDisk estimates that about 1 billion floppy disks, CDs, and DVDs end up in landfills every year.

U.S. landfills already hold more than 2 million tons of computer and electronic parts, which contain toxic substances such as lead, cadmium, and mercury. A computer monitor, for example, can contain up to eight pounds of lead. An Environmental Protection Agency (EPA) report sums up the situation: "In this world of rapidly changing technology, disposal of computers and other electronic equipment has created a new and growing waste stream."

Many computers end up in landfills because their owners are unaware of potential environmental hazards and simply toss them in the garbage. In addition, PC owners typically are not given information on options for disposing of their old machines. Instead of throwing away your old computer, you might be able to sell it; donate it to a local school, church, or community program; have it hauled away by a professional recycling firm; or send it back to the manufacturer. Some artists even accept old computers and use parts in jewelery and craft projects.

Recycled Computer Creations by Gregory Steele, Marquette, MI

With the growing popularity of Internet auctions and dedicated computer reclamation sites, you might be able to get some cash for your old computer. At Web sites such as the Computer Recycle Center at *www.recycles.com*, you can post an ad for your "old stuff." Off the Web, you can find several businesses, such as Computer Renaissance, that refurbish old computers and sell them in retail stores.

Donating your old computer to a local organization doesn't actually eliminate the disposal problem, but it does delay it. Unfortunately, finding a new home for an old computer is not always easy. Most schools and community organizations have few resources for repairing broken equipment, so if your old computer is not in good working order, it could be more of a burden than a gift. In addition, your computer might be too old to be compatible with the other computers in an organization. It helps if you can donate software along with your old computer. To ensure a legal transfer, include the software distribution disks, manuals, and license agreement. And remember, once you donate the software, you cannot legally use it on your new computer unless it is freeware or shareware.

If you cannot find an organization to accept your computer donation, look in your local Yellow Pages or on the Internet for an electronics recycling firm, which will haul away your computer and recycle any usable materials.

Despite private sector options for selling, donating, or recycling old computers, many governments are worried that these voluntary efforts will not be enough to prevent massive dumping of an ever-growing population of obsolete computers.

During the past two years, about half the states have taken some legislative action to curtail the rampant disposal of obsolete computer equipment. For example, Massachusetts implemented a statewide ban in 2000 on disposing computers in landfills, which helped spur recycling efforts. New Jersey's tough regulations on electronics disposal apply to more than 220 pounds or 100 kilograms, which is about eight monitors. Under those regulations, disposal must be at an approved New Jersey facility and disposal records must be kept for three years. Failure to comply can result in a $2,000 fine.

Many lawmakers in the United States, Japan, and the European Union believe that more legislation is necessary, but they can't agree on an implementation plan. Basic to the issue is the question of "Who pays?" Should it be the taxpayer, the individual consumer, or the computer manufacturer?

Taxpayers typically pick up the tab for electronic waste disposal through municipal trash pick-up fees or local taxes. For example, the Silicon Valley Toxics Coalition estimates that California taxpayers will spend more than $1 billion to manage electronic waste between 2002 and 2006. But is this approach fair to individual taxpayers who generate very little electronic waste?

To make consumers responsible for the cost of recycling the products they buy, some lawmakers suggest adding a special recycling tax to computers and other electronic devices. A proposal in South Carolina, for example, would impose a $5 fee on the sale of each piece of electronic equipment containing a CRT and require the state treasurer to deposit the fees into a recycling fund for electronic equipment. Of three bills introduced in 2003 in Oregon to address the issue of managing the electronics waste stream, two would impose similar point-of-sale fees on electronic components.

Other lawmakers propose to make manufacturers responsible for recycling costs and logistics. "Extended producer responsibility" refers to the idea of holding manufacturers responsible for the environmental effects of their products through the entire product life cycle, which includes taking them back, recycling them, or disposing of them. Proposed legislation in Europe would require manufacturers to accept returns of their old equipment free of charge and take appropriate steps to recycle it. The economics of a mandatory take-back program are likely to increase product costs because manufacturers would typically pass on recycling costs to consumers.

Some companies currently participate in voluntary producer responsibility programs. Sony's take-back program in Minnesota allows residents to recycle any Sony products at no cost. Using IBM's PC Recycling Service, you can ship any make of computer, including system units, monitors, printers, and optional attachments, to a recycling center for $29.99. Such programs are important steps in the effort to keep our planet green.

INFOWEBLINKS

You'll find much more information about how you can recycle an old computer by connecting to the **Computer Recycling InfoWeb**.

www.course.com/np/concepts8/ch02

WHAT DO YOU THINK?

1. Have you ever thrown away an old computer or other electronic device? ○ Yes ○ No ○ Not sure

2. Are you aware of any options for recycling electronic equipment in your local area? ○ Yes ○ No ○ Not sure

3. Would it be fair for consumers to pay a recycling tax on any electronic equipment that they purchase? ○ Yes ○ No ○ Not sure

SAVE RESPONSES

COMPUTERS IN CONTEXT
MILITARY

In *Engines of the Mind*, Joel Shurkin writes, "If necessity is the mother of invention, then war can be said to be its grandmother." The military, an early pioneer in computer and communication technologies, continues to be the driving force behind technologies that have revolutionized everyday life. During World War II, the U.S. military initiated a classified research program, called Project PX, to develop an electronic device to calculate artillery firing tables; by hand, each table required weeks of grueling calculations. Project PX produced ENIAC (Electrical Numerical Integrator And Calculator), one of the first general-purpose electronic computers. When ENIAC was completed in 1946, the war was over, but ENIAC's versatile architecture could be used for other calculations, such as designing hydrogen bombs, predicting weather, and engineering wind tunnels. ENIAC's technology evolved into the computers used today.

After Project PX, the military continued to support computer research. Like most large corporations, the military used mainframe computers to maintain personnel, inventory, supply, and facilities records. This data was distributed to terminals at other locations via rudimentary networks. Because all data communication flowed through the mainframe, a single point of failure for the entire system was a possible risk. A malfunction or an enemy "hit" could disrupt command and control, sending the military into chaos. Therefore, the armed forces created the Advanced Research Projects Agency (ARPA) to design a distributed communications system that could continue operating without a centralized computer. The result was ARPANET, which paved the way for the data communications system we know today as the Internet.

The U.S. Department of Defense (DoD) currently maintains two data communications networks: SIPRNet, a classified (secret-level) network, and NIPRNet, which provides unclassified services. The DoD's public Web site, called DefenseLINK, provides official information about defense policies, organizations, budgets, and operations.

Computers and communications technology have also become an integral part of high-tech military operations. U.S. Apache helicopters, for example, are equipped with computer-based Target Acquisition Designation Sights, laser range finder/designators, and Pilot Night Vision Sensors. These arcade-style controls are also used by tank drivers in the U.S. Army's 4th Infantry Division. Each vehicle in this "Digitized Division" is equipped with a Force 21 Battle Command Brigade and Below system, which works like a battlefield Internet to transmit data on the location of friendly and enemy forces from one vehicle to another using wireless communication.

Much like a video game, the Force 21 touch screen shows friendly troops in blue, and a global positioning satellite (GPS) system updates their positions automatically. Enemy troops spotted by helicopters are shown as red icons. To get information on any friendly or enemy vehicle, a soldier can simply touch one of these blue or red icons. To send text messages—much like cell phone and computer instant messaging—a soldier touches the Message button.

COMPUTER HARDWARE

The built-in GPS system provides location and route information, much like sophisticated mapping programs in luxury cars.

Force 21 computers are installed in shock-resistant cases and equipped with a cooling system that eliminates the need for a fan, which might pull in dust, dirt, or water. The computers run Sun Microsystem's Solaris operating system because it is less vulnerable to viruses and intrusion attacks than Microsoft Windows. To prevent enemy capture and use, Force 21 computers have a self-destruct mechanism that can be triggered remotely.

In addition to pilots and tank drivers, battlefield soldiers will soon be equipped with "wearable" computer and communications equipment. The $2 billion Land Warrior program will provide high-tech weaponry, such as the Integrated Helmet Assembly Subsystem, for soldiers. IHAS is a helmet-mounted device that displays graphical data, digital maps, thermal images, intelligence information, and troop locations. It also includes a weapon-mounted video camera, so that soldiers can view and fire around corners and acquire targets in darkness.

The military has also conducted research in computer simulations that are similar to civilian computer games. "Live" military training is dangerous—weapons are deadly and equipment costs millions of dollars. With computer simulations, however, troops can train in a true-to-life environment without physical harm or equipment damage. Flying an F-16 fighter, for example, costs about $5,000 an hour, but flying an F-16 simulator costs only $500 per hour. The military uses simulators to teach Air Force pilots to fly fighter jets, Navy submarine officers to navigate in harbors, and Marine infantry squads to handle urban combat. Military trainers agree that widespread use of computer games helps prepare troops to adapt quickly to simulations.

A 24-year-old preflight student at Pensacola Naval Air Station modified the Microsoft Flight Simulator game to re-create a T-34C Turbo Mentor plane's controls. After logging 50 hours on the simulator, the student performed so well on a real plane that the Navy used his simulation to train other pilots. Today, a growing cadre of computer and communications specialists are needed to create and maintain increasingly complex military systems.

An army once depended on its infantry, but today's high-tech army depends equally on its database designers, computer programmers, and network specialists. Even previously low-tech military jobs, such as mechanics and dietitians, require some computer expertise. Happily, new recruits are finding military computer systems easy to learn, based on their knowledge of civilian technologies, such as the Internet and computer games.

Although most citizens agree that an adequate national defense is necessary, the cost of defense-related equipment, personnel, and research remains controversial. In 1961, President Dwight Eisenhower warned "We must guard against the acquisition of unwarranted influence, whether sought or unsought, by the military-industrial complex." Many socially motivated citizens and pacifists protested diverting tax dollars from social and economic programs to the military-industrial complex Eisenhower cautioned against. In retrospect, however, military funding contributed to many technologies we depend on today. For example, detractors tried to convince the government that Project PX was doomed to failure, but without ENIAC research, computers might not exist today. Skeptics saw no future for the fruits of ARPANET research, but it led to the Internet, which has changed our lives significantly.

INFOWEBLINKS

You'll find lots more information related to this Computers in Context topic at the **Computers and the Military InfoWeb**.

www.course.com/np/concepts8/ch02

INTERACTIVE SUMMARY

To review important concepts from this chapter, fill in the blanks to best complete each sentence. When using the NP8 BookOnCD, click the Check Answers buttons to automatically score your answers. Place your Tracking Disk in the floppy disk drive if you want to save your scores.

Most of today's computers are electronic, digital devices that work with data coded as binary digits, also known as [_____]. To represent numeric data, a computer can use the [_____] number system. To represent character data, a computer uses Extended [_____], EBCDIC, or Unicode. These codes also provide digital representations for the numerals 0 through 9 that are distinguished from numbers by the fact that they are not typically used in mathematical operations. Computers also [_____] sounds, pictures, and videos into 1s and 0s.

An [_____] is a single 1 or 0, whereas a [_____] is a sequence of eight 1s and 0s. Transmission speeds are usually measured in [_____], but storage space is usually measured in [_____] or gigabytes. In the context of computing, the prefix "kilo" means exactly 1,024. Kb stands for [_____], while the abbreviation KB stands for [_____]. The prefix [_____] means precisely 1,048,576, or about 1 million. The prefix "giga" means about 1 billion; "tera" means about 1 trillion; and "exa" means about 1 quintillion.

The terms "computer chip," "microchip," and "chip" originated as techie jargon for [_____] circuits. These chips are made from a super-thin slice of semiconducting material and are packed with millions of microscopic circuit elements. In a computer, these chips include the [_____], memory modules, and other support circuitry. They are housed inside the computer's system unit on a large circuit board called the [_____].

CHECK ANSWERS

The microprocessor and memory are two of the most important components in a computer. The microprocessor is an [_____] circuit, which is designed to process data based on a set of instructions. Its miniaturized circuitry is grouped into important functional areas. The microprocessor's ALU performs arithmetic and [_____] operations. The [_____] unit fetches each instruction, interprets it, loads data into the ALU's registers, and directs all the processing activities within the microprocessor. In most of today's personal computers, microprocessor performance is measured in [_____]—the number of cycles per second, or clock rate. Other factors affecting overall processing speed include word size, cache size, instruction set complexity, parallel processing, and pipelining.

RAM is a special holding area for data, program instructions, and the [_____] system. It stores data on a temporary basis while it waits to be processed. In most computers, RAM is composed of integrated circuits called [_____] or RDRAM. The speed of RAM circuitry is measured in [_____] or in megahertz (MHz). RAM is different from disk storage because it is [_____], which means that it can hold data only when the computer power is turned on. Computers also contain [_____], which is a type of memory that provides a set of "hard-wired" instructions that a computer uses to boot up. A third type of memory, called [_____], is battery powered and contains configuration settings.

CHECK ANSWERS

COMPUTER HARDWARE

Today's personal computers use a variety of storage technologies, including floppy disks, hard disks, CDs, DVDs, tapes, and flash drives. Each storage device essentially has a direct pipeline to a computer's _____ so that data and instructions can move from a more permanent storage area to a temporary holding area and vice versa.

Magnetic storage technology stores data by magnetizing microscopic particles on the surface of a disk or tape. Optical storage technologies store data as a series of _____ and lands on the surface of a CD or DVD. _____ storage technology stores data by activating electrons in a microscopic grid of circuitry.

A standard 3.5" floppy disk formatted for a PC stores _____ MB of data. Zip disks have a higher disk _____, which provides significantly more storage capacity than a standard floppy disk.

A hard disk provides multiple platters for data storage, and these platters are sealed inside the drive case or cartridge to prevent airborne contaminants from interfering with the read-write heads. These disks are less durable than floppy disks, so it is important to make a _____ copy of the data they contain. Computer ads usually contain information about a hard disk's capacity and its _____ card type: SATA, EIDE, Ultra ATA, or SCSI.

Optical storage technologies, such as CD- and DVD- _____, provide good data storage capacity, but do not allow you to alter the disks' contents. _____ technology allows you to write data on a CD or DVD, but you cannot delete or change that data. _____ technology allows you to write and rewrite data on a CD or DVD.

USB _____ drives provide portable, solid state storage.

✦ CHECK ANSWERS

Most computer systems include a keyboard and some type of _____ device for basic data input. A mouse is standard equipment with most desktop computer systems, but alternatives include pointing _____, trackpads, and trackballs.

For output, most computers include a display device. A _____ produces an image by spraying electrons toward the screen. _____ technology produces an image by manipulating light within a layer of liquid crystal cells. _____ screen technology creates an on-screen image by illuminating miniature fluorescent lights arrayed in a panel-like screen. Image quality for a display device is a factor of screen size, dot _____, _____ of viewing angle, resolution, refresh rate, and color _____. A typical computer display system consists of the display device and a _____ card.

For printed output, most PC owners turn to _____ jet printers, although _____ printers are a popular option when low operating costs and high _____ cycle are important. A dot _____ printer is sometimes used for back-office applications and printing multipart forms.

Installing a peripheral device is not difficult when you remember that it is all about using the _____ bus to make a connection between the computer's _____ and a peripheral device. The cable you use must match the peripheral device and a _____ on the computer. If the right type of port is not available, you might have to add an _____ card. Once the connection is made, _____ should recognize the new device. If not, you'll probably have to install device _____ software.

✦ CHECK ANSWERS

INTERACTIVE KEY TERMS

Make sure you understand all the boldfaced key terms presented in this chapter. If you're using the NP8 BookOnCD, you can use this list of terms as an interactive study activity. First, try to define a term in your own words, and then click the term to compare your definition with the definition presented in the chapter.

Access time, 81
AGP, 97
ALU, 68
Analog device, 60
ASCII, 61
Benchmarks, 71
Binary digits, 60
Binary number system, 60
Cache, 70
Capacitors, 73
Card reader, 80
CD, 86
CD-DA, 87
CD-R, 87
CD-ROM, 87
CD-RW, 87
Character data, 61
CISC, 70
CMOS memory, 75
Color depth, 93
CompactFlash, 89
Control unit, 68
Controller, 83
CRT, 92
Data bus, 97
Data representation, 60
Data transfer rate, 81
Device driver, 98
Digital device, 60
Digitize, 62
DIMMs, 65
DIPs, 65
Disk density, 82
Dot matrix printer, 94
Dot pitch, 92
Double layer DVD, 86
Drive bays, 80
Duty cycle, 95
DVD, 86
DVD+R, 87
DVD-ROM, 87
DVD+RW, 87
DVD-Video, 87
Dye sublimation printer, 95
EBCDIC, 61
Expansion bus, 97
Expansion card, 97
Expansion port, 98

Expansion slot, 97
Extended ASCII, 61
File header, 63
Floppy disk, 81
Gigabit, 63
Gigabyte, 63
Gigahertz (GHz), 69
Graphics card, 93
Hard disk platter, 83
Head crash, 84
Ink jet printer, 94
Instruction cycle, 101
Instruction set, 69
Integrated circuit, 64
ISA, 97
Joystick, 91
Kilobit, 63
Kilobyte, 63
Lands, 79
Laser printer, 94
LCD, 92
Level 1 cache, 70
Level 2 cache, 70
Machine code, 100
Magnetic storage, 79
Megabit, 63
Megabyte, 63
Megahertz (MHz), 69
Microprocessor, 68
Microprocessor clock, 69
MultiMedia cards, 89
Nanosecond, 74
Numeric data, 60
Op code, 100
Operands, 100
Optical storage, 79
Parallel processing, 70
PC card, 98
PCI, 97
PCMCIA slot, 97
PGAs, 65
Pipelining, 70
Pits, 79
Pixels, 92
Plasma screen, 92
Plug and Play, 98
Pointing device, 91
Pointing stick, 91

PostScript, 96
Printer Control Language (PCL), 96
RAM, 72
Random access, 81
RDRAM, 74
Read-write head, 79
Recordable technology, 86
Refresh rate, 92
Registers, 68
Resolution, 93
Rewritable technology, 86
RISC, 70
ROM, 74
ROM BIOS, 74
SDRAM, 74
SEC cartridges, 65
SecureDigital, 89
Semiconducting materials, 64
Sequential access, 81
Serial processing, 70
SmartMedia, 89
Solid ink printer, 95
Solid state storage, 80
Storage device, 78
Storage medium, 78
SVGA, 93
SXGA, 93
System board, 65
Tape backup, 85
Thermal transfer printer, 95
Trackball, 91
Trackpad, 91
Unicode, 61
USB flash drive, 88
UXGA, 93
VGA, 93
Viewable image size, 92
Viewing angle width, 92
Virtual memory, 73
Volatile, 73
Word size, 70
Write-protect window, 82
XGA, 93

COMPUTER HARDWARE

INTERACTIVE SITUATION QUESTIONS

Apply what you've learned to some typical computing situations. When using the NP8 BookOnCD, you can type your answers, and then use the Check Answers button to automatically score your responses. Place your Tracking Disk in the floppy disk drive if you want to save your scores.

1. Suppose you're reading a computer magazine and you come across the ad pictured to the right. By looking at the specs, you can tell that the microprocessor was manufactured by which company? _____

2. The capacity of the hard disk drive in the ad is _____ and the memory capacity is _____.

3. The computer in the ad appears to have a(n) _____ controller card for the hard disk drive.

4. You are thinking about upgrading the microprocessor in your three-year-old computer, which has a 2.6 MHz Pentium microprocessor and 32 MB of RAM. Would it be worthwhile to spend $500 to install a 3.0 GHz Pentium processor? Yes or no? _____

5. You're in the process of booting up your computer and suddenly the screen contains an assortment of settings for date and time, hard disk drive, and memory capacity. From what you've learned in this chapter, you can surmise that these are settings stored in the _____ memory, and that they are best left unmodified.

6. You're looking for a portable storage device that you can use to transport a few files between your home computer and your school computer lab. The school lab computers have no floppy disk drives, but do have USB ports. You should be able to transport your files using a USB _____ drive.

HOME/SMALL BUSINESS DESKTOP MODEL XP2002

- Pentium 4 560 3.6 GHz
- 1 GB 533 MHz SDRAM
- 80 GB UltraATA HD (7200 rpm)
- 32 X Max CD-RW
- 3.5" 1.44 MB FDD
- 21" 24 dp monitor
- 256 MB AGP graphics card
- Sound Blaster 64v PCI sound card
- Altec Lansing speakers
- U.S. Robotics 56 Kbps modem
- 3-year limited warranty*

$ 1299

7. You want to add a storage device to your computer that reads CD-ROMs, DVD-ROMs, DVD-Videos, and CD-Rs. A DVD/CD-RW will do the job. True or false? _____

8. You are a professional graphics designer. A(n) _____ is likely to give you the best colors from all viewing angles, whereas a(n) _____ may not show true colors when viewed from some angles.

9. Suppose that you volunteer to produce a large quantity of black-and-white leaflets for a charity organization. It is fortunate that you have access to a(n) _____ printer with a high duty cycle and low operating costs.

CHECK ANSWERS

INTERACTIVE PRACTICE TESTS

Practice tests that consist of 10 multiple-choice, true/false, and fill-in-the-blank questions are available on both the NP8 BookOnCD and the NP8 Web site. The questions are selected at random from a large test bank, so each time you take a test, you'll receive a different set of questions. Your tests are scored immediately, and you can print study guides that help you find the correct answers for any questions that you missed.

www.course.com/np/concepts8/ch02

CLICK TO START

REVIEW
ON THE WEB

PROJECTS

An NP8 Project is an open-ended activity that helps you apply the concepts you have learned. Many projects require resources in addition to your textbook, such as current magazines, library materials, or Web access. When you tackle a project, be prepared to use your critical thinking skills, logical analysis, and creativity. Projects for this chapter include:

- Issue Research: Computers and the Environment
- Buying a New Computer
- Computers in the Military
- Calculating Storage Requirements
- Sizing Up Future Storage Technologies
- Can a Computer Make Errors?
- The Jargon of Computer Ads

To work with the Projects for this chapter, connect to the **New Perspectives NP8 Web Site**.

www.course.com/np/concepts8/ch02

TECHTV VIDEO PROJECT

The TechTV segment *Getting Started* demonstrates the basic parts needed to construct a personal computer. While watching the video, make a list of the parts. Use the Web to find an example of each part. Add the manufacturer, model number, and price in your list. Calculate the price of assembling a computer from these parts.

To work with the Video Projects for this chapter, connect to the **New Perspectives NP8 Web Site**.

www.course.com/np/concepts8/ch02

STUDY TIPS

Study Tips help you to organize and consolidate the information in a chapter by making lists, outlines, charts, and sketches. You can use paper and pencil or word processing software to complete most of the Study Tips.

To work with the Study Tips for this chapter, connect to the **New Perspectives NP8 Web Site**.

www.course.com/np/concepts8/ch02

ONLINE GAMES

Test your comprehension of the concepts introduced in Chapter 2 by playing the NP8 Online Games. At the end of each game, you have three options:

- Print a comprehensive study guide complete with page references
- Print your results to be submitted to your instructor
- Save your results to be submitted to your instructor via e-mail

To work with the Online Games for this chapter, connect to the **New Perspectives NP8 Web Site**.

www.course.com/np/concepts8/ch02

COMPUTER HARDWARE 113

STUDENT EDITION LABS

Extend your knowledge of binary numbers and computer hardware with the Chapter 2 Student Edition Labs.

The following Student Edition Labs are offered with Chapter 2:
- Using Input Devices
- Peripheral Devices
- Binary Numbers
- Understanding the Motherboard

Go to the NP8 New Perspectives Web site for specific lab topics.

To work with the Chapter 2 Student Edition Labs and their corresponding lab assignments, connect to the **New Perspectives NP8 Web Site**.

www.course.com/np/concepts8/ch02

Work hands-on in structured simulations practicing important skills and concepts

Test your comprehension of the lab topics through a series of objective-based questions

Track Your Progress with the Student Edition Labs

- Student Edition Labs test your comprehension of the lab topics through a series of trackable objective-based questions. Your instructor will direct you to either print your results or submit them via e-mail.

- Student Edition Lab Assignments, available on the New Perspectives NP8 Web site, require you to apply the skills learned through the lab in a live environment. Go to the New Perspectives NP8 Web site for detailed instruction on individual Student Edition Lab Assignments.

If you have a SAM user profile, you have access to even more interactive content. Log in to your SAM account and go to your assignments page to see what your instructor has assigned for this chapter.

3

COMPUTER SOFTWARE

CONTENTS

✻ SECTION A: SOFTWARE BASICS

Software: The Inside Story
Programmers and Programming Languages
How Software Works
Application Software and System Software

✻ SECTION B: COMPUTER OPERATING SYSTEMS

Operating System Overview
Windows, Mac OS, UNIX, Linux, and DOS
Handheld and Tablet Operating Systems

✻ SECTION C: APPLICATION SOFTWARE

Document Production Software
Spreadsheet Software
"Number Crunching" Software
Database Software
Graphics Software
Music Software
Video Editing and DVD Authoring Software
Software Suites
Educational and Reference Software
Entertainment Software
Business Software

✻ SECTION D: SOFTWARE INSTALLATION AND COPYRIGHTS

Installation Basics
Installing from Distribution Media
Installing Downloaded Software
Uninstalling Software
Software Copyrights
Software Licenses

✻ TECHTALK: THE WINDOWS REGISTRY

✻ ISSUE: SOFTWARE PIRACY

✻ COMPUTERS IN CONTEXT: JOURNALISM

✻ REVIEW ACTIVITIES

Interactive Summary
Interactive Key Terms
Interactive Situation Questions
Interactive Practice Tests
Review on the Web

LABS

✻ Using the Windows Interface
✻ Installing and Uninstalling Software

TIP

When using the BookOnCD, the ✻ icons are "clickable" to access resources on the CD. The ✚ icons are clickable to access resources on the Web. You can also access Web resources by using your browser to connect directly to the NP8 New Perspectives Web site at:

www.course.com/np/concepts8/ch03

COMPUTER SOFTWARE

CHAPTER PREVIEW

Before you begin Chapter 3, you can use the Web-based preview activities to hear an overview of the chapter, check your current level of expertise about key concepts, and look through a list of learning objectives. You can access the preview activities by clicking the ✣ icon when using the BookOnCD or going to the New Perspectives NP8 Web site.

CHAPTER OVERVIEW

Software essentially transforms a computer from one kind of machine to another—from a drafting station to a typesetting machine, from a flight simulator to a calculator, from a filing system to a music remixing turntable. Get your book and highlighter ready, then connect to the New Perspectives NP8 Web site where you can listen to an overview that points out the most important concepts for this chapter.

www.course.com/np/concepts8/ch03 ✣

CHAPTER PRE-ASSESSMENT

How much do you know about installing and using software? To gauge your level of knowledge before beginning the chapter, try the pre-assessment quiz at the New Perspectives NP8 Web site. Armed with your results from this quiz, you can focus your study time on concepts that will round out your knowledge of software and improve your test scores.

www.course.com/np/concepts8/ch03 ✣

LEARNING OBJECTIVES

When you complete this chapter you should be able to:

- Describe the components of a typical software package, including executable files, support modules, and data modules
- Trace the development of a computer program from its inception as a set of high-level language instructions through its translation into machine language
- Describe the differences between system software and application software
- Describe the way an operating system manages each computer resource
- Identify operating systems for personal computers, PDAs, and servers
- Explain the key features and uses for word processing, desktop publishing, and Web authoring software
- Describe the major features of spreadsheet software
- Describe the key features of database software
- List the types of software available for graphics, video, music, education and reference, entertainment, and business
- Explain how to install and uninstall software, whether it is supplied on CDs or as a Web download
- Describe the differences among new software versions, software patches, and service packs
- Describe the rights granted by copyright law, commercial software licenses, shareware licenses, freeware licenses, open source licenses, and public domain software

A detailed list of learning objectives is provided at the New Perspectives NP8 Web site
www.course.com/np/concepts8/ch03 ✣

SECTION A
SOFTWARE BASICS

Computer software determines the types of tasks a computer can help you accomplish. Some software helps you create documents, while other software helps you edit home videos, prepare your tax return, or design the floor plan for a new house. But how does software transform your computer into a machine that can help with so many tasks? Section A delves into the characteristics of computer software and explains how it works.

SOFTWARE: THE INSIDE STORY

What is software? As you learned in Chapter 1, the instructions that tell a computer how to carry out a task are referred to as a computer program. These programs form the software that prepares a computer to do a specific task, such as document production, video editing, graphic design, or Web browsing. Software is usually distributed on CDs or DVDs, as shown in Figure 3-1. It also can be made available as a Web download.

What kinds of files are included in a typical software product? Whether it's on a CD or downloaded from the Web, today's software is typically composed of many files. You might be surprised by the number of files that are necessary to make software work. For example, the eVideo-In Pro software includes numerous files with extensions such as .exe, .dll, and .hlp, as shown in Figure 3-2.

FIGURE 3-1
In popular usage, the term "software" usually refers to one or more computer programs and any additional files that are provided to carry out a specific type of task.

FIGURE 3-2
The files required by the eVideo-In Pro software contain user-executable programs, support programs, and data.

Files containing support programs often have .dll file extensions.

User-executable program files have .exe file extensions.

Data files have a variety of file extensions, including .dat, .hlp, .bmp, and .txt.

COMPUTER SOFTWARE

At least one of the files included in a software package contains an executable program designed to be launched, or started, by users. On PCs, these programs are stored in files that typically have .exe file extensions and are sometimes referred to as "executable files" or "user-executable files." When using a Windows PC, you can start an executable file by clicking its icon, selecting it from the Start menu, or entering its name in the Run dialog box.

Other files supplied with a software package contain programs that are not designed to be run by users. These "support programs" contain instructions for the computer to use with the main user-executable file. A support program can be "called," or activated, by the main program as needed. In the context of Windows software, support programs often have file extensions such as .dll and .ocx.

In addition to program files, many software packages also include data files. As you might expect, these files contain any data that is necessary for a task, but not supplied by the user, such as Help documentation, a word list for an online spell checker, synonyms for a thesaurus, or graphics for the software's toolbar icons. The data files supplied with a software package sport file extensions such as .txt, .bmp, and .hlp. Figure 3-3 illustrates the relationship between the various files distributed with a typical software package.

TERMINOLOGY NOTE

The term "software" was once used for all non-hardware components of a computer. In this context, software referred to computer programs and to the data the programs used. It could also refer to any data that existed in digital format, such as documents or photos. Using today's terminology, however, the documents and photos you create are usually classified as "data" rather than as "software."

FIGURE 3-3
The main executable file provides the primary set of instructions for the computer to execute and calls various support programs and data files as needed.

Why does software require so many files? The use of a main user-executable file plus several support programs and data files offers a great deal of flexibility and efficiency for software developers. Support programs and data files can usually be modified without changing the main executable file. This modular approach can significantly reduce the time required to create and test the main executable file, which usually contains a long and fairly complex program. The modular approach also allows software developers to reuse their support programs and adapt preprogrammed support modules for use in their own software.

Modular programming techniques are of interest mainly to people who create computer programs; however, these techniques affect the process of installing and uninstalling software, discussed later in this chapter. It is important, therefore, to remember that computer software typically consists of many files that contain user-executable programs, support programs, and data.

PROGRAMMERS AND PROGRAMMING LANGUAGES

Who creates computer software? **Computer programmers** write instructions for the computer programs that become the components of a computer software product. The finished software product is then distributed by the programmers or by **software publishers**—companies that specialize in marketing and selling commercial software.

At one time, businesses, organizations, and individuals had to write most of the software they used. Today, however, most businesses and organizations purchase commercial software (also referred to as "off-the-shelf software") to avoid the time and expense of writing their own. Individuals rarely write software for their personal computers, preferring to select from thousands of software titles available in stores, from catalogs, and on the Internet. Although most computer owners do not write their own software, working as a computer programmer for a government agency, business, or software publisher can be a challenging career.

How does a programmer "write" software? Most software is designed to provide a task-related environment, which includes a screen display, a means of collecting commands and data from the user, the specifications for processing data, and a method for displaying or outputting data. Figure 3-4 illustrates a very simple software environment that converts a Fahrenheit temperature to Celsius and displays the result.

FIGURE 3-4
Today's software includes menus, buttons, and other control objects. These controls are defined by a programmer, who designates their properties. For example, one property of the Convert button specifies how to convert Fahrenheit temperatures to Celsius.

To create a software environment, a programmer must define **properties** for each element in the environment, such as where an object appears, its shape, its color, and its behavior. For the example shown in Figure 3-4, the programmer must define many properties for the Convert button, including:

- Its height: 375
- Its label (caption): Convert
- What happens when you click it: Subtract 32 from Fahrenheit, divide by 1.8, and then display the answer

COMPUTER SOFTWARE

A **programming language** (sometimes referred to as a "computer language") provides the tools a programmer uses to create software and produce a lengthy list of instructions, called **source code**, which defines the software environment in every detail—what it looks like, how the user enters commands, and how it manipulates data. Most programmers today prefer to use a **high-level language**, such as C++, Java, COBOL, and Visual Basic. These languages have some similarities to human languages and produce programs that are fairly easy to test and modify.

HOW SOFTWARE WORKS

How does a computer process a program? A computer's microprocessor understands only **machine language**—the instruction set that is "hard wired" within the microprocessor's circuits. Therefore, instructions written in a high-level language must be translated into machine language before a computer can use them. Figure 3-5 gives you an idea of what happens to a high-level instruction when it is converted into machine language instructions.

FIGURE 3-5
A simple instruction to add two numbers becomes a long series of 0s and 1s in machine language.

High-level Language Instruction	Machine Language Equivalent	Description of Machine Language Instructions
Answer=FirstNumber+SecondNumber	10001000 00011000 010000000	Load FirstNumber into Register 1
	10001000 00010000 00100000	Load SecondNumber into Register 2
	00000000 00011000 00010000	Perform ADD operation
	10100010 00111000	Move the number from the accumulator to the RAM location called Answer

How are instructions converted to machine language? The process of translating instructions from a high-level language into machine language can be accomplished by two special types of programs: compilers and interpreters. A **compiler** translates all the instructions in a program as a single batch, and the resulting machine language instructions, called **object code**, are placed in a new file (Figure 3-6). Most of the program files on a distribution CD for commercial software are compiled so that they contain machine language instructions that are ready for the processor to execute.

FIGURE 3-6
A compiler converts high-level instructions into a new file containing machine language instructions.

As an alternative to a compiler, an **interpreter** converts one instruction at a time while the program is running. An interpreter reads the first instruction, converts it into machine language, and then sends it to the microprocessor. After the instruction is executed, the interpreter converts the next instruction, and so on (Figure 3-7 on the next page).

FIGURE 3-7

An interpreter converts high-level instructions into machine language instructions while the program is running.

An interpreted program runs more slowly than a compiled program because the translation process happens while the program is running.

CLICK TO START

So how does software work? Assume that a video editing program, such as eVideo-In Pro, is installed on your computer, which is running Windows. Figure 3-8 illustrates how the files included in this software package interact when you edit videos.

FIGURE 3-8

The main executable file loads into RAM when the program runs, and can call various other files as needed.

1. When you start the eVideo-In Pro software, the instructions in the file eVidpro.exe are loaded from disk into RAM and then sent to the microprocessor.

2. eVidpro.exe is a compiled program, so its instructions are immediately executed by the processor.

3. As processing begins, the eVideo-In Pro window opens and the graphical controls for video editing tasks appear. The program waits for you to select a control by clicking it with the mouse.

4. Based on your selection, eVidpro.exe follows its instructions and performs the actions you specify. Many of the instructions for these actions are included in the main executable file. If not, eVidpro.exe calls a support program, such as Sftrans.dll.

5. If you access eVideo-In Pro Help, eVidpro.exe loads the data file eVidpro.hlp.

6. eVidpro.exe continues to respond to the controls you select until you click the Close button, which halts execution of the program instructions, closes the program window, and releases the space the program occupied in RAM for use by other programs or data.

APPLICATION SOFTWARE AND SYSTEM SOFTWARE

How is software categorized? Software is categorized as application software or system software. When you hear the word "application," your first reaction might be to envision a financial aid application or a form you fill out to apply for a job, a club membership, or a driver's license. The word "application" has other meanings, however. One of them is a synonym for the word "use." A computer certainly has many uses, such as creating documents, crunching numbers, drawing designs, and editing photographs.

COMPUTER SOFTWARE

121

Each use is considered an "application," and the software that provides the computer with instructions for each use is called **application software**, or simply an "application." The primary purpose of application software is to help people carry out tasks using a computer.

In contrast, the primary purpose of **system software**—your computer's operating system, device drivers, and utilities—is to help the computer carry out its basic operating functions. Figure 3-9 illustrates the division between system software and application software. You'll learn more about these software categories in Sections B and C.

FIGURE 3-9
Software can be classified into categories.

QUICKCHECK......SECTION A

1. When using a Windows PC, you can start a(n) [_____] file by clicking its icon, selecting it from the Start menu, or entering its name in the Run dialog box.

2. A programming language provides tools for creating a lengthy list of instructions called [_____] code.

3. Instructions that are written in a(n) [_____]-level language must be translated into machine language before a computer can use them.

4. As a program is running, a(n) [_____] converts one instruction at a time into machine language.

5. Computer software can be divided into two major categories: [_____] software and system software.

CHECK ANSWERS

SECTION B
COMPUTER OPERATING SYSTEMS

Chapter 1 explained that an operating system is one factor that determines a computer's platform and compatibility. The term operating system (abbreviated OS) is defined as system software, which acts as the master controller for all activities that take place within a computer system.

An operating system is an integral part of virtually every computer system. It fundamentally affects how you can use your computer. Can you run two programs at the same time? Can you connect your computer to a network? Does your computer run dependably? Does all your software have a similar "look and feel," or do you have to learn a different set of controls and commands for each new program you acquire?

To answer questions like these, it is helpful to have a clear idea about what an operating system is and what it does. Section B provides an overview of operating systems and compares some of the most popular operating systems for personal computers.

OPERATING SYSTEM OVERVIEW

What does an operating system do? A computer's software is similar to the chain of command in an army. You issue a command using application software. Application software tells the operating system what to do. The operating system tells the device drivers, device drivers tell the hardware, and the hardware actually does the work. Figure 3-10 illustrates this chain of command for printing a document or photo.

FIGURE 3-10

A command to print a document is relayed through various levels of software, including the operating system, until it reaches the printer.

1. You issue the Print command while using application software, such as a word processor.

2. The word processing application signals the operating system that a document must be sent to the printer.

3. The operating system communicates the document data to the device driver for the printer.

4. The device driver controls the printer as it prints the document.

COMPUTER SOFTWARE

The operating system interacts with application software, device drivers, and hardware to manage a computer's resources. In the context of a computer system, the term **resource** refers to any component that is required to perform work. For example, the processor is a resource. RAM, storage space, and peripherals are also resources. While you interact with application software, your computer's operating system is busy behind the scenes with tasks such as those listed in Figure 3-11.

- Manage processor resources
- Manage memory
- Keep track of storage resources
- Ensure that input and output proceed in an orderly manner
- Establish basic elements of the user interface

FIGURE 3-11
Operating System Tasks

How does the operating system manage processor resources? Chapter 2 explained how the control unit directs activities within the microprocessor. The operating system also controls the microprocessor—just at a slightly higher level. Every cycle of a computer's microprocessor is a resource for accomplishing tasks.

Many activities—called "processes"—compete for the attention of your computer's microprocessor. Commands are arriving from programs you're using, while input is arriving from the keyboard and mouse. At the same time, data must be sent to the display device or printer, and Web pages are arriving from your Internet connection. To manage all these competing processes, your computer's operating system must ensure that each one receives its share of microprocessor cycles.

Ideally, the operating system should be able to help the microprocessor switch tasks so that, from the user's vantage point, everything seems to be happening at the same time. The operating system also must ensure that the microprocessor doesn't "spin its wheels" waiting for input while it could be working on some other processing task.

Why does an operating system manage memory? A microprocessor works with data and executes instructions stored in RAM—one of your computer's most important resources. When you want to run more than one program at a time, the operating system has to allocate specific areas of memory for each program, as shown in Figure 3-12.

When multiple programs are running, the OS must ensure that instructions and data from one area of memory don't "leak" into an area allocated to another program. If an OS falls down on the job and fails to protect each program's memory area, data can get corrupted, programs can "crash," and your computer displays error messages, such as "General Protection Fault." Your PC can sometimes recover from memory leak problems if you use the Ctrl+Alt+Del key sequence to close the corrupted program.

FIGURE 3-12
The operating system allocates a specific area of RAM for each program that is open and running. The operating system is itself a program, so it requires RAM space, too.

RAM
- Operating system
- Document
- Word processing software
- Photo data
- Graphics software

How does the OS keep track of storage resources? Behind the scenes, an operating system acts as a filing clerk that stores and retrieves files from your disks and CDs. It remembers the names and locations of all your files and keeps track of empty spaces where new files can be stored. Chapter 4 explores file storage in more depth and explains how the operating system affects the way you create, name, save, and retrieve files.

Why does the operating system get involved with peripheral devices? Every device connected to a computer is regarded as a resource. Your computer's operating system communicates with device driver software so that data can travel smoothly between the computer and these peripheral resources. If a peripheral device or driver is not performing correctly, the operating system makes a decision about what to do—usually it displays an on-screen message to warn you of the problem.

Your computer's operating system ensures that input and output proceed in an orderly manner, using "buffers" to collect and hold data while the computer is busy with other tasks. By using a keyboard buffer, for example, your computer never misses one of your keystrokes, regardless of how fast you type or what else is happening in your computer system at the same time.

How does the operating system affect the user interface? A **user interface** can be defined as the combination of hardware and software that helps people and computers communicate with each other. Your computer's user interface includes a display device, mouse, and keyboard that allow you to view and manipulate your computing environment. It also includes software elements, such as menus and toolbar buttons. The operating system's user interface defines the "look and feel" for all its compatible software. For example, application software that runs under Windows uses a standard set of menus, buttons, and toolbars based on the operating system's user interface.

Most computers today feature a graphical user interface. Abbreviated "GUI" (sometimes pronounced as "gooey"), a **graphical user interface** provides a way to point and click a mouse to select menu options and manipulate graphical objects displayed on the screen. GUIs were originally conceived at the prestigious Xerox PARC research facility. In 1984, Apple Computer turned the idea into a commercial success with the launch of its popular Macintosh computer, which featured a GUI operating system and applications. Graphical user interfaces didn't really catch on in the PC market until 1992 when Windows 3.1 became standard issue on most PCs, replacing a **command-line interface** that required users to type memorized commands to run programs and accomplish tasks (Figure 3-13).

TERMINOLOGY NOTE

The term "buffer" is technical jargon for a region of memory that holds data waiting to be transferred from one device to another.

FIGURE 3-13

A graphical user interface (below left) features menus and icons that you can manipulate with the click of a mouse.

A command-line interface (below right) requires you to memorize and type commands.

COMPUTER SOFTWARE

Where is the operating system stored? In some computers—typically handhelds and videogame consoles—the entire operating system is small enough to be stored in ROM. For nearly all personal computers, servers, workstations, mainframes, and supercomputers, the operating system program is quite large, so most of it is stored on a hard disk. The operating system's small **bootstrap program** is stored in ROM and supplies the instructions needed to load the operating system's core into memory when the system boots. This core part of the operating system, called the **kernel**, provides the most essential operating system services, such as memory management and file access. The kernel stays in memory all the time your computer is on. Other parts of the operating system, such as customization utilities, are loaded into memory as they are needed.

Do I ever interact directly with the OS? Although its main purpose is to control what happens "behind the scenes" of a computer system, many operating systems provide helpful tools, called **utilities**, that you can use to control and customize your computer equipment and work environment. Utilities, like those listed below, are typically accessed by using a GUI, such as the familiar Windows desktop.

- **Launch programs.** When you start your computer, Windows displays graphical objects, such as icons, the Start button, and the Programs menu, which you can use to start programs.

- **Manage files.** Another useful utility, called Windows Explorer, allows you to view a list of files, move them to different storage devices, copy them, rename them, and delete them.

- **Get help.** Windows offers a Help system you can use to find out how various commands work.

- **Customize the user interface.** The Control Panel, accessible from the Start menu, provides utilities that help you customize your screen display and work environment.

- **Configure equipment.** The Control Panel also provides access to utilities that help you set up and configure your computer's hardware and peripheral devices (Figure 3-14).

FIGURE 3-14
Many Windows utilities can be accessed from the Control Panel. You'll find it by clicking the Start button. If it does not appear on the Start menu, click Settings and then Control Panel.

Are different operating systems needed for different computing tasks? One operating system might be better suited to some computing tasks than others. To provide clues to their strengths and weaknesses, operating systems are informally categorized and characterized using one or more of the following terms:

A **single-user operating system** expects to deal with one set of input devices—those that can be controlled by one user at a time. Operating systems for handheld computers and many personal computers fit into the single-user category. DOS is an example of a single-user operating system.

A **multiuser operating system** allows a single computer—often a mainframe—to deal with simultaneous input, output, and processing requests from many users. One of its most difficult responsibilities is to schedule all the processing requests that a centralized computer must perform. IBM's OS/390 is one of the most popular mainframe multiuser operating systems.

A **network operating system** (also referred to as a "server operating system") provides communications and routing services that allow computers to share data, programs, and peripheral devices. Novell NetWare, for example, is almost always referred to as a network operating system. The difference between network services and multiuser services can seem a little hazy—especially because operating systems such as UNIX, Linux, and Sun Microsystem's Solaris offer both. The main difference, however, is that multiuser operating systems schedule requests for processing on a centralized computer, whereas a network operating system simply routes data and programs to each user's local computer, where the actual processing takes place.

A **multitasking operating system** provides process and memory management services that allow two or more programs to run simultaneously. Most of today's operating systems, including the OS on your personal computer, offer multitasking services.

A **desktop operating system** is one that's designed for a personal computer—a desktop, notebook, or tablet computer. The computer you use at home, at school, or at work is most likely configured with a desktop operating system, such as Windows or Mac OS. Typically, these operating systems are designed to accommodate a single user, but might also provide networking capability. Today's desktop operating systems invariably provide multitasking capabilities.

Some operating system vendors characterize their products as "home" or "professional" versions. The home version usually has fewer network management tools than the professional version.

WINDOWS, MAC OS, UNIX, LINUX, AND DOS

What's the best-selling operating system? **Microsoft Windows** is installed on more than 80% of the world's personal computers. The number and variety of programs that run on Windows are unmatched by any other operating system, a fact that contributes to its dominant position as the most widely used desktop operating system. Since its introduction in 1985, Windows has evolved through several versions, listed in Figure 3-15.

FIGURE 3-15
Windows Timeline

2001 Windows XP
Featured an updated user interface, used the Windows 2000 32-bit kernel, and supported FAT32 and NTFS file systems.

2000 Windows Me
Featured enhanced multimedia utilities.

2000 Windows 2000
Billed as a "multipurpose network OS for businesses of all sizes" and featured enhanced Web services.

1998 Windows 98
The last Windows version to use the original Windows kernel that accesses DOS.

1995 Windows 95
Featured a revised user interface. Supported 32-bit processors, TCP/IP, dial-up networking, and long file names.

1993 Windows NT
Provided management and security tools for network servers and the NTFS file system.

1992 Windows for Workgroups
Provided peer-to-peer networking, e-mail, group scheduling, and file and printer sharing.

1992 Windows 3.1
Introduced program icons and the file folder metaphor.

1990 Windows 3.0
Introduced graphical controls.

1987 Windows 2.0
Introduced overlapping windows and expanded memory access.

1985 Windows 1.0
Divided the screen into "windows" that allowed users to work with several programs at the same time.

COMPUTER SOFTWARE

The first versions of Windows, including Windows 3.1, were sometimes referred to as "operating environments" rather than operating systems because they required DOS to supply the operating system kernel. Windows operating environments primarily supplied a point-and-click user interface, complete with graphical screen displays and mouse input. Windows operating environments evolved into today's comprehensive operating systems, that do not require the DOS kernel.

The Windows operating system gets its name from the rectangular work areas that appear on the screen-based desktop. Each work area (or "window") can display a different document or program, providing a visual model of the operating system's multitasking capabilities (Figure 3-16).

INFOWEBLINKS

You'll find lots of current information about Windows at the **Microsoft Windows InfoWeb**.

www.course.com/np/concepts8/ch03

FIGURE 3-16
If you find a Start button sporting the Windows logo in the lower-left corner of the screen, it is a good bet that the computer is running some version of Windows.

The graphical user interface for Windows NT, 98, 2000, and Me (shown at left) features many similarities and some cosmetic differences when compared to the interface for Windows XP (shown below).

- Icons represent computer hardware and software.
- When set for the classic menu style, the left side of the Start menu displays the Windows OS version in use.
- The Start button provides access to a menu of programs, documents, and utilities.
- The taskbar indicates which programs are running.
- Start menu
- Start button
- Icons
- Taskbar
- Programs run in separate windows.

Microsoft currently offers several types of operating systems. Home, Professional, and Workstation editions are designed for personal computers. Server editions are designed for LAN, Internet, and Web servers. Embedded editions are designed for handheld devices, such as PDAs and mobile phones. Figure 3-17 categorizes Windows offerings.

FIGURE 3-17
Microsoft offers several versions of Windows, designed for different computing tasks and equipment.

Personal Computers

Windows XP Home Edition
Windows XP Professional
Windows XP Tablet PC Edition
Windows 2000 Professional
Windows NT Workstation
Windows Me
Windows 98
Windows 95
Windows 3.1

LAN, Internet, and Web Servers

Windows Server 2005
Windows Server 2003
Windows 2000 Server
Windows NT Server

PDAs, Mobile Phones, and Non-personal Computer Devices

Windows Mobile OS
Pocket PC OS 2002
Pocket PC OS 2000
Windows CE
Windows XP Embedded

Is Mac OS similar to Windows? Although **Mac OS** was developed several years before Windows, both operating systems base their user interfaces on the graphical model pioneered at Xerox PARC. Like Windows, Mac OS has been through a number of revisions, including OS X "Tiger" (X meaning version 10), released in 2004.

A quick comparison of Figures 3-16 and 3-18 shows that both Mac and Windows interfaces use a mouse to point and click various icons and menus. Both interfaces feature rectangular work areas to reflect multitasking capabilities. Both operating systems provide basic networking services. A decent collection of software is available for computers that run Mac OS, although the selection is not as vast as the Windows collection. Many of the most prolific software publishers produce one version of their software for Windows and another, similar version for Mac OS.

INFOWEBLINKS

The **Apple InfoWeb** links you to the official site for Apple Computer, Inc.

www.course.com/np/concepts8/ch03

FIGURE 3-18
The Apple logo at the top of the screen is your clue that a computer is running Mac OS.

- The Apple logo provides access to a menu.
- Two different programs can run in two separate windows.
- Menus and other on-screen objects are manipulated by using a mouse.
- Icons represent computer hardware components and software.

COMPUTER SOFTWARE   **129**

Are UNIX and Linux the same? The **UNIX** operating system was developed in 1969 at AT&T's Bell Labs. It gained a good reputation for its dependability in multiuser environments, and many versions of it became available for mainframes and microcomputers. In 1991, a young Finnish student named Linus Torvalds developed the **Linux** (pronounced LIH nucks) operating system. Linux was inspired by and loosely based on a UNIX deriviative called MINIX, created by Andrew Tanenbaum.

Linux is rather unique because it is distributed along with its source code under the terms of a General Public License (GPL), which allows everyone to make copies for their own use, to give to others, or to sell. This licensing policy has encouraged programmers to develop Linux utilities, software, and enhancements. Linux is primarily distributed over the Web.

Although Linux is designed for microcomputers, it shares several technical features with UNIX, such as multitasking, virtual memory, TCP/IP drivers, and multiuser capabilities. These features make Linux a popular operating system for e-mail and Web servers as well as for local area networks. Linux has been gaining popularity as a desktop operating system, and some new personal computers now come configured with Linux instead of Windows or Mac OS. Linux typically requires a bit more tinkering than the Windows and Mac desktop operating systems. The comparatively limited number of programs that run under Linux also discourages many nontechnical users from selecting it as the OS for their desktop and notebook computers.

Several Web sites offer a Linux "distribution," which is a package that contains the Linux kernel, system utilities, applications, and an installation routine. Beginner-friendly Linux distributions include Mandrakelinux, Linspire, College Linux, and Xandros Desktop. Most of these distributions include a GUI module that provides a user interface similar to the one pictured in Figure 3-19.

INFOWEBLINKS

If you're interested in exploring the world of "open source" operating systems, start your journey at the **Linux InfoWeb**.

www.course.com/np/concepts8/ch03

FIGURE 3-19

Linux users can choose from several graphical interfaces. Pictured here is the popular KDE graphical desktop.

- Desktop icons look similar to those on the Windows and Macintosh desktops.
- Two different programs can run in two separate windows.
- A horizontal option bar combines features of the Windows Start menu, Control Panel, and taskbar.

Why do I keep hearing about DOS? Old-timers in the computer industry sometimes reminisce about DOS. It was the first operating system that many of them used, and its cryptic command-line user interface left an indelible impression. **DOS** (which rhymes with "toss") stands for Disk Operating System. It was developed by Microsoft—the same company that later produced Windows—and introduced on the original IBM PC in 1982. Although IBM called this operating system PC-DOS, Microsoft marketed it to other companies under the name MS-DOS.

After more than 20 years, remnants of DOS still linger in the world of personal computers because it provides part of the operating system kernel for Windows versions 3.1, 95, 98, and Me. Users rarely interact with DOS, however, because it is well hidden by the Windows graphical user interface.

During the peak of its popularity, thousands of software programs were produced for computers running DOS. You can occasionally find some of these programs on the Internet, and run them using the MS-DOS Prompt option (Windows 98, Me, NT, and 2000) or the Command Prompt option (Windows XP) on the Windows Start menu. DOS programs look rather unsophisticated by today's standards, so for most of us, DOS and DOS software are nothing more than footnotes in the history of the computer industry.

HANDHELD AND TABLET OPERATING SYSTEMS

What are the options for handheld operating systems? Two operating systems dominate the realm of handheld computers: Palm OS and Windows Mobile OS, shown in Figure 3-20.

INFOWEBLINKS

If you want to find out more about this venerable operating system, connect to the **DOS InfoWeb**.

www.course.com/np/concepts8/ch03

FIGURE 3-20
Palm OS (left) and Windows Mobile OS (right) are two popular PDA operating systems.

Palm OS is produced by PalmSource, a spinoff of the company that produced some of the first commercially successful PDAs. Palm OS is currently used for popular PDAs such as palmOne Zire and Sony CLIE. It also powers Fossil's wristwatch PDA and smartphones from manufacturers such as palmOne, Samsung, and Kyocera.

Windows Mobile OS is an operating system built on the Microsoft Windows CE technology. As a cousin to Windows XP, Windows Mobile OS sports some features similar to those found on the Windows desktop. Windows Mobile OS is the operating system for a variety of PDAs, phone-enabled PDAs, and smartphones.

COMPUTER SOFTWARE

Are operating systems for handheld devices similar to desktop operating systems? Operating systems for handheld and desktop devices provide many similar services, such as scheduling processor resources, managing memory, loading programs, managing input and output, and establishing the user interface. But because handheld devices tend to be used for less sophisticated tasks, their operating systems are somewhat simpler and significantly smaller.

By keeping the operating system small, it can be stored in ROM. Without the need to load the OS from disk into RAM, a handheld device's operating system is ready almost instantly when the unit is turned on. Operating systems for handheld devices provide built-in support for touch screens, handwriting input, wireless networking, and cellular communications.

What about operating systems for tablet computers? Windows XP Tablet Edition is the operating system supplied with just about every tablet computer. Its main feature is handwriting recognition, which accepts printed input from the touch-sensitive screen and then converts it into ASCII text, as shown in Figure 3-21.

FIGURE 3-21
Handwriting recognition is one of the main services a tablet computer OS provides.

QUICKCHECK......SECTION B

1. An operating system manages a computer's [_____], such as RAM, storage space, and peripherals.

2. To run more than one program at a time, the operating system must allocate specific areas of [_____] for each program.

3. A graphical [_____] interface provides a way to point and click a mouse to select menu options and manipulate objects that appear on the screen.

4. ROM contains a(n) [_____] program that supplies instructions for loading key parts of the operating system when the computer starts.

5. The core part of an operating system is called its [_____].

6. A desktop operating system, such as Windows, is designed for personal computers. True or false? [_____]

7. Handheld devices, such as PDAs and smartphones typically feature multiuser operating systems. True or false? [_____]

CHECK ANSWERS

LAB 3-B
USING THE WINDOWS INTERFACE

In this lab, you'll learn:

- Why the standard Windows controls make it easy to learn new Windows software
- What happens when you use the mouse pointer to click, double-click, and right-click an object
- How ToolTips or ScreenTips help you identify icons and toolbar buttons
- How to use the Maximize, Minimize, Restore, and Close buttons
- How to use scroll bars
- How to navigate through a series of menus
- Which menus are common to most Windows applications
- The meaning of menu conventions, such as the ellipsis and triangle
- How to use standard dialog box controls, such as option buttons, spin boxes, tabs, check boxes, and lists
- How to use toolbar buttons
- How to adjust toolbars
- How to take a screenshot and print it

INTERACTIVE LAB

CLICK TO START THE LAB

LAB ASSIGNMENTS

1. Start the interactive part of the lab. Insert your Tracking Disk if you want to save your QuickCheck results. Perform each lab step as directed, and answer all the lab QuickCheck questions. When you exit the lab, your answers are automatically graded and your results are displayed.

2. Draw a sketch or print a screenshot of the Windows desktop on any computer you use. Use ToolTips (or ScreenTips) to identify all the icons on the desktop and the taskbar.

3. Use the Start button and Accessories menu to start an application program called Paint. (If Paint is not installed on your computer, you can use any application software, such as a word processing program.) Draw a sketch or print a screenshot of the Paint (or other application) window and label the following components: window title, title bar, Maximize/Restore button, Minimize button, Close button, menu bar, toolbar, and scroll bar.

4. Look at each of the menu options the Paint software (or other application) provides. Make a list of those that seem to be standard Windows menu options.

5. Draw a sketch of Paint's Print dialog box (or other application's Print dialog box). Label the following parts: buttons, spin bar, pull-down list, option button, and check boxes.

COMPUTER SOFTWARE

SECTION C
APPLICATION SOFTWARE

Most computers include some basic word processing, e-mail, and Internet access software, but computer owners invariably want additional software to increase their computers' repertory of productivity, business, learning, or entertainment activities. Section C provides an overview of the vast array of application software that's available for personal computers.

DOCUMENT PRODUCTION SOFTWARE

How can my computer help me with my writing? Whether you are writing a 10-page paper, writing software documentation, designing a brochure for your new startup company, or laying out the school newspaper, you will probably use some form of **document production software**. This software assists you with composing, editing, designing, printing, and electronically publishing documents. The three most popular types of document production software are word processing, desktop publishing, and Web authoring (Figure 3-22).

Word processing software, such as Microsoft Word, has replaced typewriters for producing documents such as reports, letters, memos, papers, and manuscripts. Word processing software gives you the ability to create, spell-check, edit, and format a document on the screen before you commit it to paper.

Desktop publishing software (abbreviated DTP) takes word processing software one step further by helping you use graphic design techniques to enhance the format and appearance of a document. Although today's word processing software offers many page layout and design features, DTP software products, such as QuarkXPress and Adobe PageMaker, have sophisticated features to help you produce professional-quality output for newspapers, newsletters, brochures, magazines, and books.

Web authoring software helps you design and develop customized Web pages that you can publish electronically on the Internet. Only a few years ago, creating Web pages was a fairly technical task that required authors to insert special formatting HTML tags, such as <a href="contents.htm">. Now Web authoring software products, such as Microsoft FrontPage and Macromedia Dreamweaver, help nontechnical Web authors by providing easy-to-use tools for composing the text for a Web page, assembling graphical elements, and automatically generating HTML tags.

How does document production software help me turn my ideas into sentences and paragraphs? Document production software makes it easy to let your ideas flow because it automatically handles many tasks that might otherwise distract you. For example, you don't need to worry about fitting words within the margins. A feature called "word wrap" determines how your text will flow from line to line by automatically moving words down to the next line as you reach the right margin. Imagine that the sentences in your document are ribbons of text; word wrap bends the ribbons. Changing the margin size just means bending the ribbon in different

FIGURE 3-22
Popular document production software includes Microsoft Word, QuarkXPress, and Macromedia Dreamweaver.

INFOWEBLINKS

This InfoWeb is your guide to today's best-selling **Document Production Software**.

www.course.com/np/concepts8/ch03

places. Even after you type an entire document, adjusting the size of your right, left, top, and bottom margins is simple (Figure 3-23).

FIGURE 3-23
Document production software makes it easy to get your ideas down on your screen-based "paper." Start the video to see word wrap and the spelling checker in action.

CLICK TO START

Document production software automatically tries to fit your text within the margins using word wrap.

As you type, the spelling checker compares your words with a list of correctly spelled words. Words not included in the list are marked with a wavy line as possible misspellings.

What if I'm a bad speller? Most document production software includes a **spelling checker** that marks misspelled words in a document. You can easily correct a misspelled word as you type, or you can run the spelling checker when you finish entering all the text. Some software even has an autocorrecting capability that automatically changes a typo, such as "teh," to the correct spelling ("the").

Although your software's spelling checker helps you correct misspellings, it cannot guarantee an error-free document. A spelling checker works by comparing each word from your document to a list of correctly spelled words that is stored in a data file called a **spelling dictionary**. If the word from your document is in the dictionary, the spelling checker considers the word correctly spelled. If the word is not in the dictionary, the word is counted as misspelled. Sounds okay, right? But suppose your document contains a reference to the city of "Negaunee." This word is not in the dictionary, so the spelling checker considers it misspelled, even though it is spelled correctly. Proper nouns and scientific, medical, and technical words are likely to be flagged as misspelled, even if you spell them correctly, because they do not appear in the spelling checker's dictionary.

Now suppose that your document contains the phrase "a pear of shoes." Although you meant to use "pair" rather than "pear," the spelling checker will not catch your mistake because "pear" is a valid word in the dictionary. Your spelling checker won't help if you have trouble deciding whether to use "there" or "their," "its" or "it's," or "too" or "to." Remember, then, that a spelling checker cannot substitute for a thorough proofread.

Can document production software improve my writing? Because word processing software tends to focus on the writing process, it offers several features that can improve the quality of your writing. These features may not be available in desktop publishing software or Web authoring software, which focus on the format of a document.

COMPUTER SOFTWARE   135

Your word processing software is likely to include a **thesaurus**, which can help you find a synonym for a word so that you can make your writing more varied and interesting. A **grammar checker** "reads" through your document and points out potential grammatical trouble spots, such as incomplete sentences, run-on sentences, and verbs that don't agree with nouns.

Your word processing software might also be able to analyze the reading level of your document using a standard **readability formula**, such as the Flesch-Kincaid reading level. You can use this analysis to find out if your writing matches your target audience, based on sentence length and vocabulary.

Can document production software help me break bad writing habits? Most word processing, DTP, and Web authoring software includes a **Search and Replace** feature. You can use this feature to hunt down mistakes that you typically make in your writing. For example, you might know from experience that you tend to overuse the word "typically." You can use Search and Replace to find each occurrence of "typically," and then you can decide whether you should substitute a different word, such as "usually" or "ordinarily."

How do I get my documents to look good? The **format** for a document refers to the way that all the elements of a document—text, pictures, titles, and page numbers—are arranged on the page. The final format of your document depends on how and where you intend to use it. A school paper, for example, simply needs to be printed in standard paragraph format—perhaps double spaced and with numbered pages. Your word processing software has all the features you need for this formatting task. A brochure, newsletter, or corporate report, on the other hand, might require more ambitious formatting, such as columns that continue on noncontiguous pages and text labels that overlay graphics. You might consider transferring your document from your word processing software to your desktop publishing software for access to more sophisticated formatting tools. For documents that you plan to publish on the Web, Web authoring software usually provides the most useful set of formatting tools.

The "look" of your final document depends on several formatting factors, such as font style, paragraph style, and page layout. A **font** is a set of letters that share a unified design. Font size is measured as **point size**, abbreviated pt. (One point is about 1/72 of an inch.) Figure 3-24 illustrates several popular fonts included with document production software.

INFOWEBLINKS

You can add to your font collection by downloading font files from the **Font InfoWeb**.

www.course.com/np/concepts8/ch03

Times New Roman Font	8 pt.
Times New Roman Font	10 pt.
Times New Roman Font	12 pt.
Times New Roman Font	16 pt.
Times New Roman Font	**16 pt. Bold**
Times New Roman Font	16 pt. Green
Arial Font	16 pt.
Comic Sans MS	16 pt.
Georgia Font	**16 pt. Bold Gold**
Dotto	24 pt. Orange

FIGURE 3-24

You can vary the font style by selecting character formatting attributes, such as bold, italics, underline, superscript, and subscript. You can also select a color and size for a font. The font size for the text in a typical paragraph is set at 8, 10, or 12 pt. Titles can be as large as 72 pt.

Paragraph style includes the alignment of text within the margins and the space between each line of text. **Paragraph alignment** refers to the horizontal position of text—whether it is aligned at the left margin, aligned at the right margin, or **fully justified** so that the text is aligned evenly on both the right and left margins. Your document will look more formal if it is fully justified, like the text in this paragraph, than if it has an uneven or "ragged" right margin. **Line spacing** (also called **leading**, pronounced "LED ing") refers to the vertical spacing between lines. Documents are typically single spaced or double spaced, but word processing and DTP software allow you to adjust line spacing in 1 pt. increments.

Instead of individually selecting font and paragraph style elements, document production software typically allows you to define a **style** that lets you apply several font and paragraph elements with a single click (Figure 3-25). For example, instead of applying bold to a title, changing its font to Times New Roman, and then adjusting the font size to 24 pt., you can simply define a Title style as 24 pt., Times New Roman, bold. You can then apply all three style elements at once simply by selecting the Title style.

FIGURE 3-25
By defining a style, you can apply multiple font attributes with a single click.

CLICK TO START

Page layout refers to the physical position of each element on a page. In addition to paragraphs of text, these elements might include:

- **Headers and footers.** A **header** is text that you specify to automatically appear in the top margin of every page. A **footer** is text that you specify to automatically appear in the bottom margin of every page. You might put your name and the document title in the header or footer of a document so that its printed pages won't get mixed up with those of another printed document.

- **Page numbers.** Word processing and DTP software automatically number the pages of a document according to your specifications, usually placing the page number within a header or footer. A Web page, no matter what its length, is all a single page, so Web authoring software typically doesn't provide page numbering.

COMPUTER SOFTWARE

- **Graphical elements.** Photos, diagrams, graphs, and charts can be incorporated in your documents. **Clip art**—a collection of drawings and photos designed to be inserted in documents—is a popular source of graphical elements.

- **Tables.** A **table** is a grid-like structure that can hold text or pictures. For printed documents, tables are a popular way to produce easy-to-read columns of data and to position graphics. It may sound surprising, but for Web pages, tables provide one of the few ways to precisely position text and pictures. As a result, Web page designers make extensive and very creative use of tables.

Most word processing is page-oriented because it treats each page as a rectangle that can be filled with text and graphics. Text automatically flows from one page to the next. In contrast, most DTP software is frame-oriented because it allows you to divide each page into several rectangular-shaped **frames** that you can fill with text or graphics. Text flows from one frame to the next, rather than from page to page (Figure 3-26).

FIGURE 3-26

Frames give you exact control over the position of elements on a page, such as a figure and a caption on top of it.

CLICK TO START

Attack on Everest
by Janell Chalmers

Mountain climbing was once the domain of professional explorers, whose bodies and minds were honed to a long assault against weather, ice, and rock.

Wrapping text around a frame adds interest to the layout.

Tenzing Norkay, reached the summit. Hillary was knighted for this accomplishment.

Sir Edmund Hillary would be amazed to discover that today Mount Everest has become something of a tourist destination. Guided "adventure" tours head toward the summit like cruise ships plying

"Because it's there."
George Mallory

Caribbean ports. This $65,000 trek is not without risk. In 1996 a sudden storm killed eight climbers.

Back in 1923, British mountaineer George Mallory was asked, why climb Everest? His reply, "Because it's there." A new answer to this question, "Because we can" may be largely attributable to new high-tech mountain gear. Nylon, polypropylene and Gore-Tex clothing provide light, yet warm protection from the elements. New high-tech ultraviolet lenses protect eyes from dangerous "snowblindness."

An other gear makes the mountain seem less

One frame holds the centered title and author's byline. This text is linked to the text in subsequent frames.

"Guide lines" that do not appear on printouts help align text and graphical elements.

Text can link to frames on the next page or on any page of the document.

Does document production software increase productivity? Word processing software, in particular, provides several features that automate tasks and allow you to work more productively. For example, suppose that you want to send prospective employers a letter and your resume. Instead of composing and addressing each letter individually, your software can perform a **mail merge** that automatically creates personalized letters by combining the information in a mailing list with a form letter. Some additional capabilities of word processing software include:

- Automatically generating a table of contents and an index for a document

- Automatically numbering footnotes and positioning each footnote on the page where it is referenced

- Providing document templates and document wizards that show you the correct content and format for a variety of documents, such as business letters, fax cover sheets, and memos

- Exporting a document into HTML format

SPREADSHEET SOFTWARE

What is a spreadsheet? A **spreadsheet** uses rows and columns of numbers to create a model or representation of a real situation. For example, your checkbook register is a type of spreadsheet because it is a numerical representation of the cash flowing in and out of your bank account. Today, **spreadsheet software**, such as Microsoft Excel, provides tools to create electronic spreadsheets. It is similar to a "smart" piece of paper that automatically adds up the columns of numbers you write on it. You can use it to make other calculations, too, based on simple equations that you write or more complex, built-in formulas. As an added bonus, spreadsheet software helps you turn your data into a variety of colorful graphs. It also includes special data-handling features that allow you to sort data, search for data that meets specific criteria, and print reports.

Spreadsheet software was initially popular with accountants and financial managers who dealt with paper-based spreadsheets, but found the electronic version far easier to use and less prone to errors than manual calculations. Other people soon discovered the benefits of spreadsheets for projects that require repetitive calculations—budgeting, maintaining a grade book, balancing a checkbook, tracking investments, calculating loan payments, and estimating project costs.

Because it is so easy to experiment with different numbers, spreadsheet software is particularly useful for **what-if analysis**. You can use what-if analyses to answer questions such as "What if I get an A on my next two economics exams? But what if I get only Bs?" "What if I invest $100 a month in my retirement plan? But what if I invest $200 a month?"

What does a computerized spreadsheet look like? You use spreadsheet software to create an on-screen **worksheet**. A worksheet is based on a grid of columns and rows. Each **cell** in the grid can contain a value, label, or formula. A **value** is a number that you want to use in a calculation. A **label** is any text used to describe data. For example, suppose that your worksheet contains the value $486,000. You could use a label to identify this number as "Income" (Figure 3-27).

INFOWEBLINKS

For links to today's best-selling spreadsheet software, connect to the **Spreadsheet InfoWeb**.

www.course.com/np/concepts8/ch03

FIGURE 3-27
In a worksheet, each column is lettered and each row is numbered. The intersection of a column and row is called a cell. Each cell has a unique cell reference, or "address," derived from its column and row location. For example, A1 is the cell reference for the upper-left cell in a worksheet because it is in column A and row 1. You can select any cell and make it the active cell by clicking it. Once a cell is active, you can enter data into it.

COMPUTER SOFTWARE   139

You can format the labels and values on a worksheet in much the same way as you would format text in a word processing document. You can change fonts and font size, select a font color, and select font styles, such as bold, italic, and underline.

How does spreadsheet software work? The values contained in a cell can be manipulated by formulas placed in other cells. A **formula** works behind the scenes to tell the computer how to use the contents of cells in calculations. You can enter a simple formula in a cell to add, subtract, multiply, or divide numbers. More complex formulas can be designed to perform just about any calculation you can imagine. Figure 3-28 illustrates how a formula might be used in a simple spreadsheet to calculate savings.

FIGURE 3-28
When a cell contains a formula, it displays the result of the formula rather than the formula itself. To view and edit the formula, you use the Formula bar.

You can think of the formula as working "behind the scenes" to perform calculations and then display the result.

CLICK TO START

FIGURE 3-29
Functions are special formulas provided by spreadsheet software.

A formula, such as =D4-D5+((D8/B2)*110), can contain **cell references** (like D4 and D5), numbers (like 110), and **mathematical operators**, such as the multiplication symbol (*), the division symbol (/), the addition symbol, and the subtraction symbol. Parts of a formula can be enclosed in parentheses to indicate the order in which the mathematical operations should be performed. The operation in the innermost set of parentheses—in this case, (D8/B2)— should be performed first.

You can enter a formula "from scratch" by typing it into a cell, or you can use a built-in **function** provided by the spreadsheet software. To use a function, you simply select one from a list, as shown in Figure 3-29, and then indicate the cell references of any values you want to include in the calculation.

What happens when I modify a worksheet? When you change the contents of any cell in a worksheet, all the formulas are recalculated. This **automatic recalculation** feature ensures that the results in every cell are accurate for the information currently entered in the worksheet.

Your worksheet is also automatically updated to reflect any rows or columns that you add, delete, or copy within the worksheet. Unless you specify otherwise, a cell reference is a **relative reference**—that is, a reference that can change from B4 to B3, for example, if row 3 is deleted and all the data moves up one row.

If you don't want a cell reference to change, you can use an absolute reference. An **absolute reference** never changes when you insert rows or copy or move formulas. Understanding when to use absolute references is one of the key aspects of developing spreadsheet design expertise. Figure 3-30 and its associated tour provide additional information about relative and absolute references.

FIGURE 3-30

As shown in the examples, relative references within a formula can change when you change the sequence of a worksheet's rows and columns.

An absolute reference is "anchored" so that it always refers to a specific cell.

CLICK TO START

How will I know which formulas and functions to use when I create a worksheet? To create an effective and accurate worksheet, you typically must understand the calculations and formulas that are involved. If, for example, you want to create a worksheet that helps you calculate your final grade in a course, you need to know the grading scale and understand how your instructor plans to weight each assignment and test.

Most spreadsheet software includes a few templates or wizards for pre-designed worksheets, such as invoices, income-expense reports, balance sheets, and loan payment schedules. Additional templates are available on the Web. These templates are typically designed by professionals and contain all the necessary labels and formulas. To use a template, you simply plug in the values for your calculation.

COMPUTER SOFTWARE

141

"NUMBER CRUNCHING" SOFTWARE

Aside from spreadsheets, what other "number crunching" software is available? Spreadsheet software provides a sort of "blank canvas" on which you can create numeric models by simply "painting" values, labels, and formulas. The advantage of spreadsheet software is the flexibility it provides—flexibility to create customized calculations according to your exact specifications. The disadvantage of spreadsheet software is that—aside from a few predesigned templates—you are responsible for entering formulas and selecting functions for calculations. If you don't know the formulas or don't understand the functions, you're out of luck.

In contrast to the "blank canvas" approach provided by spreadsheet software, other "number crunching" software works more like "paint by numbers." It provides a structured environment dedicated to a particular number crunching task, such as statistical analysis, mathematical modeling, or money management.

Statistical software helps you analyze large sets of data to discover relationships and patterns. Products such as SPSS and Statsoft STATISTICA are helpful tools for summarizing survey results, test scores, experiment results, or population data. Most statistical software includes graphing capability so that you can display and explore your data visually.

Mathematical modeling software provides tools for solving a wide range of math, science, and engineering problems. Students, teachers, mathematicians, and engineers, in particular, appreciate how products such as Mathcad and Mathematica help them recognize patterns that can be difficult to identify in columns of numbers (Figure 3-31).

> **INFOWEBLINKS**
>
> For more information about popular "number crunching" software, take a look at the **Numeric Software InfoWeb**.
>
> www.course.com/np/concepts8/ch03

FIGURE 3-31
Mathematical modeling software helps you visualize the product of complex formulas. Here the points from a sphere are graphed onto a plane, to demonstrate the principles behind the Astronomical Clock of Prague.

Money management software offers a variety of tools for tracking monetary transactions and investments. In this software category, **personal finance software**, such as Microsoft Money and Intuit Quicken, is designed to keep records of income, expenses, assets, and liabilities using a simple checkbook-like user interface. This software also automates routine financial tasks, such as budgeting, investing, check writing, and bill paying. Many personal financial software products provide direct links to online banking services, so you can use them to check account balances, transfer funds, and pay bills.

Personal financial software produces reports and graphs that show you where your money goes. For example, you can analyze various aspects of your cash flow, such as how much you spent on entertainment last month and how that compares to the previous month.

Tax preparation software is a specialized type of personal finance software designed to help you gather your annual income and expense data, identify deductions, and calculate tax payments. Popular products, such as Intuit TurboTax, even accept data directly from personal finance software to eliminate hours of tedious data entry.

DATABASE SOFTWARE

What is a database? The term "database" has evolved from a specialized technical term into a part of our everyday vocabulary. In the context of modern usage, a **database** is simply a collection of data that is stored on one or more computers. A database can contain any sort of data, such as a university's student records, a library's card catalog, a store's inventory, an individual's address book, or a utility company's customers. Databases can be stored on personal computers, LAN servers, Web servers, mainframes, and even handheld computers.

What is database software? **Database software** helps you enter, find, organize, update, and report information stored in a database. Microsoft Access, FileMaker Pro, and askSam are three of the most popular examples of database software for personal computers. Oracle and MySQL are popular server database software packages. For PDAs, popular choices include HanDBase, Mobile DB, dBNow, and JFile.

How does a database store data? Database software stores data as a series of records, which are composed of fields that hold data. A **record** holds data for a single entity—a person, place, thing, or event. A **field** holds one item of data relevant to a record. You can envision a record as a Rolodex or index card and a series of records as a table (Figure 3-32).

INFOWEBLINKS

For more information about popular database software, connect to the **Database Software InfoWeb**.

www.course.com/np/concepts8/ch03

TERMINOLOGY NOTE

Database software is also referred to as database management software (DBMS).

FIGURE 3-32

A single database record is similar to a Rolodex or an index card. A series of records is usually depicted in table format.

Song Title	Performer	Composer	CD	Date	Record Label	Length
Seven Years	Norah Jones	Lee Alexander	Come Away with Me	02/01/2002	Blue Note	2:24
Shoot the Moon	Norah Jones	Jesse Harris	Come Away with Me	02/01/2002	Blue Note	3:57
Summertime	Janis Joplin	George Gershwin	Greatest Hits	08/31/1999	Sony	3.28
Summertime	Sarah Vaughan	George Gershwin	Compact Jazz	06/22/1987	Polygram	4:34

Database software provides tools to work with more than one collection of records, as long as the records are somehow related to each other. For example, MTV might maintain a database pertaining to jazz music. One series of database records might contain data about jazz songs. It could contain fields such as those shown in Figure 3-32. Another series of records might contain biographical data about jazz performers, including name, birth date, and home town. It might even include a field for the performer's photo.

COMPUTER SOFTWARE

These two sets of records can be related by the name of the performing artist, as shown in Figure 3-33.

JAZZ PERFORMERS

Performer	Birth Date	Home Town
Ella Fitzgerald	04/25/1918	Newport News, VA
Norah Jones	03/30/1979	New York, NY
Billie Holiday	04/07/1915	Baltimore, MD
Lena Horne	06/17/1917	Brooklyn, NY

JAZZ SONGS

Song Title	Performer	Composer	CD	Date	Record Label	Length
Seven Years	Norah Jones	Lee Alexander	Come Away with Me	02/01/2002	Blue Note	2:24
Shoot the Moon	Norah Jones	Jesse Harris	Come Away with Me	02/01/2002	Blue Note	3:57
Summertime	Janis Joplin	George Gershwin	Greatest Hits	08/31/1999	Sony	3.28
Summertime	Sarah Vaughan	George Gershwin	Compact Jazz	06/22/1987	Polygram	4:34

FIGURE 3-33
The two sets of records are related by the Performer field. The relationship allows you to select Norah Jones from the Jazz Performers records and jump to any records in the Jazz Songs records that Norah Jones performed.

How do I create records? Database software provides the tools you need to define fields for a series of records. Figure 3-34 shows a simple form you might use to specify the fields for a database.

1. Enter field names.
2. Specify the type of data the field will hold.
3. Provide an explanation of the field's contents.
4. Enter additional specifications for the field.

FIGURE 3-34
Database software provides tools for specifying fields for a series of records.

CLICK TO START

When can I enter data? After you've defined fields for a series of records, you can enter the data for each record. Your database software provides a simple-to-use data entry form that allows you to easily fill in the data for each field. Instead of typing data into a database, you can also import data from a commercial database, such as a customer mailing list—you can even download databases from the Web, and then import the data into fields you have defined with your database software.

How do I locate specific data? Many databases contain hundreds or thousands of records. If you want to find a particular record or a group of records, scrolling through every record is much too cumbersome. Instead, you can enter a query, and the computer will quickly locate the records you seek.

Most database software provides one or more methods for making queries. A **query language**, such as SQL (Structured Query Language), provides a set of commands for locating and manipulating data. To locate all performances of *Summertime* before 1990 from a Jazz Songs database, you might enter a query such as:

Select * from JazzSongs where SongTitle = 'Summertime' and Date < '1990'

In addition to a formal query language, some database software provides **natural language query** capabilities. To make such queries, you don't have to learn an esoteric query language. Instead, you can simply enter questions, such as:

Who performed Summertime before 1990?

As an alternative to a query language or a natural language query, your database software might allow you to **query by example** (QBE), simply by filling out a form with the type of data you want to locate. Figure 3-35 illustrates a query by example for *Summertime* performances before 1990.

> **TERMINOLOGY NOTE**
>
> You encountered the term "query" in Chapter 1 in the context of search engines, which allow you to search through a database of information pertaining to the content of Web pages.
>
> A query is a set of keywords and operators that describe information you want to find.

FIGURE 3-35
When you query by example, your database software displays a blank form on the screen, and you enter examples of the data that you want to find.

How can I use search results? Your database software can typically help you print reports, export data to other programs (such as to a spreadsheet where you can graph the data), convert the data to other formats (such as HTML so that you can post the data on the Web), and transmit data to other computers.

Whether you print, import, copy, save, or transmit the data you find in databases, it is your responsibility to use it appropriately. Never introduce inaccurate information into a database. Respect copyrights, giving credit to the person or organization that compiled the data. You should also respect the privacy of the people who are the subject of the data. Unless you have permission to do so, do not divulge names, social security numbers, or other identifying information that might compromise someone's privacy.

GRAPHICS SOFTWARE

What kind of software do I need to work with drawings, photos, and other pictures? In computer lingo, the term **graphics** refers to any picture, drawing, sketch, photograph, image, or icon that appears on your computer screen. **Graphics software** is designed to help you create, manipulate, and print graphics. Some graphics software products specialize in a particular type of graphic, while others allow you to work with multiple graphics formats. If you are really interested in working with graphics, you will undoubtedly end up using more than one graphics software product.

Paint software (sometimes called "image editing software") provides a set of electronic pens, brushes, and paints for painting images on the screen. A simple program called Microsoft Paint is included with Windows. More sophisticated paint software products include JASC Paint Shop Pro and Procreate Painter. Many graphic artists, Web page designers, and illustrators use paint software as their primary computer-based graphics tool.

Photo editing software, such as Adobe Photoshop, includes features specially designed to fix poor-quality photos by modifying contrast and brightness, cropping out unwanted objects, and removing "red eye." Photos can also be edited using paint software, but photo editing software typically offers tools and wizards that simplify common photo editing tasks.

Drawing software provides a set of lines, shapes, and colors that can be assembled into diagrams, corporate logos, and schematics. The drawings created with tools such as Adobe Illustrator and Macromedia Freehand tend to have a "flat" cartoon-like quality, but they are very easy to modify, and look good at just about any size. Figure 3-36 illustrates a typical set of tools provided by drawing software.

FIGURE 3-36
Drawing software provides tools for manipulating graphics.

3-D graphics software provides a set of tools for creating "wireframes" that represent three-dimensional objects. A wireframe acts much like the framework for a pop-up tent. Just as you would construct the framework for the tent and then cover it with a nylon tent cover, 3-D graphics software can cover a wireframe object with surface texture and color to create a graphic of a 3-D object (Figure 3-37 on the next page).

FIGURE 3-37

3-D graphics software provides tools for creating a wireframe that represents a 3-D object.

Some 3-D software specializes in engineering-style graphics, while other 3-D software specializes in figures.

CAD software (computer-aided design software) is a special type of 3-D graphics software designed for architects and engineers who use computers to create blueprints and product specifications. AutoCAD is one of the best-selling professional CAD products. TurboCAD is a low-cost favorite. Scaled-down versions of professional CAD software provide simplified tools for homeowners who want to redesign their kitchens, examine new landscaping options, or experiment with floor plans.

Presentation software supplies the tools you need for combining text, photos, clip art, graphs, animations, and sound into a series of electronic slides, like those in Figure 3-38. You can display electronic slides on a color monitor for a one-on-one presentation or use a computer projection device for group presentations. You can also output the presentation as overhead transparencies, paper copies, or 35 mm slides. Popular presentation software products include Microsoft PowerPoint and Harvard Graphics.

FIGURE 3-38

A computer-based presentation consists of a series of slides, created with presentation software.

CLICK TO START

COMPUTER SOFTWARE

MUSIC SOFTWARE

Why would I need music software? You don't have to be a musician or composer to have a use for music software. Many types of music software are available. You might be surprised to find how many of them come in handy.

It is possible—and easy—to make your own digital voice and music recordings, which you store on your computer's hard disk. Windows and Mac OS operating system utilities usually supply the necessary **audio editing software**—Sound Recorder on PCs (Figure 3-39) and iTunes on Macs.

FIGURE 3-39
Audio editing software, such as Sound Recorder, provides controls much like those on a tape recorder. Menus offer additional digital editing features, such as speed control, volume adjustments, clipping, and mixing.

Audio editing software typically includes playback as well as recording capabilities. A specialized version of this software called karaoke software integrates music files and on-screen lyrics—everything you need to sing along with your favorite tunes.

Music can be stored in a variety of digital formats on a computer or on a portable audio player, such as Apple's iPod. Digital music formats, such as MP3 and AAC, are not the same formats used to store music on commercial audio CDs. These file formats take up much less storage space than on the original CD.

A variety of software allows you to convert music from commercial CDs for use on computers and portable audio players. **CD ripper software** pulls a track off an audio CD and stores it in "raw" digital format on your computer's hard disk. **Audio encoding software** (sometimes called an "audio format converter") converts the raw audio file into a format such as MP3 or AAC. After the file is converted, you can listen to it on your computer, or you can transfer it to a portable MP3 player.

Ear training software targets musicians and music students who want to learn to play by ear, develop tuning skills, recognize notes and keys, and develop other musical skills. **Notation software** is the musician's equivalent of a word processor. It helps musicians compose, edit, and print the notes for their compositions. For non-musicians, **computer-aided music software** is designed to generate unique musical compositions simply by selecting the musical style, instruments, key, and tempo. **MIDI sequencing software** and software synthesizers are an important part of the studio musician's toolbox. They're great for sound effects and for controlling keyboards and other digital instruments.

TERMINOLOGY NOTE

Some CD ripper software also includes audio encoding software so that ripping and encoding seem to happen within a single operation.

INFOWEBLINKS

At the **Music Software InfoWeb**, you'll find detailed information on popular software in this category.

www.course.com/np/concepts8/ch03

VIDEO EDITING AND DVD AUTHORING SOFTWARE

Is video editing software difficult to use? The popularity of computer-based video editing can be attributed to video editing software, such as Windows Movie Maker and Apple iMovie, now included with Windows computers and Macs. **Video editing software** provides a set of tools for transferring video footage from a camcorder to a computer, clipping out unwanted footage, assembling video segments in any sequence, adding special visual effects, and adding a sound track. Despite an impressive array of features, video editing software is relatively easy to use, as explained in Figure 3-40.

INFOWEBLINKS

Learn more about Apple iMovie and Adobe Premiere at the **Video Editing Software InfoWeb**.

www.course.com/np/concepts8/ch03

FIGURE 3-40
Video editing software, such as Adobe Premiere, helps you import a series of video clips from a camera or VCR, arrange the clips in the order of your choice, add transitions between clips, and add an audio track.

- Use the timeline to indicate the sequence for your video clips and transitions.
- Add transitions between clips.
- Arrange the audio tracks to synchronize with each video clip.
- The video and sound clips you import for the project are displayed in a list so that you can easily select them in sequence.
- Preview your video to see how the clips, transitions, and soundtrack all work together.

With the growing popularity of writable DVD drives, desktop video authors now want to transfer their productions to DVDs and watch them on standard DVD players connected to television sets or projectors. **DVD authoring software** offers tools for creating DVDs with Hollywood-style menus. Just like commercial movies, desktop videos can now include menu selections such as Play Movie, Scene Selection, and Special Features. You can use the remote control for your DVD player to scroll through and select menu options. Examples of DVD authoring software include Sonic DVDit!, ULead DVD MovieFactory, Apple iDVD, and Adobe EncoreDVD.

SOFTWARE SUITES

What is a software suite? A **software suite** is a collection of application software sold as a single package. Office suites, such as Microsoft Office, Star Office, Open Office, and WordPerfect Office, include applications to boost basic productivity: word processing, spreadsheet, and e-mail software. Graphics suites, such as Adobe Creative Suite, Macromedia Studio MX, and CorelDRAW Graphics Suite, typically include paint, draw, and Web graphics tools. Figure 3-41 on the next page lists the components of several popular software suites.

COMPUTER SOFTWARE   149

Microsoft Office XP Professional
Word
Excel
Outlook
PowerPoint
Publisher
Access

Norton SystemWorks
Norton AntiVirus
Norton Utilities
Norton CleanSweep
Norton Goback PE
Norton Password Manager

Adobe Creative Suite
Adobe Illustrator
Adobe Photoshop
Adobe InDesign
Adobe Acrobat Professional
Adobe GoLive

FIGURE 3-41
Software suites are available in many applications categories, such as productivity, antivirus, and graphics.

What are the advantages and disadvantages of software suites? Purchasing a software suite is usually much less expensive than purchasing the applications separately. Another advantage is usability. Because all the applications in a suite are produced by the same software publisher, they tend to use similar user interfaces and provide an easy way to transport data from one application to another.

The disadvantage of a software suite is that it might include applications you don't need. If that is the case, you should calculate the price of the applications you *do* need and compare that to the cost of the suite.

EDUCATIONAL AND REFERENCE SOFTWARE

How can I use my computer to learn new things? **Educational software** helps you learn and practice new skills. For the youngest students, educational software, such as MindTwister Math and 3-D Froggy Phonics, teaches basic arithmetic and reading skills. Instruction is presented in game format, and the levels of play are adapted to the player's age and ability.

For older students and adults, software is available for such diverse educational endeavors as learning languages, training yourself to use new software, learning how to play the piano or guitar, improving keyboarding skills, and even learning managerial skills for a diverse workplace. Exam preparation software is available for standardized tests such as the SAT, GMAT, and LSAT. Web-based distance education software tools, such as WebCT and BlackBoard, help instructors keep track of student progress and provide students with interactive study and testing activities.

What's reference software? **Reference software** provides a collection of information and a way to access that information. This type of software includes massive amounts of data—unlike database software, which is shipped without any data. The reference software category spans a wide range of applications—from encyclopedias to medical references, from map software to trip planners, and from cookbooks to telephone books. The options are as broad as the full range of human interests.

Because of the quantity of data it includes, reference software is generally shipped on a CD or DVD, or can be accessed on the Web. Encyclopedias are the most popular software packages in this category. Bestsellers include Microsoft Encarta and Britannica's CD. An encyclopedia on CD-ROM or the Web has several advantages over its printed counterpart. Finding information is easier, for example. Also, electronic formats take up less space on your bookshelf and include interesting video and audio clips. A single CD is cheaper to produce than a shelf full of hard-bound printed books. These lower production costs translate to more affordable products and allow an average person to own a comprehensive encyclopedia.

INFOWEBLINKS

What can you learn on your computer? Check out the **Educational and Reference Software InfoWeb**.

www.course.com/np/concepts8/ch03

ENTERTAINMENT SOFTWARE

What's the best-selling entertainment software? Although some people might get a kick out of watching an animated screen saver, computer games are the most popular type of entertainment software. Over $6 billion of computer and video games are sold each year in the United States alone. Contrary to popular belief, teenage boys are not the only computer game enthusiasts. According to the Interactive Digital Software Association, 90% of all computer games are purchased by people 18 and older. Thirteen percent of gamers are over 50, and about 43% are women.

Computer games are generally classified into subcategories, such as role-playing, action, adventure, puzzles, simulations, and strategy/war games, as described in Figure 3-42.

INFOWEBLINKS

The **Entertainment Software InfoWeb** is your link to the best game sites on the Internet.

www.course.com/np/concepts8/ch03

FIGURE 3-42
Game Categories

Type of Game	Description	Examples
Role-playing	Based on a detailed story line—often one that takes place in a medieval world populated with dastardly villains and evil monsters—the goal is to build a character into a powerful entity that can conquer the bad guys and accumulate treasure.	Diablo, EverQuest, Icewind Dale, Planescape
Action	Like arcade games, action games require fast reflexes as you maneuver a character through a maze or dungeon.	Quake, Doom, Unreal Tournament, Enter the Matrix, Tomb Raider
Adventure	Similar to role-playing games except that the focus is on solving problems rather than building a character into a powerful wizard or fighter.	Myst, The Longest Journey, Return to Monkey Island
Puzzle	Include computerized versions of traditional board games, card games, and Rubik's cube-like challenges.	Tetris, Lemmings
Simulation	Provide a realistic setting, such as the cockpit of an airplane. Players must learn to manipulate controls using the keyboard, joystick, or special-purpose input device. A great way to get your adrenaline pumping without expenses or risks.	Flight Simulator, NASCAR Racing, Mech Warrior
Sports	Place participants in the midst of action-packed sports events, such as a football game, baseball game, hockey final, soccer match, or golf tournament. Most sports games offer arcade-like action and require quick reflexes.	NBA Live, MVP Baseball, SimGolf
Strategy	Players (one player might be the computer) take turns moving characters, armies, and other resources in a quest to capture territory.	Age of Empires, Sim City, Warcraft

How do multiplayer games work? Multiplayer games provide an environment in which two or more players can participate in the same game. Even some of the earliest computer games, like Pong, supplied joysticks for two players. Today's multiplayer games are a far cry from those simplistic games. Now numerous players can use Internet technology to band together or battle one another in sophisticated visual environments.

Massively multiplayer games, such as Battlefield 1942 and EverQuest, operate on multiple Internet servers, each one with the capacity to handle thousands of players at peak times. A new twist in online multiplayer games is "persistent metaworlds," in which objects remain even when play ends. If one player drops an object, for example, it will be there when other players pass by.

Are computer games rated like movies and music? Since it was established in 1994, the Entertainment Software Rating Board (ESRB) has rated more than 10,000 video and computer games. Rating symbols can usually be found in the lower-right corner of the game box. In past years, about 57% of the rated games received an "Everyone" rating. About 32% received a "Teen" rating, and about 10% received a "Mature" rating.

INFOWEBLINKS

Who rates software and how do they do it? Find out at the **Software Ratings InfoWeb**.

www.course.com/np/concepts8/ch03

COMPUTER SOFTWARE

BUSINESS SOFTWARE

Do businesses use specialized software? The term "business software" is a broad umbrella for vertical and horizontal market software, which are designed to help businesses and organizations accomplish routine or specialized tasks.

What is vertical market software? Vertical market software is designed to automate specialized tasks in a specific market or business. Examples include patient management and billing software that is specially designed for hospitals, job estimating software for construction businesses, and student record management software for schools. Today, almost every business has access to some type of specialized vertical market software designed to automate, streamline, or computerize key business activities.

What is horizontal market software? Horizontal market software is generic software that just about any kind of business can use. **Payroll software** is a good example of horizontal market software. Almost every business has employees and must maintain payroll records. No matter what type of business uses it, payroll software must collect similar data and make similar calculations to produce payroll checks and W-2 forms. Accounting software and project management software are additional examples of horizontal market software. **Accounting software** helps a business keep track of the money flowing in and out of various accounts. **Project management software** is an important tool for planning large projects, scheduling project tasks, and tracking project costs.

What is groupware? Groupware is a type of horizontal market software, designed to help several people collaborate on a single project using LAN or Internet connections. It usually provides the capability to maintain schedules for group members, automatically select meeting times for the group, facilitate communication by e-mail or other channels, distribute documents according to a prearranged schedule or sequence, and allow multiple people to contribute to a single document.

QUICKCHECK......SECTION C

1. Various kinds of _____ production software provide tools for creating and formatting printed and Web-based materials.

2. A spelling checker will find an error in "The sailor tied a complex not." True or false? _____

3. _____ software provides a sort of "blank canvas" on which you can create numeric models by simply "painting" values, labels, and formulas.

4. _____ software stores data as a series of records and allows you to establish relationships between different types of records.

5. CD _____ software transfers files from an audio CD to your computer's hard disk.

6. _____ authoring software allows you to add Hollywood-style menus to digital videos.

CHECK ANSWERS

SECTION D
SOFTWARE INSTALLATION AND COPYRIGHTS

Software is sold in some surprising places. You might find graphics software at your local art supply store. Your favorite beauty salon might carry *Cosmopolitan*'s makeup and hairstyle makeover software. You might even find homeopathic medicine software on sale at a health food store. Of course, software is also available from traditional sources, including office stores, computer superstores, electronics superstores, and discount stores as well as local computer stores. You can buy software from mail-order catalogs, the software publisher's Web site, and software download sites.

Regardless of how you obtain a new software package, you must install it on your computer before you can use it. That is the first topic in Section D. From time to time, you might want to eliminate some of the software on your computer. The procedure for uninstalling software is the second topic in this section. The section ends with a discussion of software copyrights—important information that will help you understand the difference between legal and illegal software copying.

INSTALLATION BASICS

What's included in a typical software package? The key "ingredients" necessary to install new software are the files that contain the programs and data. These files might be supplied on **distribution media**—one or more CDs or DVDs that are packaged in a box, along with an instruction manual. The files might also be supplied as an Internet download that contains program modules and the text of the instruction manual.

How do I know if a software program will work on my computer? Tucked away at the software publisher's Web site or printed on the software package (Figure 3-43), you'll find **system requirements**, which specify the operating system and minimum hardware capacities necessary for a software product to work correctly.

FIGURE 3-43
System requirements typically can be found on the software box or posted on the download site.

System Requirements
Operating Systems: Windows 95/98/2000/Me/XP
Processor: Pentium class computer
Memory: 16 MB or more
Hard Disk Space: 10 MB free
Network Protocol: TCP/IP
Network Connection: 10/100 Ethernet LAN/WAN, cable modem, DSL router, ISDN router, or dial-up modem

eCourse Internet Works
2005 eCourseWare Corp. All rights reserved. eCourse is a registered trademark of eCourseWare Corp.

COMPUTER SOFTWARE

Why is it necessary to install most software? When you **install** software, the new software files are placed in the appropriate folders on your computer's hard disk, and then your computer performs any software or hardware configurations necessary to make sure the program is ready to run. During the installation process, your computer usually performs the following activities:

- Copies files from distribution media or downloads files to specified folders on the hard disk
- Uncompresses files that have been distributed in compressed format
- Analyzes the computer's resources, such as processor speed, RAM capacity, and hard disk capacity, to verify that they meet or exceed the minimum system requirements
- Analyzes hardware components and peripheral devices to select appropriate device drivers
- Looks for any system files and players, such as Internet Explorer or Windows Media Player, that are required to run the program but not supplied on the distribution media or download
- Updates necessary system files, such as the Windows Registry and the Windows Start menu, with information about the new software

Are all files for the software provided on the distribution media?
With Windows and other operating systems, application software programs share some common files. These files are often supplied by the operating system and perform routine tasks, such as displaying the Print dialog box, which allows you to select a printer and specify how many copies of a file you want to print. These "shared" files are not typically provided on the new software's distribution media or download because the files should already exist on your computer. The installation routine attempts to locate these files. It then notifies you if any files are missing, and provides instructions for installing them.

Are all the files for the new software installed in the same folder?
Most executable files and data files for new software are placed in the folder you specify. Some support programs for the software, however, might be stored in other folders, such as Windows/System. The location for these files is determined by the software installation routine. Figure 3-44 maps out the location of files for a typical Windows software installation.

FIGURE 3-44
When you install software, its files might end up in different folders. Files for the eVideo-In Pro software are installed in two folders.

Distribution CD

Windows\System

File name	Size	Type
eVidmdbg.dll	20 KB	Support Program
eVidodec32.dll	92 KB	Support Program
eVidwave.dll	37 KB	Support Program
Version.dll	24 KB	Support Program
eVidpodbc.dll	955 KB	Support Program
eVidgain.dll	116 KB	Support Program
eVgateway.ocx	42 KB	Support Program

Program Files\eVideo-In Pro

File name	Size	Type
eVidpro.exe	5,500 KB	Main Executable Program
eVidpro.hlp	275 KB	Help File
eVidcore.hlp	99 KB	Help File
eVidcore.dll	1,425 KB	Support Program
eVidpro.dll	1,517 KB	Support Program
Readme.doc	65 KB	Data File
eVdplugin.dll	813 KB	Support Program
eVdtrans.dll	921 KB	Support Program

INSTALLING FROM DISTRIBUTION MEDIA

How do I install software from distribution media? Installation procedures vary, depending on a computer's operating system. Take a look at the installation process on a computer running Windows.

Windows software typically contains a **setup program** that guides you through the installation process. Figure 3-45 shows you what to expect when you use a setup program.

FIGURE 3-45
Installing from Distribution Media

1 Insert the first distribution CD, or DVD. The setup program should start automatically. If it does not, look for a file called Setup.exe and then run it.

2 Read the license agreement, if one is presented on the screen. By agreeing to the terms of the license, you can proceed with the installation.

3 Select the installation option that best meets your needs. If you select a full installation, the setup program copies all files and data from the distribution medium to the hard disk of your computer system. A full installation gives you access to all features of the software.

If you select a custom installation, the setup program displays a list of software features for your selection. After you select the features you want, the setup program copies only the selected program and data files to your hard disk. A custom installation can save space on your hard disk.

4 Follow the prompts provided by the setup program to specify a folder to hold the new software program. You can use the default folder specified by the setup program or a folder of your own choosing, You can also create a new folder during the setup process.

5 If the software includes multiple distribution CDs, insert each one in the specified drive when the setup program prompts you.

6 When the setup is complete, start the program you just installed to make sure it works.

COMPUTER SOFTWARE

155

INSTALLING DOWNLOADED SOFTWARE

Is the installation process different for downloaded software? The installation process is slightly different for Windows software that you download. Usually all the files needed for the new software are **zipped** to consolidate them into one large file, which is compressed to decrease its size and reduce the download time. As part of the installation process, this downloaded file must be reconstituted, or **unzipped**, into the original collection of files (Figure 3-46).

FIGURE 3-46
Installing Downloaded Software

1 At the distribution Web site, locate any information pertaining to installing the software. Read it. You might also want to print it.

2 Click the download link.

3 If you are downloading from a trusted site and have antivirus software running, click the Open button in the File Download dialog box.

4 Wait for the download to finish. Typically, the setup program included in the download starts automatically.

5 Use the setup program to specify a folder to hold the new software program. You can use the default folder specified by the setup program or a folder of your own choosing. You can also create a new folder during the setup process.

6 Wait for the setup program to uncompress the downloaded file and install the software in the selected directory. During this process, respond to license agreement and other prompts. When the installation is complete, test the software to make sure it works.

Downloadable software can be provided in several different formats. Some automatically install themselves, but others require manual procedures. A downloadable file typically is set up as a **self-installing executable file**, **self-executing zip file**, or **non-executing zip file** (Figure 3-47).

FIGURE 3-47
Downloadable File Formats

Self-installing Executable Files
Under the most automated installation system, the process of downloading new software automatically initiates the entire installation process.

The software download is packaged as one large file with an .exe extension. This file automatically unzips itself and starts the setup program. You simply follow the setup program prompts to acknowledge the license agreement, indicate the folder for the software files, and complete the installation.

Self-executing Zip Files
Downloaded files with .exe extensions do not always install themselves. Some are simply self-executing zip files, which automatically unzip the software's files, but do not automatically start the setup program.

To install software from a self-executing zip file, you start the executable file to unzip the files for the new software. One of these files will be the Setup.exe program. Next, you manually start the setup program and follow its prompts to complete the installation.

Non-executing Zip Files
If you download software and it arrives as one huge file with a .zip extension, you must locate this file on your hard disk and then use Windows XP or a program such as WinZip to unzip it.

After unzipping the file, you must run the setup program to acknowledge the license agreement, indicate the folder for the software files, and complete the installation.

Is installing a software update different from installing the original version? After you purchase and install software, you might have the opportunity to update it. A software update can be distributed as a new version, patch, or service pack. A new version of software entirely replaces an old version, and is installed in much the same way as the original.

In contrast, a **software patch** is a small section of program code that replaces part of the software you currently have installed. The term **service pack**, which usually applies to operating system updates, is a set of patches that correct problems and address security vulnerabilities. Patches and service packs are usually distributed via the Internet and automatically install themselves when you download them. It is always a good idea to install patches and service packs when they become available.

UNINSTALLING SOFTWARE

How do I get rid of software? With some operating systems, such as DOS, you can remove software simply by deleting its files. Other operating systems, such as Windows and Mac OS, include an **uninstall routine**, which deletes the software's files from various folders on your computer's hard disk. The uninstall routine also removes references to the program from the desktop and from operating system files, such as the file system and, in the case of Windows, the Windows Registry (Figure 3-48).

TERMINOLOGY NOTE

Some software provides an Automatic Update option that periodically checks the software publisher's Web site for updates, downloads updates automatically, and installs them without user intervention.

The advantage of Automatic Update is convenience. The disadvantage is that changes are made to your computer without your knowledge.

FIGURE 3-48
To uninstall any Windows application software, first look for an Uninstall option listed on the same menu you use to start the program. If that option is not available, use Add/Remove Programs from the Control Panel.

COMPUTER SOFTWARE

SOFTWARE COPYRIGHTS

Is it legal to copy software? After you purchase a software package, you might assume that you can install it and use it in any way you like. In fact, your "purchase" entitles you to use the software only in certain prescribed ways. In most countries, computer software, like a book or movie, is protected by a copyright. A **copyright** is a form of legal protection that grants the author of an original "work" an exclusive right to copy, distribute, sell, and modify that work, except under special circumstances described by copyright laws. These exceptions include:

1. The purchaser has the right to copy software from distribution media or a Web site to a computer's hard disk in order to install it.

2. The purchaser can make an extra, or backup, copy of the software in case the original copy becomes erased or damaged.

3. The purchaser is allowed to copy and distribute sections of a software program for use in critical reviews and teaching.

Most software displays a **copyright notice**, such as "© 2005 eCourse," on one of its screens. This notice is not required by law, however, so programs without a copyright notice are still protected by copyright law. People who circumvent copyright law and illegally copy, distribute, or modify software are sometimes called software pirates, and their illegal copies are referred to as pirated software.

SOFTWARE LICENSES

What is a software license? In addition to copyright protection, computer software is often protected by the terms of a software license. A **software license**, or "license agreement," is a legal contract that defines the ways in which you may use a computer program. For personal computer software, you will find the license on the outside of the package, on a separate card inside the package, on the CD packaging, or in one of the program files.

Typically, computer owners purchase the right to use software that is distributed under a **single-user license** that limits use of the software to only one person at a time. Schools, organizations, and businesses sometimes purchase a **site license**, **multiple-user license**, or **concurrent-use license**, which allows more than one person to use the software.

Most legal contracts require signatures before the terms of the contract take effect. This requirement becomes unwieldy with software—imagine having to sign a license agreement and return it before you can use a new software package. To circumvent the signature requirement, software publishers typically use two techniques to validate a software license: shrink-wrap licenses and installation agreements.

When you purchase computer software, the distribution media are usually sealed in an envelope, plastic box, or shrink wrapping. A **shrink-wrap license** goes into effect as soon as you open the packaging. Figure 3-49 explains more about the mechanics of a shrink-wrap license.

An **installation agreement** is displayed on-screen when you first install software. After reading the software license on the screen, you can indicate that you accept the terms of the license by clicking a designated button—usually labeled "OK," "I agree," or "I accept." If you do not accept the terms, the software does not load and you will not be able to use it.

INFOWEBLINKS

To read the actual text of software copyright laws, connect to the **Software Copyright InfoWeb**.

www.course.com/np/concepts8/ch03

TERMINOLOGY NOTE

A site license is generally priced at a flat rate and allows software to be used on all computers at a specific location.

A multiple-user license is priced per user and allows the allocated number of people to use the software at any time.

A concurrent-use license is priced per copy and allows a specific number of copies to be used at the same time.

FIGURE 3-49

When software has a shrink-wrap license, you agree to the terms of the software license by opening the package. If you do not agree with the terms, you should return the software in its unopened package.

Software licenses are often lengthy and written in "legalese," but your legal right to use the software continues only as long as you abide by the terms of the software license. Therefore, you should understand the software license for any software you use. To become familiar with a typical license agreement, you can read through the one in Figure 3-50.

> **Software License Agreement**
> **Important - READ CAREFULLY:** This License Agreement ("Agreement") is a legal agreement between you and eCourse Corporation for the software product, eCourse GraphWare ("The SOFTWARE"). By installing, copying, or otherwise using the SOFTWARE, you agree to be bound by the terms of this Agreement. The SOFTWARE is protected by copyright laws and international copyright treaties. The SOFTWARE is licensed, not sold.
> **GRANT OF LICENSE.** This Agreement gives you the right to install and use one copy of the SOFTWARE on a single computer. The primary user of the computer on which the SOFTWARE is installed may make a second copy for his or her exclusive use on a portable computer.
> **OTHER RIGHTS AND LIMITATIONS.** You may not reverse engineer, decompile, or disassemble the SOFTWARE except and only to the extent that such activity is expressly permitted by applicable law.
> The SOFTWARE is licensed as a single product; its components may not be separated for use on more than one computer. You may not rent, lease, or lend the SOFTWARE.
> You may permanently transfer all of your rights under this Agreement, provided you retain no copies, you transfer all of the SOFTWARE, and the recipient agrees to the terms of this Agreement. If the software product is an upgrade, any transfer must include all prior versions of the SOFTWARE.
> You may receive the SOFTWARE in more than one medium. Regardless of the type of medium you receive, you may use only one medium that is appropriate for your single computer. You may not use or install the other medium on another computer.
> **WARRANTY.** eCourse warrants that the SOFTWARE will perform substantially in accordance with the accompanying written documentation for a period of ninety (90) days from the date of receipt. TO THE MAXIMUM EXTENT PERMITTED BY APPLICABLE LAW, eCourse AND ITS SUPPLIERS DISCLAIM ALL OTHER WARRANTIES AND CONDITIONS EITHER EXPRESS OR IMPLIED, INCLUDING, BUT NOT LIMITED TO, IMPLIED WARRANTIES OF MERCHANTABILITY, FITNESS FOR A PARTICULAR PURPOSE, TITLE, AND NON-INFRINGEMENT, WITH REGARD TO THE SOFTWARE PRODUCT.

FIGURE 3-50
When you read a software license agreement, look for answers to the following questions:

Am I buying the software or licensing it?

When does the license go into effect?

Under what circumstances can I make copies?

Can I rent the software?

Can I sell the software?

What if the software includes a distribution CD and a set of distribution floppy disks?

Does the software publisher provide a warranty?

Can I loan the software to a friend?

Are all software licenses similar? Copyright laws have fairly severe restrictions on copying, distributing, and reselling software; however, a license agreement might offer additional rights to consumers. The licenses for commercial software, shareware, freeware, open source, and public domain software specify different levels of permission for software use, copying, and distribution.

Commercial software is typically sold in computer stores or at Web sites. Although you "buy" this software, you actually purchase only the right to use it under the terms of the software license. A license for commercial software typically adheres closely to the limitations provided by copyright law, although it might give you permission to install the software on a computer at work and on a computer at home, provided that you use only one of them at a time.

Shareware is copyrighted software marketed under a "try before you buy" policy. It typically includes a license that permits you to use the software for a trial period. To use it beyond the trial period, you must pay a registration

COMPUTER SOFTWARE

fee. A shareware license usually allows you to make copies of the software and distribute them to others. If they choose to use the software, they must pay a registration fee as well. These shared copies provide a low-cost marketing and distribution channel. Registration fee payment relies on the honor system, so unfortunately many shareware authors collect only a fraction of the money they deserve for their programming efforts. Thousands of shareware programs are available, encompassing just about as many applications as commercial software.

Freeware is copyrighted software that—as you might expect—is available for free. Because the software is protected by copyright, you cannot do anything with it that is not expressly allowed by copyright law or by the author. Typically, the license for freeware permits you to use the software, copy it, and give it away, but does not permit you to alter it or sell it. Many utility programs, device drivers, and some games are available as freeware.

Open source software makes the uncompiled program instructions—the source code—available to programmers who want to modify and improve the software. Open source software may be sold or distributed free of charge in complied form, but it must, in every case, also include the source code. Linux is an example of open source software, as is FreeBSD—a version of UNIX designed for personal computers.

Public domain software is not protected by copyright because the copyright has expired, or the author has placed the program in the public domain, making it available without restriction. Public domain software may be freely copied, distributed, and even resold. The primary restriction on public domain software is that you are not allowed to apply for a copyright on it.

QUICKCHECK......SECTION D

1. System [_____] specify the operating system and minimum hardware capacities required for software to work correctly.

2. During the [_____] process, your computer performs many tasks, including updating the Windows Registry and Start menu.

3. The [_____] program typically asks for your consent to the license agreement and confirms the folder into which you want files copied.

4. The files for downloaded software are usually [_____] into one large compressed file.

5. You can [_____] software using the Control Panel's Add/Remove Programs option.

6. Linux is an example of [_____] source software.

7. [_____] domain software is not copyrighted, making it available for use without restriction, except that you cannot apply for a copyright on it.

CHECK ANSWERS

LAB 3-D
INSTALLING AND UNINSTALLING SOFTWARE

In this lab, you'll learn:

- How to use a setup program to install Windows application software from a distribution CD
- What to do if the setup program doesn't automatically start
- The difference between typical, compact, and custom installation options
- How to specify a folder for a new software installation
- How to install downloaded software
- How to install an upgrade
- How to uninstall a Windows application
- What happens, in addition to deleting files, when you uninstall a software application
- How to locate the program that will uninstall a software application
- Why you might not want to delete all of the files associated with an application

INTERACTIVE LAB

CLICK TO START THE LAB

LAB ASSIGNMENTS

1. Start the interactive part of the lab. Insert your Tracking Disk if you want to save your QuickCheck results. Perform each lab step as directed, and answer all the lab QuickCheck questions. When you exit the lab, your answers are automatically graded and your results are displayed.

2. Browse the Web and locate a software application that you might like to download. Use information supplied by the Web site to answer the following questions:
   a. What is the name of the program and the URL of the download site?
   b. What is the size of the download file?
   c. According to the instructions, does the download file appear to require manual installation, is it a self-executing zip file, or is it a self-installing executable file?

3. On the computer you typically use, look through the list of programs (click Start, then select Programs to see a list of them). List the names of any programs that include their own uninstall routines.

4. On the computer you typically use, open the Control Panel and then open the Add/Remove Programs dialog box. List the first 10 programs that are currently installed on the computer.

COMPUTER SOFTWARE

TECHTALK
THE WINDOWS REGISTRY

To many computer owners, the Windows Registry is simply a mysterious "black box" that is mentioned occasionally in articles about computer troubleshooting. Certainly, it is possible to use a computer without intimate knowledge of the Registry; however, the Registry is the "glue" that binds together many of the most important components of a PC—the computer hardware, peripheral devices, application software, and system software. After reading this TechTalk section, you should have a basic understanding of the Registry and its role in the operation of a computer system.

Why does a PC need the Registry? Reflect back for moment on what you know so far about how a computer works. You know that you use menus, dialog boxes, and other controls provided by application software to direct the operations a computer carries out. For some operations—particularly those involving hardware—the application software communicates with the operating system. The operating system might communicate with device drivers or, in some cases, it can directly communicate with a peripheral device.

To act as an intermediary between software and peripheral devices, your operating system needs information about these components—where they are located, what's been installed, how they are configured, and how you want to use them. CMOS memory holds the most essential data about your computer's processing and storage hardware, but the **Windows Registry** keeps track of your computer's peripheral devices and software so that the operating system can access the information it needs to coordinate the activities in a computer system. Figure 3-51 lists some of the items the Registry tracks.

Where can I find the Registry? The contents of the Registry are stored in multiple files in the Windows folder of your computer's hard disk and combined into a single database when Windows starts. Although each version of Windows uses a slightly different storage scheme, the basic organization and function of the Registry are similar in all versions.

Windows 95, 98, and Me store the entire contents of the Registry in two files: System.dat and User.dat. System.dat includes configuration data for all the hardware and software installed on a computer. User.dat contains user-specific information, sometimes called a "user profile," which includes software settings and desktop settings. Windows 2000 and XP divide Registry data among about two dozen files.

What does the Registry look like? The Registry has a logical structure that appears as a hierarchy of folders, similar to the directory structure of your hard disk, as shown in Figure 3-52.

FIGURE 3-51
Items Tracked by the Windows Registry

- User preferences for desktop colors, icons, pointers, shortcuts, and display resolution
- Sounds that are assigned to various system events, such as clicking and shutting down
- The capability of your CD-ROM drive for playing audio CDs and autorunning computer CDs
- The options that appear on a shortcut menu when you right-click an object
- The computer's network card settings and protocols
- The location of the uninstall routines for all installed software

FIGURE 3-52
The Windows Registry is organized as a hierarchy of folders and files.

- My Computer
  - HKEY_CLASSES_ROOT
  - HKEY_CURRENT_USER
  - HKEY_LOCAL_MACHINE
  - HKEY_USERS
  - HKEY_CURRENT_CONFIG
  - HKEY_DYN_DATA

162 TECHTALK, CHAPTER 3

There are six main folders in the Registry, and their names begin with HKEY. Each folder contains data that pertains to a particular part of a computer system, as described in Figure 3-53.

FIGURE 3-53
Registry Folder Contents

Folder	Contents
HKEY_CLASSES_ROOT	This folder contains data that associates file extensions with a particular application and a list of desktop shortcuts to programs.
HKEY_CURRENT_USER	Information for the current user is transferred here from the HKEY_USERS folder.
HKEY_LOCAL_MACHINE	This folder contains computer-specific information about hardware configuration and software preferences. This information is used for all users who log on to this computer.
HKEY_USERS	This folder contains individual preferences for each person who uses the computer.
HKEY_CURRENT_CONFIG	This folder links to the section of HKEY_LOCAL_MACHINE appropriate for the current hardware configuration.
HKEY_DYN_DATA	This folder points to the part of HKEY_LOCAL_MACHINE that maintains data for Plug and Play devices. This data is dynamic and can change as devices are added and removed from the system.

What does the Registry data look like? The Registry contains thousands of esoteric-looking data entries, such as those shown in Figure 3-54.

FIGURE 3-54
The Registry entries for Display Settings specify such settings as DPI, display fonts, and resolution.

- DPI refers to the number of dots displayed per inch on this computer's display device.
- The Registry database is open to the Display Settings records.
- The resolution is set at 640 x 480 pixels.
- The font settings specify which font Windows will use on the desktop.

COMPUTER SOFTWARE   163

Can I make changes to the Registry? You change the Registry indirectly whenever you install or remove software or hardware. The setup program for your software automatically updates the Registry with essential information about the program's location and configuration. Device drivers and the Windows Plug and Play feature provide similar update services for hardware.

You can also make changes to the Windows Registry by using the dialog boxes for various configuration routines provided by the operating system and application software. For example, if you want to change the desktop colors for your user profile, you can do so by selecting the Settings option from the Start menu, clicking Control Panel, and then selecting the Display option. Any changes you make to settings in the Display Properties dialog box (Figure 3-55) will be recorded in the Windows Registry.

FIGURE 3-55
Changes that you make when using the Display Properties dialog box automatically update the corresponding entries in the HKEY_CURRENT_CONFIG folder of the Registry.

QUICKCHECK........TECHTALK

1. The Windows Registry contains settings and preferences for the peripheral devices and software that are installed on a computer. True or false? _____

2. The Registry is stored in the _____ folder.

3. In the hierarchy of Registry folders, each folder name begins with _____.

4. The _____ program automatically updates the Registry when you install software.

CHECK ANSWERS

ISSUE
SOFTWARE PIRACY

Software is easy to steal. You don't have to walk out of a Best Buy store with a $495 DVD Workshop software box under your shirt. You can simply borrow your friend's DVD Workshop distribution CDs and install a copy of the program on your computer's hard disk. It seems so simple that it couldn't be illegal. But it is.

Piracy takes many forms. End-user piracy includes friends loaning distribution disks to each other and installing software on more computers than the license allows.

Counterfeiting is the large-scale illegal duplication of software distribution media and sometimes even its packaging. According to Microsoft, many software counterfeiting groups are linked to organized crime and money-laundering schemes that fund a diverse collection of illegal activities, such as smuggling, gambling, extortion, and prostitution. Counterfeit software is sold in retail stores and through online auctions—often the packaging looks so authentic that buyers have no idea they have purchased illegal goods.

Internet piracy uses the Web as a way to illegally distribute unauthorized software. In "Net" jargon, the terms "appz" and "warez" (pronounced as "wares" or "war EZ") refer to pirated software. Some warez has even been modified to eliminate serial numbers, registration requirements, expiration dates, or other forms of copy protection. The Business Software Alliance (BSA) estimates that more than 800,000 Web sites illegally sell or distribute software.

In many countries, including the United States, software pirates are subject to civil lawsuits for monetary damages and criminal prosecution, which can result in jail time and stiff fines. Nonetheless, software piracy continues to have enormous impact. According to the Software and Information Industry Association (SIIA), a leading anti-piracy watchdog, revenue losses from business software piracy typically exceed $2 billion per year. This figure reveals only part of the piracy problem—it does not include losses from rampant game and educational software piracy, which are estimated to exceed $12 billion a year.

A small, but vocal, minority of software users, such as members of GNU (which stands for "Gnu's Not UNIX"), believes that data and software should be freely distributed. Richard Stallman writes in the GNU Manifesto, "I consider that the golden rule requires that if I like a program I must share it with other people who like it. Software sellers want to divide users and conquer them, making each user agree not to share with others. I refuse to break solidarity with other users in this way. I cannot in good conscience sign a nondisclosure agreement or a software license agreement."

Is software piracy really damaging? Who cares if you use a program without paying for it? Software piracy is damaging because it has a negative effect on the economy. Software production makes a major contribution to the United States economy, employing more than 2 million people and accounting for billions of dollars in corporate revenue. A BSA economic impact study concluded that lowering global piracy from an average of 36% to only 26% would add more that 1 million jobs and $400 billion in worldwide economic growth.

Decreases in software revenues can have a direct effect on consumers, too. When software publishers are forced to cut corners, they tend to reduce customer service and technical support. As a result, you, the consumer, get put on hold when you call for technical support, find fewer free technical support sites, and encounter customer support personnel who are only moderately knowledgeable about their products. The bottom line—software piracy negatively affects customer service.

COMPUTER SOFTWARE

As an alternative to cutting support costs, some software publishers might build the cost of software piracy into the price of the software. The unfortunate result is that those who legitimately license and purchase software pay an inflated price.

According to a 2003 BSA/IDC report on global software piracy, about 36% of the software currently in use is pirated. China has the world's highest piracy rate—92% of the software used in China is believed to be pirated. In Russia the piracy rate is 87%. In the United States, an estimated 22% of software is pirated. In Japan, the rate is 29%.

Piracy Rates by Region (as percent of total in use)

Region	Rate
Middle East/Africa	56
Latin America	63
Western Europe	36
Eastern Europe	70
Asia	53
North America	23

Source: BSA/IDC Global Piracy Report 2003

Although the rate of business software piracy might be declining, total piracy appears to be growing by one or two percentage points each year. Analysts fear that the Internet is a major factor in piracy increases. As Internet access becomes available to subscribers in countries such as China, piracy could skyrocket. To make matters worse, increased access to high-speed Internet connections makes it much easier to quickly download large software files.

As a justification of high piracy rates, some observers point out that people in many countries simply might not be able to afford software priced for the U.S. market. This argument could apply to China, where the average annual income is equivalent to about U.S.$3,500, and in North Korea, where the average income is only U.S.$900. A Korean who legitimately purchases Microsoft Office for U.S.$250 would be spending more than one-quarter of his or her annual income.

Many countries with a high incidence of software piracy, however, have strong economies and respectable per capita incomes. To further discredit the theory that piracy stems from poverty, India—which has a fairly large computer-user community, but a per capita income of only U.S.$1,600—is not among the top 10 countries with high rates of software piracy.

If economic factors do not account for the pervasiveness of software piracy, what does? The incidence of piracy seems to be higher among small business and consumer personal computer users than corporations and government agencies. Some analysts suggest that people need more education about software copyrights and the economic implications of piracy. Other analysts believe that copyright enforcement must be increased by implementing more vigorous efforts to identify and prosecute pirates.

INFOWEBLINKS

You can read the GNU Manifesto and other thought-provoking articles about software piracy by going to the **Copyright and Piracy InfoWeb**.

www.course.com/np/concepts8/ch03

WHAT DO YOU THINK?

1. Do you believe that software piracy is a serious issue? ◯ Yes ◯ No ◯ Not sure
2. Do you know of any instances of software piracy? ◯ Yes ◯ No ◯ Not sure
3. Do you think that most software pirates understand that they are doing something illegal? ◯ Yes ◯ No ◯ Not sure
4. Should software publishers try to adjust software pricing for local markets? ◯ Yes ◯ No ◯ Not sure

SAVE RESPONSES

COMPUTERS IN CONTEXT

JOURNALISM

In the ancient world, news spread by word of mouth, relayed by bards and merchants who traveled from town to town—in essence, the first reporters to "broadcast" the news. The news business is all about gathering and disseminating information as quickly as possible. Technology has played a major role in news reporting's evolution from its bardic roots to modern 24-hour "live" news networks.

Johann Gutenberg's printing press (ca. 1450), the first technological breakthrough in the news business, made it feasible to publish news as printed notices tacked to walls in the town square. As paper became more economical, resourceful entrepreneurs sold broadsheets to people eager for news, and the concept of a newspaper was born. The first regularly published newspapers appeared in Germany and Holland in 1609, and the first English newspaper, the *Weekly News*, was published in 1622.

But the news spread slowly. In the early 1800s, it took four weeks for newspapers in New York to receive reports from London. With the advent of the telegraph in 1844, however, reporters from far-flung regions could "wire" stories to their newspapers for publication the next day. The first radio reporters in the 1920s offered live broadcasts of sports events, church services, and variety shows. Before the 1950s, black-and-white newsreels shown in movie theaters provided the only visual imagery of news events, but television gave viewers news images on a nightly basis.

Technology has benefited print journalism, too. For decades, typesetters transferred reporters' handwritten stories into neatly set columns of type. Today, reporters use computers and word processing software to tap out their stories and run a preliminary check of spelling and grammar.

Stories are submitted via computer network to editors, who use the same software to edit stories to fit time and space constraints. The typesetting process has been replaced by desktop publishing software and computer to plate (CTP) technology. Digital pages produced with desktop publishing software are sent to a raster image processor (RIP), which converts the pages into dots that form words and images. After a page has been RIPed, a platesetter uses lasers to etch the dots onto a physical plate, which is then mounted on the printing press to produce printed pages. CTP is much faster and more flexible than typesetting, so publishers can make last-minute changes to accommodate late-breaking stories.

Personal computers have also added a new dimension to the news-gathering process. Reporters were once limited to personal interviews, observation, and fact gathering at libraries, but can now make extensive use of Internet resources and e-mail. Web sites and online databases provide background information on all sorts of topics. Other resources include newsgroups and chat rooms, where reporters can monitor public opinion on current events and identify potential sources.

Most major networks maintain interactive Web sites that offer online polls and bulletin boards designed to collect viewers' opinions. Although online poll respondents are not a representative sample of the population, they can help news organizations gauge viewer opinions and determine whether news coverage is comprehensive and effective.

E-mail has changed the way reporters communicate with colleagues and sources. It's often the only practical method for contacting people in remote locations or distant time zones, and it's useful with reluctant sources, who feel more comfortable providing information under the cloak of anonymous Hotmail or Yahoo! accounts. "Vetting" e-mail sources—verifying credentials such as name, location, and occupation—can be difficult, however, so reporters tend not to rely on these sources without substantial corroboration.

For broadcast journalism, digital communications play a major role in today's "live on the scene" television reporting. Most news organizations maintain remote production vans, sometimes called "satellite news gathering (SNG) trucks," that travel to the site of breaking news, raise their antennas, and begin to broadcast. These complete mobile production facilities include camera control units, audio and video recording equipment, and satellite or microwave transmitters.

On-the-scene reporting no longer requires a truck full of equipment, however. Audiovisual editing units and video cameras have gone digital, making them easier to use and sized to fit in a suitcase. A new breed of "backpack journalists" carry mini-DV cameras, notebook computers, and satellite phones. Jane Ellen Stevens, a pioneer backpack journalist specializing in science and technology, has reported since 1997 from remote locations, such as a space camp in Russia.

Backpack journalists can connect their minicams to notebook computers with a FireWire cable, transfer their video footage to the hard disk, and then edit the footage using consumer-level video editing software. The resulting video files, compressed for transmission over a satellite phone, are sent to newsroom technicians, who decompress and then broadcast them—all in a matter of seconds.

One drawback of backpack journalists' use of minicams and compression is that the video quality usually isn't as crisp as images filmed with studio cameras. News organizations with high standards were hesitant to use this lower quality video, but have found that viewers would rather see a low-quality image now than a high-quality image later. To many viewers, a few rough edges just make the footage seem more compelling, more "you are there."

A recent tour de force in SNG was the brainchild of David Bloom, an NBC reporter embedded with the U.S. Army 3rd Infantry Division during Operation Iraqi Freedom. He helped modify an M-88 tank recovery vehicle into a high-tech, armored SNG vehicle. The $500,000 "Bloommobile" featured a gyrostabilized camera that could produce jiggle-free video as the tank blasted over sand dunes at 50 mph. Tragically, Bloom died while covering the conflict, but many viewers vividly remember his exhilarating reports as the Bloommobile raced down desert roads, trundled along with army supply convoys, and narrowly escaped enemy fire.

Computers, the Internet, and communications technology make it possible to instantly broadcast live reports across the globe, but live reporting is not without controversy. A reporter who arrives at the scene of a disaster with microphone in hand has little time for reflection, vetting, and cross-checking, so grievous errors, libelous images, or distasteful video footage sometimes find their way into news reports. Jeff Gralnick, former executive producer for ABC News, remarks, "In the old days, we had time to think before we spoke. We had time to write, time to research and time to say, 'Hey, wait a minute.' Now we don't even have the time to say, 'Hey, wait a nanosecond.' Just because we can say it or do it, should we?" Technology has given journalists a powerful arsenal of tools for gathering and reporting the news, but has also increased their accountability for accurate, socially responsible reporting.

INFOWEBLINKS

You'll find lots more information related to this topic at the **Computers and Journalism InfoWeb**.

www.course.com/np/concepts8/ch03

INTERACTIVE SUMMARY

To review important concepts from this chapter, fill in the blanks to best complete each sentence. When using the NP8 BookOnCD, click the Check Answers buttons to automatically score your answers. Place your Tracking Disk in the floppy disk drive if you want to save your scores.

_____ consists of computer programs and data files that work together to provide a computer with the instructions and data necessary for carrying out a specific type of task, such as document production, video editing, graphic design, or Web browsing. Computer _____ write instructions for the programs that become the components of a computer software product. To understand how software is installed and uninstalled, it is important for computer owners to recognize that today's software typically consists of many files.

To create a software environment, a programmer must define the _____ for each element in the environment, such as where an object appears, its shape, its color, and its behavior. A computer programming _____ provides the tools a programmer uses to create software. Most programmers today prefer to use _____ languages, such as C, C++, Java, Ada, COBOL, and Visual Basic. A computer's microprocessor understands only _____ language, however, so a program that is written in a high-level language must be compiled or interpreted before it can be processed. A _____ translates all the instructions in a program as a single batch, and the resulting machine language instructions, called _____ code, are placed in a new file. An alternative method of translation uses an _____ to translate instructions one at a time while the program runs.

CHECK ANSWERS

A computer's software is like the chain of command in an army. _____ software tells the operating system what to do. The operating system tells the device drivers, device drivers tell the hardware, and the hardware actually does the work. The operating system interacts with application software, device drivers, and hardware to manage a computer's _____. In addition, many operating systems also influence the "look and feel" of your software, or what's known as the user _____.

The core part of an operating system is called the _____. In addition to this core, many operating systems provide helpful tools, called _____, that you can use to control and customize your computer equipment and work environment. Operating systems are informally categorized and characterized using one or more of the following terms: A _____ operating system expects to deal with one set of input devices—those that can be controlled by one person at a time. A _____ operating system is designed to deal with input, output, and processing requests from many users. A _____ operating system provides process and memory management services that allow two or more programs to run simultaneously. A _____ operating system is one that's designed for a personal computer—either a desktop or notebook computer. Popular desktop operating systems include Windows 95/98/Me/XP and Mac OS. Popular _____ operating systems include Windows NT/2000, Linux, and UNIX. Operating systems for PDAs are typically smaller than PC operating systems and can fit in _____.

CHECK ANSWERS

COMPUTER SOFTWARE

Document _____ software assists you with composing, editing, designing, printing, and electronically publishing documents. The three most popular types of document production software include word processing, desktop publishing, and Web authoring. _____ software is similar to a "smart" piece of paper that automatically adds up the columns of numbers you write on it. You can use it to make other calculations, too, based on simple equations that you write or more complex, built-in formulas. Because it is so easy to experiment with different numbers, this type of software is particularly useful for _____ analyses. _____ software helps you store, find, organize, update, and report information stored in one or more tables. When two sets of records are _____, database software allows you to access data from both tables at the same time. _____ software, including paint, photo editing, drawing, CAD, 3-D, and presentation software, is designed to help you create, manipulate, and print images.

Music and video editing software, educational and reference software, and entertainment software round out the most popular categories of personal computer software. A software _____ is a "bundled" collection of application software sold as a single package.

For businesses, _____ market software is designed to automate specialized tasks in a specific market or business. _____ market software is generic software that can be used by just about any kind of business. _____ is a type of horizontal market software designed to help several people collaborate on a single project using LAN or Internet connections.

CHECK ANSWERS

When you _____ software, the new software files are placed in the appropriate folders on your computer's hard disk, and then your computer performs any software or hardware configurations that are necessary to make sure the program is ready to run. The _____ files and data files for the software are placed in the folder you specify. Some _____ programs for the software, however, might be stored in different folders, such as Windows\System. Windows software typically contains a _____ program that guides you through the installation process.

To install application software from a _____ CD, simply place the CD in the drive and wait for the setup program to begin. The installation process is slightly different for application software that you download. Usually all the files needed for the new software are consolidated into one large file, which is _____ to decrease its size and reduce the download time. This large, downloaded file must be reconstituted, or _____, into the original collection of files as a first step in the installation process. A self-installing _____ file automatically unzips the downloaded file and starts the setup program. A self-executing _____ file automatically unzips the software's files, but does not automatically start the setup program.

A _____ is a form of legal protection that grants the author of an original "work" an exclusive right to copy, distribute, sell, and modify that work, except under special circumstances described by copyright laws. A software _____ is a legal contract that defines the ways in which you may use a computer program. Licenses for commercial, shareware, freeware, open source, and public domain software provide consumers with different sets of rights pertaining to copying and distribution.

CHECK ANSWERS

INTERACTIVE KEY TERMS

Make sure that you understand all of the boldfaced key terms presented in this chapter. If you're using the NP8 BookOnCD, you can use this list of terms as an interactive study activity. First, try to define a term in your own words, then click the term to compare your definition with the definition that is presented in the chapter.

Absolute reference, 140
Application software, 121
Automatic recalculation, 140
Bootstrap program, 125
Cell, 138
Cell references, 139
Clip art, 137
Command-line interface, 124
Commercial software, 158
Compiler, 119
Computer programmers, 118
Concurrent-use license, 157
Copyright, 157
Copyright notice, 157
Database, 142
Desktop operating system, 126
Distribution media, 152
DOS, 130
Field, 142
Font, 135
Footer, 136
Format, 135
Formula, 139
Frames, 137
Freeware, 159
Fully justified, 136
Function, 139
Grammar checker, 135
Graphical user interface, 124
Graphics, 145
Groupware, 151
Header, 136
High-level language, 119
Install, 153
Installation agreement, 157

Interpreter, 119
Kernel, 125
Label, 138
Leading, 136
Line spacing, 136
Linux, 129
Mac OS, 128
Machine language, 119
Mail merge, 137
Mathematical operators, 139
Microsoft Windows, 126
Multiple-user license, 157
Multitasking operating system, 126
Multiuser operating system, 126
Natural language query, 144
Network operating system, 126
Non-executing zip file, 156
Object code, 119
Open source software, 159
Page layout, 136
Palm OS, 130
Paragraph alignment, 136
Paragraph style, 136
Point size, 135
Programming language, 119
Properties, 118
Public domain software, 159
Query by example, 144
Query language, 144
Readability formula, 135
Record, 142
Relative reference, 140
Resource, 123
Search and Replace, 135
Self-executing zip file, 156

Self-installing executable file, 156
Service pack, 156
Setup program, 154
Shareware, 158
Shrink-wrap license, 157
Single-user license, 157
Single-user operating system, 126
Site license, 157
Software license, 157
Software patch, 156
Software publishers, 118
Software suite, 148
Source code, 119
Spelling checker, 134
Spelling dictionary, 134
Spreadsheet, 138
Style, 136
System requirements, 152
System software, 121
Table, 137
Thesaurus, 135
Uninstall routine, 156
UNIX, 129
Unzipped, 155
User interface, 124
Utilities, 125
Value, 138
What-if analysis, 138
Windows Mobile OS, 130
Windows Registry, 161
Worksheet, 138
Zipped, 155

COMPUTER SOFTWARE

SOFTWARE KEY TERMS

3-D graphics software, 145
Accounting software, 151
Audio editing software, 147
Audio encoding software, 147
CAD software, 146
CD ripper software, 147
Computer-aided music software, 147
Database software, 142
Desktop publishing software, 133
Document production software, 133
Drawing software, 145
DVD authoring software, 148

Ear training software, 147
Educational software, 149
Graphics software, 145
Horizontal market software, 151
Mathematical modeling software, 141
MIDI sequencing software, 147
Money management software, 141
Notation software, 147
Paint software, 145
Payroll software, 151
Personal finance software, 141
Photo editing software, 145

Presentation software, 146
Project management software, 151
Reference software, 149
Spreadsheet software, 138
Statistical software, 141
Tax preparation software, 141
Vertical market software, 151
Video editing software, 148
Web authoring software, 133
Word processing software, 133

INTERACTIVE SITUATION QUESTIONS

Apply what you've learned to some typical computing situations. When using the NP8 BookOnCD, you can type your answers, then use the Check Answers button to automatically score your responses. Place your Tracking Disk in the floppy disk drive if you want to save your scores.

1. While using several programs at the same time, your computer displays an error message that refers to a general protection fault. You recognize this problem as a potential [_____] leak and decide to close the corrupted program using Ctrl+Alt+Del.

2. If your goal is to produce a printed brochure that contains numerous graphics and looks professionally typeset, you should use DTP software that provides [_____]-oriented layout, instead of a word processor that provides page-oriented layout.

3. You've volunteered to create some graphics for a nonprofit organization, but you'll need a variety of graphics software tools for the organization's computer. Your first choice is to consider a graphics [_____] that bundles together paint, draw, and Web graphics software.

4. Suppose that you've been hired to organize a professional skateboard competition. When you consider how you'll need to use computers, you realize that you must collect information on each competitor and keep track of every competitive event. With at least two types of related records, you'll probably need to use [_____] software.

5. Imagine that you just purchased a new software package. You insert the distribution CD, but nothing happens. No problem—you can manually run the [_____] program, which will start the install routine.

6. You are preparing to download a new software program from the Web. The download consists of one huge file with an .exe extension. You recognize this as a self-[_____] executable file that will automatically unzip itself and start the installation routine.

7. You download an open source software program from the Web. You assume that the download includes the uncompiled [_____] code for the program as well as the [_____] version.

CHECK ANSWERS

INTERACTIVE PRACTICE TESTS

Practice tests that consist of 10 multiple-choice, true/false, and fill-in-the-blank questions are available on both the NP8 BookOnCD and the NP8 Web site. The questions are selected at random from a large test bank, so each time you take a test, you'll receive a different set of questions. Your tests are scored immediately, and you can print study guides that help you find the correct answers for any questions that you missed.

www.course.com/np/concepts8/ch03

CLICK TO START

REVIEW ON THE WEB

PROJECTS

An NP8 Project is an open-ended activity that helps you apply the concepts you have learned. Many projects require resources in addition to your textbook, such as current magazines, library materials, or Web access. When you tackle a project, be prepared to use your critical thinking skills, logical analysis, and creativity. Projects for this chapter include:

- **Issue Research: Software Piracy**
- **Application Software**
- **Computers in Journalism**
- **Software Applications: What's Available**
- **Productivity Suites and Groupware**
- **Where's the Shareware?**
- **Legal Beagle**

To work with the Projects for this chapter, connect to the **New Perspectives NP8 Web Site**.

www.course.com/np/concepts8/ch03

TECHTV VIDEO PROJECT

The TechTV segment *Software Vending Machines* highlights an innovative way to get software into the hands of consumers. After watching the video, write a short description of how this technology works. Next, suppose you are asked to invest in this company. What do you see as the advantages and disadvantages of this technology? Do alternative technologies exist that might be more effective? Discuss your thoughts on these questions.

To work with the Video Projects for this chapter, connect to the **New Perspectives NP8 Web Site**.

www.course.com/np/concepts8/ch03

STUDY TIPS

Study Tips help you to organize and consolidate the information in a chapter by making lists, outlines, charts, and sketches. You can use paper and pencil or word processing software to complete most of the Study Tips.

To work with the Study Tips for this chapter, connect to the **New Perspectives NP8 Web Site**.

www.course.com/np/concepts8/ch03

ONLINE GAMES

Test your comprehension of the concepts introduced in Chapter 3 by playing the NP8 Online Games. At the end of each game, you have three options:

- Print a comprehensive study guide complete with page references
- Print your results to be submitted to your instructor
- Save your results to be submitted to your instructor via e-mail

To work with the Online Games for this chapter, connect to the **New Perspectives NP8 Web Site**.

www.course.com/np/concepts8/ch03

COMPUTER SOFTWARE   173

STUDENT EDITION LABS

Extend your knowledge of software with the Chapter 3 Student Edition Labs.

The following Student Edition Labs are offered with Chapter 3:
- Working with Windows
- Word Processing
- Spreadsheets
- Databases
- Presentation Software
- Installing and Uninstalling Software
- Advanced Spreadsheets

Go to the NP8 New Perspectives Web site for specific lab topics.

To work with the Chapter 3 Student Edition Labs and their corresponding lab assignments, connect to the **New Perspectives NP8 Web Site**.

www.course.com/np/concepts8/ch03

Work hands-on in structured simulations practicing important skills and concepts

Test your comprehension of the lab topics through a series of objective-based questions

Track Your Progress with the Student Edition Labs

- Student Edition Labs test your comprehension of the lab topics through a series of trackable objective-based questions. Your instructor will direct you to either print your results or submit them via e-mail.

- Student Edition Lab Assignments, available on the New Perspectives NP8 Web site, require you to apply the skills learned through the lab in a live environment. Go to the New Perspectives NP8 Web site for detailed instruction on individual Student Edition Lab Assignments.

If you have a SAM user profile, you have access to even more interactive content. Log in to your SAM account and go to your assignments page to see what your instructor has assigned for this chapter.

FILE MANAGEMENT, VIRUS PROTECTION, AND BACKUP

CONTENTS

✺ **SECTION A: FILE BASICS**

File Names, Extensions, and Formats
File Locations, Folders, and Paths
File Sizes and Dates

✺ **SECTION B: FILE MANAGEMENT**

Application-based File Management
File Management Utilities
File Management Metaphors
Windows Explorer
File Management Tips
Physical File Storage

✺ **SECTION C: COMPUTER VIRUSES**

Viruses, Trojan Horses, and Worms
Antivirus Software
Virus Hoaxes

✺ **SECTION D: DATA BACKUP**

Backup and Restore Procedures
Disk, CD, and DVD Backup
Network and Internet Backup
Hard Disk and Tape Backup
Boot and Recovery Disks

✺ **TECHTALK: FILE FORMATS**

✺ **ISSUE: COMPUTER CRIME**

✺ **COMPUTERS IN CONTEXT: LAW ENFORCEMENT**

✺ **REVIEW ACTIVITIES**

Interactive Summary
Interactive Key Terms
Interactive Situation Questions
Interactive Practice Tests
Review on the Web

LABS

✺ Working with Windows Explorer
✺ Backing Up Your Computer

TIP

When using the BookOnCD, the ✺ icons are "clickable" to access resources on the CD. The ✢ icons are clickable to access resources on the Web. You can also access Web resources by using your browser to connect directly to the NP8 New Perspectives Web site at:

www.course.com/np/concepts8/ch04

FILE MANAGEMENT, VIRUS PROTECTION, AND BACKUP   175

CHAPTER PREVIEW

Before you begin Chapter 4, you can use the Web-based preview activities to hear an overview of the chapter, check your current level of expertise about key concepts, and look through a list of learning objectives. You can access the preview activities by clicking the ⚓ icon when using the BookOnCD or going to the New Perspectives NP8 Web site.

CHAPTER OVERVIEW

Your important documents, music collection, and digital photos are stored in files on your computer. This chapter tells you how to organize your files for easy access and how to protect them from viruses and equipment failures. Get your book and highlighter ready, then connect to the New Perspectives NP8 Web site where you can listen to an overview that points out the most important concepts for this chapter.

www.course.com/np/concepts8/ch04 ⚓

CHAPTER PRE-ASSESSMENT

How much do you know about computer file management and viruses? To gauge your level of knowledge before beginning the chapter, take the pre-assessment quiz at the New Perspectives NP8 Web site. Armed with your results from this quiz, you can focus your study time on concepts that will round out your knowledge of computer files and improve your test scores.

www.course.com/np/concepts8/ch04 ⚓

LEARNING OBJECTIVES

When you complete this chapter you should be able to:

- Create valid names for files and folders, plus demonstrate that you can construct and trace file paths
- Demonstrate how to use file management features of application software and operating system utilities
- Describe how a computer physically stores data on disks, but represents this storage system with a logical model
- Explain how file viruses, boot sector viruses, macro viruses, Trojan horses, worms, and Denial of Service attacks affect files and disrupt computer operations
- Describe how a computer owner can use antivirus software to avoid, find, and remove viruses
- Demonstrate that you can implement a viable backup and restore plan
- Compare the advantages and disadvantages of using tapes, floppy disks, a second hard disk, CDs, Zip disks, networks, and Web sites for backups

A detailed list of learning objectives is provided at the New Perspectives NP8 Web site

www.course.com/np/concepts8/ch04 ⚓

SECTION A
FILE BASICS

The term "file" was used for filing cabinets and collections of papers long before it became part of the personal computer lexicon. Today, a computer file—or simply a "file"— is defined as a named collection of data that exists on a storage medium, such as a disk, CD, DVD, or tape. A file can contain a group of records, a document, a photo, music, a video, an e-mail message, or a computer program.

Computer files have several characteristics, such as a name, format, location, size, and date. To make effective use of computer files, you'll need a good understanding of these file basics, and that is the focus of Section A.

FILE NAMES, EXTENSIONS, AND FORMATS

What are the rules for naming files? Every file has a name and might also have a file extension. When you save a file, you must provide a valid file name that adheres to specific rules, referred to as **file-naming conventions**. Each operating system has a unique set of file-naming conventions. You can use Figure 4-1 to determine whether file names, such as *Nul*, *My File.doc*, *Report:2002*, and *Bud01/02.txt*, are valid under the operating system you use.

FIGURE 4-1
File-Naming Conventions

	DOS and Windows 3.1	Windows 95/98/Me/XP/NT/2000	Mac OS (Classic)	UNIX/Linux
Maximum length of file name	8-character file name plus an extension of 3 characters or less	File name and extension cannot exceed 255 characters	1–31 characters	14–256 characters (depending on UNIX/Linux version), including an extension of any length
Spaces allowed	No	Yes	Yes	No
Numbers allowed	Yes	Yes	Yes	Yes
Characters not allowed	* / [ ] ; " = \ : , | ?	* \ : < > | " / ?	:	* ! @ # $ % ^ & ( ) { } [ ] " \ ? ; < > /
File names not allowed	Aux, Com1, Com2, Com3, Com4, Con, Lpt1, Lpt2, Lpt3, Prn, Nul	Aux, Com1, Com2, Com3, Com4, Con, Lpt1, Lpt2, Lpt3, Prn, Nul	Any file name is allowed	Any filename is allowed
Case sensitive	No	No	No	Yes (use lowercase)

FILE MANAGEMENT, VIRUS PROTECTION, AND BACKUP

Why are certain characters and words not allowed in a file name? If an operating system attaches special significance to a symbol, you might not be able to use it in a file name. For example, DOS and Windows use the colon (:) character to separate the device letter from a file name or folder, as in *C:Music*. A file name such as *Report:2002* is not valid because the operating system would become confused about how to interpret the colon.

Some operating systems also contain a list of **reserved words** that are used as commands or special identifiers. You cannot use these words alone as a file name. You can, however, use these words as part of a longer file name. For example, under Windows XP, the file name *Nul* would not be valid, but you could name a file something like *Nul Committee Notes.doc* or *Null Set.exe*.

Are file extensions important? As explained in Chapter 1, a file extension is an optional file identifier that is separated from the main file name by a period, as in *Paint.exe*. With some operating systems, such as Windows and DOS, file extensions work like tickets that admit people to different plays, movies, or concerts. If you have the right ticket, you get in. If a file has the right extension for a particular application program, you'll see it in the list of files you can open with that software. For example, files with a .doc extension appear in the Open and Save As lists when you're working with Microsoft Word software.

A file extension is usually related to the **file format**, which is defined as the arrangement of data in a file and the coding scheme used to represent the data. Files containing graphics are usually stored using a different file format than files containing text. Hundreds of file formats exist, and you'll encounter many of them as you use a variety of software. Most software programs have what's called a **native file format** for storing files. For example, Microsoft Word stores files in DOC format, whereas Adobe Illustrator stores graphics files in AI format. When using a software application such as Microsoft Word to open a file, the program displays any files that have the file extension for its native file format, as shown in Figure 4-2.

FIGURE 4-2

The next time you use software, take note of the file extensions that appear when you look at the list of files in the Open dialog box. If you don't see any file extensions, you've discovered the results of a Windows setting that can hide (but not erase) file extensions.

If Windows is set to hide file extensions, you can view them by opening Windows Explorer, selecting the Tools menu, selecting Folder Options, then changing the "Hide file extensions" option.

CLICK TO START

FILE LOCATIONS, FOLDERS, AND PATHS

How do I designate a file's location? To designate a file's location, you must first specify where the file is stored. As shown in Figure 4-3, each of a PC's storage devices is identified by a device letter—a convention that is specific to DOS and Windows. The floppy disk drive is usually assigned device letter A and is referred to as "drive A." A device letter is usually followed by a colon, so drive A could be designated as A: or as 3.5" Floppy (A:). The main hard disk drive is usually referred to as "drive C." Additional storage devices can be assigned letters D through Z. Although most PCs stick to the standard of drive A for the floppy disk drive and drive C for the hard disk drive, the device letters for CD, Zip, and DVD drives are not standardized. For example, the CD-writer on your computer might be assigned device letter E, whereas the CD-writer on another computer might be assigned device letter R.

FIGURE 4-3
The Windows operating system labels storage devices with letters, such as A: and C:.

Name	Type
Hard Disk Drives	
Local Disk (C:)	Local Disk
Devices with Removable Storage	
3½ Floppy (A:)	3½-Inch Floppy Disk
DVD/CD-RW Drive (D:)	CD Drive
Network Drives	
files on 'Mtcnas' (H:)	Network Drive

What's the purpose of folders? An operating system maintains a list of files called a **directory** for each storage disk, tape, CD, or DVD. The main directory of a disk is referred to as the **root directory**. On a PC, the root directory is identified by the device letter followed by a backslash. For example, the root directory of the hard disk drive would be C:\. You should try to avoid storing your data files in the root directory of your hard disk; instead, store them in a subdirectory.

A root directory can be subdivided into smaller lists. Each list is called a **subdirectory**. When you use Windows, Mac OS, or a Linux graphical file manager, these subdirectories are depicted as **folders** because they work like folders in a filing cabinet to store an assortment of related items. Each folder has a name, so you can easily create a folder called *Documents* to hold reports, letters, and so on. You can create another folder called *My Music* to hold your MP3 files. Folders can be created within other folders. You might, for example, create a folder within the *My Music* folder to hold your jazz collection and another folder to hold your reggae collection.

A folder name is separated from a drive letter and other folder names by a special symbol. In DOS and Microsoft Windows, this symbol is the backslash (\ ). For example, the folder for your reggae music (within the *My Music* folder on drive C) would be written as *C:\ My Music\Reggae*.

Imagine how hard it would be to find a specific piece of paper in a filing cabinet that was stuffed with a random assortment of reports, letters, and newspaper clippings. By storing a file in a folder, you assign it a place in an organized hierarchy of folders and files.

A computer file's location is defined by a **file specification** (sometimes called a **path**), which includes the drive letter, folder(s), file name, and extension. Suppose that you have stored an MP3 file called *Marley One Love* in the *Reggae* folder on your hard disk drive. Its file specification would be as follows:

C:\My Music\Reggae\Marley One Love.mp3

Drive letter | **Primary folder** | **Secondary folder** | **File name** | **File extension**

FILE MANAGEMENT, VIRUS PROTECTION, AND BACKUP

FILE SIZES AND DATES

What's the significance of a file's size? A file contains data, stored as a group of bits. The more bits, the larger the file. **File size** is usually measured in bytes, kilobytes, or megabytes. Knowing the size of a file can be important. Compared to small files, large files fill up storage space more quickly, require longer transmission times, and are more likely to be stripped off e-mail attachments by a mail server. Your computer's operating system keeps track of file sizes and supplies that information when you request a listing of files.

Is the file date important? Your computer keeps track of the date that a file was created or last modified (Figure 4-4). The **file date** is useful if you have created several versions of a file and want to make sure you know which version is the most recent. It can also come in handy if you have downloaded several updates of a software package, such as an MP3 player, and you want to make sure you install the latest version.

Name	Size	Type	Date Modified
Folder Settings		File Folder	4/17/2004 2:56 PM
My Music		File Folder	12/6/2004 4:57 PM
My Pictures		File Folder	12/6/2004 4:57 PM
My Webs		File Folder	7/13/2004 5:00 PM
Temp		File Folder	3/26/2004 3:16 PM
ABC.doc	33 KB	Microsoft Word Document	9/16/2004 6:59 PM
Application Letter.doc	24 KB	Microsoft Word Document	7/16/2004 6:22 PM
Home Inventory.mdb	360 KB	Microsoft Office Access Application	4/21/2003 1:21 PM
Jazz Recordings.mdb	176 KB	Microsoft Office Access Application	3/31/2004 1:23 PM

FIGURE 4-4
File sizes and dates can provide information that is useful when working with files.

QUICKCHECK......SECTION A

1. Windows file-naming _____ are different than for Linux.

2. When using Windows, you cannot use a reserved word, such as Aux, as a file name. True or false? _____

3. Microsoft Word uses DOC as its _____ file format.

4. On a computer running Windows, the hard disk letter is usually designated as _____.

5. The root directory of a disk can be divided into smaller lists called _____, that are depicted as folders.

6. A file's location is defined by a file path, which includes the drive letter, one or more _____, file name, and extension.

7. A file's _____ can be important information when you are planning to transmit it to another computer over a network.

CHECK ANSWERS

SECTION B
FILE MANAGEMENT

File management encompasses any procedure that helps you organize your computer-based files so that you can find and use them more efficiently. Depending on your computer's operating system, you can organize and manipulate your files from within an application program or by using a special file management utility the operating system provides. Section B offers an overview of application-based and operating system-based file management.

APPLICATION-BASED FILE MANAGEMENT

How does a software application help me manage files? Applications, such as word processing software or graphics software, typically provide a way to open files and save them in a specific folder on a designated storage device. An application might also have additional file management capabilities, such as deleting, copying, and renaming files. Take a look at an example of the file management capabilities in a typical Windows application—Microsoft Word.

Suppose you want to write a letter to the editor of your local newspaper about the rising tide of graffiti in your neighborhood. You would open your word processing software and type the document. As you type, the document is held in RAM. At some point, you'll want to save the document. To do so, you click File on the menu bar, and then select the Save As option. The Save As dialog box, shown in Figure 4-5, opens and allows you to specify a name for the file and its location on one of your computer's storage devices.

FIGURE 4-5
The Save As dialog box is used to name a file and specify its storage location.

1. Begin by clicking this arrow button to display a list of storage devices. Double-clicking any device displays its folders.

2. Select a storage device and folder to indicate where you want the file to be stored.

3. Type a name for the file.

4. Click the Save button.

FILE MANAGEMENT, VIRUS PROTECTION, AND BACKUP

What's the difference between the Save option and the Save As option? Most Windows applications provide a curious set of options on the File menu. In addition to the Save As option, the menu contains a Save option. The difference between the two options is subtle, but useful. The Save As option allows you to select a name and storage device for a file, whereas the Save option simply saves the latest version of a file under its current name and at its current location.

A potentially confusing aspect of these options occurs when you try to use the Save option for a file that doesn't yet have a name. Because you can't save a file without a name, your application displays the Save As dialog box, even though you selected the Save option. The flowchart in Figure 4-6 will help you decide whether to use the Save or Save As command.

What other options are available in the Save As dialog box? The Save As dialog box displayed by Windows applications allows you to do more than just save a file. You can use it to rename a file, delete a file, or create a folder, as shown in Figure 4-7.

FIGURE 4-6
Should I use the Save or Save As command?

- Does the file have a name yet? — **No** → Use Save As
- Yes ↓
- Do you want to change the name of the file, or save your current work as a separate file from the original? — **No** → Use Save
- Yes ↓
- Use Save As

FIGURE 4-7
The Save As dialog box not only helps you select a name and destination drive for a file, but also allows you to rename files, delete files, create folders, and rename folders.

CLICK TO START

Use this icon to create a new folder.

To rename or delete a folder, right-click it and then use one of the options on the pop-up menu.

Use any of the options on this pop-up menu to manipulate the highlighted file or folder.

To rename or delete a file, right-click the file name, and then select a command from the pop-up menu that appears. In addition to the Rename and Delete options, this menu might include options to copy the file, e-mail it, or scan it for viruses.

181

FILE MANAGEMENT UTILITIES

How does the operating system help me manage files? Although most application software gives you access to commands you can use to save, open, rename, and delete individual files, you might want to work with groups of files or perform other file operations that are inconvenient within the Open or Save dialog boxes.

Most operating systems provide **file management utilities** that give you the "big picture" of the files you have stored on your disks and help you work with them. For example, Windows provides a file management utility that can be accessed from the My Computer icon or from the Windows Explorer option on the Start menu. On computers with Mac OS, the file management utility is called the "Finder." These utilities, shown in Figure 4-8, help you view a list of files, find files, move files from one place to another, make copies of files, delete files, discover file properties, and rename files.

FIGURE 4-8

The Windows file management utility can be tailored to show files as icons (top) or as a list (middle).

Mac OS provides a file management utility called the Finder (bottom).

FILE MANAGEMENT, VIRUS PROTECTION, AND BACKUP   183

FILE MANAGEMENT METAPHORS

How can a file management utility help me visualize my computer's file storage? File management utilities often use some sort of **storage metaphor** to help you visualize and mentally organize the files on your disks and other storage devices. These metaphors are also called **logical storage models** because they are supposed to help you form a mental (logical) picture of the way in which your files are stored.

What storage metaphors are typically used for personal computers? After hearing so much about files and folders, you might have guessed that the filing cabinet is a popular metaphor for computer storage. In this metaphor, each storage device of a computer corresponds to one of the drawers in a filing cabinet. The drawers hold folders and the folders hold files.

Another storage metaphor is based on a hierarchical diagram that is sometimes referred to as a "tree structure." In this metaphor, a tree represents a storage device. The trunk of the tree corresponds to the root directory. The branches of the tree represent folders. These branches can split into small branches representing folders within folders. The leaves at the end of a branch represent the files in a particular folder. Figure 4-9 illustrates the tree lying on its side so that you can see the relationship to the metaphor shown in the next figure, Figure 4-10.

The tree structure metaphor offers a useful mental image of the way in which files and folders are organized. It is not, however, particularly practical as a user interface. Imagine the complexity of the tree diagram from Figure 4-9 if it were expanded to depict branches for hundreds of folders and leaves for thousands of files.

For practicality, storage metaphors are translated into more mundane screen displays. Figure 4-10 shows how Microsoft programmers combined the filing cabinet metaphor with the tree structure metaphor in the Windows Explorer file management utility.

FIGURE 4-9
You can visualize the directory of a disk as a tree on its side. The trunk corresponds to the root directory, the branches to folders, and the leaves to files.

FIGURE 4-10
Windows Explorer borrows folders from the filing cabinet metaphor and places them in a hierarchical structure similar to a tree on its side.

WINDOWS EXPLORER

How do I use a file management utility? As an example of a file management utility, take a closer look at **Windows Explorer**, a utility program bundled with the Windows operating system and designed to help you organize and manipulate the files stored on your computer.

The Windows Explorer window is divided into two "window panes." The pane on the left side of the window lists each of the storage devices connected to your computer, plus several important system objects, such as My Computer, My Network Places, and the Desktop.

An icon for a storage device or other system object can be "expanded" by clicking its corresponding plus-sign icon. Expanding an icon displays the next level of the storage hierarchy—usually a collection of folders.

A device icon or folder can be "opened" by clicking directly on the icon rather than on the plus sign. Once an icon is opened, its contents appear in the pane on the right side of the Windows Explorer window. Figure 4-11 illustrates how to manipulate the directory display.

FIGURE 4-11

Windows Explorer makes it easy to drill down through the levels of the directory hierarchy to locate a folder or file.

CLICK TO START

- The left pane displays your computer's hierarchy of storage devices and folders.
- The minus-sign icon can be used to collapse a device or folder to hide levels of the hierarchy.
- The plus-sign icon can be used to expand a device or folder to display the next level of the hierarchy.
- The right pane displays the folders and files contained in the device or folder that is currently open in the left pane.
- Any device or system object can be opened by clicking it.

Can I work with more than one file or folder at a time? To work with a group of files or folders, you must first select them. You can accomplish this task in several ways. You can hold down the Ctrl key as you click each item. This method works well if you are selecting files or folders that are not listed consecutively. As an alternative, you can hold down the Shift key while you click the first item and the last item you want to select. By using this method, you select the two items that you clicked and all the items in between. Windows Explorer displays all the items you selected by highlighting them. After a group of items is highlighted, you can use the same copy, move, or delete procedure that you would use for a single item.

What can I do with the folders and files that are listed in Windows Explorer? In addition to locating files and folders, Windows Explorer provides a set of procedures (shown in Figure 4-12 on the next page) that help you manipulate files and folders in the following ways:

- **Rename.** You might want to change the name of a file or folder to better describe its contents.

FILE MANAGEMENT, VIRUS PROTECTION, AND BACKUP

- **Copy.** You can copy a file from one device to another—for example, from a floppy disk in drive A to the hard disk in drive C. You can also make a copy of a document so that you can revise the copy and leave the original intact.

- **Move.** You can move a file from one folder to another or from one storage device to another. When you move a file, it is erased from its original location, so make sure you remember the new location of the file. You can also move folders from one storage device to another or move them to a different folder.

- **Delete.** You can delete a file when you no longer need it. You can also delete a folder. Be careful when you delete a folder because most file management utilities also delete all the files within a folder.

FIGURE 4-12

Windows Explorer helps you delete, copy, move, and rename files.

To copy a file or folder, right-click it, and then select Copy. Right-click the new location for the file or folder, and then select Paste.

To move a file or folder, you can use the mouse to drag it to a different device or folder icon.

To delete a file or folder, click it, and then press the Delete key.

To rename a file or folder, right-click it, and then select Rename. A box appears around the current name so that you can modify it.

FILE MANAGEMENT TIPS

A file management utility provides tools and procedures to help you keep track of your program and data files, but these tools are most useful when you have a logical plan for organizing your files and when you follow some basic file management guidelines. The following tips pertain to managing files on your own computer. When working with files on lab computers, follow the guidelines from your instructor or lab manager.

- **Use descriptive names.** Give your files and folders descriptive names, and avoid using cryptic abbreviations.

- **Maintain file extensions.** When renaming a file, keep the original file extension so that you can easily open it with the correct application software.

- **Group similar files.** Separate files into folders based on subject matter. For example, store your creative writing assignments in one folder and your MP3 music files in another folder.

- **Organize your folders from the top down.** When devising a hierarchy of folders, consider how you want to access files and back them up. For example, it is easy to specify one folder and its subfolders for a backup. If your important data is scattered in a variety of folders, however, making backups is more time consuming.

- **Consider using the My Document default directory.** Windows software typically defaults to the *My Documents* folder for storing data files. You might want to use *My Documents* (Figure 4-13) as your main data folder, and add subfolders as necessary to organize your files.

- **Do not mix data files and program files.** Do not store data files in the folders that hold your software—on Windows systems, most software is stored in subfolders of the *Program Files* folder.

- **No files in the root directory.** Although it is acceptable to create folders in the root directory, it is not a good practice to store programs or data files in the root directory of your computer's hard disk.

- **Access files from the hard disk.** For best performance, copy files from floppy disks or CDs to your computer's hard disk before accessing them.

- **Follow copyright rules.** When copying files, make sure you adhere to copyright and license restrictions.

- **Delete files you no longer need.** Deleting unneeded files and folders helps keep your list of files from growing to an unmanageable size.

- **Be aware of storage locations.** When you save files, make sure the drive letter and folder name specify the correct storage location.

- **Back up!** Back up your folders regularly.

PHYSICAL FILE STORAGE

Is data stored in specific places on a disk? So far, you've seen how an operating system such as Windows can help you visualize computer storage as files and folders. This logical storage model, however, has little to do with what actually happens on your disk. The structure of files and folders you see in Windows Explorer is called a "logical" model because it is supposed to help you create a mental picture. The **physical storage model** describes what actually happens on the disks and in the circuits. As you will see, the physical model is quite different from the logical model.

Before a computer can store a file on a disk, CD, or DVD, the storage medium must be formatted. The **formatting** process creates the equivalent of electronic storage bins by dividing a disk into **tracks** and then further dividing each track into **sectors**. Tracks and sectors are numbered to provide addresses for each data storage bin. The numbering scheme depends on the storage device and the operating system. On floppy, Zip, and hard disks, tracks are arranged as concentric circles; on CDs and DVDs, one or more tracks spiral out from the center of the disk (Figure 4-14).

FIGURE 4-13
Windows XP supplies a series of default folders, including *My Documents*, that many users find convenient for storing their data.

FIGURE 4-14
A process called formatting prepares the surface of a disk to hold data.

Disks are divided into tracks and wedge-shaped sectors—each side of a floppy disk typically has 80 tracks divided into 18 sectors. Each sector holds 512 bytes of data.

On a typical CD, a single track is about three miles long and is divided into 336,000 sectors. Each sector holds 2,048 bytes of data.

FILE MANAGEMENT, VIRUS PROTECTION, AND BACKUP

How does a disk get formatted? Today, most floppy, Zip, and hard disks are preformatted at the factory; however, computer operating systems provide **formatting utilities** you can use to reformat some storage devices—typically floppy and hard disks. Formatting utilities are also supplied by the companies that manufacture hard disk drives, writable CD drives, and writable DVD drives.

When you use a formatting utility, it erases any data that happens to be on the disk, and then prepares the tracks and sectors necessary to hold data. You might consider reformatting some of your old floppy disks (instead of just deleting the files they contain) if you really want to make them blank before you reuse them. The screen tour associated with Figure 4-15 demonstrates how to use Windows to format a floppy disk.

FIGURE 4-15
Windows includes a floppy disk formatting utility, which can be accessed from the A: (Floppy disk) icon in the My Computer window or Windows Explorer.

CLICK TO START

How does the operating system keep track of a file's location? The operating system uses a **file system** to keep track of the names and locations of files that reside on a storage medium, such as a hard disk. Different operating systems use different file systems. Most versions of Mac OS use the Macintosh Hierarchical File System (HFS). Ext2fs (extended 2 file system) is the native file system for Linux. Windows NT, Windows 2000, and Windows XP use a file system called **NTFS** (New Technology File System). The file system for Windows 3.1 was called FAT16. Windows 95, 98, and Me use a file system called **FAT32**.

To speed up the process of storing and retrieving data, a disk drive usually works with a group of sectors called a **cluster** or a "block." The number of sectors that form a cluster varies, depending on the capacity of the disk and the way the operating system works with files. A file system's primary task is to maintain a list of clusters and keep track of which are empty and which hold data. This information is stored in a special index file. If your computer uses the FAT32 file system, for example, this index file is called the **File Allocation Table** (FAT). If your computer uses NTFS, it is called the **Master File Table** (MFT).

Each of your disks contains its own index file so that information about its contents is always available when the disk is in use. Unfortunately, storing this crucial file on disk also presents a risk because if the index file is damaged by a hard disk head crash or scratch, you'll generally lose access to all the data stored on the disk. Index files become damaged all too frequently, so it is important to back up your data.

When you save a file, your PC's operating system looks at the index file to see which clusters are empty. It selects one of these clusters, records the file data there, and then revises the index file to include the file name and its location.

A file that does not fit into a single cluster spills over into the next contiguous (meaning adjacent) cluster unless that cluster already contains data. When contiguous clusters are not available, the operating system stores parts of a file in noncontiguous (nonadjacent) clusters. Figure 4-16 helps you visualize how an index file, such as the MFT, keeps track of file names and locations.

Master File Table

File	Cluster	Comment
MFT	1	Reserved for MFT files
DISK USE	2	Part of MFT that contains list of empty sectors
Bio.txt	3, 4	Bio.txt file stored in clusters 3 and 4
Jordan.wks	7, 8, 10	Jordan.wks file stored noncontiguously in clusters 7, 8, and 10
Pick.wps	9	Pick.wps file stored in cluster 9

FIGURE 4-16
Each colored cluster on the disk contains part of a file. Bio.txt is stored in contiguous clusters. Jordan.wks is stored in noncontiguous clusters.

A computer locates and displays the Jordan.wks file by looking for its name in the Master File Table.

When you want to retrieve a file, the OS looks through the index for the file name and its location. It moves the disk drive's read-write head to the first cluster that contains the file data. Using additional data from the index file, the operating system can move the read-write heads to each of the clusters containing the remaining parts of the file.

What happens when a file is deleted? When you click a file's icon and then select the Delete option, you might have visions of the read-write head somehow scrubbing out the clusters that contain data. That doesn't happen. Instead, the operating system simply changes the status of the file's clusters to "empty" and removes the file name from the index file. The file name no longer appears in a directory listing, but the file's data remains in the clusters until a new file is stored there. You might think that this data is as good as erased, but it is possible to purchase utilities that recover a lot of this "deleted" data—law enforcement agents, for example, use these utilities to gather evidence from deleted files on the computer disks of suspected criminals.

To delete data from a disk in such a way that no one can ever read it, you can use special **file shredder software** that overwrites "empty" sectors with random 1s and 0s. You might find this software handy if you plan to donate your computer to a charitable organization, and you want to make sure your personal data no longer remains on the hard disk.

FILE MANAGEMENT, VIRUS PROTECTION, AND BACKUP

Can deleted files be undeleted? The Windows Recycle Bin and similar utilities in other operating systems are designed to protect you from accidentally deleting hard disk files you actually need. Instead of marking a file's clusters as available, the operating system moves the file to the Recycle Bin folder. The "deleted" file still takes up space on the disk, but does not appear in the usual directory listing.

Files that appear in the directory listing for the Recycle Bin folder can be undeleted so that they again appear in the regular directory. The Recycle Bin can be emptied to permanently delete any files it contains.

How does a disk become fragmented? As a computer writes files on a disk, parts of files tend to become scattered all over the disk. These **fragmented files** are stored in noncontiguous clusters. Drive performance generally declines as the read-write heads move back and forth to locate the clusters containing the parts of a file. To regain peak performance, you can use a **defragmentation utility** to rearrange the files on a disk so that they are stored in contiguous clusters (Figure 4-17).

FIGURE 4-17
Defragmenting a disk helps your computer operate more efficiently. Consider using a defragmentation utility at least once a month to keep your computer running in top form.

On the fragmented disk (left), the purple, yellow, and blue files are stored in noncontiguous clusters.

When the disk is defragmented (right), the sectors of data for each file are moved to contiguous clusters.

Fragmented disk

Defragmented disk

QUICKCHECK......SECTION B

1. The _____ option on an application's File menu allows you to save the latest version of a file under its current name and at its current location.

2. A storage _____, such as a filing cabinet or tree, helps you visualize and mentally organize your computer files.

3. Windows _____ is software provided by the operating system and designed to help you organize and manipulate files.

4. A hard disk stores data in concentric _____, which are divided into wedge-shaped _____.

5. File _____ software overwrites deleted files with random 1s and 0s.

CHECK ANSWERS

LAB 4-B
WORKING WITH WINDOWS EXPLORER

In this lab, you'll learn:

- How to access Windows Explorer
- How to expand and collapse the directory structure to locate folders and files
- How to rename or delete a file or folder
- The basic principles for creating an efficient directory structure for your files
- How to create a folder
- How to select a single file or a group of files
- How to move files from one folder to another

INTERACTIVE LAB

CLICK TO START THE LAB

LAB ASSIGNMENTS

1. Start the interactive part of the lab. Insert your Tracking Disk if you want to save your QuickCheck results. Perform each lab step as directed, and answer all the lab QuickCheck questions. When you exit the lab, your answers are automatically graded and your results are displayed.

2. Use Windows Explorer to look at the directory of the hard disk or floppy disk that currently contains most of your files. Draw a diagram showing the hierarchy of folders. Write a paragraph explaining how you could improve this hierarchy, and draw a diagram to illustrate your plan.

3. Use a new floppy disk or format an old disk that doesn't contain important data. Create three folders on the disk: Music, Web Graphics, and Articles. Within the Music folder, create four additional folders: Jazz, Reggae, Rock, and Classical. Within the Classical folder, create two more folders: Classical MIDI and Classical MP3. If you have Internet access, go on to #4.

4. Use your browser software to connect to the Internet, and then go to a Web site, such as *www.zdnet.com* or *www.cnet.com*. Look for a small graphic (remember, you have only 1.44 MB of space on your floppy disk!) and download it to your Web Graphics folder. Next, use a search engine such as *www.google.com* or *www.yahoo.com* to search for "classical MIDI music." Download one of the compositions to the Music\Classical\Classical MIDI folder. Open Windows Explorer and expand all the directories for drive A. Open the Music\Classical\Classical MIDI folder and make sure your music download appears. Capture a screenshot. Follow your instructor's directions to submit this screenshot as a printout or an e-mail attachment.

SECTION C
COMPUTER VIRUSES

Viruses are one of the biggest threats to the security of your computer files. In 1981, there was one known computer virus. Today, the count exceeds 70,000. Between 600 and 900 new viruses appear every month. Viruses are spreading more rapidly than ever. The Michelangelo virus infected 75,000 computers in seven months; the Melissa virus reached 3.5 million computers in 10 hours; and a virus called I-love-you took only three hours to reach 72 million. Today, MyDoom, Sasser, and Netsky infections affect hundreds of millions of computers despite vigorous eradication efforts.

Computer viruses invade all types of computers, including mainframes, servers, personal computers, and even handheld computers. To defend your computer against viruses, you should understand what they are, how they work, and how to use antivirus software.

VIRUSES, TROJAN HORSES, AND WORMS

What kind of code can attack my computer? The term **malicious code** (sometimes called "malware") refers to any program or set of program instructions designed to surreptitiously enter a computer and disrupt its normal operations. Malicious code, including viruses, worms, and Trojan horses, is created and unleashed by individuals referred to as "hackers" or "crackers."

The term "hacker" originally referred to a highly skilled computer programmer. Today, however, the terms "hacker" and "cracker" usually refer to anyone who uses a computer to gain unauthorized access to data, steal information, distribute viruses, or crash a computer system. Spreading a computer virus is a crime in many countries, including the United States.

What is a computer virus? A **computer virus** is a set of program instructions that attaches itself to a file, reproduces itself, and spreads to other files. It can corrupt files, destroy data, display an irritating message, or otherwise disrupt computer operations. A common misconception is that viruses spread themselves from one computer to another, but they can replicate themselves only on the host computer. Viruses spread because people distribute infected files by exchanging disks and CDs, sending e-mail attachments, exchanging music on file-sharing networks, and downloading software from the Web. Be cautious of floppy disks, homemade CDs, and Web sites that contain games and other supposedly fun stuff. Check these files with antivirus software before you copy or use them.

Many computer viruses infect files executed by your computer—files with extensions such as .exe, .com, or .vbs. When your computer executes an infected program, it also executes the attached virus instructions. These instructions then remain in RAM, waiting to infect the next program your computer runs or the next disk it accesses.

In addition to replicating itself, a virus might deliver a **payload**, which could be as harmless as displaying an annoying message or as devastating as corrupting the data on your computer's hard disk. A **trigger event**, such as a specific date, can unleash some viruses. For example, the Michelangelo virus triggers on March 6, the birthday of artist Michelangelo.

TERMINOLOGY NOTE

Viruses that deliver their payloads on a specific date are sometimes referred to as "time bombs."

Viruses that deliver their payloads in response to some other system event are referred to as "logic bombs."

A key characteristic of viruses is their ability to "lurk" in a computer for days or months, quietly replicating themselves. While this replication takes place, you might not even know that your computer has contracted a virus; therefore, it is easy to inadvertently spread infected files to other people's computers.

A virus can be classified as a file virus, boot sector virus, or macro virus. A **file virus** infects application programs, such as games. A **boot sector virus** Infects the system files your computer uses every time you turn it on. These viruses can cause widespread damage and recurring problems. A **macro virus** infects a set of instructions called a "macro"—a miniature program that usually contains legitimate instructions to automate document and worksheet production. When you view a document containing an infected macro, the macro virus duplicates itself into the general macro pool, where it is picked up by other documents (Figure 4-18).

FIGURE 4-18
Today, programs with macro capabilities warn you if a document contains a macro and allow you to disable macros. Macro security warnings do not necessarily mean that a document contains a macro infected with a virus. Scanning the macro with antivirus software, however, can detect the presence of a virus.

How is a Trojan horse different from a virus? A **Trojan horse** is a computer program that seems to perform one function while actually doing something else. Technically, it is not the same as a virus because, unlike a virus, a Trojan horse is not designed to make copies of itself. Trojan horses are notorious for stealing passwords. For example, one Trojan horse arrives as an e-mail attachment named Picture.exe, which leads you to believe you've received some type of graphics software. If you open this file, however, it searches for America Online (AOL) user information and tries to steal your login and e-mail passwords. Trojan horses can also generate official-looking forms that are actually fake (Figure 4-19).

FIGURE 4-19
A Trojan horse called Padodor watches your browser window for text strings such as "Sign in" and "Log in." It then displays a fake login screen like the one shown here to collect your credit card numbers and ATM PIN code.

Messages that demand your PayPal account number, your AOL password, or your ATM PIN are additional examples of Trojan horses currently making the rounds.

FILE MANAGEMENT, VIRUS PROTECTION, AND BACKUP

Many Trojan horses have **backdoor** capability, which allows unauthorized access to victims' computers. A backdoor allows remote hackers to download and execute files on your computer, upload a list of other infected computers, and use your computer as a relay station for breaking into other computers.

Some Trojan horses delete files and cause other trouble. Although a Trojan horse is not defined as a program that replicates itself, some Trojan horses do contain a virus, which can replicate and spread. Other Trojan horses are carried by worms. Virus experts use the term **blended threat** to describe threats that combine more than one type of malicious program. Common blended threats include Trojan-horse/virus combinations and worm/virus combinations.

What's a worm? With the proliferation of network traffic and e-mail, worms have become a major concern in the computing community. Unlike a virus, which is designed to spread from file to file, a **worm** is designed to spread from computer to computer. Most worms take advantage of communications networks—especially the Internet—to travel within e-mail and TCP/IP packets, jumping from one computer to another. Some worms simply spread throughout a network. Others also deliver payloads that vary from harmless messages to malicious file deletions.

How do worms spread? Mass-mailing worms have become especially troublesome. A **mass-mailing worm** spreads by sending itself to every address in the address book of an infected computer. Mass-mailing worms such as Klez, Netsky, MyDoom, and Bagle have made headlines and caused havoc on personal computers, LANs, and Internet servers. To make these worms difficult to track, the "From" line of the infected message sometimes contains a **spoofed address** of a randomly selected person from the address book rather than the address of the computer that actually sent the mail.

Mass-mailing worms often include an attachment that contains the worm. Opening the attachment unleashes the worm. Some mass-mailing worms contain a Web link that installs a worm, Trojan horse, or virus (Figure 4-20). Sasser and other mass-mailing worms, however, require no user interaction to infect a computer.

FIGURE 4-20
A mass-mailing worm called Wallon contains a link to a Web site. Clicking the link downloads several files, including the worm, which replicates by sending itself to addresses listed on the infected computer.

The conventional wisdom for avoiding e-mail-borne infections is not to open suspicious attachments—especially those with executable file extensions, such as .exe. Most computer owners recognize that an attachment called Amazing Photo.exe that arrives from an unknown sender probably contains a virus. Hackers, however, have become proficient at using "social engineering" techniques to make e-mail messages and their attachments seem legitimate. For example, a virus called Netsup looks like a message from your e-mail postmaster that says, "A message sent could not be delivered to one or more of its recipients correctly. This is a permanent error. Attached is a copy of the original message." Opening the attachment to view the undelivered mail triggers the worm.

Another prevalent example of social engineering is a message that appears to have been sent by Microsoft imploring you to install software updates (Figure 4-21). The so-called update contains a worm. If you're uncertain about the legitimacy of an e-mail that arrives from a reputable organization, check its Web site before responding.

FIGURE 4-21
You might be tempted to install the operating system service pack in this e-mail that seems to have been sent by Microsoft. Don't do it! This worm is an example of social engineering techniques used to make infected e-mail messages look legitimate.

Worms can also spread via HTML scripts. Chapter 1 explained that you can set your e-mail software to use HTML format, which provides a variety of font colors, types, and sizes for your messages. Unfortunately, e-mail that's in HTML format can harbor worms hidden in program-like "scripts" that hackers embed in the HTML tags. These worms are difficult to detect—even for antivirus software. As a result, many people stick with plain-text, non-HTML e-mail.

Although e-mail is currently the primary vehicle used to spread worms, hackers have also devised ways to spread worms over file-sharing networks, such as Kazaa. Some worms are designed to spread over instant messaging links. Worms such as Cabir can even infect mobile phones.

What are the most common threats? Before widespread use of the Internet, viruses were the biggest threat to computer security. Today, however, worms have become the biggest threat. Looking toward the future,

INFOWEBLINKS

The old saying "know thy enemy" applies to viruses and worms. To learn more details about current threats, visit the **Virus Descriptions InfoWeb**.

www.course.com/np/concepts8/ch04

FILE MANAGEMENT, VIRUS PROTECTION, AND BACKUP

experts predict an increase of blended threats that combine worm-like distribution with virus payloads. Worms that spread through channels other than e-mail are likely to become more prevalent, too. Figure 4-22 highlights some landmarks and trends in the development of malicious code.

FIGURE 4-22
Malicious Code Trends

Date	Threats	Trends
1981	Cloner	The first known virus begins to spread. Cloner infects files on disks formatted for Apple II computers. The prevalence of disk-borne viruses continues well into the1990s with Jerusalem (1987), Michelangelo (1992), and others.
1988	Internet Worm	The first major worm attack via the Internet sets the stage for today's prolific crop of mass-mailing worms.
1998	Back Orifice	First Trojan horse designed to allow a remote hacker to gain unauthorized access to a computer.
1999	Melissa	Macro viruses, such as Melissa and Laroux, are prevalent for several years and cause trouble by infecting Microsoft Word and Excel files.
2000	Love Letter	One of the fastest spreading mass-mailing worms of all time. Followed by Sobig, Blaster, and MyDoom (2004).
2001	Code Red	Worms designed for Denial of Service attacks gather steam. Code Red, which targeted the White House, is followed by Blaster (2001) and Slammer (2003).
2002	Klez	Klez is a mass-mailing worm that is particularly difficult to eradicate. Because the "From" address is spoofed, it is is almost impossible to locate infected computers.
2003	Mimail	Social engineering takes center stage and users are confused by fake e-mails from seemingly legitimate companies, such as PayPal, Microsoft, and Wells Fargo.
2004	Sasser Netsky Xombe MyDoom, Zafi Bagle	Worms, such as Sasser, begin to emerge that infect computers without user interaction, such as opening an infected e-mail attachment. Mass-mailing worms are still most prevalent. Worms that spread via instant messaging and handheld devices begin to emerge.

What are the symptoms of a malicious code attack? Some viruses have noticeable—and usually annoying—symptoms. Remember, however, that many infections have no recognizable symptoms. Your computer can contract a worm, for example, that never displays an irritating message or attempts to delete your files, but merrily replicates itself through your e-mail until it eventually arrives at a server where it can do some real damage to a network communication system.

What kind of damage is caused by malicious code? The current crop of viruses, Trojan horses, and worms cause various problems, ranging from displaying harmless messages to bringing down Web sites. The list of malware activities below illustrates why everyday computer users and security specialists are concerned.

Network traffic jam. When worms are active, they generate traffic on LANs and the Internet. Service deteriorates as download time increases for files, Web pages, and e-mail messages.

Denial of Service. A **Denial of Service attack** is designed to generate a lot of activity on a network by flooding its servers with useless traffic—enough traffic to overwhelm the server's processing capability and essentially bring all communications to a halt. Successful DoS attacks have been launched against Microsoft, the White House, and the controversial Internet ad agency DoubleClick.

Browser reconfiguration. Some worms block users from accessing certain Web sites and can change your home page setting. They can also set up a redirection routine that downloads malicious code from an infected Web site, even when you enter a legitimate Web address.

Delete and modify files. Many viruses are designed to delete files on a personal computer's hard disk. Some malicious code modifies the Windows Registry and can cause system instability.

Access confidential information. Trojan horses are notorious for using backdoors to steal passwords and credit card numbers. Worms can also scan files and Web sites for e-mail addresses.

Performance degradation. Malicious code requires system resources to send mail and scan files. While a virus or worm is active, your computer might seem to perform slower than normal.

Disable antivirus and firewall software. Some viruses—called **retro viruses**—are designed to attack antivirus software by deleting the files that contain virus descriptions or corrupting the main executable virus-scanning program. One antivirus vendor calls them "anti-antivirus viruses."

ANTIVIRUS SOFTWARE

How can I avoid viruses and worms? Keeping viruses, Trojan horses, and worms out of your computer is preferable to trying to eliminate these pesky programs after they have taken up residence. After malicious code infiltrates your computer, it can be difficult to eradicate. Certain viruses are particularly tenacious—just the process of booting up your computer can trigger their replication sequence or send them into hiding.

These are the top three steps you can take to prevent your computer from becoming infected:

- ✓ Use antivirus software on every computing device you own.
- ✓ Keep software patches and operating system service packs up to date.
- ✓ Do not open suspicious e-mail attachments.

What is antivirus software? **Antivirus software** is a set of utility programs that can look for and eradicate viruses, Trojan horses, and worms. This essential software is available for handheld computers, personal computers, and servers. Popular antivirus software for personal computers includes McAfee VirusScan, Norton AntiVirus, and F-Secure Anti-Virus.

How does antivirus software work? Antivirus software uses several techniques to find viruses. As you know, some viruses attach themselves to an existing program. The presence of such a virus often increases the length of the original program. The earliest antivirus software simply examined the programs on a computer and recorded their length. A change in the length of a program from one computing session to the next indicated the possible presence of a virus.

To counter early antivirus software, hackers became more cunning. They created viruses that insert themselves into unused portions of a program file without changing its length. Antivirus software developers fought back. They designed software that examines the bytes in an uninfected application program and calculates a checksum. A **checksum** is a number calculated by combining the binary values of all bytes in a file. Each time you run an application program, antivirus software calculates the checksum and compares it with the previous checksum. If any byte in the application program has changed, the checksum will be different, and the antivirus software assumes that a virus is present.

Today's viruses, Trojan horses, and worms are not limited to infecting program files, so modern antivirus software attempts to locate viruses by

---

INFOWEBLINKS

If you don't have antivirus software for your computer, you should get it. Use the **Antivirus Software InfoWeb** to link to Web sites where you can purchase and download antivirus software.

www.course.com/np/concepts8/ch04

FILE MANAGEMENT, VIRUS PROTECTION, AND BACKUP   **197**

searching your computer's files and memory for virus signatures. A **virus signature** is a section of the virus program, such as a unique series of instructions, that can be used to identify a known virus, much as a fingerprint is used to identify an individual.

When should I use antivirus software? The short answer is "all the time." Most antivirus software allows you to specify what to check and when to check it. You can, for example, fire it up only when you receive a suspicious e-mail attachment, or you can set it to look through all the files on your computer once a week. The best practice, however, is to keep your antivirus software running full-time in the background so that it scans all files the moment they are accessed and checks every e-mail message as it arrives. The scanning process requires a short amount of time, which creates a slight delay in downloading e-mail and opening files. The wait is worth it, however, when you can feel confident that the files you open have been scanned for viruses.

How often should I get an update? The information antivirus software uses to identify and eradicate viruses, Trojan horses, and worms is stored in one or more files usually referred to as "virus definitions." New viruses and variations of old viruses are unleashed just about every day. To keep up with these newly identified pests, antivirus software vendors provide virus definition updates, which are usually available as Web downloads (Figure 4-23). You should check your antivirus vendor's Web site for the latest updates of antivirus software every few weeks or when you hear of a new virus making headlines.

How reliable is antivirus software? Considering the number of existing viruses and the number of viruses debuting every month, antivirus software is surprisingly reliable. Viruses try to escape detection in many ways. **Multi-partite viruses** (pronounced multi-PAR-tite) are able to infect multiple types of targets. For example, a multi-partite virus might combine the characteristics of a file virus (which hides in .exe files) and a boot sector virus (which hides in the boot sector). If your antivirus software looks for that particular virus only in .exe files, the virus could escape detection by hiding in the boot sector as well.

Polymorphic viruses mutate to escape detection by changing their signatures. **Stealth viruses** remove their signatures from a disk-based file and temporarily conceal themselves in memory. Antivirus software can find stealth viruses only by scanning memory.

Unfortunately, antivirus software is not 100% reliable. On rare occasions, it might not identify a virus, or it might conclude that your computer has a virus when one does not actually exist. Despite these rare mistakes, the protection you get is worth the required investment of time and money. Remember that without antivirus software, your computer is susceptible to all the nasty little programs that can cause damage to your files and irritate the friends whose computers you infect.

VIRUS HOAXES

What's a virus hoax? Some virus threats are very real, but you're also likely to get e-mail messages about "viruses" that don't really exist. A **virus hoax** usually arrives as an e-mail message containing dire warnings about a supposedly new virus on the loose (Figure 4-24 on the next page).

TERMINOLOGY NOTE

Because today's antivirus software scans for virus signatures, it is sometimes referred to as "virus scanning software."

FIGURE 4-23
It is important to get regular updates for your antivirus software. Some antivirus vendors feature an electronic update service that you can set to automatically download and install updated virus definitions.

FIGURE 4-24

A virus hoax tends to contain telltale characteristics, such as:

- Warns of a "new" or "dangerous" virus spreading on the Internet.
- Contains a long list of people in the To: or Cc: boxes.
- Cites some "authority" to make you think the alert is official.
- Includes some technical jargon that supposedly explains the virus attack.
- Provides instructions, such as reformatting your computer's hard disk drive or deleting a file, for eradicating the virus. The instructions can cause more damage than the virus itself!
- Urges you to send the e-mail message to everyone in your address book.

What should I do about virus hoaxes? When you receive an e-mail message about a virus, don't panic. Many of them are hoaxes. If you are uncertain, check one of the many antivirus Web sites. There you can look up the alleged virus by name to see if it is a real threat or a hoax.

If the virus is a real threat, the antivirus Web site can provide information to determine whether your computer has been infected. You can also find instructions for eradicating the virus and updating the list of virus definitions your computer's antivirus software uses. If the virus threat is a hoax, you can ignore it. Under no circumstances should you forward virus hoax messages to other people.

INFOWEBLINKS

Some Web sites specialize in tracking hoaxes. For links to these sites, visit the **Hoax InfoWeb**.

www.course.com/np/concepts8/ch04

QUICKCHECK......SECTION C

1. The key characteristic of a virus is that it can replicate itself. True or false? [____]

2. Many Trojan horses have [____] capability, which allows unauthorized access to victims' computers.

3. Many mass-mailing worms are difficult to trace because they contain [____] addresses.

4. Social [____] is a technique used by hackers to make e-mail messages and their attachments seem legitimate.

5. A virus [____] is a section of the virus program, such as a unique series of instructions, that can be used to identify a known virus.

6. [____] viruses mutate to escape detection by changing their signatures.

CHECK ANSWERS

FILE MANAGEMENT, VIRUS PROTECTION, AND BACKUP 199

SECTION D
DATA BACKUP

Computer experts universally recommend that you make backups of your data. It sounds pretty basic, right? Unfortunately, this advice tells you what to do, not how to do it. It fails to address some key questions, such as: Do I need special backup equipment and software? How often should I make a backup? How many of my files should I back up? What should I do with the backups?

In this last section of Chapter 4, you'll find the answers to your questions about backing up data that's stored on a personal computer. You'll begin by looking at how to devise a backup plan that's right for you, and then review your equipment and software options. Along the way, you should pick up lots of practical tips to help you keep your data safe.

BACKUP AND RESTORE PROCEDURES

Why do I need to make backups? Have you ever mistakenly copied an old version of a document over a new version? Has your computer's hard disk drive gone on the fritz? Did a virus wipe out your files? Has lightning "fried" your computer system? These kinds of data disasters are not rare; they happen to everyone. You can't always prevent them, so you need a backup plan that helps you recover data that's been wiped out by operator error, viruses, or hardware failures.

How do I make a backup? A **backup** is a copy of one or more files that has been made in case the original files become damaged. A backup is usually stored on a different storage medium from the original files. For example, you can back up files from your hard disk to a different hard disk, a writable CD or DVD, tape, floppy disk, or Web site. The exact steps you follow to make a backup depend on your backup equipment, the software you use to make backups, and your personal backup plan. That said, the list in Figure 4-25 gives you a general idea of the steps in a typical backup session.

FIGURE 4-25
These are the steps in a typical backup session.

CLICK TO START

1. Insert the disk, CD, or tape on which you'll store the backup.
2. Start the software you're using for the backup.
3. Select the folders and files you want to back up.
4. Give the "go ahead" to start copying data.
5. Feed in additional disks, CDs, or tapes if prompted to do so.
6. Clearly label each disk, CD, or tape.
7. Test your backup.

How do I restore data? In technical jargon, you **restore** data by copying files from a backup to the original storage medium or its replacement. As with the procedures for backing up data, the process you use to restore data to your hard disk varies, depending on your backup equipment and software. It also depends on exactly what you need to restore.

After a hard disk crash, for example, you'll probably need to restore all your backup data to a new hard disk. On the other hand, if you inadvertently delete a file or mistakenly copy one file over another, you might need to restore only a single file from the backup. Most software designed to back up and restore data allows you to select which files you want to restore. A typical session to restore data follows the steps in Figure 4-26.

What's the best backup plan? A good backup plan allows you to restore your computing environment to its pre-disaster state with a minimum of fuss. Unfortunately, no single backup plan fits everyone's computing style or budget. You must devise your own backup plan that's tailored to your particular computing needs.

The checklist in Figure 4-27 outlines factors you should consider as you formulate your own backup plan.

FIGURE 4-26
These are the steps in a typical restore session.

1. Start the software you used to make the backup.
2. Select the file or files you want to restore.
3. Insert the appropriate backup tape or disk.
4. Wait for the files to be copied from the backup to the hard disk.

FIGURE 4-27
Backup Tips

- ☑ Decide how much of your data you want, need, and can afford to back up.
- ☑ Create a realistic schedule for making backups.
- ☑ Make sure you have a way to avoid backing up files that contain viruses.
- ☑ Find out what kind of boot disks you might need to get your computer up and running after a hard disk failure or boot sector virus attack.
- ☑ Make sure you can test your restore procedure so that you can successfully retrieve the data you've backed up.
- ☑ Find a safe place to store your backups.
- ☑ Decide what kind of storage device you'll use to make backups.
- ☑ Select software to handle backup needs.

Do I have to back up every file? A **full-system backup** contains a copy of every program, data, and system file on a computer. The advantage of a full-system backup is that you can easily restore your computer to its pre-disaster state simply by copying the backup files to a new hard disk. A full-system backup takes a lot of time, however, and automating the process requires a large-capacity tape backup device or a second hard disk drive.

A workable alternative to a full system backup is a "selective" backup that contains only your most important data files. A backup of these files ensures that your computer-based documents and projects are protected from many data disasters. You can back up these files on floppy disks, Zip disks, removable hard disks, an external hard disk, CDs, or DVDs. The disadvantage of this backup strategy is that because you backed up only data files, you must manually reinstall all your software in addition to restoring your data files.

If your strategy is to back up your important data files, the procedure can be simplified if you've stored all these files in one folder or its subfolders. For

FILE MANAGEMENT, VIRUS PROTECTION, AND BACKUP

example, Windows users might store their data files in folders contained in the *My Documents* folder. A folder called *My Documents\Music* might hold MP3 files, a *My Documents\Reports* folder can hold reports, a *My Documents\Art* folder can hold various graphics files, and so on. With your data files organized under the umbrella of a single folder, you are less likely to omit an important file when you make backups.

Some applications, such as financial software, create files and update them without your direct intervention. If you have the option during setup, make sure these files are stored under the My Documents umbrella. Otherwise, you must discover the location of the files and make sure they are backed up with the rest of your data.

In addition to data files you create, a few other types of data files might be important to you. Consider making backups of the files listed in Figure 4-28.

FIGURE 4-28
Back up these files in addition to your documents, graphics, and music files.

> **Internet connection information.** Your ISP's phone number and IP address, your user ID, and your password are often stored in an encrypted file somewhere in the *Windows\System* folder. Your ISP can usually help you find this file.
>
> **E-mail folders.** If you're using POP e-mail software, your e-mail folder contains all the e-mail messages you've sent and received, but not deleted. Check the Help menu on your e-mail program to discover the location of these files.
>
> **E-mail address book.** Your e-mail address book might be stored separately from your e-mail messages. To find the file on a Windows computer, use the Search or Find option on the Start menu to search for "Address Book."
>
> **Favorite URLs.** If you're attached to the URLs you've collected in your Favorites or Bookmarks list, you might want to back up the file that contains this list. To find the file, search your hard disk for "Favorites" or "Bookmarks."
>
> **Downloads.** If you paid to download any files, you might want to back them up so that you don't have to pay for them again. These files include software, which usually arrives in the form of a compressed .exe file that expands into several separate files as you install it. For backup purposes, the compressed .exe file should be all you need.

What about backing up the Windows Registry? Windows users often hear a variety of rumors about backing up the Windows Registry. The Registry, as it is usually called, is an important group of files the Windows operating system uses to store configuration information about all the devices and software installed on a computer system. If the Registry becomes damaged, your computer might not be able to boot up, launch programs, or communicate with peripheral devices. It is a good idea to have an extra copy of the Registry in case the original file is damaged.

As simple as it sounds, backing up the Registry can present a bit of a problem because the Registry is always open while your computer is on. Some software that you might use for backups cannot copy open files. If you use such software, the Registry will never make its way onto a backup. Windows users whose backup plans encompass all files on the hard disk must make sure their backup software provides an option for including the Windows Registry. Even if a full-system backup is not planned, many experts recommend that you at least copy the Registry to a separate folder on the hard disk or to a floppy disk. If you do so, you should update this copy whenever you install new software or hardware.

INFOWEBLINKS

For more detailed information on backup techniques, such as backing up the Registry, take a look at the **Backup Techniques InfoWeb**.

www.course.com/np/concepts8/ch04

How do I avoid backing up files that contain viruses? Viruses can damage files to the point that your computer can't access any data on its hard disk. In this case, it is really frustrating when you restore data from a backup only to discover that the restored files contain the same virus that wiped out your data. If your antivirus software is not set to constantly scan for viruses on your computer system, you should run an up-to-date virus check as the first step in your backup routine.

How often should I back up my data? Your backup schedule depends on how much data you can afford to lose. If you're working on an important project, you might want to back up the project files several times a day. Under normal use, however, most people schedule a once-a-week backup. If you work with a To Do list, use it to remind yourself when it is time to make a backup.

Where should I store my backups? Store your backups in a safe place. Don't keep them at your computer desk because a fire or flood that damages your computer could also wipe out your backups. In addition, a thief who steals your computer might also scoop up nearby equipment and media. Storing your backups at a different location is the best idea, but at least store them in a room apart from your computer.

How do I choose a backup device? The backup device you select depends on the value of your data, your current equipment, and your budget. If you can afford a tape drive, buy one, install it, and use it. Otherwise, use what you have—your writable CD drive, Zip drive, or floppy disk drive. If you have several backup options available, use the table in Figure 4-29 to evaluate the strengths and weaknesses of each one.

FIGURE 4-29
Storage Capacities of Backup Media

	Device Cost	Media Cost	Capacity	Comments
Floppy disk	$20–$50	25¢	1.44 MB	Low capacity means that you have to wait around to feed in disks
Zip disk	$200 (average)	$9	750 MB	Holds much more than a floppy but a backup still requires multiple disks
External hard disk	$200 (average)	N/A	80 GB (average)	Fast and convenient, but might hold only one backup
Removable hard disk	$149 (average)	$100	2 GB (average)	Fast, limited capacity, but disks can be removed and locked in a secure location
CD-R	$50 (average)	50¢	680 MB	Limited capacity, can't be reused, long shelf life
CD-RW	$50 (average)	75¢	680 MB	Limited capacity, reusable, very slow
Writable DVD	$100 (average)	50¢	4.7 GB	Good capacity, reasonable media cost
Tape	$300 (average)	$50	40 GB (average)	Great capacity, reasonable media cost, convenient—you can let backups run overnight
USB Flash drive	$15–$500	N/A	32 MB–4 GB	Convenient and durable, but high-capacity models are expensive
Web site	N/A	$5.95 per month	N/A	Transfer rate depends on your Internet connection; security and privacy of your data might be a concern

DISK, CD, AND DVD BACKUP

What's the easiest way to back up my important data? Today, most computers are equipped with a writable CD or DVD drive with adequate storage capacity for a typical computer owner's data files. An easy way to back up your important data is simply copying selected files to a writable CD or DVD. No special software is necessary for this task. The software supplied with your CD or DVD writer includes a formatting routine that prepares a disk to hold data and allows you to select the files you want to copy, or "burn," as a backup.(Figure 4-30).

FIGURE 4-30
Use the software supplied with your CD or DVD drive to format disks and copy files.

What are the limitations of CDs and DVDs? The major disadvantage of backing up your data on CDs and DVDs is that the writing process is slow—slower than writing data to tape or a removable hard disk. Further, although it is feasible to back up your entire system on a series of CDs or DVDs, you would have to use special backup software, monitor the backup process, and switch disks occasionally. CDs and DVDs are more practical for backing up a select group of important data files.

Unfortunately, if you simply back up data files, the process of restoring a crashed computer is cumbersome. You must load the operating system, device drivers, and application software from original distribution disks before copying your data from CDs or DVDs to your computer's hard disk.

Can I use floppy disks and Zip disks to back up my data? Floppy disks are inexpensive and just about every computer has a floppy disk drive. The 1.44 MB capacity of a floppy disk is suitable for storing several documents, but does not provide enough capacity for digital photos or most MP3 music files. If you have no other means to back up your data, at least copy your e-mail address book and important document files to floppy disks.

Zip disks with 100 MB or 250 MB capacity are sufficient for backups of documents and most digital graphics files. Several 750 MB Zip disks might be enough for backing up all your data files and could be feasible for a full-system backup if you have not installed lots of application software.

NETWORK AND INTERNET BACKUP

Can I store backup files on a network server? If your computer is connected to a local area network, you might be able to use the network server as a backup device. Before entrusting your data to a server, check with the network administrator to make sure you are allowed to store a large amount of data on the server. Because you might not want strangers to access your data, you should store it in a password-protected, non-shared folder. You also should make sure the server is backed up on a regular basis so that your backup data won't be wiped out by a server crash.

Can I store my backups on the Internet? Several Web sites offer fee-based backup storage space. When needed, you can simply download backup files from the Web site to your hard disk. These sites are practical for backups of your data files, but space limitations and download times make them impractical for a full-system backup. Experts suggest that you should not rely on a Web site as your only method of backup. If a site goes out of business or is the target of a Denial of Service attack, your backup data might not be accessible.

HARD DISK AND TAPE BACKUP

Can I back up to a second hard disk? A second hard disk drive is a good backup option—especially if it has equivalent capacity to your main hard disk. This capacity allows the backup process to proceed unattended because you won't have to swap disks or CDs. Speed-wise, a hard disk is faster than many tape drives. Unfortunately, like your computer's main hard disk, a backup hard disk is susceptible to head crashes, making it one of the least reliable storage options.

Internal hard disk drives are inexpensive, but they are not desirable backup devices because they are susceptible to electrical damage and any other catastrophe that besets your computer. External hard disk drives, like the one shown in Figure 4-31, are preferred for backups because they can be disconnected from your computer and stored in a safe place. An internal hard disk drive with removable disks is also an acceptable option because the disks can be removed for safe storage.

What about using a tape drive for backups? Tape drives are typically used in business computing situations, when a full-system backup is desirable. Some computer owners with a large amount of important data also install tape drives for their home systems. Tape drives are fairly inexpensive and fast enough to back up an entire hard disk in less than two hours. A tape drive with the capacity to hold the entire contents of a computer's hard disk can be left unattended as the backup proceeds. To make a tape backup, you typically use **backup software**—a set of utility programs designed to back up and restore files.

What does backup software do? Backup software usually includes options that make it easy to schedule periodic backups, define a set of files that you want to regularly back up, and automate the restoration process.

Backup software differs from most copy routines because it typically compresses all the files for a backup and places them in one large file. Under the direction of backup software, this file can spread across multiple tapes if necessary. The file is indexed so that individual files can be located, uncompressed, and restored.

Where can I get backup software? Backup software is supplied with most tape drives. Some versions of Windows include Microsoft Backup software, which you can usually find by clicking the Start button, and then

---

INFOWEBLINKS

Interested in using a Web site for your backup? You can evaluate several of these sites by following the links at the **Web-based Backup InfoWeb**.

www.course.com/np/concepts8/ch04

FIGURE 4-31
An external hard disk drive typically connects to your computer's USB port. The drive can easily be disconnected when not in use and stored in a safe place.

INFOWEBLINKS

For current links to backup software information, reviews, and manufacturers, visit the **Backup Software InfoWeb**.

www.course.com/np/concepts8/ch04

selecting Accessories and System Tools. You can also purchase and download backup software from companies that specialize in data protection software.

Whatever backup software you use, remember that it needs to be accessible when it comes time to restore your data. If the only copy of your backup software exists on your backup tapes, you will be in a Catch-22 situation. You won't be able to access your backup software until you restore the files from your backup, but you won't be able to restore your files until your backup software is running! Make sure you keep the original distribution CD for your backup software or a disk-based copy of any backup software you downloaded from the Web.

How do I use backup software? Backup software provides tools for scheduling backup dates and selecting the files you want to back up. The scheduling feature allows you to automate the backup process and reduces the chance that you'll forget to make regular backups. Backup software can also save time and storage space by offering options for full, differential, or incremental backups.

What is a full backup? A **full backup** makes a fresh copy of every file in the folders you've specified for the backup. In contrast to a full-system backup, a full backup does not necessarily contain every file on your computer. A full backup might contain only your data files, for example, if those are the files you want to regularly back up.

What is a differential backup? A **differential backup** makes a backup of only those files that were added or changed since your last full backup session. After making a full backup of your important files, you can make differential backups at regular intervals. If you need to restore all your files after a hard disk crash, first restore the files from your full backup, and then restore the files from your latest differential backup.

What is an incremental backup? An **incremental backup** makes a backup of the files that were added or changed since the last backup—not necessarily the files that changed from the last full backup, but the files that changed since any full or incremental backup. After making a full backup of your important files, you can make your first incremental backup containing the files that changed since the full backup. When you make your second incremental backup, it will contain only the files that changed since the first incremental backup. To restore files from an incremental backup, files from a full backup are restored first, followed by files from each incremental backup, starting with the oldest and ending with the most recent. The video associated with Figure 4-32 describes the difference between full, differential, and incremental backups.

FIGURE 4-32
Full, incremental, and differential backups each take a slightly different approach to backing up files.

CLICK TO START

How many backup tapes do I need? Computer systems with tape backup usually contain essential business data, and it is critical that data from the backups can be restored in case of a hard disk crash. In this situation, one backup tape is not sufficient. Data security experts recommend maintaining a rotating set of backups—typically using three backup tapes.

To maintain a rotating backup, use one tape for the first backup, and then use a different tape for the next backup. Use another tape for the third backup. For the fourth backup, you can overwrite the data on the first backup tape; for the fifth backup, overwrite the data on the second tape, and so on. So that you know which backup is the most recent, write the date of the backup on the tape label.

How can I be sure that my tape backup works? If your computer's hard disk crashes, you do not want to discover that your backup tapes are blank! To prevent such a disastrous situation, it is important to enable the "read after write" or "compare" option backup software provides. These options force the software to check the data in each sector as it is written to make sure it is copied without error. You should also test your backup by trying to restore one file. Try it with one of your least important data files, just in case your backup is faulty.

BOOT AND RECOVERY DISKS

What is a boot disk? If your computer's hard disk is out of commission, you might wonder how it can access the operating system files needed to carry out the boot process. If your hard disk failed or a virus wiped out the boot sector files on your hard disk, you will not be able to use your normal boot procedure.

A **boot disk** is a floppy disk or CD containing the operating system files needed to boot your computer without accessing the hard disk. A barebones boot disk simply loads the operating system kernel. You can make a boot disk using My Computer or Windows Explorer, as shown in Figure 4-33. The boot disk you create, however, boots DOS, not Windows.

FIGURE 4-33
To create an MS-DOS boot disk, insert a blank floppy disk in drive A. Open My Computer or Windows Explorer, and then right-click the Drive A icon. Select Format and check the box labeled Create an MS-DOS startup disk.

FILE MANAGEMENT, VIRUS PROTECTION, AND BACKUP   **207**

A more sophisticated boot disk—sometimes referred to as a **recovery CD**—loads hardware drivers and user settings as well as the operating system. Recovery CDs are sometimes included with new computer systems. Some computer manufacturer Web sites offer a download that creates a recovery CD. The operating system might also supply a method for creating recovery CDs. For example, the Windows XP Backup utility creates a set of **Automated System Recovery** disks (Figure 4-34).

FIGURE 4-34
Windows XP includes an Automated System Recovery Wizard that helps you create a boot disk containing your system settings.

The contents and capabilities of recovery CDs vary. Some are designed to restore your computer to its "like new" state and wipe out all your data. Others attempt to restore user settings, programs, and data. Before you depend on a recovery CD, make sure you know what it contains and how to use it in case of a system failure.

QUICKCHECK......SECTION D

1. When backing up selected files, rather than making a full backup, you should make a copy of the Windows ⬜ and keep it updated every time you install new hardware or software.

2. The backup process is simplified if you store all your important data files in a single ⬜.

3. One of the best devices for home backup is a(n) ⬜ hard disk drive.

4. A(n) ⬜ backup copies only those files that have changed since your last backup session.

5. A(n) ⬜ CD helps restore a computer system by loading hardware drivers and user settings as well as the operating system.

CHECK ANSWERS

LAB
LAB 4-D
BACKING UP YOUR COMPUTER

In this lab, you'll learn:

- How to start the Windows Backup utility
- How to use the Backup Wizard
- How to create a backup job
- Which files to select for a backup job
- How to back up the Windows Registry
- The advantages and disadvantages of using a password to protect your backup data
- The implications of compressing your backup data
- How to restore data from an entire backup job
- How to restore a single file from a backup

INTERACTIVE LAB

CLICK TO START THE LAB

LAB ASSIGNMENTS

1. Start the interactive part of the lab. Insert your Tracking Disk if you want to save your QuickCheck results. Perform each lab step as directed, and answer all the lab QuickCheck questions. When you exit the lab, your answers are automatically graded and your results are displayed.

2. Describe where most of your data files are stored, and estimate how many megabytes of data (not programs) you have in all these files. Next, take a close look at these files and estimate how much data (in megabytes) you cannot afford to lose. Finally, explain what you think would be the best hardware device for backing up this amount of data.

3. Draw a sketch or capture a screenshot of the Microsoft Backup window's toolbar. Use ToolTips, ScreenTips, or the window's status bar to find the name of each toolbar button. Use this information to label the buttons on your sketch or screenshot.

4. Assume that you will use Microsoft Backup to make a backup of your data files. Describe the backup job you would create—specify the folders you must include. It is not necessary to list individual files unless they are not within one of the folders you would back up. Make sure you indicate whether you would use password protection, the type of compression you would select, and how you would handle the Windows Registry.

FILE MANAGEMENT, VIRUS PROTECTION, AND BACKUP

TECHTALK
FILE FORMATS

As you learned earlier in the chapter, the way data is stored in a file is referred to as its file format (or file type) and is indicated by its file extension. Most computer users quickly catch on to the basic idea that a file extension provides a clue as to which application software is needed to open the file. For example, files with .doc extensions typically can be opened using Microsoft Word.

Although a basic understanding of file formats might be sufficient for computer "newbies," a more in-depth understanding can come in handy. This TechTalk is designed to take your current knowledge of file formats in the Windows environment and kick it up a notch so that you'll become more adept at using and manipulating the files stored on your computer.

Why should I know about file formats? Some operating systems do a fairly good job of shielding users from the intricacies of file formats. For example, Windows uses a file association list to link a file extension to its corresponding application software. This handy feature allows you to open a data file without first opening an application, simply by double-clicking the file from within Windows Explorer or selecting it from the Documents list that's accessible from the Start menu.

Of course, your application software also shields you from the messy task of searching through directories to find the files it will open. When you use the Open dialog box, most applications automatically comb through the files on a specified device and in a specified folder to display only those that have the "right" file extensions.

With all this help from the operating system and your application software, it might seem that knowing about file formats is unimportant. You might, however, find it useful to understand file formats so that you can easily accomplish tasks such as those listed in Figure 4-35.

What determines a file's format? Although a file extension is a good indicator of a file's format, it does not really define the format. You could use the Rename command to change a QuickTime movie called Balloons.mov to Balloons.doc. Despite the .doc extension, the file is still in QuickTime format because the data elements in the file are arranged in a specific configuration unique to QuickTime.

The format of a file might include a header, data, and possibly an end-of-file marker. You might recall that file headers were defined in Chapter 2. A file header is a section of data at the beginning of a file that contains information about a file—typically the date it was created, the date it was last updated, its size, and its file type.

A file header should not be confused with the headers appearing at the top of each page in a document created with a word processor. Instead, envision a file header as a hidden Post-It note that's attached to the beginning of a file. Although it is hidden to users, computers can read the information in a file header to determine the file's format.

FIGURE 4-35
Understanding file formats helps you perform the following tasks:

- Figure out the correct format for e-mail attachments that you send to friends or colleagues.
- Find the right player software for music and media files that you download from the Web.
- Discover how to work with a file that doesn't seem to open.
- Convert files from one format to another.

The remaining contents of a file depend on whether it contains text, graphics, audio, or multimedia data. A text file, for example, might contain sentences and paragraphs interspersed with codes for centering, boldfacing, and margin settings. A graphics file might contain color data for each pixel, followed by a description of the color palette. The file format dictates the arrangement of this data. Figure 4-36 illustrates the layout for a Windows bitmap file and contrasts it with the layout of a GIF file.

Bitmap File Format
- File header
- Bitmap header
- Color palette
- Bitmap data

GIF File Format
- File header
- Logical screen descriptor
- Global color table
- Local image descriptor
- Local color table
- Image data
- End-of-file character

FIGURE 4-36
Although bitmap and GIF file formats contain graphics, the file layouts differ.

Which file formats am I most likely to encounter? A software program typically consists of at least one executable file with an .exe file extension. It might also include a number of support programs with extensions such as .dll, .vbx, and .ocx. Configuration and startup files usually have .bat, .sys, .ini, and .bin extensions. In addition, you'll find files with .hlp and .tmp extensions. Files with .hlp extensions hold the information for a program's Help utility. Files with .tmp extensions are temporary files. When you open a data file with software applications, such as word processors, spreadsheets, and graphics tools, your operating system makes a copy of the original file and stores this copy on disk as a temporary file. It is this temporary file that you work with as you view and revise a file.

To the uninitiated, the file extensions associated with programs and the operating system might seem odd. Nevertheless, executable and support files—even so-called temporary files—are crucial for the correct operation of your computer system. You should not manually delete them unless they become corrupted. The table in Figure 4-37 lists the file extensions typically associated with the operating system and executable files.

INFOWEBLINKS

The **File Formats InfoWeb** provides a list of file extensions and their corresponding software.

www.course.com/np/concepts8/ch04

FIGURE 4-37
OS and Executable Extensions

Type of File	Description	Extension
Batch file	A sequence of operating system commands executed automatically when the computer boots	.bat
Configuration file	Information about programs the computer uses to allocate the resources necessary to run them	.cfg .sys .mif .bin .ini
Help	The information displayed by online Help	.hlp
Temporary file	A sort of "scratch pad" that contains data while a file is open, but is discarded when you close the file	.tmp
Support program	Program instructions executed along with the main .exe file for a program	.ocx .vbx .vbs .dll
Program	The main executable files for a computer program	.exe .com

FILE MANAGEMENT, VIRUS PROTECTION, AND BACKUP

The list of data file formats is long, but becoming familiar with the most popular formats and the type of data they contain is useful. Figure 4-38 provides this information in a convenient table. Where noted, a file format is associated with a particular software program.

FIGURE 4-38
Data File Extensions

Type of File	Extension
Text	.txt .dat .rtf .doc (Microsoft Word and WordPad) .wpd (WordPerfect)
Sound	.wav .mid .mp3 .au .ra (RealAudio)
Graphics	.bmp .pcx .tif .wmf .gif .jpg .png .eps .ai (Adobe Illustrator)
Animation/video	.flc .fli .avi .mpg .mov (QuickTime) .rm (RealMedia)
Web pages	.htm .html .asp .vrml
Spreadsheets	.xls (Microsoft Excel) .wks (Lotus 1-2-3) .dif
Database	.mdb (Microsoft Access)
Miscellaneous	.pdf (Adobe Acrobat) .ppt (Microsoft PowerPoint) .zip (WinZip) .pub (Microsoft Publisher) .qxd (QuarkExpress)

How do I know which files a program will open? A software application can open files that exist in its native file format, plus several additional file formats. For example, Microsoft Word opens files in its native DOC format, plus files in formats such as HTML (.htm or .html), Text (.txt), and Rich Text Format (.rtf). Within the Windows environment, you can discover which formats a particular software program can open by looking at the *Files of type* list in the Open dialog box, as shown in Figure 4-39.

FIGURE 4-39
An application's *Files of type* list usually displays the file formats a program can open. You can also look for an Import option on the File menu.

Why can't I open some files? Suppose you receive an e-mail attachment called Cool.tif. "Aha!" you say to yourself, "My Photoshop software ought to open that file." You try—several times—but all you get is an error message. When a file doesn't open, one of three things probably went wrong:

- The file might have been damaged—a techie would call it "corrupted"—by a transmission or disk error. Although you might be able to use special file recovery software to repair the damage, it is usually easier to obtain an undamaged copy of the file from its original source.

- Someone might have inadvertently changed the file extension. While renaming the Cool file, perhaps the original .bmp extension was changed to .tif. If you have a little time, you can change the file extension and try to open the file. If a file contains a graphic, chances are that it should have the extension for one of the popular graphics formats, such as .bmp, .gif, .jpg, .tif, or .pcx. Otherwise, you should contact the source of the file to get accurate information about its real format.

- Some file formats exist in several variations, and your software might not have the capability to open a particular variation of the format. You might be able to open the file if you use different application software. For example, Photoshop might not be able to open a particular file with a .tif file extension, but CorelDraw might open it.

What if all my software fails to open a particular file format? Although a computer might be able to discover a file's format, it might not necessarily know how to work with it. Just as you might be able to identify a helicopter, you can't necessarily fly it without some instructions. Your computer also requires a set of instructions to use most file formats. These instructions are provided by software. To use a particular file format, you must make sure your computer has the corresponding software.

Suppose you download a file with a .rm extension and none of your current software works with this file format. Several Web sites provide lists of file extensions and their corresponding software. By looking up a file extension in one of these lists, you can find out what application software you'll need to find, buy, download, and install.

Many files downloaded from the Web require special "player" or "reader" software. For example, PDF text files require software called Acrobat Reader, MP3 music files require software called an MP3 player, and RM video files require the RealMedia Player software. Typically, you can follow a link from the Web page that supplied your file download to find a site from which you can download the necessary player or reader software.

How do I know what kinds of file formats I can send to my friends, colleagues, and instructor? Unless you know what application software is installed on your friends' computers, you won't know for certain whether they can open a particular file you've sent. There's a good chance, however, that your friends can open files saved in common file formats represented by the extensions listed in Figure 4-40. You should check with the recipient before sending files in less common, proprietary formats, such as Adobe Illustrator's AI format and QuarkExpress's QXD format.

Is it possible to convert a file from one format to another? Perhaps you created a Word document on your PC, but you need to convert it into a format that's usable by your colleague who owns a Mac. Or suppose you want to convert a Word document into HTML format so that you can post it on the Web. You might also want to convert a Windows bitmap (.bmp)

FIGURE 4-40
Extensions for Common File Formats

.bmp	.tif
.gif	.doc
.txt	.wav
.jpg	.mid
.htm	.html
.xls	.rtf
.mp3	.aac
.wmv	.wma

FILE MANAGEMENT, VIRUS PROTECTION, AND BACKUP

graphic into GIF format so that you can include it on a Web page. The easiest way to convert a file from one format to another is to find an application program that works with both file formats. Open the file using that software, and then use the Export option, or the Save As dialog box, to select a new file format, assign the file a new name, and save it (Figure 4-41).

FIGURE 4-41
An easy way to convert a file from one format to another is to open it with an application that supports both file formats, and then use the Save As dialog box to select an alternative file format.

CLICK TO START

1. Open the file, and then open the Save As dialog box.
2. Use the *Save as type* list box to select an alternative file format.
3. Provide a file name, as usual.
4. Click the Save button.

Many file formats convert easily to another format, and the resulting file is virtually indistinguishable from the original. Some conversions, however, do not retain all the characteristics of the original file. When you convert a DOC file into HTML format, for example, the HTML page does not contain any of the headers, footers, superscripts, page numbers, special characters, or page breaks that existed in the original DOC file.

When you need a conversion routine for an obscure file format, or if you need to convert between many different file formats, consider specialized conversion software, available through commercial or shareware outlets.

INFOWEBLINKS

Conversion software runs the gamut from simple shareware to "industrial-strength" commercial packages. The **Conversion Software InfoWeb** will help you compare what's available.

www.course.com/np/concepts8/ch04

QUICKCHECK........TECHTALK

1. A file _____ is a section of data at the beginning of a file that contains information about the file type.

2. File extensions, such as .ocx, .vbx, .vbs, and .dll, typically indicate _____ programs.

3. The _____ file format for Microsoft Word is DOC.

4. _____ software can help you transform one file type into a different file type.

CHECK ANSWERS

ISSUE
COMPUTER CRIME

It doesn't take any special digital expertise to mastermind some computer crimes. Setting fire to a computer doesn't require the same finesse as writing a stealthy virus, but both can have the same disastrous effect on data. "Old-fashioned" crimes, such as arson, that take a high-tech twist because they involve a computer can be prosecuted under traditional laws.

Traditional laws do not, however, cover the range of possibilities for computer crimes. Suppose a person unlawfully enters a computer facility and steals backup tapes. That person might be prosecuted for breaking and entering. But would common breaking and entering laws apply to a person who uses an off-site terminal to "enter" a computer system without authorization? And what if a person copies a data file without authorization? Has that file really been "stolen" if the original remains on the computer?

Many countries have computer crime laws that specifically define computer data and software as personal property. These laws also define as crimes the unauthorized access, use, modification, or disabling of a computer system or data. But laws don't necessarily stop criminals. If they did, we wouldn't have to deal with malicious code and intrusions.

Computer Crime Gambits

Data diddling: Unauthorized alterations to data stored on a computer system, such as a student changing grades stored in a school's computer.

Identity theft: Unauthorized copying of personal information, such as credit card numbers, passwords, social security numbers, and bank account PINs.

Salami shaving: Redirecting small, unnoticeable amounts of money from large amounts.

Denial of Service: An attempt to disrupt the operations of a network or computer system, usually by flooding it with data traffic.

Information theft: Unauthorized access to a computer system, such as military or government computers, to gain restricted information.

Virus distribution: Launching viruses, worms, and Trojan horses.

Vandalism: Intentional defacement of Web sites.

Computer crimes—costly to organizations and individuals—include a variety of gambits, such as virus distribution, data diddling, identity theft, and salami shaving.

One of the first computer crime cases involved a worm unleashed on the ARPANET in 1990 that quickly spread through government and university computer systems. The worm's author, Robert Morris, was convicted and sentenced to three years' probation, 400 hours of community service, and a $10,000 fine. This relatively lenient sentence was imposed because Morris claimed he had not intended to cripple the entire network.

A 1995 high-profile case involved a computer hacker named Kevin Mitnick, who was accused of breaking into dozens of corporate, university, government, and personal computers. Although vilified in the media, Mitnick had the support of many hackers and other people who believed that the prosecution grossly exaggerated the extent of his crimes. Nonetheless, Mitnick was sentenced to 46 months in prison and ordered to pay restitution in the amount of $4,125 during his three-year period of supervised release. The prosecution was horrified by such a paltry sum—an amount that was much less than its request for $1.5 million in restitution.

Forbes reporter Adam L. Penenberg took issue with the 46-month sentence imposed by Judge Marianne Pfaelzer and wrote, "This in a country where the average prison term for manslaughter is three years. Mitnick's crimes were curiously innocuous. He broke into corporate computers, but no evidence indicates that he destroyed data. Or sold anything he copied. Yes, he pilfered software—but in doing so left it behind. This world of bits is a strange one, in which you can take something and still leave it for its rightful owner. The theft laws designed for payroll sacks and motor vehicles just don't apply to a hacker."

In 1999, Melissa virus author David L. Smith pleaded guilty in federal court to purposely spreading a computer virus with the intent to cause damage. The charge carried a maximum prison sentence of five years and a $250,000 fine. Smith received a more lenient sentence: 20 months in prison, 3 additional years of supervised release, 100 hours of community service, and a $5,000 fine. Analyst Lorna Koetzle remarked: "It is a stiff sentence akin to a zero tolerance approach, but the people who commit these attacks believe that only the stupid get caught and that they are not stupid."

More recently, officials made two arrests in connection with the Blaster worm. A 24-year-old Romanian and an American teenager apparently downloaded copies of the worm source code, altered it slightly, and sent their versions back out again. The Romanian was allegedly angered by his treatment by one of his professors. The American teenager was just trying to see what he could get away with.

Under Romanian law, distributing a virus can mean a 15 year prison sentence. The U.S. Patriot Act and the Cyber-Security Enhancement Act carry even stiffer penalties—anywhere from 10 years to life in prison.

A CNET reporter questions the fairness of such penalties: "What bothers me most is that here in the United States, rapists serve, on average, 10 years in prison. Yet if, instead of assaulting another human being, that same person had released a virus on the Net, the criminal would get the same or an even harsher sentence."

Law makers hope that stiff penalties will deter cyber criminals. U.S. Attorney John McKay is quoted as saying, "Let there be no mistake about it, cyber-hacking is a crime. It harms persons, it harms individuals, it harms businesses. We will investigate, track down and prosecute cyber-hackers."

These cases illustrate our culture's ambivalent attitude toward computer hackers. On the one hand, they are viewed as evil cyberterrorists who are set on destroying the glue that binds together the Information Age. From this perspective, hackers are criminals who must be hunted down, forced to make restitution for damages, and prevented from creating further havoc.

From another perspective, hackers are viewed more as Casper the Friendly Ghost in our complex cyber-machines—as moderately bothersome entities whose pranks are tolerated by the computer community, along with software bugs and hardware glitches. Seen from this perspective, a hacker's pranks are part of the normal course of study that leads to the highest echelons of computer expertise. "Everyone has done it," claim devotees, "even Bill Gates (founder of Microsoft) and Steve Jobs (founder of Apple Computer)."

Which perspective is right? Are hackers dangerous cyberterrorists or harmless pranksters? Before you make up your mind about computer hacking and cracking, you might want to further investigate several landmark cases by following links at the Computer Crime InfoWeb.

INFOWEBLINKS

Who's in the cybercrime news? How are cybercriminals caught? The **Computer Crime InfoWeb** provides answers to these questions and more.

www.course.com/np/concepts8/ch04

WHAT DO YOU THINK?

1. Should a computer virus distribution sentence carry the same penalty as manslaughter?   ○ Yes ○ No ○ Not sure

2. Should it be a crime to steal a copy of computer data while leaving the original data in place and unaltered?   ○ Yes ○ No ○ Not sure

3. Should hackers be sent to jail if they cannot pay restitution to companies and individuals who lost money as the result of a prank?   ○ Yes ○ No ○ Not sure

4. Do you think that a hacker would make a good consultant on computer security?   ○ Yes ○ No ○ Not sure

SAVE RESPONSES

COMPUTERS IN CONTEXT
LAW ENFORCEMENT

Sirens wail. Blue lights strobe the night. A speeding car slows and pulls off to the side of the road. It looks like a routine traffic stop, but the patrol car is outfitted with a mobile data computer. The police officers on this high-tech force have already checked the speeding car's license plate number and description against a database of stolen cars and cars allegedly used in kidnapping and other crimes.

Mounted in the dashboard of marked and unmarked police cars, a mobile data computer resembles a notebook computer with its flat-panel screen and compact keyboard. Unlike a consumer-grade notebook, however, the computers in police cruisers use hardened technology designed to withstand extreme conditions, such as high temperatures in parked vehicles. The dashboard-mounted computer communicates with an office-based server using a wireless link, such as short-range radio, CDPD (cellular digital packet data) technology, or Wi-Fi. With this wireless link, police officers can access data from local, state, and national databases.

One national database, the National Crime Information Center (NCIC), is maintained by the FBI and can be accessed by authorized personnel in local, state, and federal law enforcement agencies. The system can process more than 2.4 million queries per day related to stolen vehicles, wanted criminals, missing persons, violent gang members, stolen guns, and members of terrorist organizations.

The officers who pulled over the speeding car received information from the NCIC that the car was stolen, so they arrested the car's occupant and took him to the police station for booking.

At the police station, digital cameras flash and the suspect's mug shot is automatically entered into an automated warrants and booking system. The system stores the suspect's complete biographical and arrest information, such as name, aliases, addresses, social security number, charges, and arrest date. The system also checks for outstanding warrants against the suspect, such as warrants for other thefts. Booking agents can enter those charges into the system, assign the new inmate to a cell, log his personal items, and print a photo ID or wrist band.

Automated warrants and booking systems have been proved to increase police productivity. New York City's system handles more than 300,000 bookings per year, with gains in productivity that have put nearly 300 officers back into action investigating crimes and patrolling neighborhoods.

As part of the booking process, the suspect is fingerprinted. A standard fingerprint card, sometimes called a "ten-print card," contains inked prints of the fingers on each hand, plus name, date of birth, and other arrest information. Now, however, instead of using ink, a biometric scanning device can electronically capture fingerprints. Text information is entered via keyboard and stored with digital fingerprint images.

The fingerprint information can be transmitted in digital format from local law enforcement agencies to the FBI's Automated Fingerprint Identification System

(AFIS). This biometric identification methodology uses digital imaging technology to analyze fingerprint data. Using sophisticated algorithms, AFIS can classify arriving prints for storage or search the collection of 600 million fingerprint cards for matching prints.

Conventional crimes, such as car theft, are often solved by using standard investigative techniques with information from computer databases. To solve cybercrimes, however, often the special skills of computer forensic investigators are required.

Computer forensics is the scientific examination and analysis of data located on computer storage media, conducted to offer evidence of computer crimes in court. Computer crimes can be separated into two categories. The first includes crimes that use computers, such as transmitting trade secrets to competitors, reproducing copyrighted material, and distributing child pornography. The second includes crimes targeted at computers, such as Denial of Service attacks on servers, Web site vandalism, data theft, and destructive viruses. Computer forensics can be applied to both categories.

Whether a computer is suspected as the origin of a cyber attack or is suspected of holding evidence, the first step in the forensic process is to use disk imaging software to make an exact replica of the information stored on the hard disk. The disk image is then collected on a write-once medium that cannot be altered with "planted" evidence, and the forensic scientist begins analyzing the disk image data with simple search software that looks through files for keywords related to the crime. In the case of the "Gap-Toothed Bandit" who was convicted for robbing nine banks, analysis of the disk image revealed word processing files containing notes he handed to tellers demanding money.

Criminals typically attempt to delete files with incriminating evidence, but a good forensic scientist can retrieve data from deleted files with undelete software or data recovery software. Temporary Internet or cache files can also yield evidence, pointing law enforcement officers to Web sites the suspect visited that might be fronts for illegal activity.

When a computer is a target of a cyber attack, forensic investigators use three techniques to track the source. The first option is to make an immediate image of the server's hard disk and look through its log files for evidence of activity coming from unauthorized IP addresses. A second technique is to monitor the intruder by watching login attempts, changes to log files, and file access requests. Sophisticated intruders might be able to detect such monitoring, however, and cover their tracks. A third technique is to create a "honeypot"—an irresistible computer system or Web site containing fake information that allows investigators to monitor hackers until identification is possible.

Despite the many techniques and tools available to forensic investigators, they have three main constraints. First, they must adhere to privacy regulations and obtain warrants to set up wiretaps or gather information from ISPs about their customers. Second, they must scrupulously document their procedures so that the evidence they produce cannot be discredited in court as "planted" or fabricated. Third, forensic investigators must examine a wide range of alternatives pertaining to the crime, such as the chance that an IP or e-mail address used to commit a cybercrime doesn't belong to an innocent bystander being spoofed by the real hacker.

Privacy, documentation, and evidentiary constraints cost forensic investigators time, and failure to adhere to strict standards can sometimes allow criminals to avoid conviction and penalties. But even within these constraints, careful forensic investigation is an important aspect of catching and convicting high-tech criminals.

INFOWEBLINKS

For more information about police and FBI technology, connect to the **Computers in Law Enforcement InfoWeb**.

www.course.com/np/concepts8/ch04

INTERACTIVE SUMMARY

To review important concepts from this chapter, fill in the blanks to best complete each sentence. When using the NP8 BookOnCD, click the Check Answers buttons to automatically score your answers. Place your Tracking Disk in the floppy disk drive if you want to save your scores.

A computer [_____] is a named collection of data that exists on a storage medium, such as a hard disk, floppy disk, CD, DVD, or tape. Every file has a name and might also have a file extension. The rules for naming a file are called file-naming [_____]. These rules typically do not allow you to use certain characters or [_____] words in a file name. A file [_____] is usually related to a file format, which is defined as the arrangement of data in a file and the coding scheme used to represent the data. A software program's [_____] file format is the default format for storing files created with that program.

A file's location is defined by a file [_____] (sometimes called a "path"), which includes the storage device, folder(s), file name, and extension. In Windows, storage devices are identified by a drive letter, followed by a [_____]. An operating system maintains a list of files called a directory for each storage disk, tape, CD, or DVD. The main directory of a disk is sometimes referred to as the [_____] directory, which can be subdivided into several smaller lists called subdirectories that are depicted as [_____].

CHECK ANSWERS

File [_____] encompasses any procedure that helps you organize your computer-based files so that you can find and use them more effectively. [_____]-based file management uses tools provided with a software program to open and save files. Additional tools might also allow you to create new folders, rename files, and delete files. The Save and Save As dialog boxes are examples of these file management tools.

Most operating systems provide file management [_____] that give you the "big picture" of the files you have stored on your disks. The structure of folders that you envision on your disk is a logical model, which is often represented by a storage [_____], such as a tree structure or filing cabinet. Windows Explorer is an example of a file management utility provided by an operating system. Windows Explorer allows you to find, rename, copy, move, and delete files and folders. In addition, it allows you to perform these file management activities with more than one file at a time.

The way that data is actually stored is referred to as the [_____] storage model. Before a computer stores data on a disk, CD, or DVD, it creates the equivalent of electronic storage bins by dividing the disk into [_____], and then further dividing the disk into [_____]. This dividing process is referred to as [_____]. Each sector of a disk is numbered, providing a storage address that the operating system can track. Many computers work with a group of sectors, called a [_____], to increase the efficiency of file storage operations. An operating system uses a file system to track the physical location of files. The file system for Windows 95, 98, and Me is called FAT32; for Windows NT, 2000, and XP, it is called [_____].

CHECK ANSWERS

FILE MANAGEMENT, VIRUS PROTECTION, AND BACKUP

A computer virus is a set of program instructions that attaches itself to a file, reproduces itself, and spreads to other files. You might encounter several types of viruses. A virus that attaches itself to an application program, such as a game utility, is known as a _____ virus. A boot _____ virus infects the system files your computer uses every time you turn it on. A _____ virus infects a set of instructions that automates document and worksheet production.

A Trojan horse is a computer program that seems to perform one function while actually doing something else. Such programs are notorious for stealing _____, although some delete files and cause other problems.

A _____ is a program designed to spread from computer to computer. Most take advantage of communications networks—especially the Internet—to travel within e-mail and TCP/IP packets, jumping from one computer to another. Today, mass _____ worms, such as MyDoom, are one of the most common threats to computer networks. Many worms are designed to trigger Denial of _____ attacks that flood networks and block access to servers.

_____ threats that combine a worm or Trojan horse with a virus are becoming more prevalent.

Viruses can slip into your computer from a variety of sources, such as floppy disks, homemade CDs, and Web sites that contain games and other supposedly fun stuff. E-mail _____ are another common source of viruses. HTML-formatted e-mail is susceptible to viruses and worms hidden in program-like "scripts" that are embedded in HTML tags.

_____ software can help prevent viruses from invading your computer system and can root out viruses that take up residence. This software typically scans for a virus _____ and is sometimes referred to as virus scanning software.

CHECK ANSWERS

A backup is a copy of one or more files that has been made in case the original files become damaged. For safety, a backup is usually stored on a different storage medium from the original files. A good backup plan allows you to _____ your computing environment to its pre-disaster state with a minimum of fuss.

No single backup plan fits everyone's computing style or budget. Your personal backup plan depends on the files you need to back up, the hardware you have available to make backups, and your backup software. In any case, it is a good idea to back up the Windows _____ and make sure your files are free of _____. Backups should be stored in a safe place, away from the computer.

Backups can be recorded on floppy disks, writable CDs and DVDs, networks, Web sites, a second hard disk, or tapes. Many computer owners depend on writable CDs for backups, and use My Computer or Windows _____ to simply select files and copy files to the backup. _____ drives and backup software are typically used in business situations when a full-system backup is desirable. Backup software differs from most copy routines because it _____ all the files for a backup into one large file.

In addition to file backups, you should have a _____ disk containing the operating system files and settings needed to start your computer without accessing the hard disk.

CHECK ANSWERS

INTERACTIVE KEY TERMS

Make sure you understand all the boldfaced key terms presented in this chapter. If you're using the NP8 BookOnCD, you can use this list of terms as an interactive study activity. First, try to define a term in your own words, and then click the term to compare your definition with the definition presented in the chapter.

Antivirus software, 196	Formatting, 186	Subdirectory, 178
Automated System Recovery, 207	Formatting utilities, 187	Tracks, 186
Backdoor, 193	Fragmented files, 189	Trigger event, 191
Backup, 199	Full backup, 205	Trojan horse, 192
Backup software, 204	Full-system backup, 200	Virus hoax, 197
Blended threat, 193	Incremental backup, 205	Virus signature, 197
Boot disk, 206	Logical storage models, 183	Windows Explorer, 184
Boot sector virus, 192	Macro virus, 192	Worm, 193
Checksum, 196	Malicious code, 191	
Cluster, 187	Mass-mailing worm, 193	
Computer virus, 191	Master File Table, 187	
Defragmentation utility, 189	Multi-partite viruses, 197	
Denial of Service attack, 195	Native file format, 177	
Differential backup, 205	NTFS, 187	
Directory, 178	Path, 178	
FAT32, 187	Payload, 191	
File Allocation Table, 187	Physical storage model, 186	
File date, 179	Polymorphic viruses, 197	
File format, 177	Recovery CD, 207	
File management utilities, 182	Reserved words, 177	
File-naming conventions, 176	Restore, 200	
File shredder software, 188	Retro viruses, 196	
File size, 179	Root directory, 178	
File specification, 178	Sectors, 186	
File system, 187	Spoofed address, 193	
File virus, 192	Stealth viruses, 197	
Folders, 178	Storage metaphor, 183	

FILE MANAGEMENT, VIRUS PROTECTION, AND BACKUP

INTERACTIVE SITUATION QUESTIONS

Apply what you've learned to some typical computing situations. When using the NP8 BookOnCD, you can type your answers, and then use the Check Answers button to automatically score your responses. Place your Tracking Disk in the floppy disk drive if you want to save your scores.

1. Suppose you are using Microsoft Word and you want to open a file. When your software lists the documents you can open, you can expect them to be in Word's _____ file format, which is DOC.

2. Can you use a Windows application, create a document, and store it using the file name I L*ve NY ? Yes or no? _____

3. When you want to work with several files—to move them to different folders, for example—it would be most efficient to use a file management utility, such as Windows _____.

4. When specifying a location for a data file on your hard disk, you should avoid saving it in the _____ directory.

5. Suppose you have a floppy disk containing data you no longer need. You can use a(n) _____ utility to erase the data on the disk and re-create all the tracks and sectors on the disk.

6. You have an old computer that you will donate to a school, but you want to make sure its hard disk contains no trace of your data. To do so, you should use file _____ software that overwrites "empty" sectors with random 1s and 0s.

7. You receive e-mail from PayPal asking you to renew your account by entering your current user ID and password. You assume that a hacker is using _____ engineering to make a Trojan horse appear to be a legitimate message.

8. You receive an e-mail message that says, "Your computer has contracted a virus. You can remove it by using the program attached to this message." Would you assume that this message is a hoax? Yes or no? _____

9. You just bought a tape drive and you make a full-system backup. Before you depend on this backup, you should _____ it to make sure you can successfully restore the data in the event of a hard disk crash.

10. Your hard disk crashed for some unknown reason. Now when you switch on the computer power, all you get is an "Error reading drive C:" message. Your first reaction should be to reach for a(n) _____ CD that contains the operating system files and device drivers needed to start your computer without accessing the hard disk.

CHECK ANSWERS

INTERACTIVE PRACTICE TESTS

Practice tests that consist of 10 multiple-choice, true/false, and fill-in-the-blank questions are available on both the NP8 BookOnCD and the NP8 Web site. The questions are selected at random from a large test bank, so each time you take a test, you'll receive a different set of questions. Your tests are scored immediately, and you can print study guides that help you find the correct answers for any questions that you missed.

www.course.com/np/concepts8/ch04

CLICK TO START

REVIEW
ON THE WEB

PROJECTS

An NP8 Project is an open-ended activity that helps you apply the concepts you have learned. Many projects require resources in addition to your textbook, such as current magazines, library materials, or Web access. When you tackle a project, be prepared to use your critical thinking skills, logical analysis, and creativity. Projects for this chapter include:

- **Issue Research: Computer Crime**
- **Hoax!**
- **Computer Forensics**
- **Antivirus Software**
- **Cyber Crime**
- **Biometrics**
- **Web Backup Sites**

To work with the Projects for this chapter, connect to the **New Perspectives NP8 Web Site**.

www.course.com/np/concepts8/ch04

TECHTV VIDEO PROJECT

The TechTV segment *MS Windows Security Hole* highlights one of many security problems that plague computer owners. After watching the video, write a short description of the security hole, and discuss how it relates to hackers, viruses, and worms. Explore the Microsoft Web site *www.microsoft.com* and list any security updates needed by your computer. If you are using your own personal computer, you can install these updates. If you are working on a lab computer, obtain permission from the lab manager before installing Windows updates.

To work with the Video Projects for this chapter, connect to the **New Perspectives NP8 Web Site**.

www.course.com/np/concepts8/ch04

STUDY TIPS

Study Tips help you to organize and consolidate the information in a chapter by making lists, outlines, charts, and sketches. You can use paper and pencil or word processing software to complete most of the Study Tips.

To work with the Study Tips for this chapter, connect to the **New Perspectives NP8 Web Site**.

www.course.com/np/concepts8/ch04

ONLINE GAMES

Test your comprehension of the concepts introduced in Chapter 4 by playing the NP8 Online Games. At the end of each game, you have three options:

- Print a comprehensive study guide complete with page references
- Print your results to be submitted to your instructor
- Save your results to be submitted to your instructor via e-mail

To work with the Online Games for this chapter, connect to the **New Perspectives NP8 Web Site**.

www.course.com/np/concepts8/ch04

FILE MANAGEMENT, VIRUS PROTECTION, AND BACKUP 223

STUDENT EDITION LABS

Extend your knowledge of file management and backup procedures with the Chapter 4 Student Edition Labs.

The following Student Edition Labs are offered with Chapter 4:
- Maintaining a Hard Drive
- Managing Files and Folders
- Keeping Your Computer Virus Free
- Backing Up Your Computer

Go to the NP8 New Perspectives Web site for specific lab topics.

To work with the Chapter 4 Student Edition Labs and their corresponding lab assignments, connect to the **New Perspectives NP8 Web Site**.

www.course.com/np/concepts8/ch04

Work hands-on in structured simulations practicing important skills and concepts

Test your comprehension of the lab topics through a series of objective-based questions

Track Your Progress with the Student Edition Labs

- Student Edition Labs test your comprehension of the lab topics through a series of trackable objective-based questions. Your instructor will direct you to either print your results or submit them via e-mail.

- Student Edition Lab Assignments, available on the New Perspectives NP8 Web site, require you to apply the skills learned through the lab in a live environment. Go to the New Perspectives NP8 Web site for detailed instruction on individual Student Edition Lab Assignments.

If you have a SAM user profile, you have access to even more interactive content. Log in to your SAM account and go to your assignments page to see what your instructor has assigned for this chapter.

TECHBUZZ

PREVIEW

Every year, the computer press falls in love with some cool gadget, new technology, great piece of software, or hot Web site. Industry analysts predict great things for these technology darlings. Some of their predictions are correct and innovative products, such as digital music players, become popular. Other products get lots of hype, but seem to go nowhere. TechBuzz takes a look at some of the products that have recently had industry analysts buzzing.

GADGETS

Last year, the iPod made a big splash as a handy audio player and portable backup device. USB continued its move to replace serial, parallel, SCSI, and PS/2 ports. Keychain USB Flash drives increased in popularity as a convenient way to transport data. That's all mainstream news. What else is on the horizon gadget-wise? Here are a few that analysts like.

Tiny, Tiny Hard Disk Drives

In late 2004, Toshiba introduced a hard disk drive with an .85-inch storage surface that's about the size of a nickel. The disk holds 2 GB of data and consumes about half the power of 1.8-inch drives currently used for portable multimedia devices, such as Apple's iPod. Toshiba expects to increase storage capacity to 30 GB before the end of the decade. These drives have potential applications for digital music players, portable movie players, digital cameras, and cell phones.

But how do these drives stack up to solid state storage memory cards? They are currently less expensive per GB of storage, but on the downside, they are somewhat less durable and 2GB is not quite enough for most media applications. Tiny hard drives are likely to fill the bill for some applications, but are an evolutionary, rather than revolutionary, technology.

RFID Lost and Found

The applications of disposable RFID chips keep expanding. Reminiscent of Harry Potter's Maurader's Map that showed the whereabouts of everyone at Hogwarts, families visiting LegoLand in Denmark can rent wristbands containing an RFID tag that can pinpoint a child's location in the park in less than 20 seconds. Wi-Fi signals emitted by the RFID tags are monitored by 38 receiver units within the park. Parents with lost children can ask for location coordinates simply by sending a text message from their cell phones to the tracking system.

Find That Hotspot

You're all signed up for Wi-Fi service. Now how do you find hotspots? You can check one of the many hotspot maps on the Web, but that assumes you're already connected. Suppose you're toting your Wi-Fi enabled notebook computer on a trip and want to find the nearest hotspot without digging out lots of equipment. A company called Chrysalis thinks it has the answer in a little gadget that fits on your key ring. Just press a button on the Wi-Fi Seeker, and a series of LED lights help you home in on the nearest hotspot. Is this product a very cool idea or just another toy for gadget fans? Let's wait and see if consumers add these devices to their key rings alongside USB flash drives and garage door openers.

TECHBUZZ

New Horizons in Backup

Here's the problem: You've got a home network and you want to back up data from all your computers, but you hesitate to back up everyone's data to your main computer. What if it gets fried? Now Linksys offers an inexpensive server device called a Network Storage Link for USB 2.0 (NSLU2) that you can connect to your network hub. Then attach one USB hard drive for your everyday storage tasks, and when you're ready to back up, connect a second USB hard drive. Built-in utilities let you schedule backups from your computer's hard disk to the USB hard disk and from one USB disk to the other.

This is a very neat solution, but it's still not perfect. Current versions of the Linksys server store data in a different format than the Windows file system. That means you can access data from the disks only when they are attached to the Linksys server. You cannot, for example, connect one of the USB drives directly to your computer and access the data.

High-end Handhelds

Hewlett-Packard's iPaq h6315 pushed the technology envelope by incorporating three connectivity bands: cellular, Wi-Fi, and Bluetooth. For the consumer, these options provide flexibility and cost savings. Wi-Fi service is faster (and often cheaper) than cellular service, so most handheld owners prefer to use it if available. The iPaq switches seamlessly between networks so that users don't have to fiddle with IP addresses and intermittent connections. As with standard handhelds, the multiband iPaq defaults to the cell system's cellular technology. When a Wi-Fi network is nearby, however, the iPaq connects to it in standby mode. At the end of the current HTTP session—for example, after a Web page graphic has been displayed—the iPaq switches to the Wi-Fi network.

Multiband capability does not come cheap, however. Retail pricing for the iPaq h6315 is about $500 with a 1-year T-Mobile service contract that will set you back almost $80 per month. And yet, this seems to be the future of PDAs and cell phones. Maybe as use increases, prices will come down.

Wi-Fi Boombox

In the past few years, Internet radio has become increasingly popular. Listeners can connect to radio station Web sites anywhere in the world for live audio feeds of music, news, sports, and talk radio. Listeners also tune into their favorite local stations via the Internet when reception is bad. Depending on the station, streaming audio might be available in formats such as Windows Media, Real Audio, or MusicMatch. If your computer doesn't have the right player, most Internet radio sites offer a link for downloading it.

What if you'd like to listen to Internet radio while on the go? Some PDAs include Wi-Fi radios that connect to hotspots using client services, such as Boingo, but the sound quality is not great. For better sound, you need a better box.

Philips offers a high-end stereo system with built-in 802.11b circuitry that streams Internet radio to a pair of powerful woofer-equipped speakers. It includes cool features such as the Info button that e-mails the title of any song you're listening to but can't identify. Unfortunately, the Wi-Fi capabilities are designed for use on a LAN, not as you wander around town from hotspot to hotspot. But you can expect portable Wi-Fi boomboxes to be available soon.

BITTORRENT: SOLUTION TO THE BANDWIDTH BOTTLENECK?

Napster and other music file swap sites, such as Kazaa and eDonkey, turned peer-to-peer networking technology into an overnight sensation. Now the computer press is focused on another peer-to-peer technology called BitTorrent. According to an *InfoWorld* article, BitTorrent has "taken the Internet by storm."

What It Does
A BitTorrent network is designed to reduce the bandwidth bottleneck that occurs when many people attempt to download the same very large file, such as a feature-length film, application software, or an interactive 3-D computer game.

With conventional uploading and downloading technology, simultaneous requests for large files can easily max out a central server's capacity. This bottleneck has made nationwide movie distribution over the Internet impractical. Imagine the server capacity needed to handle simultaneous download requests on the release date of big box office hits. Many industry analysts expect BitTorrent technology to kick-start the online movie download business, making film fans less reliant on trips to their local video stores.

How It Works
BitTorrent reduces download bottlenecks by using computers that download a file to also upload that file to other computers.

Suppose that 100 computers request the film *Robots* at about the same time. A server breaks the movie file into pieces and begins to download those pieces to the first computer that requested the movie. As more computers request the file, they become part of a "swarm" that uses peer-to-peer technology to exchange file pieces with each other. After the server has downloaded all the file pieces to the swarm, its job is complete and it can service other requests. The swarm continues to exchange file pieces until every computer in the swarm has the entire file.

BitTorrent client software is currently available from several Web sites. After installing the client, you can use it to download from any BitTorrent-enabled site simply by clicking the file you want. The BitTorrent client handles the entire file-swapping procedure. After getting the entire file, good etiquette requires clients to remain connected to the swarm so that they can "seed" (see BitTorrent Lingo box below) file pieces to others.

Where It's Headed
Industry analysts seem to anticipate that BitTorrent will power commercial movie download sites similar to music sites, such as iTunes and MSN Music. BitTorrent technology, however, is currently more like Napster and other music-swapping technologies that ran afoul of the recording industry. Pirates use it to transfer illicit copies of software, music, and movies. Watch for future developments to see if BitTorrent can be tamed to serve commercial interests.

BITTORRENT LINGO

Swarm: A group of computers temporarily networked to download a file.

Tracker: Server software that helps establish a swarm of end-user computers.

Seed or seeder: A computer that has downloaded an entire file and can upload pieces to other clients in a swarm.

Leech or leecher: A computer in the process of obtaining file pieces from a swarm.

Chokers: Clients that don't allow other clients to download file pieces.

SECURITY, BOTNETS, AND ZOMBIES: WHY HAS THE INTERNET BECOME SO DANGEROUS?

In the near future, hackers and their troublesome viruses might seem like a civilized group compared to the organized crime syndicates now emerging as the Internet's newest threat. At a Gartner IT Security Summit, author Bruce Sterling offered a bleak depiction of cybersecurity, saying "We had a digital revolution in the 1990s—now we've slid into digital terror." He went on to add "Today's Internet is a dirty mess—it's revolution failed."

To support his criticism, Sterling points out that many of the most recent "innovations" on the Internet include spam, phishing, mass-mailing worms, and viruses that can activate even before an e-mail message is opened.

JPEG of Death
Sterling neglected to mention one of the latest hacker exploits: the JPEG of Death. A critical flaw in Windows XP allows hackers to hide malicious code in JPEG images, which are indistinguishable from uncorrupted images. Typically, corrupted images are posted on porn sites that attract lots of download traffic. When a corrupted image is opened, malicious code turns the infected computer into a "zombie."

Zombies
A "zombie" is a computer that can be remotely controlled by a hacker. In addition to the JPEG of Death, viruses, worms, and e-mail attachments can also harbor code that creates zombies.

Botnets
Getting control of one computer is just a start. Hackers create hundreds or even thousands of zombie computers and link them into temporary peer-to-peer or grid systems called "botnets." In one highly publicized investigation, a botnet of more than 10,000 zombies was discovered and dismantled. Rogue botnets run by hackers can launch denial-of-service attacks or send spam that bypasses IP address blacklists and is difficult to trace. Although some botnets are harmless pranks launched by teenagers, many botnets are highly profitable criminal enterprises that are leased to spammers and used to extort money from owners of sites targeted for denial-of-service attacks.

Law enforcement officials and IT security experts are becoming increasingly worried about terrorist use of botnets. One participant in a *comp.security.UNIX* chast forum draws this disturbing picture: "If you were to execute the world's largest Internet terrorist attack, the best way to go about it would be via a massive botnet. With a large enough botnet, you could bring down the entire Internet." Botnet attacks could disable power grids, banking systems, and communications networks.

Computer owners can take steps to prevent their computers from being used for criminal or terrorist activity by activating firewall software, using antivirus software, and keeping operating system patches up-to-date.

WI-FI GETS SERIOUS

Wireless networks remain in the tech news headlines. Most people today are familiar with popular Wi-Fi technology used for college LANs and Starbuck's hotspots. The basic 802.11b Wi-Fi standard uses the 2.4 GHz band and transmits at 2 Mbps. The follow-up 802.11g Wi-Fi technology also uses the 2.4 GHz band, but transmits at a much faster 54 Mbps. Wi-Fi's major advantage is its unlicensed spectrum that allows anyone to set up a wireless network and offer wireless hotspots. The drawback of Wi-Fi is its limited coverage area, which maxes out at about 300 feet. Directional antennas can increase Wi-Fi's range to a few miles, but that distance limits service to LANs and small hotspots in airports or coffeehouses. Technologies such as WiMax, Mobile-Fi, Wi-Media, and ZigBee might extend Wi-Fi's reach and open new possibilities.

WiMAX

A technology called WiMAX (or Broadband Wireless) has the potential to overcome Wi-Fi's range and data transmission rate limitations. Based on the 802.16 standard, WiMAX has a range of 30 miles and data transmission rates of 70 Mbps. In addition to citywide coverage, WiMAX is being hailed as the ideal technology to provide broadband Internet access in rural areas where DSL and cable Internet service are not available.

Some analysts predict that 100 million people will be using WiMAX by 2006. More conservative industry watchers estimate that widespread WiMAX deployment won't occur for another decade. WiMAX availability might be curtailed by contention among variations of the technology. Some versions of WiMAX use licensed spectrums and seem to be the focus of commercial service providers who'd like to operate local monopolies similar to cable TV and Internet services. Other versions of WiMAX use the unlicensed spectrum and offer opportunities for local service providers or community governments.

Mobile-Fi

Another wireless standard, known as Mobile-Fi, lets people access the Internet while traveling by train, bus, bike, or car. The Mobile-Fi 802.20 standard offers speeds up to 16 Mbps within a range of several miles. It operates in a licensed part of the spectrum, presumably to allow service providers to establish comprehensive networks that hand off signals to neighboring transmitters as users travel along. As with most technologies in the licensed spectrum, Mobile-Fi requires customers to pay for access.

Wi-Media

Another wireless technology called Wi-Media is also in the pipeline. The goal is for Wi-Media to move massive files quickly (up to 500 Mbps) over short distances (100 meters). Its main application is to transfer files between devices within a PAN (personal area network). For example, Wi-Media enabled devices might be used to wirelessly transfer a feature-length film download from a PC to a TV or transfer video footage from a camera to a PC. As this book went to press, work was progressing on an 802.15.3 Wi-Media standard. However, it offers transmission rates of only 55 Mbps on the 2.4 GHz unlicensed band. That's not optimal for real-time media transfers. Clearly, Wi-Media has not yet hit is stride.

Zigbee

In 2003, a ZDNet reporter wrote "Look out for Zigbee, the low power, low speed technology promises to be cheaper than Bluetooth and to run for months on ordinary batteries." ZigBee technology is based on the 802.15.4 standard with the potential to transmit data at 250 Kbps over a 2.4 GHz band in a range of a few hundred feet. Currently, it is used mainly for monitoring and automating utility and alarm systems in homes and offices. In the future, you might find it in home security systems and medical monitoring equipment. Cute name, but not the kind of application that's likely to wow consumers.

Wi-Fi is definitely on the move as technology innovations increase its speed and bandwidth. Some futurists envision a wireless environment where Internet access to data, voice, movies, and music is everywhere!

TECHBUZZ

VOICE OVER IP: IS IT FINALLY READY FOR PRIME TIME?

VoIP (Voice over IP) has languished in the technology doldrums since its lackluster introduction in 1995. Its early promise of free voice calling over the Internet was sabotaged by slow dial-up connections that produced easily dropped and static-filled conversations. Every few years, the computer press got on the VoIP bandwagon, touted its advantages, and predicted a bold new world without monthly telephone bills. That just didn't happen, but recent developments, such as increased broadband use and support from communications companies, might give VoIP the boost it needs to finally gain widespread popularity.

How VoIP Works

In general, there are two ways to use VoIP. Originally, the technology required VoIP client software, such as Microsoft NetMeeting, Skype, or Internet Phone, and a headset connected to your computer. You can still use this technology and it's free. However, you and the person you're calling must have the same software client.

The second VoIP technology is more versatile, but requires you to pay for a service provider's VoIP plan. After connecting an adapter to your computer and telephone, you can dial as usual. Your calls are routed through your VoIP provider, and then to the telephone of the person you're calling.

As 2004 came to a close, AT&T and Vonage were two of the biggest VoIP service providers. Both offer monthly service plans under $30 with unlimited local and domestic long-distance calling, plus extras such as call forwarding. Other telcos and cable companies are evaluating the VoIP market, however, and service plan prices are expected to fall.

VoWLAN and VoWi-Fi

Following close on the heels of VoIP are VoWLAN (Voice over Wireless LAN) and VoWi-Fi (Voice over Wi-Fi). Whereas VoIP has the potential to replace standard wired telephone service, VoWLAN and VoWi-Fi have the potential to replace cellular phone service. In a perfect world of wireless voice technology, callers could stroll down the street connecting seamlessly to local Wi-Fi hotspots to place free voice calls to anyone in the world via the Internet. Unfortunately, wireless voice technologies have been plagued by technical problems that result in poor quality of service. Most Wi-Fi access points have bandwidth to handle fewer than 10 simultaneous calls.

Current adopters of VoIP and VoWLAN tend to be businesses. Individuals who examine the pros and cons of VoIP might decide to stick with their land and cellular service just a little longer.

VOIP PROS

- Unlike cell phones, no per-minute charges
- Can be free or less expensive than standard or cellular monthly service plans
- Allows callers to share data during calls
- Conference calls are as simple as two-party calls
- A single phone number travels with you, wherever you take your VoIP-enabled computer

VOIP CONS

- Audio quality might not be as high as with a wired telephone
- Requires a broadband Internet connection
- Calls to standard handsets require monthly service contracts
- No phone service during a power outage unless your equipment runs on battery back-up

WIKI

A Wiki is a collaborative Web site that allows anyone to edit, modify, or delete elements displayed on Wiki-enabled Web pages. In some ways, Wikis are similar to blogs. Both are accessible with a browser and allow anyone to add comments. Wikis, however, allow participants to alter the original posting and even delete postings made by other participants.

Participants can also create new Wiki pages simply by adding a link to an existing Wiki. All changes are stored in a history file, so participants can trace the evolution of a page and see when changes were made and who made them.

Editing Wiki pages is easy. Simply click the "edit page" link. You can add, modify, or delete the text and graphics displayed on the page. Some Wikis require participants to log in before making changes, presumably to reduce the number of spurious, malicious, and erroneous postings. A list of Wikis can be found by connecting to Internet sites such as www.worldwidewiki.net/wiki/SwitchWiki.

Wikipedia

One of the most extensive Wikis is an encyclopedia called Wikipedia located at www.wikipedia.org. Connect to Wikipedia and you'll find word definitions, articles about news and events, and extensive entries about a wide range of topics. It's a great source for technical information, with definitions and articles provided by well-known experts.

Wikipedia encourages everyone to contribute to the knowledge base by writing articles, checking facts, adjusting page format, and copyediting. To find a current list of tasks, connect to Wikipedia and click the Community Portal link. Make sure you read through the instructions, policy guidelines, and style manual so that your contribution conforms to the Wikipedia style. You wouldn't want to waste your time making substandard edits, only to have them deleted by another contributor who is more familiar with Wikipedia style.

Wiki Apps

Small standalone Wikis are being tried for collaborative business projects as an alternative to expensive groupware. It might turn out, however, that Wikipedia becomes the cornerstone of the Wiki world and serves as the core body of information to which contributor-sponsored links and pages can be added.

For anyone who is disillusioned by the runaway commercialization, hacking, defacement, disinformation, and just plain rudeness on today's Web, Wikipedia offers the promise of a serious community of scholars dedicated to open and logical discussion. Once again a technology has appeared with the potential to encourage every voice to speak, but within a process of natural selection that essentially weeds out erroneous information. Whether active vigilance and editing on the part of contributors can fend off hackers and grandstanders is yet to be seen.

WIKI GLOSSARY

Wikitext: User editable source code, which the Wiki server converts into HTML.

Wiki Markup Standard: The syntax used to create and edit Wiki pages; similar to HTML tags used to mark up HTML pages.

CamelCase: A style for generating links on Wiki pages, recognizable because spaces are removed from the words for links, as in ClickToSeeLargePhoto.

WikiGnome: A contributor who makes helpful edits to Wiki pages without much fanfare.

WikiGremlin: A vandal or hacker who defaces or makes malicious edits to Wiki pages.

Wikify: Standardize the format for a Wiki page.

Games Gone Retro: Kingdom of Loathing

3-D computer games have become more sophisticated, with stunning graphics, extensive playing environments, surround sound effects, online access, and multiplayer interaction. Massively multiplayer online games (MMOGs) attract thousands of new players daily. EverQuest remains one of the most popular online games for U.S. players. Another all-time favorite, Doom, is now in its third major revision and attracts scads of devoted followers. These big-budget megahits keep gamers on a steady hardware upgrade path for faster processors and graphics cards.

Stick Figures in a 2-D World

In the pack of online games vying for recognition, the Kingdom of Loathing offers a unique and quirky gaming experience that appeals to a remarkably wide audience. Like popular favorites EverQuest and Doom, Kingdom of Loathing players select characters and guide them on a quest where they fight monsters, solve riddles, gain treasure, and accumulate skills. But Kingdom of Loathing eschews fancy graphics and surround sound for crude stick drawings that give the game a retro quality and appeal similar to text-based adventure-game classics, such as Zork and Colossal Cave.

Pastamancers and Sorcerers

As with conventional role-playing games, characters are categorized as fighters, magic users, or thieves. But in the wacky Kingdom of Loathing, sorcerers are saucepan-wielding "Sorcerers" and spaghetti-tossing "pastamancers." Accordion Thieves, Disco Bandits, Turtle Tamers, and Seal Clubbers round out the character choices.

Characters venture through sites, such as the Misspelled Cemetary and the Orchish Frat House, where they might encounter a ferocious Sabre-toothed Lime, Stone Mariachis, the Fickle Finger of F8, or a Beer Batter.

Players can band together to share useful items, battle monsters, or fend off rival bands of online players. A community of Kingdom fans has its own chat sites, forums, and an online magazine. Chat participants swap strategies, attempt to solve tricky riddles, and barter for loot such as the meatloaf helmet.

Players get a limited number of turns per day—about an hour's worth of play time—and that seems to be just about enough to keep gamers coming back for more.

Built Like a Classic

Classic games, such as Zork and Colossal Cave, were written by a single programmer or small team and released as freeware or shareware on university networks and the ARPANet. Originally designed for mainframe computers without graphics capability, these games were text-based. Gamers read a description of a scene and then used a command-line interface to type their next move. User input like "go straight" or "pickup sword" was interpreted by a noun-verb parser—a sophisticated technology at the time. The games were simple yet challenging, and that was their appeal.

In the style of classic adventure games, the Kingdom of Loathing was created by a single programmer, Zack Johnson, and his "idea man," Josh Nite. A CNET article describes their efforts as "one of the brightest—and weirdest—lights of the independent game development world," then goes on to say that projects with shoestring budgets can still flourish, even though professional game development has become mired in multibillion-dollar budgets and strings of sequels.

Playing Kingdom of Loathing is free. Gamers can support the site by purchasing "An Adventurer is Me!" T-shirts, coffee cups, and mousepads.

QUICK CHECK ANSWERS

ORIENTATION

QuickCheck A
1. unit
2. Start
3. mouse
4. False
5. Backspace

QuickCheck B
1. Start
2. save
3. File
4. Glossary
5. Help

QuickCheck C
1. Internet
2. Web
3. browser
4. search

QuickCheck D
1. @
2. mailbox
3. Inbox
4. delete, erase, remove

CHAPTER 1

QuickCheck A
1. central
2. stored
3. system
4. False
5. False
6. operating

QuickCheck B
1. backbone
2. TCP, Transmission Control Protocol
3. servers
4. voice
5. False
6. False
7. national, dial-up
8. False
9. logging
10. False

QuickCheck C
1. URL, Uniform Resource Locator
2. case
3. HTML, Hypertext Markup Language
4. home
5. True
6. False
7. query, search terms
8. directory, index, category list

QuickCheck D
1. header
2. MIME, Multi-Purpose Internet Mail Extension
3. True
4. server
5. POP, Post Office Protocol; SMTP, Simple Mail Transfer Protocol
6. Inbox; Outbox

QuickCheck TechTalk
1. operating system
2. POST, power-on self-test
3. Safe
4. True

CHAPTER 2

QuickCheck A
1. digital; analog
2. binary, base 2
3. True
4. Unicode
5. character; binary
6. True
7. integrated

QuickCheck B
1. ALU, Arithmetic Logic Unit
2. microprocessor
3. True
4. clock, system clock
5. megabytes, MB
6. capacitors
7. ROM, read-only memory
8. CMOS, complementary metal oxide semiconductor

QuickCheck C
1. pits
2. Access
3. random; sequential
4. density, capacity
5. False
6. controller
7. False
8. DVD-R, DVD

QuickCheck D
1. optical
2. resolution
3. depth
4. ink jet
5. expansion
6. slots
7. driver

QuickCheck TechTalk
1. Machine
2. op, operation
3. pointer
4. accumulator, register

ANSWERS

CHAPTER 3

QuickCheck A
1. executable
2. properties
3. high; machine
4. compiler
5. system

QuickCheck B
1. resource
2. memory, RAM
3. interface
4. kernel
5. multiuser
6. network, server
7. PDAs, handheld computers

QuickCheck C
1. production
2. spreadsheet
3. Database
4. graphics
5. digital
6. Vertical

QuickCheck D
1. setup
2. zipped, compressed
3. uninstall
4. Copyright
5. Shareware
6. source
7. domain

QuickCheck TechTalk
1. True
2. system
3. User
4. setup program, setup

CHAPTER 4

QuickCheck A
1. conventions
2. reserved
3. format
4. root
5. specification, path
6. date

QuickCheck B
1. Save As
2. logical
3. tracks; sectors
4. file
5. Master

QuickCheck C
1. extension, filename extension
2. sector
3. worm
4. blended
5. True
6. checksum
7. stealth
8. hoax

QuickCheck D
1. restore
2. Registry
3. folder
4. differential
5. boot

QuickCheck TechTalk
1. header
2. support
3. native
4. conversion, import, export

CREDITS

Cover ©PhotoDisc/Getty Images
Figure 1-2 Courtesy of Fujitsu Ltd. And Microsoft Corp.
Figure 1-3 Courtesy of Handspring
Figure 1-4 Courtesy of Sun Microsystems
Figure 1-5 Courtesy of Microsoft Corp.
Figure 1-6 Courtesy of IBM Corporation
Figure 1-7a Courtesy of Alienware
Figure 1-7b Courtesy of Apple Computer, Inc.
Figure 1-7c Courtesy of IBM Corporation
Figure 1-7d Courtesy of Sony Electronics, Inc.
Figure 1-7e Courtesy of Acer Inc. and Microsoft Corp.
Figure 1-7f Courtesy of Apple Computer, Inc. Apple IMAC 17"
Figure 1-10a Courtesy of Epson America, Inc.
Figure 1-10b Courtesy of Olympus
Figure 1-10c Courtesy of Epson America, Inc.
Figure 1-10d Courtesy of Wacom Tech Corp.
Figure 1-16 Courtesy of Linksys
Issue-1a ©Ron Chapple/Getty Images
Issue-1b ©Dennis MacDonald/Photoedit
CinC-1a Courtesy of the Department of Homeland Security
CinC-1b Courtesy of the Department of Homeland Security
Figure 2-11 Courtesy of Intel Corporation
Figure 2-23 Courtesy of IBM Research
Figure 2-24 Courtesy of Intel Corporation
Figure 2-34a Courtesy of Sony Electronics, Inc.
Figure 2-34b Courtesy of Kingston Technology
Figure 2-34c Courtesy of SanDisk Corp.
Figure 2-34d Courtesy of SanDisk Corp.
Figure 2-34e Courtesy of Kingston Technology
Figure 2-35a Courtesy of Logitech Inc.
Figure 2-35b Courtesy of Microsoft Corp.
Figure 2-35c Courtesy of Think Outside Inc. and Palm Inc.
Figure 2-35d Courtesy of Research in Motion
Figure 2-37a Courtesy of IBM Corporation
Figure 2-37b Courtesy of Kensington Technology Group
Figure 2-37c Courtesy of X-Gaming Inc.
Figure 2-38a Courtesy of Sony Electronics, Inc.
Figure 2-38b Couresy of Sony Electronics, Inc.
Figure 2-38c Courtesy of ViewSonic
Figure 2-41 Courtesy of ATI Technologies, Inc.
Figure 2-42 Courtesy of Epson America, Inc.
Issue-2a ©Gabe Palmer/CORBIS
Issue-2b Courtesy of Lexmark International
CinC-2a ©Computer History Museum
CinC-2b ©Courtesy of Business Wire and Lages & Assoc.

Figure 3-20a Courtesy of Handspring
Figure 3-20b Courtesy of Microsoft Corp.
Figure 3-21 Courtesy of Microsoft Corp.
Figure 3-22a Courtesy of Microsoft Corp.
Figure 3-22b Reprint with permission of Quark Inc., and its affiliates
Figure 3-22c Courtesy of Macromedia, Inc.
Figure 3-31a Courtesy of Wolfram Research
Figure 3-31b ©Julie Cooke, *www.lightdrawing.com*
Figure 3-41a Courtesy of Microsoft Corporation
Figure 3-41b Courtesy of Symantec Corp.
Figure 3-41c Courtesy of Adobe Systems Inc.
Issue-3a Courtesy of Software and Information Industry Association
CinC-3a ©Eli Reed/ MAGNUM Photos
CinC-3b ©Ashley GILBERTSON/AURORA
Figure 4-14a Courtesy of Dell, Inc.
Figure 4-14b Courtesy of Intel Corporation
Figure 4-14c Courtesy of Microsoft Corporation
Figure 4-14d ©AP/Wide World Photos
Figure 4-14e ©AP/Wide World Photos
Figure 4-31 Courtesy of Maxtor Corporation ©2003
Issue-4a ©Dennis O'Clair/ Getty Images
CinC-4a ©A. Ramey/PhotoEdit
CinC-4b ©PETER MACDIARMID/Reuters/Corbis
Orientation Fig. 2 Courtesy of Sony Electronics, Inc.
Orientation Fig. 6 Courtesy of Kensington Technology Group
Orientation Fig. 7 ©PhotoDisc/Getty Images
Orientation Fig. 18 Courtesy of ART + COM AG

TECH BUZZ
Kingdom of Loathing ©2004, Asymmetric Publications, LLC
BitTorrent: Beehive ©Isaac Newman/Alamy
Voice over IP Marnie Burkhart/Masterfile
WiMax ©Scott Stulberg/Alamy
Zombie WARNER BROS / THE KOBAL COLLECTION / IOVINO, PETER
Toshiba ./Nickel image ©Eric Antoniou Photography
Lego Land ©2002 The LEGO Group
Linksys Courtesy of Linksys

CREDITS

GLOSSARY

3-D graphics A type of digital graphics format that displays a three dimensional image on a two dimensional space. 362

3-D graphics software The software used to create three-dimensional wireframe objects, then render them into images. 145

Absolute reference In a worksheet formula, cell references (usually preceded by a $ symbol) that cannot change as a result of a move or copy operation. 140

Access time The estimated time for a storage device to locate data on a disk, usually measured in milliseconds. 81

Accounting software A category of software that includes accounting, money management, and tax preparation software. 151

AGP Short for accelerated graphics port, an AGP is a type of interface, or slot, that provides a high-speed pathway for advanced graphics. 97

ALU (arithmetic logic unit) The part of the CPU that performs arithmetic and logical operations on the numbers stored in its registers. 68

Always-on connection A permanent connection, as opposed to a connection that is established and dropped as needed. 19

Analog device A device that operates on continuously varying data, such as a dimmer switch or a watch with a sweep second hand. 60

Antivirus software A computer program used to scan a computer's memory and disks to identify, isolate, and eliminate viruses. 196

Application software Computer programs that help you perform a specific task such as word processing. Also called application programs, applications, or programs. 12, 121

ASCII (American Standard Code for Information Interchange) A code that represents characters as a series of 1s and 0s. Most computers use ASCII code to represent text, making it possible to transfer data between computers. 61

Audio editing software A program that enables users to create and edit digital voice and music recordings. 147

Audio encoding software A computer program designed to convert sound files into a digital sound format, such as MP3 or AAC. 147

Automated system recovery A set of recovery disks that users are able to create using the Windows XP Backup utility. 207

Automatic recalculation A feature found in spreadsheet software that automatically recalculates every formula after a user makes a change to any cell. 140

Backdoor In the context of computer security, a backdoor is a method of bypassing normal procedures to gain access to a computer system. Some backdoors, such as a hidden password, are inadvertently or intentionally left open, whereas others are opened by viruses and worms. 193

Backup A backup is a duplicate copy of a file, disk, or tape. Also refers to a Windows utility that allows you to create and restore backups. 199

Backup software A set of utility programs that performs a variety of backup related tasks, such as helping users select files for backup. 204

Beep code A series of audible beeps used to announce diagnostic test results during the boot process. 45

Benchmarks A set of tests used to measure computer hardware or software performance. 71

Binary digits Series of 1s and 0s representing data. 60

Binary number system A method for representing numbers using only two digits, 0 and 1. Contrast to the decimal number system, which uses ten digits: 0, 1, 2, 3, 4, 5, 6, 7, 8, and 9. 60

Bit The smallest unit of information handled by a computer. A bit is one of two values, either a 0 or a 1. Eight bits comprise a byte, which can represent a letter or number. 11

Blended threat A combination of more than one type of malicious program. 193

Blog (WeB LOG) A publicly-accessible personal journal posted on the Web. Blogs often reflect the personality of the author and are typically updated daily. 17

Boot disk A floppy disk or CD that contains the files needed for the boot process. 206

Boot process The sequence of events that occurs within a computer system between the time the user starts the computer and the time it is ready to process commands. 44

Boot sector virus A computer virus that infects the sectors on a disk that contain the data a computer uses during the boot process. The virus spreads every time the infected disk is in the computer when it boots. 192

Bootstrap program A program stored in ROM that loads and initializes the operating system on a computer. 125

Browser A program that communicates with a Web server and displays Web pages. 28

Byte An 8-bit unit of information that represents a single character. 11

Cable modem A communications device that can be used to connect a computer to the Internet via the cable TV infrastructure 19

Cache Special high-speed memory that gives the CPU rapid access to data that would otherwise be accessed from disk. Also called RAM cache or cache memory. 70

CAD software (Computer-Aided Design software) A program designed to draw 3-D graphics for architecture and engineering tasks. 146

Capacitors Electronic circuit components that store an electrical charge; in RAM, a charged capacitor represents an "on" bit, and a discharged one represents an "off" bit. 73

Card reader A device that can be used to read and record data on a solid stage storage device. 80

Case sensitive A condition in which uppercase letters are not equivalent to their lowercase counterparts. 22

CD (Compact disc) An optical storage medium used to store digital information. CD-ROMs are read only. CD-R and CD-RWs can be used to record data. 86

CD drive An optical drive that can work with one or more CD formats, such as CD-ROM, CD-R, or CD-RW. 10

CD ripper software Software that converts the music on an audio CD to a WAV file. 147

CD-R An acronym for compact disc-recordable. CD-R is a type of optical disk technology that allows the user to create CD-ROMs and audio CDs. 87

GLOSSARY

CD-RW An acronym for compact disc-rewritable. CD-RW is a type of optical disk technology that allows the user to write data onto a CD, then change that data much like on a floppy or hard disk. 87

Cell In spreadsheet terminology, the intersection of a column and a row. In cellular communications, a limited geographical area surrounding a cellular phone tower. 138

Cell references The column letter and row number that designate the location of a worksheet cell. For example, the cell reference C5 refers to a cell in column C, row 5. 139

Central Processing Unit (CPU) The main processing unit in a computer, consisting of circuitry that executes instructions to process data. 4

Character data Letters, symbols, or numerals that will not be used in arithmetic operations (name, social security number, etc.). 61

Chat group A discussion in which a group of people communicates online simultaneously. 17

Checksum A value, calculated by combining all the bytes in a file, that is used by virus detection programs to identify whether any bytes have been altered. 196

CISC A general-purpose microprocessor chip designed to handle a wider array of instructions than a RISC chip. CISC stands for complex instruction set computer. 70

Client A computer or software that requests information from another computer or server. 9

Clip art Graphics designed to be inserted into documents, Web pages, and worksheets; available in CD-ROM or Web-based collections. 137

Cluster A group of sectors on a storage medium that, when accessed as a group, speeds up data access. 187

CMOS memory A type of battery-powered integrated circuit that holds semi-permanent configuration data (acronym for complementary metal oxide semiconductor). 75

Command-line interface A style of user interface which requires users to type commands, rather than use a mouse to manipulate graphics. 124

Commercial software Copyrighted computer applications sold to consumers for profit. 158

CompactFlash (CF) A solid state storage card designed for digital cameras with a built in controller about the size of a matchbook that provides high storage capacity and access speed. 89

Compiler Software that translates a program written in a high-level language into low-level instructions before the program is executed. 119

Computer A device that accepts input, processes data, stores data, and produces output. 4

Computer network A collection of computers and related devices, connected in a way that allows them to share data, hardware, and software. 8

Computer program A detailed set of instructions that tells a computer how to solve a problem or carry out a task. 4

Computer programmer A person who designs, codes, and tests computer programs. 118

Computer virus A program designed to attach itself to a file, reproduce, and spread from one file to another, destroying data, displaying an irritating message, or otherwise disrupting computer operations. 191

Computer-aided music software Software used to generate unique musical compositions with a simplified set of tools, such as tempo, key, and style. 147

Concurrent-user license Legal permission for an organization to use a certain number of copies of a software program at the same time. 157

Control unit The part of the ALU that directs and coordinates processing. 68

Controller A circuit board in a hard drive that positions the disk and read-write heads to locate data. 83

Copyright A form of legal protection that grants certain exclusive rights to the author of a program or the owner of the copyright. 157

Copyright notice A line such as "Copyright 2002 by ACME CO" that identifies a copyright holder. 157

CRT (cathode ray tube) A display technology that uses a large vacuum tube, similar to that used in television sets. 92

Data In the context of computing and data management, data refers to the symbols that a computer uses to represent facts and ideas. 4

Data bus An electronic pathway or circuit that connects the electronic components (such as the processor and RAM) on a computer's motherboard. 97

Data file A file containing words, numbers, and/or pictures that the user can view, edit, save, send, and/or print. 11

Data representation The use of electronic signals, marks, or binary digits to represent character, numeric, visual, or audio data. 60

Data transfer rate The amount of data that a storage device can move from a storage medium to computer memory in one second. 81

Database A collection of information that might be stored in more than one file or in more than one record type. 142

Database software The software designed for entering, finding, organizing, updating, and reporting information stored in a database. 142

Defragmentation utility A software tool used to rearrange the files on a disk so that they are stored in contiguous clusters. 189

Denial of Service attacks An attack designed to overwhelm a network's processing capabilities, shutting it down. 193

Desktop computers Computers small enough to fit on a desk and built around a single microprocessor chip. 6

Desktop operating system An operating system specifically designed for use on personal computers, such as Windows Me or Mac OSX. 126

Desktop publishing software The software used to create high-quality output suitable for commercial printing. DTP software provides precise control over layout. 133

Device driver The software that provides the computer with the means to control a peripheral device. 98

Dial-up connection A connection that uses a phone line to establish a temporary Internet connection. 18

Differential backup A copy of all the files that changed since the last full backup of a disk. 205

Digital Any system that works with discrete data, such as 0s and 1s, in contrast to analog. 11

Digital device A device that works with discrete (distinct or separate) numbers or digits. 60

Digitize To convert non-digital information or media to a digital format through the use of a scanner, sampler, or other input device. 62

DIMMs (dual in-line memory modules) A DIMM is a small circuit board that holds RAM chips. A DIMM has a 64-bit path to the memory chips. 65

DIPs (dual in-line package) A chip configuration characterized by a rectangular body with numerous plugs along its edge. 65

Directory A list of files contained on a computer storage device. 178

Disk density The closeness of the particles on a disk surface. As density increases, the particles are packed more tightly together and are usually smaller. 82

Distribution media One or more floppy disks or CDs that contain programs and data, which can be installed to a hard disk drive. 152

Document production software Computer programs that assist the user in composing, editing, designing, and printing documents. 133

DOS (Disk Operating System) The operating system software shipped with the first IBM PCs, then used on millions of computers until the introduction of Microsoft Windows. 130

Dot matrix printer A printer that creates characters and graphics by striking an inked ribbon with small wires called "pins," generating a fine pattern of dots. 94

Dot pitch The diagonal distance between colored dots on a display screen. Measured in millimeters, dot pitch helps to determine the quality of an image displayed on a monitor. 92

Double layer DVD A DVD that essentially stacks data in two different layers on the disk surface to store 8.5 GB, twice the capacity of a standard DVD. 86

Downloading The process of transferring a copy of a file from a remote computer to local computer's disk drive. 16

Drawing software Programs that are used to create images with lines, shapes, and colors, such as logos or diagrams. 145

Drive bays Areas within a computer system unit that can accommodate additional storage devices. 80

DSS (Digital Satellite System) A type of Internet connection that uses a network of satellites to transmit data. 20

Duty cycle A measurement of how many pages a printer is able to produce per day or month. 95

DVD (Digital Video Disc) An optical storage medium similar in appearance and technology to a CD-ROM but with higher storage capacity. The acronym stands for "digital video disc" or "digital versatile disc." 86

DVD authoring software Computer programs that offer tools for creating DVD menus and transferring digital video onto DVDs that can be played in a computer or standalone DVD player. 148

DVD drive An optical storage device that reads data from CD-ROM and DVD disks. 10

DVD+RW A DVD technology that allows users to record and change data on DVD disks. 87

DVD-ROM A DVD disk that contains data that has been permanently stamped on the disk surface. 87

DVD-Video A DVD format used for commercial movies shipped on DVDs. 87

Dye sublimation printer An expensive, color precise printer that heats ribbons containing color to produce consistent, photograph-quality images. 95

Ear training software Software used by musicians to develop tuning skills, recognize keys, and develop musical skills. 147

EBCDIC (Extended Binary-Coded Decimal Interchange Code) A method by which digital computers, usually mainframes, represent character data. 61

E-commerce Short for electronic commerce, it is the business of buying and selling products online. 17

Educational software Software used to develop and practice skills. 149

E-mail Messages that are transmitted between computers over a communications network. Short for electronic mail. 17

E-mail account A service that provides users with an e-mail address and a mailbox. 36

E-mail attachment A separate file that is transmitted along with an e-mail message. 37

E-mail client software Software that is installed on a client computer and has access to e-mail servers on a network. This software is used to compose, send, and read e-mail messages. 41

E-mail message A computer file containing a letter or memo that is transmitted electronically via a communications network. 36

E-mail servers A computer that uses special software to store and send e-mail messages over the Internet. 40

E-mail system The collection of computers and software that works together to provide e-mail services. 40

Executable file A file, usually with an .exe extension, containing instructions that tell a computer how to perform a specific task. 11

Expansion bus The segment of the data bus that transports data between RAM and peripheral devices. 97

Expansion card A circuit board that is plugged into a slot on a PC motherboard to add extra functions, devices, or ports. 97

Expansion port A socket into which the user plugs a cable from a peripheral device, allowing data to pass between the computer and the peripheral device. 98

Expansion slot A socket or "slot" on a PC motherboard designed to hold a circuit board called an expansion card. 97

Extended ASCII Similar to ASCII but with 8-bit character representation instead of 7-bit, allowing for an additional 128 characters. 61

FAT32 A file system used by Microsoft Windows 95, 98, and Me operating systems to keep track of the name and location of files on a hard disk. 187

Field The smallest meaningful unit of information contained in a data file. 142

File A named collection of data (such as a computer program, document, or graphic) that exists on a storage medium, such as a hard disk, floppy disk, or CD-ROM. 11

File allocation table (FAT) A special file that is used by some operating systems to store the physical location of all the files on a storage medium, such as a hard disk or floppy disk. 187

File date The date that a file was created or last modified. 179

File format The method of organization used to encode and store data in a computer. Text formats include DOC and TXT. Graphics formats include BMP, TIFF, GIF, and PCX. 177

File header Hidden information inserted at the beginning of a file to identify its properties, such as the software that can open it. 63

File extension A set of letters and/or numbers added to the end of a filename that helps to identify the file contents or file type. 11

GLOSSARY

File management utilities Software, such as Windows Explorer, that helps users locate, rename, move, copy, and delete files. 182

File name A series of letters and characters used to identify a file stored on a computer. 11

File-naming conventions A set of rules, established by the operating system, that must be followed to create a valid filename. 176

File shredder software Software designed to overwrite sectors of a disk with a random series of 1s and 0s to ensure deletion of data. 188

File size The physical size of a file on a storage medium, usually measured in kilobytes (KB). 179

File specification A combination of the drive letter, subdirectory, filename, and extension that identifies a file (for example, A:\word\filename.doc). Also called a "path." 178

File system A system that is used by an operating system to keep files organized. 187

File virus A computer virus that infects executable files, such as programs with .exe filename extensions. 192

Floppy disk A removable magnetic storage medium, typically 3.5" in size, with a capacity of 1.44 MB. 81

Floppy disk drive A storage device that writes data on, and reads data from, floppy disks. 10

Folders The subdirectories, or subdivisions of a directory, that can contain files or other folders. 178

Font A typeface or style of lettering, such as Arial, Times New Roman, and Gothic. 135

Footer Text that appears in the bottom margin of each page of a document. 136

Format Specified properties for setting a document's appearance. 135

Formatting The process of dividing a disk into sectors so that it can be used to store information. 186

Formatting utilities Software usually included in an operating system that assists with formatting disks. 187

Formula In spreadsheet terminology, a combination of numbers and symbols that tells the computer how to use the contents of cells in calculations. 139

Fragmented files Files stored in scattered, noncontiguous clusters on a disk. 189

Frames An outline or boundary, frequently defining a box. For document production software, a pre-defined area into which text or graphics may be placed. 137

Freeware Copyrighted software that is given away by the author or owner. 159

Full backup A copy of all the files for a specified backup job. 205

Full-system backup A backup, or copy, of all of the files stored on a computer. 200

Fully justified The horizontal alignment of text where the text terminates exactly at both margins of the document. 136

Function In worksheets, a built-in formula for making a calculation. In programming, a section of code that manipulates data, but is not included in the main sequential execution path of a program. 139

Gigabit (Gb or Gbit) Approximately one billion bits, exactly 1,024 megabits. 63

Gigabyte (GB) Approximately one billion bytes; exactly 1,024 megabytes (1,073,741,842 bytes). 63

Gigahertz (GHz) A measure of frequency equivalent to one billion cycles per second. 69

Grammar checker A feature of word processing software that coaches the user on correct sentence structure and word usage. 135

Graphical user interface (GUI) A type of user interface that features on-screen objects, such as menus and icons, manipulated by a mouse. Abbreviated GUI (pronounced "gooey"). 124

Graphics Any picture, photograph, or image that can be manipulated or viewed on a computer. 145

Graphics card A circuit board inserted into a computer to handle the display of text, graphics, animation, and videos. Also called a "video card." 93

Graphics software Computer programs for creating, editing, and manipulating images. 145

Groupware Software that enables multiple users to collaborate on a project, usually through a pool of data that can be shared by members of the workgroup. 151

Handheld computer A small, pocket-sized computer that is designed to run on its own power supply and provide users with basic applications. 7

Hard disk drive A computer storage device that contains a large-capacity "hard disk" sealed inside the drive case. A hard disk is NOT the same as a 3.5" floppy disk that has a rigid plastic case. 10

Hard disk platter The component of the hard disk drive on which data is stored. It is a flat, rigid disk made of aluminum or glass and coated with a magnetic oxide. 83

Head crash A collision between the read-write head and the surface of the hard disk platter, resulting in damage to some of the data on the disk. 84

Header Text that is placed in the top margin of each page of a document. 136

High-level language A programming language that allows a programmer to write instructions using human-like language. 119

Home page (1) A document that is the starting, or entry, page at a Web site. (2) The Web page that a browser displays each time it is started. 29

Horizontal market software Any computer program that can be used by many different kinds of businesses (for example, an accounting program). 151

HTML (Hypertext Markup Language) A standardized format used to specify the layout for Web page documents. 27

HTML tags A set of instructions, such as <b>, inserted into an HTML document to provide formatting and display information to a Web browser. 30

HTTP (Hypertext Transfer Protocol) The communications system used to transmit Web pages. HTTP:// is an identifier that appears at the beginning of each Web page URL (for example, http://www.fooyong.com). 26

IMAP (Internet Messaging Access Protocol) A protocol similar to POP that is used to retrieve e-mail messages from an e-mail server, but offers additional features, such as choosing which e-mails to download from the server. 40

Incremental backup A copy of the files that changed since the last backup. 205

Information The words, numbers, and graphics used as the basis for human actions and decisions. 11

Ink jet printer A non-impact printer that creates characters or graphics by spraying liquid ink onto paper or other media. 94

Input As a noun, "input" means the information that is conveyed to a computer. As a verb, "input" means to enter data into a computer. 4

Install The process by which programs and data are copied to the hard disk of a computer system and otherwise prepared for access and use. 153

Installation agreement A version of the license agreement that appears on the computer screen when software is being installed and prompts the user to accept or decline. 157

Instant messaging A private chat in which users can communicate with each other in real time using electronically transmitted text messages. 17

Instruction cycle The steps followed by a computer to process a single instruction; fetch, interpret, execute, then increment the instruction pointer. 101

Instruction set The collection of instructions that a CPU is designed to process. 69

Integrated circuit (IC) A thin slice of silicon crystal containing microscopic circuit elements such as transistors, wires, capacitors, and resistors; also called chips and microchips. 64

Internet The worldwide communication infrastructure that links computer networks using TCP/IP protocol. 15

Internet backbone The major communications links that form the core of the Internet. 15

Internet telephony A set of hardware and software that allows users to make phone-style calls over the Internet, usually without a long-distance charge. 17

Interpreter A program that converts high-level instructions in a computer program into machine language instructions, one instruction at a time. 119

ISA (Industry Standard Architecture) A standard for moving data on the expansion bus. Can refer to a type of slot, a bus, or a peripheral device. An older technology, it is rapidly being replaced by PCI architecture. 97

ISDN (Integrated Services Digital Network) A telephone company service that transports data digitally over dial-up or dedicated lines. 20

ISP A company that provides Internet access to businesses, organizations, and individuals. 20

Joystick An input device that looks like a small version of a car's stick shift. Popular with gamers, moving the stick moves objects on the screen. 91

Kernel The core module of an operating system that typically manages memory, processes, tasks and disks. 125

Keyword 1) A word or term used as the basis for a Web page search. 2) A command word provided by a programming language. 32

Kilobit (Kbit or Kb) 1024 bits. 63

Kilobyte (KB) Approximately one thousand bytes; exactly 1,024 bytes. 63

Label In the context of spreadsheets, any text used to describe data. 138

LAN (Local Area Network) An interconnected group of computers and peripherals located within a relatively limited area, such as a building or campus. 8

Lands Non-pitted surface areas on a CD that represent digital data. (See also Pits.) 79

Laser printer A printer that uses laser-based technology, similar to that used by photocopiers, to produce text and graphics. 94

LCD (liquid crystal display) A type of flat panel computer screen, typically found on notebook computers. 92

LCD screen (liquid crystal display) A type of flat panel computer screen, typically found on notebook computers. (See LCD.) 10

Leading Also called line spacing, the vertical spacing between lines of text. 136

Level 1 cache (L1 cache) Cache memory built into a microprocessor chip. L1 cache typically can be read in one clock cycle. 70

Level 2 cache (L2 cache) Cache memory that is located in a chip separate from the microprocessor chip. 70

Line spacing Also called leading, the vertical spacing between lines of text. (See leading.) 136

Links Underlined areas of text that allow users to jump between Web pages. 26

Linux A server operating system that is a derivative of UNIX and available as freeware. 129

Logical storage models Also referred to as metaphors, are any visual aid that helps a computer user visualize a file system. 183

Mac OS The operating system software designed for use on Apple Macintosh and iMac computers. 128

Machine code Program instructions written in binary code that the computer can execute directly. 100

Machine language A low-level language written in binary code that the computer can execute directly. 119

Macro virus A computer virus that infects the macros that are attached to documents and spreadsheets. (See macro.) 192

Macs (Macintosh computers) A personal computer designed and manufactured by Apple Computers. 13

Magnetic storage The recording of data onto disks or tape by magnetizing particles of an oxide-based surface coating. 79

Mail merge A feature of document production software that automates the process of producing customized documents, such as letters and advertising flyers. 137

Mailing list server Any computer and software that maintains a list of people who are interested in a topic, and facilitates message exchanges among all members of the list. 17

Mainframe computer A large, fast, and expensive computer generally used by businesses or government agencies to provide centralized storage processing and management for large amounts of data. 8

Malicious code Any program or set of program instructions, such as a virus, worm, or Trojan horse, designed to surreptitiously enter a computer and disrupt its normal operations. 191

Mass mailing worm A worm that sends itself to every e-mail address in the address book of an infected computer. 193

Master File Table An index file used in NTFS systems used to maintain a list of clusters and keep track of their contents. 187

Mathematical modeling software Software for visualizing and solving a wide range of math, science, and engineering problems. 141

Mathematical operators Symbols such as + - / * that represent specific mathematical functions in a formula. 139

GLOSSARY

Megabit (Mb or Mbit) 1,048,576 bits. 63

Megabyte (MB) Approximately one million bytes; exactly 1,048,576 bytes. 63

Megahertz (MHz) A measure of frequency equivalent to 1 million cycles per second. 69

Memory The computer circuitry that holds data waiting to be processed. 5

Message header The section of an e-mail document that contains the address, subject, and file attachment information. 36

Microcomputer A category of computer that is built around a single microprocessor chip. The computers typically used in homes and small businesses (also called a personal computer). 6

Microprocessor An integrated circuit that contains the circuitry for processing data. It is a single-chip version of the central processing unit (CPU) found in all computers. 6, 68

Microprocessor clock A device on the motherboard of a computer responsible for setting the pace of executing instructions. 69

Microsoft Windows An operating system, developed by Microsoft Corporation, that provides a graphical interface. Versions include Windows 3.1, Windows 95, Windows 98, Windows Me, Windows NT, Windows 2000, and Windows XP. 126

MIDI sequencing software Software that uses a standardized way of transmitting encoded music or sounds for controlling musical devices, such as a keyboard or sound card. 147

MIME (Multi-purpose Internet Mail Extensions) A conversion process used for formatting non-ASCII messages so that they can be sent over the Internet. 37

Modem A device that sends and receives data to and from computers. (See voice band modem and cable modem.) 10

Money management software Software used to track monetary transactions and investments. 141

Monitor A display device that forms an image by converting electrical signals from the computer into points of colored light on the screen. 10

Motherboard (See System board.)

Mouse An input device that allows the user to manipulate objects on the screen by clicking, dragging, and dropping. 10

Multimedia card (MMC) A solid state storage card about the size of a stamp with a built in controller used in mobile phones, pagers, MP3 players and some digital cameras. 89

Multi-partite viruses A computer virus that is able to infect many types of targets by hiding itself in numerous locations on a computer. 197

Multiple-user license Legal permission for more than one person to use a particular software package. 157

Multitasking operating system An operating system that runs two or more programs at the same time. 126

Multiuser operating system An operating system that allows a single computer to deal with simultaneous processing requests from multiple users. 126

Nanoseconds Units of time representing 1 billionth of a second. 74

Native file format A file format that is unique to a program or group of programs and has a unique file extension. 177

Natural language query A query using language spoken by human beings, as opposed to an artificially constructed language such as machine language. 144

Netiquette Internet etiquette or a set of guidelines for posting messages and e-mails in a civil, concise way. 39

Network card An expansion board mounted inside a computer to allow access to a local area network. Also called a network interface card (NIC). 9

Network operating system Programs designed to control the flow of data, maintain security, and keep track of accounts on a network. 126

Newsgroups An online discussion group that focuses on a specific topic. 17

Non-executing zip files A type of file that has to be unzipped manually to extract the file or files contained within it. 156

Notation software Software used to help musicians compose, edit, and print their compositions. 147

Notebook computers Small, lightweight, portable computers that usually run on batteries. Sometimes called laptops. 6

NTFS (New Technology File System) A file system used by Microsoft Windows NT, 2000, and XP operating systems to keep track of the name and location of files on a hard disk. 187

Numeric data Numbers that represent quantities and can be used in arithmetic operations. 60

Object code The low-level instructions that result from compiling source code. 119

Op code Short for operation code, an op code is an assembly language command word that designates an operation, such as add (ADD), compare (CMP), or jump (JMP). 100

Open source software Software that includes its source code, allowing programmers to modify and improve it. 159

Operands The part of an instruction that specifies the data, or the address of the data, on which the operation is to be performed. 100

Operating system The software that controls the computer's use of its hardware resources, such as memory and disk storage space. Also called OS. 12

Optical storage A means of recording data as light and dark spots on a CD, DVD, or other optical media. 79

Output The results produced by a computer (for example, reports, graphs, and music). 5

Page layout The physical positions of elements on a document page such as headers, footers, page numbering, and graphics positioning. 136

Paint software The software required to create and manipulate bitmap graphics. 145

Palm OS A popular type of operating system produced by PalmSource specifically for handheld computers. 130

Paragraph alignment The horizontal position (left, right, justified, centered, for example) of the text in a document. 136

Paragraph style A specification for the format of a paragraph, which includes the alignment of text within the margins and line spacing. 136

Parallel processing The simultaneous use of more than one processor to execute a program. 70

Password A special set of symbols used to restrict access to a user's computer or network. 22

Path A file's location in a file structure. (See File specification.) 178

Payload The action taken by a virus, ranging from displaying annoying message to corrupting the data on a computer's hard disk. 191

Payroll Software A type of horizontal market software used to maintain payroll records. 151

PC card (PCMCIA card) A credit card-sized circuit board used to connect a modem, memory, network card, or storage device to a notebook computer. 98

PCI (Peripheral Component Interconnect) A method for transporting data on the expansion bus. Can refer to type of data bus, expansion slot, or transport method used by a peripheral device. 97

PCMCIA slot A PCMCIA (Personal Computer Memory Card International Association) slot is an external expansion slot typically found on notebook computers. 97

PCs (Derived from the term Personal Computers) Microcomputers that use Windows software and contain Intel-compatible microprocessors. 13

PDA (personal digital assistant) A computer that is smaller and more portable than a notebook computer (also called a palm-top or handheld computer). 7

Peer-to-peer The process by which one workstation/server shares resources with another. Refers to the capability of a network computer to act as both a file server and workstation. 16

Peripheral device A component or equipment that expands a computer's input, output, and storage capabilities, such as a printer or scanner. 11

Personal computer A microcomputer designed for use by an individual user for applications such as Internet browsing and word processing. 6

Personal finance software Software geared toward individual finances that helps track bank account balances, credit card payments, investments, and bills. 141

PGAs A pin-grid array is a common chip design used for microprocessors. 65

Photo editing software The software used to edit, enhance, retouch, and manipulate digital photographs. 145

Physical storage model A representation of data as it is physically stored. 186

Pipelining A technology that allows a processor to begin executing an instruction before completing the previous instruction. 70

Pits Spots on a CD that are "burned," representing digital data. 79

Pixels Short for picture element, a pixel is the smallest unit in a graphic image. Computer display devices use a matrix of pixels to display text and graphics. 92

Plasma screen A compact, lightweight, flat panel computer screen that displays the pixels of an image using a technology similar to that of neon lights. 92

Platform A "family" or category of computers based on the same underlying software and hardware of a computer. 13

Plug and Play The ability of a computer to automatically recognize and adjust the system configuration for a newly added device. 98

Point size A unit of measure (1/72 of an inch) used to describe the height of characters. 135

Pointing device An input device such as a mouse, trackball, pointing stick, or trackpad, that allows users to manipulate an on-screen pointer and other screen-based graphical controls. 91

Pointing stick A mouse-substitute input device that looks like the tip of an eraser embedded in the keyboard of a notebook computer. 91

Polymorphic viruses Viruses that can escape detection from antivirus software by changing their signatures. 19196

POP The Post Office Protocol (POP) is used to retrieve e-mail messages from an e-mail server. 40

POP server A computer that receives and stores e-mail data until retrieved by the e-mail account holder. 41

PostScript A printer language, developed by Adobe Systems, which uses a special set of commands to control page layout, fonts, and graphics. 96

Power-on self-test (POST) A diagnostic process that runs during startup to check components of the computer, such as the graphics card, RAM, keyboard, and disk drives. 44

Presentation software Software that provides tools to combine text, graphics, graphs, animation, and sound into a series of electronic "slides" that can be output on a projector, or as overhead transparencies, paper copies, or 35-millimeter slides. 146

Printer Control Language (PCL) PCL is the unofficial standard language used to send page formatting instructions from a PC to a laser or ink jet printer. 96

Processing The manipulation of data using a systematic series of actions. 4

Programming language A set of keywords and grammar (syntax) that allows a programmer to write instructions that a computer can execute. 119

Project management software Software specifically designed as a tool for planning, scheduling, and tracking projects and their costs. 151

Properties The characteristics of an object in a program. 118

Proprietary services Services specific to or offered by one company. 21

Public domain software Software that is available for public use without restriction except that it cannot be copyrighted. 159

Query A search specification that prompts the computer to look for particular records in a file. 32

Query by example (QBE) A type of database interface in which the user fills in a field with an example of the type of information that she is seeking. 144

Query language A set of command words that can be used to direct the computer to create databases, locate information, sort records, and change the data in those records. 144

RAM Random access memory is a type of computer memory circuit that holds data, program instructions, and the operating system while the computer is on. 72

Random access The ability of a storage device (such as a disk drive) to go directly to a specific storage location without having to search sequentially from a beginning location. 81

RDRAM Rambus dynamic RAM is a fast (up to 600 MHz) type of memory used in newer personal computers. 74

Readability formula A feature found in some word processing software that can estimate the reading level of a written document. 135

Read-write head The mechanism in a disk drive that magnetizes particles on the storage disk surface to write data, or senses the bits that are present to read data. 79

GLOSSARY

Record In the context of database management, a record is the fields of data that pertain to a single entity in a database. 142

Recordable technology (R) A technique of writing data permanently on CD and DVD disks, the data cannot be changed once it has been recorded. 86

Reference software Software that contains a large database of information with tools for sorting, viewing, and accessing specific topics. 149

Refresh rate The speed at which a computer monitor is rewritten, measured in Hertz. Faster refresh rates reduce flickering. 92

Registers A sort of "scratch pad" area of the ALU and control unit into which data or instructions are moved so that they can be processed. 68

Relative reference In a worksheet, cell references that can change if cells change position as a result of a move or copy operation. 140

Reserved words Special words used as commands in some operating systems that may not be used in filenames. 177

Resolution The density of the grid used to display or print text and graphics. The greater the horizontal and vertical density, the higher the resolution. 93

Resource A component, either hardware or software, that is available for use by a computer's processor. 123

Restore The act of moving data from a backup storage medium to a hard disk in the event original data has been lost. 200

Retro viruses Viruses designed to corrupt antivirus software. 196

Rewritable technology (RW) A technique of writing data on CD and DVD disks that is rewritable. The data can be changed, or deleted after being recorded. 86

RISC (Reduced Instruction Set Computer) Refers to a microprocessor chip designed for rapid and efficient processing of a small set of simple instructions. 70

ROM (Read-Only Memory) Refers to one or more integrated circuits that contain permanent instructions that the computer uses during the boot process. 74

ROM BIOS A small set of basic input/output system instructions stored in ROM, which causes the computer system to load critical operating files when the user turns on the computer. 74

Root directory The main directory of a disk. 178

Safe Mode A menu option that appears when Windows is unable to complete the boot sequence. By entering Safe Mode, a user can gracefully shut down the computer, then try to reboot it. 46

SDRAM Short for synchronous dynamic RAM, it is a type of RAM that synchronizes itself with the CPU, thus enabling it to run at much higher clock speeds than conventional RAM. 74

Search and Replace A feature of document production software that allows the user to automatically locate all instances of a particular word or phrase and substitute another word or phrase. 135

Search engine A program that uses keywords to find information on the Internet and returns a list of relevant documents. 31

Search operator A word or symbol that has a specific function within a search, such as "AND or +". 32

SEC cartridges A single edge contact is a common, cassette-like chip design for microprocessors. 65

Sectors Subdivisions of the tracks on a storage medium that provide a storage area for data. 186

SecureDigital (SD) A solid state storage card based on MultiMedia card technology, but features significantly faster data transfer rates and cryptographic security protection. Usually used for MP3 storage. 89

Self-executing zip files A type of file that can be run to unzip the file or files contained within it. 156

Self-installing executable file A program that automatically unzips and then initiates and runs its setup program. 156

Semiconducting materials (semiconductors) Substances, such as silicon or germanium, that can act either as a conductor or insulator. Used in the manufacture of computer chips. 64

Sequential access A form of data storage, usually on computer tape, that requires a device to read or write data one record after another, starting at the beginning of the medium. 81

Serial processing Processing of data one instruction at a time, completing one instruction before beginning another. 70

Server A computer or software on a network that supplies the network with data and storage. 9

Service pack A collection of patches designed to correct bugs and/or add features to an existing software program. 158

Setup program A program module supplied with a software package for the purpose of installing the software. 154

Shareware Copyrighted software marketed under a license that allows users to use the software for a trial period and then send in a registration fee if they wish to continue to use it. 158

Shrink-wrap license A legal agreement printed on computer software packaging, which becomes binding when the package is opened. 157

Single-user license Legal permission for one person to use a particular software package. 157

Single-user operating system A type of operating system that is designed for one user at a time with one set of input devices. 126

Site license Legal permission for software to be used on any and all computers at a specific location (for example, within a corporate building or on a university campus). 157

SmartMedia The least durable portable solid state storage medium that does not include a built-in controller. 89

Smileys Text-based symbols used to express emotion. 39

SMTP server (Simple Mail Transfer Protocol Server) A computer used to send e-mail across a network or the Internet. 42

Software The instructions that direct a computer to perform a task, interact with a user, or process data. 4

Software license A legal contract that defines the ways in which a user may use a computer program. 157

Software patch A section of software code designed to modify an existing program to fix a specific error or add a feature. 156

Software publishers Companies that produce computer software. 118

Software suite A collection of individual applications sold as one package. 148

Solid ink printer A printer that melts a stick of solid ink and sprays it onto paper where it is fused to produce photograph-quality images without the use of special paper. 95

Solid state storage A technology that records data and stores it in a microscopic grid of cells on a non-volatile, erasable, low-power chip. 80

Sound card A circuit board that gives the computer the ability to accept audio input from a microphone, play sound files stored on disks and CD-ROMs, and produce audio output through speakers or headphones. 10

Source code Computer instructions written in a high-level language. 119

Spam Unsolicited e-mail typically sent as a bulk or mass-mailing and used for fraudulent of deceptive marketing. 40

Spam filter Software that identifies unsolicited and unwanted e-mail messages and blocks them from the recipient's inbox. 40

Spelling checker A feature of document production software that checks each word in a document against an electronic dictionary of correctly spelled words, then presents a list of alternatives for possible misspellings. 134

Spelling dictionary A data module that is used by a spelling checker as a list of correctly spelled words. 134

Spoofed address A fake return address on an e-mail message designed to hide the address of the real sender. 193

Spreadsheet A numerical model or representation of a real situation, presented in the form of a table. 138

Spreadsheet software Software for creating electronic worksheets that hold data in cells and perform calculations based on that data. 138

Statistical software Software for analyzing large sets of data to discover patterns and relationships within them. 141

Stealth viruses Viruses that can escape detection from antivirus software by removing their signatures and hiding in memory. 197

Storage The area in a computer where data is retained on a permanent basis. 5

Storage device A mechanical apparatus that records data to and retrieves data from a storage medium. 78

Storage medium The physical material used to store computer data, such as a floppy disk, a hard disk, or a CD-ROM. 78

Storage metaphor A likeness or analogy that helps people visualize the way that computers store files. 183

Store-and-forward technology A technology used by communications networks in which an e-mail message is temporarily held in storage on a server until it is requested by a client computer. 40

Stored program A set of instructions that resides on a storage device, such as a hard drive, and can be loaded into memory and executed. 5

Style A feature in many desktop publishing and word processing programs that allows the user to apply numerous format settings in a single command. 136

Subdirectory A directory found under the root directory. 178

Supercomputer The fastest and most expensive type of computer, capable of processing more than 1 trillion instructions per second. 8

SVGA (Super Video Graphics Array) SVGA typically refers to 800 x 600 resolution. 93

SXGA (Super eXtended Graphics Array) A screen resolution of 1280 x 1024. 93

System board The main circuit board in a computer which houses chips and other electronic components. 65

System requirements The specifications for the operating system and hardware configuration necessary for a software product to work correctly. 152

System software Computer programs that help the computer carry out essential operating tasks. 12, 121

System unit The case or box that contains the computer's power supply, storage devices, main circuit board, processor, and memory. 10

Table An arrangement of data in a grid of rows and columns. In a relational database, a collection of record types with their data. 137

Tablet computer A small, portable computer with a touch-sensitive screen that can be used as a writing or drawing pad. 7

Tape backup A copy of data from a computer's hard disk, stored on magnetic tape and used to restore lost data. 85

Tax preparation software Personal finance software that is specifically designed to assist with tax preparation. 141

TCP/IP Acronym for Transmission Control Protocol/Internet Protocol. A standard set of communication rules used by every computer that connects to the Internet. 15

Thermal transfer printer An expensive, color-precise printer that uses wax containing color to produce numerous dots of color on plain paper. 95

Thesaurus A feature of documentation software that provides synonyms. 135

Topic directory A list of topics and subtopics arranged in a hierarchy from general to specific. 33

Trackball An input device that looks like an upside down mouse. The user rolls the ball to move the on-screen pointer. 91

Trackpad A touch-sensitive surface on which you slide your fingers to move the on-screen pointer. 91

Tracks A series of concentric or spiral storage areas created on a storage medium during the formatting process. 186

Trigger event An event that activates a task, often associated with a computer virus. 191

Trojan horse A computer program that appears to perform one function while actually doing something else, such as inserting a virus into a computer system or stealing a password. 192

Unicode A 16-bit character-representation code that can represent more than 65,000 characters. 61

Uninstall routine A program that removes software files, references, and registry entries from a computer's hard disk. 156

UNIX A multi-user, multitasking server operating system developed by AT&&T's Bell Laboratories in 1969. 129

Unzipped Refers to files that have been uncompressed. 155

Uploading The process of sending a copy of a file from a local computer to a remote computer. 16

URL A Uniform Resource Locator is the address of a Web page. 27

GLOSSARY

USB flash drive A portable solid state storage device nicknamed "pen drive" or "keychain drive" that plugs directly into a computer's USB port. 88

Usenet A worldwide Internet bulletin board system of newsgroups that share common topics. 17

User ID A combination of letters and numbers that serves as a user's "call sign" or identification. Also referred to as a user name. 22

User interface The software and hardware that enable people to interact with computers. 124

Utilities A subcategory of system software designed to augment the operating system by providing ways for a computer user to control the allocation and use of hardware resources. 125

UXGA (Ultra eXtended Graphics Array) A screen resolution of 1600 x 1200. 93

Value A number used in a calculation. 138

Vertical market software Computer programs designed to meet the needs of a specific market segment or industry, such as medical record-keeping software for use in hospitals. 151

VGA (Video Graphics Array) A screen resolution of 640 x 480. 93

Video editing software Software that provides tools for capturing and editing video from a camcorder. 148

Videogame console A computer specifically designed for playing games using a television screen and game controllers. 8

Viewable image size (vis) A measurement of the maximum image size that can be displayed on a monitor screen. 92

Viewing angle width The angle at which you can still clearly see the screen image from the side. 92

Virtual memory A computer's use of hard disk storage to simulate RAM. 73

Virus hoax A message, usually e-mail, that makes claims about a virus problem that doesn't actually exist. 197

Virus signature The unique computer code contained in a virus that helps with its identification. Antivirus software searches for known virus signatures to identify a virus. 197

Voice band modem The type of modem that would typically be used to connect a computer to a telephone line. (See modem.) 18

Volatile A term that describes data (usually in RAM), which can exist only with a constant supply of power. 73

Web Short for World Wide Web. An Internet service that links documents and information from computers located worldwide, using the HTTP protocol. 26

Web authoring software Computer programs for designing and developing customized Web pages that can be published electronically on the Internet. 133

Web pages Documents on the World Wide Web that consist of a specially coded HTML file with associated text, audio, video, and graphics files. A Web page often contains links to other Web pages. 26

Web servers Computers that use special software to transmit Web pages over the Internet. 27

Web site Usually a group of Web pages that share a common domain name, such as www.cnn.com. 27

Web-based e-mail An e-mail system that allows users to access e-mail messages using a browser. 40

What-if analysis The process of setting up a model in a spreadsheet and experimenting to see what happens when different values are entered. 138

Windows Explorer A file management utility included with most Windows operating systems that helps users manage their files. 184

Windows Mobile OS An operating system designed by Microsoft for hand-held computers. 130

Windows Registry A crucial set of data files maintained by the operating system that contains the settings needed by a computer to correctly use any hardware and software that has been installed. 161

Word processing software Computer programs that assist the user in producing documents, such as reports, letters, papers, and manuscripts. 133

Word size The number of bits that a CPU can manipulate at one time, which is dependent on the size of the registers in the CPU, and the number of data lines in the bus. 70

Worksheet A computerized, or electronic, spreadsheet. 138

Workstation (1) A computer connected to a local area network. (2) A powerful desktop computer designed for specific tasks. 8

Worm A software program designed to enter a computer system, usually a network, through security "holes" and then replicate itself. 193

Write-protect window A small hole and sliding cover on a floppy disk that restricts writing to the disk. 82

XGA Extended Graphics Array or XGA usually refers to 1024 x 768 resolution. 93

Zipped Refers to one or more files that have been compressed. 155

INDEX

* (asterisk), 32
@ (at symbol), 36
\ (backslash), 178
: (colon), 176, 177, 178
" (double quotes), 32
/ (forward slash), 28

A
AAC format, 147
absolute references, 140
Access (Microsoft), 149
access time, 81
accounting software, 151
Acrobat (Adobe), 149, 212
Add/Remove Programs console, 156
Address box, 28, 30, 31
ADR (advanced digital recording), 85
ADSL (Asynchronous Digital Subscriber Line), 20
AFIS (Automated Fingerprint Identification System), 216–217
AGP (Accelerated Graphics Port) slots, 93, 97
AI format, 177
ALU (arithmetic logic unit), 68–69, 70, 101–102
always-on connections, 19–20
AMD (Advanced Micro Devices), 71
American Management Association, 48
analog devices, 60
AND operator, 32
animation, 211
antivirus software, 196–197
AOL (American Online), 20
application(s). *See also* programs; *specific applications*
-based file management, 180–181
software, overview of, 12–13, 120–121, 133–151
ARPA (Advanced Research Projects Agency), 106, 107, 214
ARPANET, 107, 214
ASCII (American Standard Code for Information Interchange), 37–38, 62–63, 131
Ask Jeeves Web site, 34
asterisk (*), 32
at symbol (@), 36
AT&T (American Telephone & Telegraph), 15, 20, 129
Athlon processors, 71
audio. *See also* music
editing software, 147
encoding software, 147
file formats, 211
AutoCAD, 146
automatic recalculation, 140
Automated System Recovery disks, 206
Automatic Updates, 156

B
backbone, 15, 20
backdoor capabilities, 193
backslash (\), 178
Backup (Microsoft), 204–205, 206
backups, 186, 199–208
batch files, 210
beep codes, 45
binary
digits, 60
number system, 60–63, 67, 78
biometric devices, 216–217
bitmaps, 210, 212. *See also* graphics
bits, 11, 63–66
BlackBoard, 149
blended threats, 193
blogs, 17
bookmarks, 29
boot
disks, 206
process, 44–47, 75–76
sector viruses, 192
broadcasting, 17
browsers, 28–31, 35, 195
BSA (Business Software Alliance), 164–165
BTTF (Back Thru The Future Micro Computer), 103
buffers, keyboard, 124
bulletin boards, 17
business
networks, 20
software, 151
buttons, properties of, 118
bytes, 11, 63

C
C++ (high-level language), 119
cable access
described, 19
ISPs and, 20, 21
cable television, 19
caches, 70
CAD software, 146
capacitors, 73
card readers, 80
CD (compact disc) drives, 80, 99. *See also* CDs (compact discs)
described, 10, 86–88
location of, 64
CDs (compact discs), 202, 203. *See also* CD (compact disc) drives
burning, 147
described, 86
formatting, 186–187
Celeron processors, 71
cell(s)
described, 138
references, 139, 140
cell phones, 88
character data, 61
chat, 17, 19
checksums, 196
CISC (complex instruction set computer), 70
clients, described, 9
clip art, 137. *See also* graphics
clusters, 187–189
CMOS (complementary metal oxide semiconductor) memory, 44, 75–76
CNET, 215
CNN Web site, 27

INDEX

COBOL, 119
colon (:), 176, 177, 178
color depth, 93
command-line interface, 124
commercial software licenses, 158. *See also* licenses
CompactFlash (CF) cards, 89
compiling, 119–120
compression, 155–156
computer(s). *See also specific types*
   -aided music software, 147
   basics, 4–13
   categories, 6–7
   cost of, 7
   early, 5
   environment and, 104–105
   purchasing, 76
   recycling, 104–105
   specifications, typical, 69
   use of the term, 4
concurrent-use licenses, 157. *See also* licenses
configuration files, 210
Control Panel, 125, 156, 163
control units, 68, 102–103
copyright laws, 157–158, 186
CPUs (central processing units). *See also* micro processors
   boot process and, 44
   described, 4
   peripheral devices and, 11
   supercomputers and, 9
crashes, 123, 188
credit-card information, 24
crime, computer, 214–215. *See also* viruses
CRT (cathode ray tube) monitors, 92. *See also* monitors
CSX file extension, 117
CTP (computer to plate) technology, 166
Cyber Security Alerts, 51

D

data
   bus, 97
   computer hardware and, 60–66
   described, 4
   diddling, 214
   information and, distinction between, 11
   Internet, storage of, 16
   locating, in databases, 144
   representation, 60–66
database software, 142–144, 211
DBMSs (database management systems), 142
DDS (digital data storage), 85
decimal number system, 61
defragmentation utilities, 189
Dell Computers, 13
Denial of Service attacks, 195, 214
Department of Defense (United States), 106
desktop computers
   described, 6, 133
   storage devices and, 80, 84
   system software and, 126, 131
device drivers, 97, 122
DHS (Department of Homeland Security), 50–51
dial-up connections, 18–21, 25
differential backups, 205. *See also* backups
digital
   cameras, 11, 99
   devices, overview of, 60
   formats, 11
DIMMs (dual in-line memory modules), 64, 66
DIPs (dual in-line packages), 64
directories
   described, 178
   root, 178
discussion forums. *See* newsgroups
disk density, 82
display devices, 10, 92–93. *See also* monitors
Display Properties dialog box, 163
distribution media, 152–154
Ditto tape drives, 85

DLL file extension, 117
DMA (direct memory access), 83–84
DOC format, 177, 211, 213
document(s)
   formatting, 135–137
   production software, 133–137
   templates, 137
DOS (Disk Operating System), 126–130, 206
   file-naming conventions, 176, 177
   uninstalling software and, 156
dot matrix printers, 94–95
dot pitch, 92
double quotes ("), 32
downloaded programs, installing, 155–156
downloading
   described, 16
   files, to create recovery CDs, 207
dpi (dots per inch), 162
drawing software, 145
Dreamweaver (Macromedia), 133
drive bays, 80
drivers, 97, 122
DSL (Digital Subscriber Line), 20
DSS (Digital Satellite Service), 20
duty cycle, 95–96
DVD (digital video disc) drive(s). *See also* DVDs (digital video discs)
   bays, 80
   described, 10, 86–88
DVDs (digital video discs). *See also* DVD (digital video disc) drives
   authoring software for, 148
   backups and, 202, 203
   formatting, 186–187
   described, 86
   double layer, 86
   playing, 99
dye sublimation printers, 95

E

ear training software, 147
Earthlink, 20
EBCDIC (Extended Binary-Coded Decimal Interchange Code), 61
e-commerce, 17, 19
educational software, 149. *See also* schools
EIDE drive controllers, 83–84
Eisenhower, Dwight, 107
Electronic Communications Privacy Act, 48
e-mail
   accounts, 36
   addresses, 36, 38, 40, 193
   attachments, 37–39
   blind carbon copy (Bcc:), 38, 39
   carbon copy (Cc:), 38, 39
   client software, 41, 42
   composing, 36–37
   connection speeds and, 19
   described, 17, 36–42
   forwarding, 37
   headers, 36, 37
   homeland security and, 51
   HTML and, 38
   journalism and, 167
   netiquette and, 38–39
   Outboxes, 41–42
   printing, 37
   privacy, 48–49
   replying to, 39
   servers, 40
   sorting, 38
   spell checking, 38
   systems, 40
   technology, 40–42
   viruses and, 191–198
   Web-based, 40–41, 42
Encarta (Microsoft), 149
EncoreDVD (Adobe), 148
encyclopedias, 149
ENIAC (Electrical Numerical Integrator And Calculator), 106, 107
entertainment software, 150
environmental issues, 103–105
errors, transient soft, 47
ESRB (Entertainment Software Rating Board), 150
eVideo-In Pro, 116–117, 120, 153
exabyte, 63
Excel (Microsoft), 138, 149
EXE file extension, 11–12, 156, 177
executable files
   described, 11–12, 117, 210
   self-installing, 156
   viruses and, 194
expansion bus, 97
expansion cards, 64, 97
expansion slots, 66, 97
Explorer (Windows), 177, 183–185, 190
   boot disks and, 206
   file formats and, 209
extension cords, 45

F

fans, 45, 64
FAT (File Allocation Table) file system, 126, 187
FAT32 file system, 126, 187
Favorites list, 29, 201
FBI (Federal Bureau of Investigation), 48, 216–217
field(s)
   described, 142
   searches, 32
   specifying, 143
file(s). *See also* file extensions; file formats; file names
   copying, 185
   dates, 179
   deleting, 185, 186, 188, 189, 196
   described, 11
   grouping, 185
   headers, 63, 209
   locators, 178
   management, 176–190
   manipulating, 184–185
   moving, 185
   paths (specifications), 178
   physical storage of, 186–189
   renaming, 184–185
   saving, 180–181
   shredder software, 188
   size, 39, 179
   undeleting, 189
file extensions, 116–117, 177. *See also* file names
   described, 11, 178–179, 210–212
   maintaining, 185, 212
   in URLs, 27
file formats
   described, 178–179, 209–213
   native, 177, 211
File menu
   Save As command, 180–181
   Save command, 181
file name(s). *See also* file extensions
   conventions, 176–179
   described, 11, 178–179
file systems, 126, 187
FireWire (IEEE 1394) ports, 99
flash drives, 88–89, 96
floppy disk drives, 10, 46, 64, 178. *See also* floppy disks
   backups and, 202, 203
   hard disks and, comparison of, 83
floppy disks. *See also* floppy disks drives
   described, 10, 81–82
   formatting, 186–187
folder(s)
   file management and, 178, 184–185
   manipulating, 184–185
   names, in URLs, 27
   organizing, 185
   renaming, 184–185
   software installation and, 153
fonts, 135, 136
footers, 136
footnotes, 137
forensics, computer, 217
formatting disks, 186–187
formulas, 139, 140
forward slash (/), 28
fragmented files, 189
frames, for text, 137
Freehand (Macromedia), 145
freeware, 159
full backups, 205
full-system backups, 200, 201
functions, 139, 140

INDEX

G
games, 76, 93, 150
Gateway, 13
GIF (Graphics Interchange Format), 210, 212
gigabytes, 63
gigahertz, 69
gigbits, 63
GoLive (Adobe), 149
Google search engine, 31
GPF (General Protection Fault), 123
GPL (General Public License), 129
GPS (global positioning satellite) systems, 106, 107
GPU (graphics processing unit), 93
grammar checkers, 135
graphic(s)
   3-D (three-dimensional), 145–146
   accelerators, 93
   attaching, to e-mail, 38
   cards, 93, 97
   digitization of, 62–33
   file formats and, 210, 211
   importing, into documents, 137
   software, 145–146
   tablets, classification of, as peripheral devices, 11
   use of the term, 145
groupware, 151
GUI (Graphical User Interface), 124, 125, 129, 164
Gutenberg, Johann, 166

H
hackers, 51, 196–197
handheld computers. *See also* PDAs (personal digital assistants)
   described, 7
   system software and, 130–131
handwriting recognition, 131
hard disk drive(s), 10–11, 64, 99
   controllers, 83–84
   described, 10, 83–84
   external, 202, 204–206
   file management and, 178
   formatting, 186–187
   platters, 83
   RAM and, comparison of, 72
   removable, 84
hardware. *See also specific types*
   data representation and, 60–66
   described, 58–113
Harvard Graphics, 146
HDTV circuitry, 92
head crashes, 84
headers and footers, 136
help, 117, 125, 210
Hewlett-Packard, 13
high-level languages, 119
History list, 29
home pages, 29
homeland security, 48–51. *See also* security
horizontal market software, 151
HTML (HyperText Markup Language)
   browsers and, 30
   described, 27
   e-mail and, 38
   file formats and, 211, 213
   format, converting documents to, 137, 212, 213
   tags, 30
   Web authoring software and, 133
   worms and, 194
HTTP (HyperText Transfer Protocol), 26, 27
hyper-threading, 70

I
IBM (International Business Machines), 13, 130
   mainframes, 8
   Recycling Service, 105
IC (integrated circuit), 64
icons, described, 12
identity theft, 214
IE (Internet Explorer) browser, 28–29. *See also* browsers
Illustrator (Adobe), 145, 149, 177, 212
images. *See* graphics
IMAP (Internet Messaging Access Protocol), 40–42
incremental backups, 205. *See also* backups
InDesign (Adobe), 149
information
   data and, distinction between, 11
   theft, 214
inkjet printers, 94
input
   described, 4
   devices, overview of, 90–107
installation
   agreements, 157
   software, 152–160
instant messaging, 17
instruction(s), 100–103, 119–120
   microprocessors and, 70–71
   sets, 68
   storage of, described, 5
Internet
   backbone, 15, 20
   basics, 15–24
   connection information, backing up, 201
   data, storage of, 16
   history of, 106
   passwords and, 22–24
   resources, 15–18
   system software and, 128
   telephony, 17
   user IDs and, 22–24
Internet Connection Wizard, 21
interpreted programs, 120
interpreters, 119–120
iPod, 83, 147
IRQs (interrupt requests), 98
ISA (Industry Standard Architecture), 97
ISDN (Integrated Services Digital Network), 20
ISPs (Internet Service Providers)
   described, 20–22
   e-mail and, 37
   information, backing up, 201
   passwords and, 22–23
   privacy and, 48, 217
   protocols and, 41
iTunes, 147

J

Java, 119
journalism, 166–167, 215
joysticks, 11, 91, 99

K

kernel, 125, 127, 129, 130
keyboards, 10, 90–91, 99
keychain drives. *See* flash drives
keywords, 32
kilobits, 63
kilobytes, 63

L

labels, 138, 139
lands, 79
LANs (local area networks), 151, 193. *See also* networks
  connection types and, 20
  described, 8
  servers and, 9
  system software and, 128
laser printers, 94
law enforcement, 216–217
LCD screens, 10, 92
leading, 136
licenses, 157–159
line spacing, 136
links, described, 26. *See also* URLs (Uniform Resource Locators)
Linux, 126–130, 176
logical storage models, 183

M

machine
  code, 100
  language, 119–120
Macintosh, 12–13, 126–130, 156, 182
  described, 13
  file-naming conventions, 176
  music software, 147
macro viruses, 192
magnetic storage devices, 79
mail merge, 137
mailing lists, 17
mainframe computers, 8
malicious code, use of the term, 191. *See also* viruses
margin settings, 133–134
mass-mailing worms, 193
mathematical
  modeling software, 141
  operators, 139
MATRIX (Multistate Antiterrorism Information Exchange System), 50
megabits, 63
megabytes, 63
megahertz, 69
memory. *See also* RAM (random access memory); ROM (read-only memory)
  boot process and, 47
  chips and, 64
  classification of, as a resource, 123
  CMOS, 44, 75–76
  described, 5
  leaks, 123
  management of, 123
  microprocessors and, 70
  printers and, 96
  shortages, 73
  storage devices and, 88
menu bar, 28
metaphors, file management, 183
MFT (Master File Table), 187, 188
microchips (computer chips), 64–66
microcomputers, described, 6
microprocessor(s), 8, 13. *See also* CPUs (central processing units)
  clocks, 69
  described, 6, 68–77
  execution of instructions by, 100–103
  location of, 64
  performance, 69–71
  resources and, 123
MIDI (Musical Instrument Digital Interface), 147
military computers, 22, 106–107
MIME (Multi-Purpose Internet Mail Extensions), 37, 38
modem(s)
  connector types, 99
  described, 10, 97
  personal computer systems and, 10
  types of, 18
money management software, 141
monitor(s). *See also* screens
  connector types, 99
  described, 10, 92–93
motherboard. *See* system board
Motorola, 71
mouse, 10, 12–13, 91, 99
MP3 files, 147, 201, 212
MP3 players, 88, 99, 179, 212
MPEG decoders, 88
MS-DOS, 130, 206. *See also* DOS (Disk Operating System)
MSN (Microsoft Network), 20
multicasting, 17
MultiMedia (MMC) cards, 89
multi-partite viruses, 197
multiple-user licenses, 157. *See also* licenses
multitasking operating systems, 126, 127
multiuser operating systems, 126
music. *See also* audio
  digitization of, 62–33
  software, 147
My Computer, 182, 206
My Documents folder, 186, 201

N

nanoseconds, 74
navigation buttons, 29
NCIC (National Crime Information Center), 50, 216–217
NEAR operator, 32
netiquette, 38–39
Netscape Navigator browser, 28. *See also* browsers
network(s). *See also specific types*
  backups and, 204
  described, 8
  operating system (NOS), 126
  traffic jams, 195

INDEX

worms and, 195
network cards, 10, 97
newsgroups, 17
non-executing zip files, 156
Norton AntiVirus, 149, 196
NOT operator, 32
notation software, 147
notebooks computers, 18, 45, 80, 84
  described, 6–7
  PC cards and, 97
  storage devices and, 88
  system software and, 126
NSA (National Security Agency), 50–51
NTFS (New Technology File System), 126, 187
number(s)
  "crunching" software, 141
  page, 136–137
numeric data, described, 60

O

object code, 119
Office (Microsoft), 148–149
Omnibus Crime Control and Safe Streets Act, 48
op codes, 100, 101
Open dialog box, 211
open source software, 159
operands, 100
operating systems software. *See also specific operating systems*
  boot process and, 45, 46
  described, 12–13, 120–126
  storage of, 125
operators, 32, 139
Opteron processors, 71
optical storage devices, 79
OR operator, 32
Oracle, 142
Outlook (Microsoft), 41, 149
output
  described, 5
  devices, overview of, 90–107

P

P2P (peer-to-peer) file sharing, 16
page(s)
  layout, 136–137
  numbering, 136–137
paint software, 145
Palm, 7, 12, 130–131. *See also* handheld computers; PDAs (personal digital assistants)
paragraphs, formatting, 135–136
parallel
  ports, 99
  processing, 70
passwords
  described, 22–24
  remote access and, 18
Patriot Act, 48, 215
payloads, 191
payroll software, 151
PC cards, 18, 97
PCI (Peripheral Component Interconnect), 97
PCL (Printer Control Language), 96
PCMCIA (Personal Computer Memory Card International Association), 97
PDAs (personal digital assistants), 7, 128, 142. *See also* handheld computers
  described, 7
  storage devices and, 88
PDF (Portable Document Format), 212
pen drives. *See* flash drives
Pentium processors, 69, 71
peripheral devices
  boot process and, 45, 46
  classification of, as resources, 123
  described, 11
  installing, 96–99
  system software and, 123, 124
personal computer(s). *See also* Windows (Microsoft)
  command-line interface, 124
  described, 6, 9–13
  operating, 14
personal finance software, 141
petabyte, 63
PGAs (pin-grid arrays), 64, 68
photo editing software, 145, 149, 212
Photoshop (Adobe), 145, 149, 212
physical file storage, 186–189
PINs (personal identification numbers), 22
pipelining, 70
pits, 79
pixels, 92
plasma screens, 92. *See also* screens
platforms, described, 13
PlayStation (Sony), 8
Plug and Play, 97, 163
PocketPC, 7. *See also* handheld computers
point size, 135
pointing devices, 91. *See also* mouse
polymorphic viruses, 197
Pong, 150
POP (Post Office Protocol), 40–42
POST (power-on self-test), 44, 46
PostScript, 96
power
  cables, 45
  light, 45
  switch, 45
PowerPoint (Microsoft), 146, 149
presentation software, 146, 149
printer(s), 10–11, 95–96, 122–123
  described, 10, 94–96
  connector types, 99
  printing Web pages with, 29
privacy, 48–49, 217
processes, described, 123
processing, described, 4

programmers, 118–119
programming languages, 118–119
programs. *See also* applications; *specific programs*
  described, 4
  file format for, 210
project management software, 151
properties, for elements in software environments, 118–119
public domain software, 159
Publisher (Microsoft), 149

Q

QBE (query by example), 144
QuarkXPress, 133, 212
queries. *See also* SQL (Structured Query Language)
  described, 32
  natural language, 34, 144
Quicken (Intuit), 141
QuickTime, 209
QWERTY keyboards, 90
QXD format, 212

R

radio shows, 17
RAM (random access memory). *See also* memory
  boot process and, 44
  cache, 70
  classification of, as a resource, 123
  CMOS and, 75–76
  control unit and, 102
  described, 72–76
  file management and, 180
  management of, 123
  storage devices and, 78, 84
  system software and, 131
  video editing software and, 120
  viruses and, 191
  volatile, 73
random-access devices, 81
RDRAM (rambus dynamic RAM), 74
readability formulas, 135
read-write heads, 79, 188
real-time clock, 66

RealMedia Player, 212
recordable technology, 86
records, creating, 142–143
recovery CDs, 207
Recycle Bin, 189
reference software, 149
refresh rates, 92
registers, 68
Registry, 156, 161–164, 201
relative references, 140
remote access, 18
reserved words, 177
resolution
  monitors and, 93
  printers and, 95, 96
resources
  described, 123
  management of, 123
  storage, 124
retro viruses, 196
rewritable technology, 86
RIP (raster image processor), 166
RISC (reduced instruction set computer), 70
ROM (read-only memory)
  BIOS (basic input/output system), 74
  bootstrap programs, 44–46, 125
  described, 74
  system software and, 131
root directories, 186
RTF (Rich Text Format), 211

S

Safe Mode, 46–47
salami shaving, 214
Save As dialog box, 180–181, 213
scanners, 11, 99
schools, 20, 48–49
screens. *See also* monitors
  handheld computers and, 7
  touch-sensitive, 6
SCSI (Small Computer Systems Interface), 83–84, 99
SD (SecureDigital) cards, 89
SDRAM (synchronous dynamic RAM), 74, 76

SDSL (Synchronous Digital Subscriber Line), 20
Search and Replace features, 135
search engines, 16, 31–35
search operators, 32
SEC (single edge contact cartridges), 64
sectors, 186
security. *See also* viruses
  e-mail and, 39, 42
  "homeland," 50–51
  passwords, 18, 22–24
self-executing zip files, 156
self-installing executable files, 156
sequential access devices, 81
serial
  ports, 99
  processing, 70
servers
  backups and, 204
  described, 9
  mailing list, 17
  storage of Internet data on, 16
  Web servers, 27, 128
  worms and, 195
service packs, 156
setup programs, 154
shareware licenses, 158–159. *See also* licenses
shrink-wrap licenses, 157. *See also* licenses
Shut Down command, 46–47
single-user licenses, 157. *See also* licenses
single-user operating systems, 126
site licenses, 157. *See also* licenses
smartphones, 7, 130
smileys, 39
SMTP (Simple Mail Transfer Protocol), 41–42
software. *See also* applications; programs; *specific software*
  described, 4, 114–173
  files required by, 117
  how it works, 119–120
  installation, 152–160

INDEX

licenses, 157–159
piracy, 164–165
publishers, 118–119
suites, 148–149
uninstalling, 156, 160
use of the term, 117
Solaris (Sun Microsystems), 107, 126
solid ink printers, 95
solid state storage devices, 80, 88–89
sound. *See* audio; sound cards
sound cards, 10, 96, 97
Sound Recorder, 147
source code, described, 119
spam, 40
speakers, 10
spelling
    checkers, 134
    dictionaries, 134
spoofed addresses, 193
spreadsheet software, 138–140, 211
Sprint, 15
SQL (Structured Query Language), 144. *See also* queries
SSI (small-scale integration), 64
statistical software, 141
status bar, 28
stealth viruses, 197
storage devices. *See also specific devices*
    classification of, as resources, 123
    described, 5, 78–89
    storage metaphors and, 183
store-and-forward technology, 40
stored programs, described, 5
subdirectories, 178
supercomputers, 8–9
support programs, 117
surge strips, 45
SVGA (Super VGA) standard, 93
SXGA (Super XGA) standard, 93
system board, 64

system requirements, 152
System Tools, 205
system units, 10, 64–66
System.dat, 161

T

tables, creating, 137
tablet computers, 6–7, 45, 126, 130–131
tape drives, 85, 99, 202, 204–206
tax preparation software, 141
TCP/IP (Transmission Control Protocol/Internet Protocol), 15, 126, 129, 193
teleconferencing, 17, 19. *See also* broadcasting
television, cable, 19
Telnet, 18
temporary files, 210
terabyte, 63
terrorism, 48. *See also* security
text
    alignment, 136
    copying/pasting, 31
    file formats, 211
    messaging, 39
    styles, 136
thermal transfer printers, 95
thesaurus, 135
title bars, 28
toolbars, 28
topic directories, 33
trackballs, 91
trackpads, 91
tracks, 186
transistors, 64
tree structure metaphor, 183
trigger events, 191
Trojan horses, 191–192, 196–197

U

ULSI (ultra large-scale integration), 64
Unicode, 61
uninstalling software, 156, 160
UNIX, 126–130, 176
updates, installing, 156
uploading, described, 16

UPS (uninterruptible power supplies), 45
URLs (Uniform Resource Locators), 27–28, 30–32, 201. *See also* links
USB (Universal Serial Bus)
    ports, 80, 97
    described, 96, 99
    flash drives, 88–89, 202
Usenet, 17
user IDs, 22–24
user interfaces, 124–125
User.dat, 161
utilities
    accessing, 125
    backup, 204–205
    file management, 182
    formatting, 187
UXGA (Ultra XGA) standard, 93

V

values, described, 138–139
vandalism, 214
vertical market software, 151
VGA (Video Graphics Array)
    ports, 93, 99
video
    cameras, 99
    connection speeds and, 19
    editing, 148
    file formats, 211
    memory, 93
videogames, 8
viewable image size, 92
viewing angle width, 92
virtual memory, 73, 76
virus(es), 39, 47, 51
    backups and, 202
    described, 191–198, 214
    signatures, 197
voiceband modems, 18

W

Web authoring software, 133–132
Web browsers, 28–31, 35, 195
Web pages, 26–27
Web servers, 27, 128
Web sites

backups via, 202, 204
described, 16
what-if analysis, 138
wildcard characters, 32
Windows (Microsoft)
    boot disks and, 206
    described, 12–13, 126–130
    file management and, 176, 177, 182, 186
    GUI, 124, 127, 132
    malicious code and, 51
    popularity of, 12
    RAM requirements, 73
    software, use of the term, 13
Windows Mobile (Microsoft), 12, 128, 130–131
WinZip, 39, 156
Word (Microsoft), 13, 133, 149
    file formats, 177, 211, 212
    file management and, 180–181
    margin settings, 134
word processing software, 133–137. *See also* Word (Microsoft)
word size, 70
word wrap features, 133–134
worksheets, 138–140
workstations, 8
World Wide Web. *See also* Web pages; Web sites
    -based e-mail, 40–42
    described, 26–34
worms, 51, 191–193, 196–197, 215. *See also* viruses

X

Xerox PARC, 124
XGA (eXtended Graphics Array) standard, 93

Y

Yahoo! search engine, 31

Z

ZIP disks, 99, 186–187
    backups and, 202, 203
    described, 82
zip files, 155–156